# The California Gothic in Fiction
# and Film

# The California Gothic in Fiction and Film

Bernice M. Murphy

EDINBURGH
University Press

Edinburgh University Press is one of the leading university presses in the UK. We publish academic books and journals in our selected subject areas across the humanities and social sciences, combining cutting-edge scholarship with high editorial and production values to produce academic works of lasting importance. For more information visit our website: edinburghuniversitypress.com

Edinburgh University Press Ltd
The Tun – Holyrood Road
12(2f) Jackson's Entry
Edinburgh EH8 8PJ

Typeset in 10.5/13 Bembo by
IDSUK (DataConnection) Ltd, and
printed and bound in Great Britain.

A CIP record for this book is available from the British Library

ISBN 978 1 4744 9786 2 (hardback)
ISBN 978 1 4744 9788 6 (webready PDF)
ISBN 978 1 4744 9789 3 (epub)

# Contents

# Acknowledgements

Much of this book was written and researched during the Covid-19 crisis. I am more grateful than ever for the support and encouragement of my family, friends and my colleagues and students in the School of English, Trinity College Dublin.

Thanks to Brian J. Showers of Swan River Press for providing me with useful additional material on Fritz Leiber. Dara Downey provided invaluable feedback when I was working on my book proposal.

Brian Cliff, Marni Rothman and Elven the dog were gracious hosts during my summer 2019 research/conference trip to California. The Trinity College Arts and Social Sciences Benefaction Fund provided the funding which enabled me to take that trip. I consider myself fortunate to work at a School (and a university) which rightly recognises the importance of fully supporting academics in their research endeavours. The College library was, as ever, an exceptionally useful resource.

I would also like to thank the editorial team at Edinburgh University Press and the peer reviewers for this volume, whose suggestions were extremely helpful.

# Introduction: 'Evil Lurks in California'

The March 1970 cover of *Esquire* magazine featured a sombre portrait of one of the leading film stars of the day and an ominous statement: 'Evil lurks in California. Lee Marvin is afraid.'[1] The implication was clear: if an exemplar of American masculinity such as Lee Marvin was freaked out, everyone else should be too. Much of the issue was devoted to articles in which a macabre portrait of the Golden State was presented. Looming over everything was the ghastly shadow of the Tate–LaBianca murders, which had taken place only seven months before. As James Riley puts it, Charles Manson came to 'signify the devil's business done; the traumatic cancellation of the hippie project; the dashing of the decade's utopian hopes; the end of the sixties'.[2]

The opening article, 'California Evil', began with an italicised list of recently deceased public figures, amongst them Robert Kennedy, Sharon Tate and her houseguests, and Hollywood star Ramon Novarro who, like Tate, had recently been murdered by strangers. 'Dead in California' was appended after each name.[3] The article's author, Craig Karpel, asked: 'What is the agency of this aberration – madness? Drugs? Or is it simply California?'

LSD was singled out as a catalysing agent. Karpel made a striking analogy between the mind-expanding potential of psychedelics and the historical event which had vastly accelerated the Americanisation of California: 'Now in 1970 the Gold Rush is on again. Only this time Leary's brain is the Sutter's Mill and some Californians are breaching the *inward* frontier, panning the trailraces of consciousness for some pinch of the precious stuff itself.'[4] But whilst the drug, Karpel claimed, allowed users to access parts of themselves that were previously unreachable, there was also a potentially devastating side effect. What if, he asked:

> it suddenly becomes too clear that the whole California trip is tainted with strychnine, that it's Death Valley Days for real now, and ain't no twenty-mule team gonna haul our asses out of here nohow? [. . .] Suddenly the

notion jells that what is going down in California might really be part of a diabolical plan that *is working*, that is hurtling towards its malignant culmination on the West Coast in 1970. What if this Walpurgistag of death and degradation and disaster suddenly resolves itself into a vision of inexpressibly painful beauty? Would not one develop, out in the Valley, up in the Hollywood Hills, along the canyons, down the Peninsula, up the Coast, more than a passing sympathy for the Devil? Worship Him? Suffer for Him? Die for Him? Kill for Him?[5]

Karpel's free-wheeling piece, and the articles which followed, were saturated by this tangible fear that California had been overtaken by the forces of chaos. 'We must ever face the possibility that California has allowed itself to become a principality of the Devil, and that the rest of the country is not far behind.'[6]

This feeling that something had gone very badly wrong in California in the years following the end of World War II – the same period during which it also became the most populous and most culturally influential state in the union – was common, and it was frequently expressed in fiction and film. Yet before and after this time the state of California was also widely perceived to be a tantalisingly utopian space. In his 1949 history of the state, Carey McWilliams argued that

> [a]lthough its derivation is unknown, California has a meaning which is as clear today as when the word stood for a place not yet discovered. It is a symbol of the mountain of paradise; the fabulous isle; the dream garden of beautiful black Amazons off the Asia coast; 'the good country' – the Zion – of which man has ever dreamed.[7]

David Wyatt observed in his 1986 book on landscape, mythology and California's literary imagination, that

> So great was the beauty of the land that it conferred on the completion of the quest the illusion of a return to a privileged source. As the sense of an ending merged with the wonder of beginnings, California as last chance merged with California as Eden.[8]

Wyatt's use of the word 'illusion' is important: along with 'dream' it tends to recur when California is under consideration. As McWilliams had earlier put it, 'Naturally, people have always been wary of this great golden dream, this highly improbable state; this symbol of a cruel illusion.'[9] James Quay also highlights this potentially misleading quality, arguing that California's 'defining cultural feature' is the state's persistence as a location where the deepest human yearnings can be realized. 'California' has sometimes been a blank screen onto which people have projected their desires, sometimes a real place that promises opportunity never before imagined, and sometimes a bitter example of disillusion and disappointment.[10]

'Modern California', Philip L. Fradkin declared in *The Seven States of California: A Natural and Human History* (1995), 'was founded on greed and violence.'[11] Fradkin was referring to the opportunistic fortune seekers who flooded the state in their thousands in the years following the discovery of gold in January 1848. This chance discovery, which happened just days before 'Mexico ceded Alta California and other territories to the United States', completely transformed the prospects and perception of the region.[12] As Kevin Starr has exhaustively chronicled, from the outset the territory was imbued by white settlers (first the Spanish, and later Anglo-Americans) and their descendants with a powerful mythic significance. However, as he puts it:

> Of course, the dream outran the reality, as it always does. California experienced more than its share of social problems because its development was so greedy and so unregulated. No evocation of imaginative inspiration can atone for the burdens of the California past, especially the violence and the brutality.[13]

It is perhaps inevitable then, that as Charles Crow puts it: 'California's literature is, mainly, a literature of disillusionment: things did not work out there, after all.'[14] In *A History of Californian Literature* (2015), Blake Allmendinger, like McWilliams and Starr before him, characterises the state as

> a place of contradictions. It is the endpoint of Manifest Destiny, the land of eternal sunshine and youth. At times, the entire state seems like a gated community inhabited by wealthy celebrities. However, California is also associated with boom-bust economies and nightmarish dystopias.[15]

Allmendinger further notes that

> California's reputation as the Golden State didn't become tarnished until the twentieth century. Industrialization, a continuing influx of immigrants, and increasing competition for the region's diminishing resources are among the many problems that have bedeviled the region. Instead of the western, which celebrates pioneer virtues and the triumph of white civilization, the genre most closely associated with California is noir [. . .] The state has also attracted science fiction writers [. . .] All of their works comment on present-day California in an unflattering way.[16]

Despite this engagement with the 'lost', 'contested' (or, as the title of one recent 2019 history of the state puts it, the 'elusive') Eden theme, to date relatively little attention has been paid to the ways in which the negative flipside of the 'California Dream' has been depicted within the horror and Gothic genres specifically.[17] Whilst there are numerous books on California's history, literature and culture (many of which are cited in this volume), at the time of writing, no single monograph devoted to California and the Gothic exists. However, I am aware of one forthcoming book chapter (in *The Haunted States of America: Gothic Regionalism in Post-war American Fiction*, by James Morgart) and a monograph-in-progress (*California Gothic: The Dark Side of the Dream* by Charles Crow). This welcome growth of interest in the topic further underlines its significance. The previously published work which overlaps most with my concerns here is the 2017 collection, *A Dark California: Essays on Dystopian Depictions in Popular Culture*, edited by Katarzyna Nowak-McNeice and Agata Zarzycka. Several of the essays featured therein usefully discuss horror and Gothic narratives and there is some reference to several of the same authors and themes dealt with in this book (particularly Joan Didion, the Hollywood Gothic and the Gothic resonances of the Donner Party, which the editors consider in their conclusion). However, my volume goes beyond this remit by explicitly defining a distinct 'California Gothic' tradition and by providing a cohesive and historically grounded thematic outline of the sub-genre, as well as situating it within the wider American Gothic tradition.

California's contribution to the development of modern horror and Gothic fiction and film is immense, but it remains sorely underappreciated. For instance, consider three of the most influential American horror novels of the twentieth century: Robert Bloch's *Psycho* (1959); Jack Finney's *The Body Snatchers* (serial 1954; novel 1955) and Richard Matheson's *I Am Legend* (1954). As befits their obvious significance, all three novels (and their many film adaptations) have been subjected to extensive academic scrutiny. Yet there is one major interpretative framework for all three texts that has thus far been largely overlooked. Most – or all – of the action in each of them takes place in specific Californian locales – the suburbs of South Central Los Angeles in *I Am Legend*, and the small towns of Fairvale and Mill Valley in *Psycho* and *The Body Snatchers* respectively. The setting in each case is more than a minor contextual detail. Like the other narratives discussed here, they are each in their own way stories *about* California, as well as stories that just happen to be set in California. The same is true of the other primary works considered here.

The California Gothic articulates anxieties rooted in the historical, cultural and geographical settings of the so-called 'Golden State'. The term will be applied here to selected works of fiction and film in which the 'California

Dream' in its various guises is undermined and themes and tropes pertaining to the 'California Nightmare' are dramatised. It was during the post-war era that modern Gothic and horror film and fiction began to most intensely engage with the very *idea* of California, and with the state's complex and often contested historical contexts. In his 1963 book, *California: The New Society*, Remi Nadeau described Californians as 'a people who appear to be moving on the frontier of American culture'.[18] He predicted that the state 'may soon become not the outpost but the wellspring of American culture'.[19] That influence, as we shall see, also extends to the Gothic and horror genres.

In *American Women's Regionalist Fiction: Mapping the Gothic* (2021), Monika Elbert and Rita Bode argue that the work of the writers featured in their volume shows 'the extent to which the Gothic played a significant part in the creative and cultural formulations of both region and nation'.[20] The same can be said of the California Gothic. In it we find both a distillation and an intensification of pre-existing American Gothic characteristics. Yet there is also a distinct regional specificity which makes it uniquely Californian. Writing about the 'problems which California took into the twentieth century from the nineteenth', Kevin Starr describes them as

> national problems – with a local texture; and that conjunction said much about the California experience as a whole. It was American and it was regional. In a very real sense, the California dream was the American dream undergoing one of its most significant variations.[21]

The same is true of the American nightmare, and of the ways in which it has found a very specific kind of regional expression within Californian fiction and film. There is, for instance, a recurrent sense of unease related to the idea that once one has reached the Pacific coast, there is nowhere else to go. As Crow observes, 'there is an urgency about California's promise of the good life: it is the last stop, the end of the road'.[22]

This volume is the fourth I have written about the relationship between place and the American Gothic. There is accordingly some occasional thematic and textual overlap between *The California Gothic in Fiction and Film* and *The Suburban Gothic in American Popular Culture* (Palgrave Macmillan, 2009); *The Rural Gothic in American Popular Culture* (Palgrave Macmillan, 2013); and *The Highway Horror Film* (Palgrave Macmillan, 2014). Indeed, it was whilst completing *The Highway Horror Film* that I began to realise that the frequency with which California featured as a setting warranted further investigation. This observation sent me back to my earlier work on the Suburban Gothic tradition, in which California was again the US state referenced most frequently.

California is the most common setting for American horror and Gothic narratives rooted in the unease associated with the unprecedented social, environmental and infrastructural changes which transformed the national landscape – and the American way of life – in the years immediately following World War II. As Michael Kowalewski notes, California is 'the state perhaps most associated with rootlessness, transience, and unchecked growth'.[23] That association has indelibly influenced its horror and Gothic traditions.

As I outlined in *The Rural Gothic*, the Southern states (and to a lesser extent, New England) have thus far provided the locales which feature most commonly in Gothic and horror narratives in which the wilderness, rural and backwoods regions – and the peoples who inhabit them – are a source of threat. California is the state most associated with works of fiction and film in which the potential horrors of modernity, personal reinvention and forward momentum are dramatised. Yet thus far, academic consideration of a specifically *Californian* Gothic tradition has for the most part been overlooked or subsumed under the broader category of 'American Gothic'.

My focus here is primarily (though not solely) directed towards works of fiction and film created in the decades following the end of World War II. I am particularly interested in the ways in which post-1945 Gothic and horror narratives have engaged with the ghosts and guilt of the Californian past, and with the complex contradictions of its present. However, this focus does not mean that the burdens of history associated with the American Gothic are absent. Despite the post-war origins of (most) of the primary texts discussed here, California's wider historical, literary and cultural contexts are of key importance. *The California Gothic in Fiction and Film* is indebted to the work of California historians and cultural commentators such as Kevin Starr, Mike Davis, Reyner Banham, Joan Didion, Philip Fradkin, Benjamin Madley and Rebecca Solnit. Starr has been a particularly important source of inspiration and historical context. His eight-volume cultural history, 'Americans and the California Dream', is the most expansive and most ambitious overview of the state's origins and development, and his discussion of the evolving concept of the 'California Dream' has greatly informed my own conception of the 'California Nightmare'.

One of the first major challenges in undertaking a project such as this one is establishing a clear rationale for selection. Which texts qualify as works of the California Gothic, and why? The question is complicated by the fact that Hollywood has for over a century been the centre of the global entertainment industry, and in that time countless movies, television shows, radio plays, screenplays, novels and stories have been generated by novelists, screenwriters, directors and other creators associated with Southern California. It is certainly not my intention then to apply the 'California Gothic' label to every single horror and Gothic narrative created within the borders of the state (not least because so many of them are explicitly set elsewhere). The volume focuses upon a selection of narratives which are both largely (or entirely) set in and in some way also *about* the state. It is also not intended to serve as a definitive survey of the *entirety* of the California Gothic. For instance, I do not engage with the work of notable late nineteenth-/early twentieth-century Gothicists such as Emma Frances Dawson, Gertrude Atherton or Mary Austin. I instead encourage readers interested in these contexts to begin by consulting the chapters written by Dara Downey and Lesley Ginsberg in *American Women's Regionalist Fiction: Mapping the Gothic* (2021).[24]

My definition of the 'California Gothic' does not always exclude texts from outside the (deeply porous) confines of the Gothic mode. As in my previous volumes, I see horror and the Gothic as genres which are intrinsically linked. Some of the literary and filmic texts discussed in this volume certainly do lie comfortably within the territory of the Gothic and explore the kind of onto-logical dread, repression and challenge to the 'rational' order traditionally asso-ciated with the mode. Several of the other narratives considered here are more usually categorised as works of horror, and the reader will observe that in these texts (which are mostly films) supernatural incidents surface frequently. In my discussions of works such as Fritz Leiber's novel *Our Lady of Darkness* (1977), John Carpenter's film *The Fog* (1980) and Matheson's *I Am Legend*, I argue, for instance, that the explicit intrusion of the uncanny here is intrinsically related to Californian contexts. Our understanding of these films – and of the other primary texts considered here – deepens when we acknowledge the extent to which they are indebted to Californian history and culture, in addition to the wider (national) contexts in which they are more usually considered.

I will also be discussing two works which are more typically classified as examples of dystopian science fiction: Philip Kaufman's 1978 film version of *Invasion of the Body Snatchers* and Dave Egger's satirical novel *The Circle* (2013). They are included here because, like Karyn Kusama's 2015 film, *The Invitation*, and Jordan Peele's 2019 film, *Us*, they depict California as 'ground zero' for the establishment of cult-like new movements which will soon overtake not only the United States, but possibly the entire world.

Additionally, no volume discussing the ways in which the 'dark side' of the Golden State has been depicted in fiction and film could neglect to mention the important role which the noir tradition has played in undermining the 'California as Eden' trope. Indeed, the relationship between noir and California – and noir and Los Angeles specifically – has been comprehensively outlined by critics such as Edward Dimendberg (2004), Sean Maher (2020), William Marling (2015) and Mike Davis (2006; for whom noir is the 'nightmare anti-myth' which helped 'make Los Angeles the city American intellectuals love to hate').[25]

I discuss two noir/neo-noir classic films which also overlap with notably Gothic themes – Billy Wilder's *Sunset Boulevard* (1950) and David Lynch's *Mulholland Drive* (2001) – in my section on 'The Hollywood Gothic'. My chapter on the role that California has played in the birth of the modern horror tradition also intersects with some notable noir themes, particularly in relation to the treatment which newly constructed 'spaces of modernity' (highways, the city, suburbia) received in both genres during the post-war era. The chapter begins with a brief discussion of Roman Polanski's remarkably bleak evocation of Southern California in *Chinatown* (1974).

Anxieties related to race and racial inequality are another important facet of this volume. The legacy of slavery may not often surface as directly within the California Gothic as it does in the Southern Gothic, for obvious historical reasons, but the ramifications of urban and suburban segregation, and the horrific ill-treatment of California's Native American tribes are significant topics of discussion. Describing the swiftness and brutality with which Yankee California took over what he calls 'Old California' in the final days of Mexican rule, Starr observes that 'Racist contempt flawed the origins of American California in hatred, injustice, and bloodshed. Tragically, one California was destroyed so that another might take its place.'[26] This sense that modern California has been built upon racially motivated violence (and then the repression of this knowledge) percolates just below the surface of many of the films and novels discussed in this book.

Kowalewski argues in his discussion of 'Contemporary Regionalism' that we can gain a sense of the 'true richness' of the state by visualising California 'not as a single entity but as a mosaic of interdependent, interlocking microregions, each with its distinctive landforms, climate zones, history and blendings of culture'.[27] However, the reader will note that the locational diversity of the California Gothic (as it is outlined here) is quite limited. Many of the texts I discuss are associated with San Francisco and Los Angeles and their surrounding environs (albeit with some notable exceptions). This geographical bias reflects the limited locational scope of the source material as well as the practical need to curtail the word count of this already sizeable volume. It has also been influenced by my interest in specific geographical and urban/suburban/coastal locales. There is certainly much scope for further work focusing upon Californian locations and regions which are only briefly mentioned here or excluded entirely.

As was the case with my 2009 definition of the Suburban Gothic (with which it occasionally overlaps) my conception of the 'California Gothic' is rooted in a series of intertwined binary oppositions.[28] This sense of California as a place that vacillates between extremes is, as many of the quotes from previous commentators have also suggested, a longstanding one. Additionally, in

*A Dark California*, Nowak-McNeice and Zarzycka also reference the 'apparent binary oppositions which often underpins the aesthetics of California themes', and persuasively argue that 'the tensions between the different facets of California are most spectacular when captured in binaries'.[29]

My own conception of these binaries (and my sense of those which are most significant) relates to the myriad ways in which, as Kevin Starr has put it, 'the dream outran the reality'. They are as follows:

## The California Dream:

1. California is a place of perpetual sunshine with a stunning natural landscape.
2. It is a 'melting pot' of peoples and cultures.
3. California is the glittering prize that concluded the nation's 'Manifest Destiny'.
4. California is a 'new' state free from the unsettling racial and historical 'baggage' associated with the East Coast and the Southern states.
5. In California, people can create themselves anew. It is associated with spiritual, economic and physical renewal.
6. For all these reasons, California is a particularly attractive destination for Americans from the Midwest who are seeking a 'fresh start'.
7. In California, the individual can pursue their personal dreams and desires.
8. California is uniquely receptive to new modes of thinking and of living.
9. California is a beacon of industrial and technological progress associated with remarkable transformations in the natural landscape and material infrastructure.
10. The 'newness' of California means that one can bypass traditional power hierarchies: anyone can make it there, if they want it badly enough.

## The California Nightmare:

1. California is beset by natural disasters, pollution, and extreme weather patterns.
2. There is a dogged persistence of stark racial, social and economic divisions.
3. California is the Dead End of the United States. Where else is there to go after this?
4. First Spanish and later Anglo-American culture and values were violently imposed upon the region's Indigenous peoples. There is a willed amnesia surrounding the many atrocities and injustices which accompanied the foundation of modern California.

5. California is fertile ground for cults and countercultural movements which quickly turn on themselves and others.

6. To paraphrase Nathanael West's *The Day of the Locust*, in the California Gothic, California is the place where Midwesterners go to die.

7. California encourages selfishness, narcissism and shallow self-interest.

8. California is dangerously receptive to harmful ideas and 'crazy' notions.

9. California prioritises 'progress' over people, and the destruction of natural environments and long-established patterns of living.

10. The initial lack of internal structures led to the establishment of corrupt and unaccountable new hierarchies and institutions: see, for example, the railroad and oil industries, battles over the control of the state's water supplies, the Hollywood studio system, the Los Angeles Police Department (LAPD) and latterly, powerful tech tycoons in Silicon Valley and beyond.

I will refer to these binaries throughout the book. As well as outlining the historical origins and characteristics of the 'California Gothic', it will discuss selected key works in which the 'California Nightmare' is outlined. The book is divided into three parts, each focusing upon a major facet of the California Gothic.

Part I, 'Foundational Horrors', incorporates discussion of events such as the establishment of the Spanish mission system; the ill-fated journey undertaken by the Donner Party; and the (allegedly) true story of the 'Winchester Mystery House' (and its relationship with the Anglo-American attempt to exterminate California's Native American population). The ramifications of these 'foundational horrors' ripple through the sub-genre up until the present day.

In Chapter 1, '"What Happened a Hundred Years Ago is Happening Again": The Ghosts of the California Past', I argue that the real-life horror story of the Donner Party holds the same foundational resonance for the California Gothic sub-genre that the Salem Witch Trials do for the New England Gothic. Evolving contemporary perceptions of the gruesome events of the winter of 1846/7 are outlined, as (briefly) is the way these events have been dramatised in horror and Gothic fiction and film. I will briefly discuss the California contexts of Antonia Bird's 1999 film, *Ravenous* (another fictionalised take on the story of the Donner Party), and of Joan Didion's fascination with the episode.

The brutal 'taming' of the frontier and the attempted extermination of California's Native American population provide the focus of the second part of this chapter. *The Fog* is discussed in relation to its nuanced but previously overlooked engagement with regional history (particularly the establishment of the Spanish mission system and the Anglo-American erasure of Hispanic and Native American history). The chapter concludes with a discussion of a foundational Californian ghost story: the legend surrounding the so-called 'Winchester Mystery House' and the ways in which it is problematically dramatized in the film *Winchester* (2018). The fabricated story attached to Sarah Winchester's architectural folly is much more than a means of tacitly acknowledging the high costs of 'Manifest Destiny': it is also a specifically *Californian* legend which reflects the often-ignored reality that many thousands of Native Americans were massacred by whites in the decades following statehood.

Chapter 2, 'The Dark Side of "the Good Life": California and the Birth of Modern Horror', begins with a discussion of a movement identified by *Los Angeles Times* critic Robert A. Kirsch. In 1965, Kirsch characterised Charles Beaumont as a leading light in the 'Southern California School of Writing', exemplifying the 'preoccupation with the present' and 'unfettered imagination' associated with the 'Southern California' literary scene. He had identified the tendency to engage with contemporary anxieties which made California the region which, more than any other, shaped the direction of post-war American horror in fiction and film. I also briefly discuss the ways in which two California-set Hitchcock films – *Shadow of a Doubt* (1943) and *Psycho* (1960) – anticipated the wider national preoccupation with the activities of dangerous (and white) 'rogue males' whose acts of psychopathic violence would, from the 1970s onwards, became irrevocably associated with California, thanks to the activities of serial killers such as Ed Kemper, the Zodiac Killer and Joseph DeAngelo, the recently unmasked 'Golden State Killer'. The chapter concludes with a discussion of Joel Schumacher's vampire film *The Lost Boys* (1987), which is set in a thinly fictionalised version of Santa Cruz, the Californian city which became irrevocably associated with the serial killer 'epidemic'.

No attempt to outline the relationship between California and the Gothic would be complete without a consideration of the central role played by depictions of Hollywood and of Hollywood stardom. This will be the focus of Part II, 'Hollywood Gothic'. 'Hollywood Gothic' presents us with a Los Angeles cityscape populated by men and women whose Tinseltown neuroses and experiences render them unable to differentiate between reality and fantasy. Amongst their number we find doomed ingénues, desperate hangers-on and fallen stars unable to accept that their time in the spotlight has come to an end. The Hollywood Gothic focuses upon the 'dark side' of a specific commercial and creative enterprise, but it also replicates many of the broader sub-genre's most notable themes and preoccupations. It also hearkens back to classic Gothic themes: here, the trope of the dangerous aristocrat is reconfigured in the form of the staple 'Hollywood Gothic' figure of the dangerously resentful 'Fallen Star'.

In Chapter 3, '"Sunshine isn't Enough": Hollywood Gothic Origins', I discuss the reasons why the business which has played such a seminal role in Southern California's cultural and economic development is also so often associated with moral corruption, madness and murder. I begin by outlining the factors behind Hollywood's establishment as the centre of the global movie-making industry. I then argue that Nathanael West's 1939 novel, *The Day of the Locust*, is a paradigmatic literary example of the 'Hollywood Gothic' because it is saturated with an awareness of Hollywood's seductive, insane, over-arching 'dream-life', and a sense that life even on the margins of the industry is inescapably chaotic and subject to the terrifying whims of the mob.

Chapter 4, 'Fallen Stars in *Sunset Boulevard* (1950) and *What Ever Happened to Baby Jane?* (1962)', begins with a discussion of the classical Gothic resonances of Wilder's *Sunset Boulevard*. In their differing ways, both *Sunset Boulevard* and *What Ever Happened to Baby Jane?* present us with a California-specific variation upon the familiar classical Gothic trope of the aristocratic villain who is a threatening relic of the feudal past, a connection reinforced by Kenneth Anger's sardonic characterisation of Hollywood's stars of the 1920s as 'the new royalty' in his book *Hollywood Babylon* (1975). Norma Desmond is also compared to a notable modern American Gothic character type: the tragic but dangerous figure who refuses to give up their own comforting but illusory private world. *What Ever Happened to Baby Jane?* is situated as a cautionary tale of childhood innocence horrifically corrupted by a youthful brush with celebrity.

The section concludes with Chapter 5, '"It's a Gateway Part!" Twenty-First-Century Hollywood Gothic'. It begins with a consideration of a more recent take on the 'embittered aristocrat' trope: David Cronenberg's 2014 film, *Maps to the Stars*. The first major variety of cinematic Hollywood Gothic narratives depicts forgotten Golden Age stars, whilst the second focuses upon the dire physical and psychological transformations undergone by those have yet to 'make it'. Beginning with a brief discussion of Lynch's neo-noir classic *Mulholland Drive*, I then discuss a more recent film in which key Hollywood Gothic tropes such as the doomed ingénue, bodily transformation and the self-destructive quest for fame are dramatised. In *Starry Eyes*, directed by Kevin Kölsch and Dennis Widmyer (2014), Hollywood is a place that creates, worships and then ruthlessly discards its 'stars'. What differentiates this film from earlier treatments of the formula is its outright supernaturalism. Here, the exploitative older white men who secretly control the 'star factory' entered into by the damned protagonist really do belong to a Satanic coven. I then briefly consider the film's overlap with a Hollywood Gothic adjacent movie which also has notably occult resonances: Nicolas Winding Refn's *The Neon Demon* (2016).

Some fascinating similarities between the seductive (but destructive) allure of Hollywood stardom and the appeal (and effects) of the cult organisations are considered in Part III, 'Cult California: New Gods and New Selves', in which I focus upon narratives in which new religious (and technological) movements promise an allegedly blissful 'new world'. Chapter 6, 'Cult Nightmares in *Our Lady of Darkness* (1977) and *Invasion of the Body Snatchers* (1978)', again notes that California has long attracted those in search of a 'fresh start', opportunity, physical renewal and spiritual fulfilment. I explore texts in which these long-standing associations become actively dystopian.

The chapter begins with a detailed discussion of the relationship between California and 'cult' organisations and an analysis of the ways in which the dystopian flipside of the 'hippie dream' emerged from the late 1960s onwards. I then discuss Leiber's *Our Lady of Darkness*, in which San Francisco is depicted as a primal locale which is particularly welcoming to charismatic charlatans. Leiber's debt to a California Gothic author of the previous generation, Clark Ashton Smith, is discussed, as is the importance of San Francisco's unique topography. As we shall see, Kaufman's 1978 version of *Invasion of the Body Snatchers* also makes the most of this setting. It is a classic urban nightmare lent additionally chilling resonance because of the ways in which the film antici-pates the real-life horrors which would soon beset the city: the Jonestown Massacre and the murders of Mayor George Moscone and LGBT rights activist Harvey Milk in City Hall (an important setting in the film).

In Chapter 7, '"The Usual Utopian Vision": Contemporary Cult California in *The Invitation* (2015), *1BR* (2019) and *The Circle* (2013)', the focus moves to modern-day Los Angeles. The chapter begins with an analysis of Kusama's *The Invitation*, a film which evokes the 1969 Manson Family murders and the 1978 Jonestown Massacre in a manner which underlines its subtly metafictional reso-nance. It is as much a film about the long-standing association between California and dangerous cult organisations as it is about a fictionalised version of one of these groups. Here, the qualities which make California an attractive locale for those seeking spiritual fulfilment again make it the perfect breeding ground for a cult which promises 'utopia', but instead delivers madness, destruction and death. This is also the case in David Marmor's *1BR*, in which a vulnerable young woman is taken captive by a cult which promises to reinvent the concept of 'community'. Finally, I argue that Eggers's *The Circle* builds upon earlier iterations of the 'California as Poisoned Eden' trope. Here, Northern California is the head-quarters of a powerful tech company which ultimately comes to resemble the cults previously discussed in this section. In *The Circle*, the supposedly progres-sive 'technological utopia' which is one of the newer manifestations of the 'Californian dream' is a dehumanizing and unstoppable nightmare.

In my Conclusion, '"It's Our Time Now": *Us* (2019) and *Desierto* (2015)', I discuss the California Gothic in relation to its tendency (thus far) to privilege the perspectives of white characters of Anglo-American descent. Jordan Peele's film *Us* subtly reminds us from the outset that it is a narrative with California-specific resonances. It also reminds us that the California Gothic is overwhelmingly associated with white creators, white protagonists and the dramatisation of middle-class white anxieties. Peele's protagonists are a Black family confronted by their (justifiably) resentful doppelgängers. To the doppelgängers and their visionary leader, the world above is a utopian paradise which must be seized by force, and a revolution which begins in California is again one that will soon expand far beyond the spatial boundaries of the state.

The final film discussed in this volume is the Mexican-made survival horror movie *Desierto*, directed by Jonás Cuarón. In *Desierto*, the desperate immigrant's journey towards the 'Promised Land' of California is relayed from a twenty-first-century genre-movie perspective. It overlaps with (and updates) many of the themes discussed in Chapter 1, particularly the feeling that the 'right' to enter the 'Eden' of California is often won at a high cost. Here, however, the travellers in peril are modern-day migrant workers desperate to make it across the border to be reunited with their family members.

Allmendinger has observed that 'California is a fanciful conceit, an elusive dream, a celluloid confection – a land where the greatest dreams and the darkest disasters come true.'[30] These dreams and disasters have, to date, largely been portrayed from the viewpoints of white Californians. As we shall see, the alternate perspectives provided in both *Us* and *Desierto* also illustrate the sub-genre's ability to dramatise the contradictions and the darkness that lie at the heart of the contemporary 'Californian Dream', while suggesting further ways in which the California Gothic may more accurately and equitably represent the state's racial and cultural make-up. Like the Golden State, the California Gothic will inevitably continue to evolve.

## Notes

1. I first came across this issue of *Esquire* when extracts were posted on the excellent 'In Search of Pagan Hollywood' blog, http://paganhollywood. blogspot.com/2018/12/evil-lurks-in-california-lee-marvin-is.html?zx= 6463411ca0013e6b (last accessed 6 August 2021).
2. Riley, *The Bad Trip*, p. 11.
3. Karpel, 'California Evil', p. 40.
4. Ibid. p. 40.
5. Ibid. p. 40

6. Ibid. p. 40.
7. McWilliams, *California*, p. 3.
8. Wyatt, *The Fall into Eden*, p. xvi.
9. McWilliams, *California*, p. 3.
10. Quay, 'Beyond Dreams and Disappointment', p. 5.
11. Fradkin, *The Seven States of California*, p. 84.
12. Ibid. p. 84.
13. Starr, *Americans and the California Dream*, p. vii.
14. Crow, 'Homecoming in the California Visionary Romance', p. 3.
15. Allmendinger, *A History of California Literature*, p. 2.
16. Ibid. p. 4.
17. Rice et al., *The Elusive Eden*.
18. Nadeau, *California*, p. 291. Kevin Starr's mention of this volume in *Golden Dreams* drew my attention to Nadeau's work.
19. Ibid. p. 9.
20. Elbert and Bode, *American Women's Regionalist Fiction*, p. 11.
21. Starr, *Americans and the California Dream*, p. 443.
22. Crow, 'Homecoming in the California Visionary Romance', p. 3.
23. Kowalewski, 'Contemporary Regionalism', p. 14.
24. See Downey, 'Emma Frances Dawson's Urban California Gothic'; Ginsberg, 'Mary Austin's California Gothic'.
25. Dimendberg, *Film Noir and the Spaces of Modernity*; Maher, *Film Noir and Los Angeles*; Marling, 'The Hard-Boiled California Novel'; Davis, *City of Quartz*, p. 21.
26. Starr, *Americans and the California Dream*, p. 21.
27. Kowalewski, 'Contemporary Regionalism', p. 16.
28. See Murphy, *The Suburban Gothic*, pp. 3–4.
29. Nowak-MacNeice and Zarzycka, *A Dark California*, pp. 2; 184.
30. Allmendinger, *A History of California Literature*, p. 13.

# PART I

# FOUNDATIONAL HORRORS

# 1

## 'What Happened a Hundred
## Years Ago is Happening Again':
## The Ghosts of the California Past

*Messiah of Evil* (1973) is set in a Northern Californian community named Point Dune. The main character is a young woman named Arletty (Marianna Hill), who has travelled there in search of her father, artist Joseph Lang (Royal Dano). Arletty relates her story in flashback from the confines of an asylum:

> Not far from here there is a small town on the coast. They used to call it New Bethlehem but they changed the name to Point Dune after the moon turned blood red. Point Dune doesn't *look* any different than a thousand other neon stucco towns. But what happened there – what they did to me – what they're doing now . . . They're coming here – they're waiting at the edge of the city. [. . .] and no one will hear you scream. No one will hear you scream!

Point Dune's profound *wrongness* becomes obvious to Arletty when she makes her first stop in town. She pulls up at an empty, neon-lit gas station, only to find the attendant firing a gun into the darkness to scare off 'stray dogs'. Within moments of her departure, the clerk is murdered. It soon becomes clear that many of the town's residents are flesh-eating zombies (of a sort) in thrall to a powerful supernatural figure known as the 'Dark Stranger'.

Jamie Russell situates *Messiah* alongside other minor-but-worthy post-*Night of the Living Dead* efforts, such as Jeff Lieberman's LSD flashback night-mare, *Blue Sunshine* (1977), David Cronenberg's *Shivers* (1975) and John D. Hancock's *Let's Scare Jessica to Death* (1971), suggesting that these movies insist upon overthrowing the ideals of the 'Flower Power' generation: 'Forming a backlash against the utopian hippie dream, these films all toy with fears about the dangers of mind-alerting drugs and rampant sexuality, while also displaying a stark mistrust of the strangeness of other people.'[1] Kim Newman, who ranks the film highly amongst the narrow but significant pantheon of 'post-hippie horror films of note', observes that it clearly draws from H. P. Lovecraft and George A. Romero.[2]

However, whilst Romero generally structured his zombie films as siege narratives, *Messiah of Evil*'s creative team Willard Huyck and Gloria Katz (they co-wrote the screenplay, which Huyck directed and Katz produced) keep their coastal Californian dead folks out and about on the streets and in the supermarkets and movie theatres of this otherwise deserted beachside locale. As Tim Lucas puts it:

> the film brilliantly captures a lightning essence of horror that no one ever bothered to bottle: the horror of neon night, of 24-hour gas stations and gro-cery stores, of muzak that sounds as if it was played by long-dead musicians, of streets lined with now defunct franchises (W. T. Grant, Florsheim Shoes), looking no different in 1971 than they did in the 1940s – in short, the horror one finds in Edward Hopper paintings.[3]

Point Dune is where the lost, the feckless and the disaffected end up, their aimless forward momentum arrested by the geographical and metaphorical endpoint of the Pacific Ocean. This sense of eerie finality extends to the languid characterisa-tion of the film's main character, Arletty, and the other urban outsiders who she befriends on her ill-fated trip – disaffected playboy Thom (Michael Greer) and his companions Toni (Joy Bang) and Laura (Anitra Ford). Although Arletty is moti-vated by the desire to find her missing father, beyond this mission she remains opaque. The character's listlessness is accentuated by the striking cadence of Hill's affected but resonant line readings.

*Messiah of Evil* is surreal and challenges conventional narrative expectations. Lucas persuasively suggests that it is

> best taken as a dream stocked with the kinds of characters David Lynch would kill for, including a blind art dealer and an albino African-American who bites the heads off rats whilst listening to 'Wagner' (mispronounced in the American way).[4]

Yet to focus only on the film's oneiric atmosphere is also to downplay the significance of the plot revelations that *do* emerge as the story unfolds. Indeed, the terrible events taking place in Point Dune are fundamentally related to the *California*-ness of the place, and the dread the film evokes is rooted in a region-ally specific undercurrent of emotional and cultural dislocation. Like the other supernatural horror films discussed in this chapter, *Messiah of Evil* suggests that

American California was tainted with corruption, madness and violence from the outset.

The film's eeriness is enhanced by the fact that much of it is set at night, in darkness enhanced by artificial lighting. As Stephen Thrower notes:

> [Huyck] turns the late-night carparks and shopping malls of the San Fernando valley into a hyperreal nightmare, where horror lurks in multiple window displays, endless storefronts, row upon row of parked cars. He captures a sense of unease that you sometimes get in our mechanized society when the fever of daily traffic is subdued by nightfall [. . .] inhuman, hostile places, emerging after dark from behind the façade of banality.[5]

The two most remarkable set-pieces take place in a supermarket and a movie theatre respectively, as Toni and Laura are (separately) stalked and then torn apart by 'infected' but soberly clad townsfolk.

Joseph Lang's scattered and increasingly fearful diaries, discovered by Arletty after she takes up residence in his beachside home, evoke the escalating horrors of Lovecraft's short story 'The Call of Cthulhu' (1928). They establish that Point Dune is still haunted by events connected to the most notorious real-life horror story associated with the Anglo-American settlement of California – the ill-fated journey to California undertaken by the Donner Party. One hundred years before, he writes, the moon turned blood red and then 'things began to happen'. These included the discovery that the town's children were eating raw meat. It is said that 'the whole town was festering with it' – 'it' being some sort of corrosive, contagious and apparently unstoppable evil. Having become aware of this rot at the heart of Point Dune, Joseph succumbed to this same malady, and slowly turned into one of the undead creatures that now stalk the town's deserted streets.

Just before Arletty kills Joseph to save herself, he haltingly explains that 'What happened a hundred years ago is happening again.' As a flashback to the late nineteenth century unfolds, Joseph's voice-over tells us that:

> A hundred years ago, a hunter first saw him. A stranger in black on a horse. He told the hunter that he had been a minster and come off the mountain with the Donner Party. He passed that horrible winter with them, and saw men commit hideous acts. He said he himself had eaten human flesh but had survived because he had faith – faith in a new master. The hunter didn't understand when the Dark Stranger said he was spreading this new religion. When they found the hunter . . . he looked as if he'd been attacked by some kind of animal – half eaten.

The 'new master' (presumably Satan), worked through the Dark Stranger, who spread his contagious 'new religion' through the town of New Bethlehem (later known as Point Dune). After biting the hunter who saw him emerge from the forest (who had to be put down like a rabid dog), the Dark Stranger 'watched the chaos' and 'walked into the sea', vowing to come back in a century to a 'world tired and disillusioned – a world looking back to Old Gods, and old, dark ways – our world'. The only way to avert this catastrophe is to destroy the infected town 'before the moon turns blood red once more, and he returns to lead them up the coast and inland into the cities'. What we have here, then, is an apocalyptic prophecy explicitly connected to a foundational historical event pertaining to the establishment of modern California – as well as a sense, as is often the case in Lovecraft, that small and nautically minded communities are particularly receptive to unwholesome and arcane belief systems. However, whereas Lovecraft's fiction, like that of Stephen King and Shirley Jackson, is associated with New England, in *Messiah of Evil* it is amidst the purportedly 'newer' landscape of Northern California that the horror takes hold.

In the film's closing moments, Arletty and Thom desperately try to flee the zombie horde which has chased them towards the beach. The townsfolk have also come to 'to stare at the ocean and wait'. Thom drowns as they try to swim towards a boat, whilst Arletty drifts into unconsciousness and is pulled from the sea as the blood-red sun sets on the horizon. After being dragged from the water she is then presented as an offering to the Dark Stranger, who has now re-emerged from the ocean. After this, Arletty is dispatched to the urban asylum (probably in San Francisco), burdened with the knowledge that the apocalyptic horrors that possess Point Dune will soon take over the rest of the world – indeed, she may be helping to spread the contagion. As the end credits roll, we are left in no doubt that a supernatural threat that first took hold on the Northern California coastline has already started to infiltrate the city. As Arletty roams the corridors of the asylum at night and 'waits', she tries to 'warn them that back there in that small town on the coast they're growing in number and moving out into the rest of the world, spreading their sickness . . . !'.

*Messiah of Evil* engages with several key thematic concerns associated with the California Gothic tradition, most notably in its reference to the cultural and historical legacy of the most notorious catastrophe associated with the mid-nineteenth-century American settlement of California. Like *Ravenous* (1999), *The Fog* (1980) and *Winchester* (2018), *Messiah of Evil* is haunted by the ghosts of the Californian past.

In the concluding chapter of *Americans and the California Dream*, Kevin Starr argues that during 'the years of its emergence as a regional civilization, what

California meant, and what it would continue to mean, was never resolvable
into a clear formula'.[6] He compared the region's sense of itself to that found in
other parts of the United States:

> Unlike the Confederate South, California could not take its identity from a
> tragic past culminating in an ordeal in which it romantically defended a deeply
> mythic conception of itself. Although just as violent, California's sins were less
> institutionalized. The Indian was not kept in formal slavery, but he was exter-
> minated at the wish and at the expense of the legislature; and for years in the
> southern part of the state under the guise of penal labor, Indians were hawked
> from the auction-block. The American South paid its price and continued
> to pay it. Complicity and atonement lay at the core of its experience, darkly
> tangled and then flowering forth in a literature great because it was earned in
> guilt and pain. But California concealed its sins and all but banished the tragic
> sense. Crimes remained unacknowledged or were sentimentalized, and, as if
> by common consent, responsibility was forgotten in the sunshine.[7]

In *Messiah of Evil*, as in the other films discussed in this chapter, California is
no longer able to conceal its sins with sunshine, and crimes committed during
the initial years of American settlement – and even further back in the regional
past – are brought to light in ways which profoundly destabilise the communities and the individuals who have profited from these acts. *Messiah of Evil*'s
surreal but effective evocation of one of the most notorious episodes in the
region's colonial history underlines the significance which this foundational
horror holds within the California Gothic.

## 'Pioneer Martyrs of California': The Gothic Legacy of the Donner Party

The Salem Witch Trials were the historical event which most influenced the
New England Gothic. The ordeal undergone by the Donner Party during the
bitter winter of 1846/7 plays a broadly equivalent role within the California
Gothic tradition.[8] Faye Ringel observes that in the weeks following the publication of Shirley Jackson's infamous 1948 short story, 'The Lottery', the author
was inundated with angry letters from people demanding to know where in
New England the events detailed took place so that they could go and see
such a ritual for themselves. Jackson did not actually specify the locale, but
that mattered little. For these correspondents, 'New England is a logical setting for Gothic Medievalism, a place where anything *could* happen, because
unthinkable, supernatural things once *did* happen there.'[9] The Witch Trials, as

W. Scott Poole further observes, 'proved that the Old World obsession with satanic pacts and supernatural evil had come to colonial America'.[10]

Like the Salem Witch Trials, the story of the Donner Party helped to establish anxieties which would be associated with the region in which these events took place thereafter. Furthermore, the Donner Party episode also occurred at a pivotal moment in regional history. The events of the winter of 1846/7 began to unfold just over a year before the discovery of gold exponentially accelerated American settlement and hastened the move towards statehood. The legend which grew up around the Donner tragedy during the early years of American California persists to this day. In his 1949 volume, *California: The Great Exception*, Carey McWilliams argued that what most differentiated California from other US states was that it had

> not grown or evolved so much as it has been hurtled forward, rocket-fashion, by a series of chain reaction explosions. [. . .] Europeans have long marveled at the driving force, the 'restless energy,' of America; but it is only in California that this energy is coeval with statehood. Elsewhere the tempo of development was slow at first, and gradually accelerated as energy accumulated. But in California the lights went on all at once, in a blaze, and they have never been dimmed.[11]

In the story of the Donner Party we see in embryonic form a recurrent California Gothic theme: the unexpected (and often violent) cost of relentless forward momentum.

As Starr (1973) argues, the 'fable' of California history at the end of the nineteenth century encompassed a 'pastoral past, progressive and colorful present, imperial future – a proud and optimistic fable, one that conferred a sense of importance and glamour upon a remote, underdeveloped region'.[12] However,

> the fable did not contain the entire truth. The California experience had its nether side, a burden of violence and frustration and failure. A sort of counter-fable ran through California historiography – which took its design from the expectations of the primary fable. Surveying their brief history, Californians detected a terrible burden as well as a glory.
> *The tragedy of the Donner party provided California with its most compelling counter-fable* [my italics].[13]

Similarly, H. Jennifer Brady (1979) has also argued that 'the experience of the family has become the original antimyth of the golden land in which the promised land becomes the heart of darkness'.[14]

The trials of the Donner Party were rapidly absorbed into the wider cultural imaginary. Their tribulations have been recounted and reimagined in countless novels, non-fiction accounts, scholarly works and works of visual media, and interest in the catastrophe remains strong. Recent works inspired by (or directly about) these events include Alma Katsu's 2018 horror novel, *The Hunger*, and the non-fiction volumes *The Indifferent Stars Above: The Harrowing Saga of a Donner Party Bride* (2009) by Daniel James Brown and *The Best Land Under Heaven: The Donner Party in the Age of Manifest Destiny* (2017) by Michael Wallis.

In Antonia Bird's 1999 film, *Ravenous*, the tale of the Donner Party is directly conflated with the violent birth of a new American state. Here, American soldiers charged with helping settlers to safely reach the 'Promised Land' beyond the Sierra Nevada mountain range are infected by an insatiable and self-interested hunger for human flesh (the parallel with the contagion in *Messiah of Evil* is obvious). Here, California becomes the staging post for a form of federally sanctioned murder that also serves as a sardonic commentary on the genocidal excesses of nineteenth-century American imperialism.

Before considering this film, I will briefly outline some of the ways in which perceptions of the episode have evolved since 1846/7, and discuss how they relate to the California Gothic characteristics outlined in my Introduction. As detailed there, my take on the sub-genre is rooted in the binary oppositions which grew out of the mismatch between the very best of what California appeared to offer to those seeking the ultimate 'good life' and the nightmarish flipside of those same qualities. As a pivotal 'counter-fable' (to recall Starr's apt phrase), the story of the Donner Party epitomises these binaries. On the one hand, it is the 'inspiring' story of white settlers whose desire to complete their journey was so powerful that they endured months of terrifying deprivation before they were rescued by valiant relief parties. On the other, many of these same survivors ate the bodies of their own dead.

Indeed, survival cannibalism has much to do with the expedition's lasting notoriety. As Donald L. Hardesty notes, the death toll for settlers travelling West during this period was relatively low, given the risks involved, but there were certainly other broadly similar calamities along the trail, and for this reason 'the tragedy is not unique'.[15] Yet, he continues,

> unlike the other tragedies of the American overland emigration, the saga of the Donner Party has persisted in memory, becoming an icon of the immigration experience. Why? [. . .] it did not even have the highest death toll – that honor belongs to the Mormon Willie Handcart Party, which lost sixty-eight members (in contrast to the thirty-six members of the Donner Party who were entrapped that winter).[16]

He argues that the story has in part had such an enduring cultural afterlife because it is an account of 'survival, heroism, conflict, greed, weakness and failure', which allowed early writers and commentators to 'play upon morality themes' that were also emphasised in many later fictional and non-fiction treatments of the event.[17] However, it was the 'alleged practice of cannibalism' which 'sets the Donner Party apart from the other tragedies of the American overland emigration'.[18]

Kristin Johnson (1996) also highlights a revealing disparity between the practical and the cultural significance of this grim regional episode. She points out that '[in] the broader historical perspective the disaster itself is of minor significance – it had little effect on subsequent events'.[19] Nevertheless,

> its impact on people has been profound. Since 1847 the ill-fated wagon train has figured in hundreds of works, not only histories and articles but also novels, short stories, juvenile literature, poems, plays, films, documentaries and even an opera and a ballet. Though the lurid act of cannibalism is the Donner party's best known aspect, the story's wide appeal cannot be attributed to mere prurience, for most of these works gloss over the horrors. Instead, the motivating factor appears to lie in the human story: unlike many epics of the American West, the Donner saga is not centered on the exploits of a few exceptional men who sought adventure, but on families, on ordinary people caught up in an extraordinary situation. It is a dreadful irony that hopes of prosperity, health and a new life in California's fertile valleys led many only to misery, hunger and death on her stony threshold.[20]

The first major book about the Donner Party, *History of the Donner Party: A Tragedy of the Sierras* (1880), was written by journalist Charles McGlashan, who corresponded with survivors, read contemporaneous diaries and claimed to have personally interviewed 'the most important actors in the tragedy'.[21] In the preface, he noted that 'New and fragmentary versions of the sad story have appeared almost every year since the unfortunate occurrence.'[22] His account, would, McGlashan asserted, at last provide the survivors with the opportunity to 'forever supplant these distorted and fabulous accounts'. There was no need for exaggeration or sensationalism, he implied, for 'The truth is sufficiently terrible.'[23]

McGlashan accurately characterised the event as a key – if 'mournful' – milestone in the origin story of the new state:

> California's history is replete with tragic, startling events. These events are landmarks by which its advancement is traced. One of the most mournful of these is recorded in this work – a work intended as a contribution, not to

the literature, but to the history of the state. More thrilling than romance, more terrible than fiction, the sufferings of the Donner party form a cold contrast to the joys of pleasure-seekers who today look down upon the lake from the windows of silver palace cars.[24]

McGlashan's preface and opening chapter emphasise that the very site where this unthinkable tragedy occurred is now, in 1880, a well-established tourist destination rendered accessible to all thanks to the railroad, and attractive to visitors not only because of its notorious backstory, but because it contains 'one of the finest and most picturesque lakes in the Sierra'.[25] The contrast between the locale's stunning natural beauty and the horror of the events for which it remains best known is emphasised.[26] For McGlashan, the travellers who perished in the snows of Truckee Lake (and the traumatised survivors) suffered for the necessary cause of a greater (American) California:

> The pioneers of a new country are deserving of a niche in the country's history. The pioneers who become martyrs to the cause of the develop-ment of an almost unknown land deserve to have a place in the hearts of its inhabitants. The far-famed Donner Party were, in a peculiar sense, pioneer martyrs of California. Before the discovery of gold, before the highway across the continent was fairly marked out, while untold dangers lurked by the wayside, and unnumbered foes awaited the emigrants, the Donner Party started for California. None but the brave and venturesome, none but the energetic and courageous, could undertake the journey.[27]

Due in part to McGlashan's retelling, during the latter half of the nineteenth century, the Donner Party began to be seen in a much more sympathetic light than was the case in the years immediately following events. They were, as in his account, often recast as tragic exemplars of the 'pioneer spirit'. The rehabilita-tion process continued well into the twentieth century. A statue was erected at Truckee Lake with considerable civic fanfare in 1918. The 'Pioneer Monument' was dedicated to 'all those who ventured across the plains to settle in California'.[28] The ceremony was attended by three of the remaining survivors, all of them elderly women who were children at the time of their ordeal.[29] Johnson notes that 'As the years passed, California's early heritage became romanticized; pioneer societies sprang up and old settlers were honored. McGlashan had rescued the Donner Party from obscurity and made them "martyr pioneers".'[30]

Yet there was no getting away from the cannibalism. In his discussion of the episode, Starr argues that one survivor – German immigrant Lewis Keseberg – became the 'Cain of California'.[31] The last member of the party rescued from

Truckee Lake, Keseberg was accused by a member of the rescue team of murdering Tamsen Donner and hiding her family's money.[32] As an earlier California historian, George R. Stewart, put it in his 1936 account, *Ordeal by Hunger: The Story of the Donner Party*, 'The deeds and character of Keseberg have caused more controversy than any other subject connected to the Donner Party.'[33] Ethan Rarick's account of Keseberg's fate post-rescue argues that '[he] suffered more than anyone else, although in many ways this had more to do with public perceptions than actual events'.[34] He continues:

> On his arrival at Sutter's Fort, whispering rumors painted him a ghoul. The gossip compounded until, motivated by an especially wagging and malevolent tongue, Keseberg sued one of his rescuers for defamation. The jury found in Keseberg's favor but concluded that his slanderers had broken tarnished goods: Damages totaled one dollar. In time he became a public caricature, the demented ogre who had relished his cannibalism.[35]

For Starr, Keseberg became a symbolic scapegoat for the new state. Whereas, with time, the other survivors 'became respected for what they had undergone', he was destined to play a very different role:

> [B]ecause atonement was necessary for their communal failure, Keseberg was made the guilty one. It was the communal failure which frightened most profoundly, and cannibalism was but its exponent. The Donner Party had crossed the outer frontier of California as dystopia. The earthly Eden could turn – for ordinary men and women – into an eating of one another's flesh. In that each wagon train was a society and California was a sum total of wagon trains, the implications of the Donner experience terrified. It provided an anti-myth to the whole myth of the West, California in particular. Keseberg ate flesh, but so did others. He bore the collective myth so that they might be free. Through circumstances, but also through design, he was forced to go through life as a warning that California's history might have locked within it some unutterable horror.[36]

In this analysis, Keseberg, the outcast survivor/villain is not allowed to be a 'pioneer martyr' in the McGlashan mode, but instead reconfigured as a kind of Californian Tessie Hutchinson (the sacrificial scapegoat in Jackson's 'The Lottery'), symbolically expelled from the community for the 'greater good' of the regional collective.

Early encounters between English colonists and what they perceived to be the frightening wilderness of the 'New World' irrevocably shaped the ways in which North American culture thereafter related to such environments and to the peoples associated with them. As Ringel notes:

From the earliest days of the New England colonies, European traditions of the monstrous took root in the stony soil and flourished; narratives of the fall from grace of those settlers, of inbred families, cruelty, and generational hauntings combined nostalgia for a medieval or colonial golden age with the stronger belief that from the past came horror and evil.[37]

Although their ill-fated journey West took place more than two centuries after the period Ringel is referring to, the disaster which struck the Donner Party is also the story of settlers who 'fall from grace' (albeit in a less theologically minded way than their Puritan predecessors). Furthermore, like many New England Gothic (and Rural Gothic) narratives, this is another cautionary tale about naive newcomers whose failure to understand their new environment has fatal consequences.

However, the relationship between past and present differs considerably between the two varieties of regional Gothic. It's a difference articulated by Joan Didion in her classic 1966 work of non-fiction reportage, 'Some Dreamers of the Golden Dream' (discussed in Chapter 2). Didion was reporting on a horrific murder which had taken place within the new suburban sprawl of the San Bernardino Valley. The case was a particularly sordid one involving a pregnant housewife sentenced to life imprisonment for setting her husband on fire. Didion wrote: 'The future looks good in the Golden Land, because no one remembers the past.'[38] The insight referred to a very particular kind of 'new California milieu'. This was a world in which the recency of SoCal suburbia meant that it served as the perfect incubator for domestic atrocity. Didion was suggesting that the promise of a beautiful life in a beautiful land was inherently linked to a bone-deep denial of the actual history of the place. This kind of willed amnesia also, Didion suggests, leaves one prone to succumbing to romantic but ill-advised flights of fancy: 'The past is not believed to have any bearing upon the present or future, out in the Golden land where every day the world is born anew.'[39]

Didion's often sinister take on her home state allies this sense of disconnection and willing blindness with the darkest aspects of Anglo-American settlement. Indeed, her non-fiction frequently evinces a decidedly Gothic sensibility. This tendency is foregrounded by her compulsive return to the story of the Donner Party, which for her has profound symbolic and familial resonances. As Robert Lacy observes:

In a very real way the fate of the Donner Party seems at the center of what makes Joan Didion tick. Her family came out West in the middle of the nineteenth century, at the same time as the Donner group. She is a fifth-generation Californian and more than a little proud of the fact. It crops up often in her writing.[40]

Didion's obsession with the Donner Party has been noted by many of those who have commentated upon her writing, including her biographer Tracy Daugherty, who also argues that the Donner 'myth' is central to Didion's sense of self, underpinning the unsentimental 'wagon train mentality' she inherited from her parents. Daugherty notes that the version of the story which Didion and her classmates read as Sacramento schoolchildren in the late 1930s/early 1940s was McGlashan's.[41] It is clearly a tale that has resonated throughout her career. The 2017 documentary about her life and work even opens by mentioning the episode's foundational place in her literary psychogeography.[42] 'I am haunted by the cannibalism of the Donner Party', Didion is reported to have declared in 1970.[43]

In *Where I Was From* (2003), Didion's later meditation on familial and regional history, she recalls being brought to visit a Sacramento asylum with her girl scout troop, and being expected to sing in the presence of 'the put away, the now intractably lost'.[44] Typically, the fate of these 'abandoned' inmates (which would one day include her own great-aunt, who was institutionalised in Napa) and the brutal pragmatism of the families who have left them behind is attributed to attitudes birthed during the arduous overland journey to California:

> Were not such abandonments the very heart and soul of the crossing story? Jettison weight? Keep moving? Bury the dead in the trail and run the wagons over it? Never dwell on what got left behind, never look back at all? *Remember*, Virginia Reed had warned attentive California children, we who had been trained since virtual infancy in the horrors she had survived, *never take no cutoffs and hurry along as fast as you can*. Once on a drive to Lake Tahoe I found myself impelled to instruct my brother's small children in the dread lesson of the Donner Party, just in case he had thought to spare them. 'Don't worry about it,' another attentive California child, Patricia Hearst, recalled having told herself during the time she was locked in a closet by her kidnappers. 'Don't examine your feelings. Never examine your feelings – they're no help at all.'[45]

The Donner Party also resurfaces in the final lines of *Where I Was From*. Didion describes a poignant deathbed scene during which her dying mother insisted on passing on a family heirloom, even though handling the object, a silver ladle, gave the mortally ill woman comfort. 'I was still pretending that she would get through the Sierra before the snows fell,' Didion recalls in closing. 'She was not.'[46] For Didion, the most infamous 'dread lesson' associated with the Anglo-American settlement of California is more than a distasteful, if fascinating historical episode. It is at the very heart of what it means to be a *true* Californian. Like the community of Point Dune in *Messiah of Evil*, Didion is haunted by, but inextricably drawn towards the bloody legacy of the pioneer past. However, in this instance, the story is presented not as a foundational evil but reframed as a fortifying, if traumatic, regional and personal origin story.

It is difficult to think of a more vivid example of real-world 'Frontier Gothic' than the scenario which unfolded at Truckee Lake during the winter of 1846/7, and yet there is no mention of the Donner Party – or the settlement of California at all (save a fleeting reference to a poem by Charlotte Perkins Gilman) – in the only volume thus far focusing on this aspect of the wider American Gothic tradition: *Frontier Gothic: Terror and Wonder at the Frontier in American Literature*, edited by David Mogen, Scott P. Sanders and Joanne B. Karpinski (1993).[47] Nevertheless, Didion's consistent engagement with the topic reflects many of the traits of the 'Frontier Gothic' as outlined therein. The editors' note that 'The associations between American frontier heritage and Gothicism are even more fundamental than many adaptations of the frontier metaphor themselves suggest', and that for white Americans, 'the most popular origin myth concerns the frontier.'[48] For Mogen, Sanders and Karpinski, 'The dark, gothic underside of American frontier literature ironically symbolizes the desolation wrought by progress, the psychological deprivation of alienation, and the threatening but revolutionary possibilities that appear when civilized conventions are left behind.'[49]

The Donner Party narrative is the white frontier experience turned worst-case scenario because it so brutally exposes the stark moral choices to be made when 'civilized' conventions collapse in the face of dire physical and environmental conditions. If, as Mogen et al. argue, 'American frontier gothic literature derives from this conflict between the inscripted history of civilization and the history of the other, somehow immanent in the landscape of the frontier', it is hard to think of a more representative 'landscape of the frontier' then California in the mid- to late nineteenth century.[50] Yet, with the promise of that frontier also came a distinctive (white) variety of cultural and historical amnesia, highlighted by Didion in *Where I Was From*.

The difference between the American West and the South, she argues, is that 'in the South they remained convinced that they had bloodied their land with history. In California we did not believe that history could bloody the land, or even touch it.'[51] It is for this same reason that the fate of the Donner Party plays a central role in the development of the 'California Gothic' tradition. Their story vividly demonstrates that the Anglo-American settlement of California was tainted with moral compromise, misery and horror from the outset. As Nowak-McNeice and Zarzycka put it in their own consideration of the relationship between the Donner Party and the Gothic:

> If we think about the phantoms of the abused and the specters of the vic-
> timized that populate California's history; if we think of the category of the
> uncanny, which makes problematic the very category of home that certain
> groups of people claim for themselves while denying the same right to oth-
> ers; if we think of the bodily harm systematically inflicted upon numerous
> Californians throughout its history, then the Gothic emerges as a highly
> adequate context for the story of California and the Donner-Reed Party.[52]

However, there is also no getting away from the fact that these horrific events were also inextricably tied to the seductive promise of a better life in a beautiful land. It is often suggested, as McGlashan did back in 1880, that the rewards of making it across the Sierra Nevadas were so considerable that it was worth the risk and the suffering. Echoing this tendency in 'Notes From a Native Daughter' (1965), Didion described the flights back home she used to make when living in New York, and speculated that she was trying to prove

> that I had not meant to leave at all, because in at least one respect, California –
> the California we are talking about – resembles Eden: it is assumed that those
> who absent themselves from its blessings have been banished, exiled by some
> perversity of heart. Did not the Donner-Reed Party, after all, eat its own dead
> to reach Sacramento?[53]

## 'It's Lonely Being a Cannibal – Hard to Make Friends': *Ravenous* (1999)

The darkly humorous historical horror film *Ravenous*, conflates the beginnings of American California with the darkest possible metaphorical reading of the Donner Party's ordeal. Here, the rapacious and seemingly unquenchable ter-ritorial appetite of the nineteenth-century United States is combined with the supernatural horror of the 'wendigo': a creature from Native American folklore which, in part thanks to the slow-burning recognition now granted *Ravenous*, is now most often associated by contemporary popular culture with the actions of monstrous white men.[54] Here, greed, relentless consumption and the high cost of 'progress' are irrevocably associated with the state's founda-tion. As Danette DiMarco observes, it 'directly establishes a specific temporal and geographical setting – during the Mexican-American War, in the wilds of Northern California – in order to consider how the wendigo serves to critique

Manifest Destiny and military resistance'.[55] Because I have discussed the film's canny deployment of the wendigo myth in detail in a previous publication, I will not engage with this aspect of the film again here, but will focus instead upon the ways in which, through its satirical recasting of the Donner narrative, it interacts with the defining tropes of the California Gothic.[56]

The nightmarish resonances of the Party's ordeal in the California wilderness are emphasised in two twenty-first-century non-fiction accounts – Rarick's *Desperate Passage* (2008) and Wallis's *The Best Land Under Heaven* (2017) – as well as horror-inflected fictional treatments such as Katsu's 2018 horror novel *The Hunger*. Wallis argues that the Donner Party story is:

> a long and complex account of how a group of people from varied backgrounds, stratified in age, wealth, education, and ethnicity, followed their different dreams. Out of necessity, they were made to unite and battle against the unknown – weather, nature and finally life and death. Their story has come to symbolize the Great American Dream gone awry. The Donner party's fate highlighted the ambitiousness, folly, recklessness, and ruthlessness that marked the great expansionist westward movement. The party becomes a microcosm of the United States which, while busily consuming other nations (Mexico and Indian tribes) that stood in the way of westward migration, had the potential to consume itself. This Gothic tale of cannibalism draws a real parallel between individuals consuming flesh and the desire of a country to consume the continent [. . .] They found that in pursuing what came to be known as the American dream, nightmares are sometimes the consequence.[57]

Wallis's suggestion that the events of that fateful winter constitute a vivid and appropriately ghastly metaphor for the rapacious imperial ambitions of the mid-nineteenth-century United States chimes precisely with the way in which the episode is fictionalised in *Ravenous*. The film is exactly the 'Gothic tale of cannibalism' evoked in his analysis.

*Ravenous* is set in 1847 – only a few months before the discovery of gold at Sutter's Mill transformed the prospects of the future state. In early 1848, the United States and Mexico signed the Treaty of Guadalupe Hidalgo, thereby 'ceding to the United States all Mexican territories north of the Rio Grande'.[58] As Starr puts it, 'After more than three hundred years of exploration, settlement, evangelization, political strife, trade, and reconnaissance, the destiny of Alta California had become clear. It would be an American province. The United States now extended from sea to shining sea.'[59] Foregrounding this connection to American imperialism from the beginning, *Ravenous* opens with a shot of the Stars and Stripes fluttering against a bright blue sky, before introducing us to a character whose arc directly challenges the self-congratulatory patriotism of the era.

Army Captain John Boyd (Guy Pearce) is a supposed 'war hero' tormented by an acute awareness of his own cowardice. Flashbacks establish that he only survived a fierce battle with Mexican troops because he played dead. Boyd was revived when the blood of his commanding officer ran down his throat. This unwitting act of cannibalism gave him a sudden burst of courage and he turned the tables on the Mexican forces, winning the contested position single-handedly. Boyd may technically be a hero, but both he and his superiors know that his commitment to the cause of relentless territorial expansion is less than absolute. When he disgraces himself by vomiting during the banquet that follows his commendation, it gives his commanding officer General Slauson (John Spencer) the excuse he needs to send him as far away as possible – to the new frontier of California. 'So, the brass decided to reward you with a little appointment to the California sun?', his latest commander, the genial Colonel Hart (Jeffrey Jones) jests, as a freezing wind howls outside Boyd's ramshackle new posting, Fort Spencer.

Soon after his arrival, Boyd and his comrades render aid to a traveller who claims to have found himself in dire peril during the journey overland. The stranger, a Scotsman calling himself Colqhoun (Robert Carlyle), tells them that he has just survived three terrible months snowbound in a cave with his fellow travellers. The starving group, he hesitantly admits, gradually resorted to eating everything that possibly could be eaten before finally turning to the bodies of the dead. However, once they ate human flesh their hunger soon returned, but was 'more . . . severe. Savage'. One of their party, Colonel Ives (who Colqhoun claims led them astray in the first place), could 'not be satisfied', and 'Things got out of hand.' The Colonel murdered everyone, but Colqhoun fled into the wilderness, allegedly leaving behind one other survivor, a woman named Mrs McCready (a possible analogue for Tamsen Donner).

Colonel Hart immediately decides that they need to send a rescue party, but his preparations are interrupted when George (Joseph Runningfox), one of the Fort's two Ojibwe servants, delivers a dire warning. As he points to gruesome images painted on deerskin, George explains that a wendigo is 'an old Indian myth from the North' which says that if a man eats the flesh of another, he steals his flesh and his spirit and the cannibal's hunger will become insatiable: 'And the more he eats the more he wants to, and the more he eats the stronger he becomes.' When Hart, polite but patronisingly sceptical, says: 'George, people don't still do that, do they?', the answer is a pointed one: 'White man eat the body of Jesus Christ every Sunday.' As DiMarco notes of this key scene, 'George serves as a physical marker for how stories migrate and change . . . [he] tells the tale of the Wendigo in his native language, translated by Colonel Hart into English.' She argues that this 'act of translation demonstrates a move whereby one culture's story is adapted by another. The native myth gets "infiltrated" by the "non-native" one.'[60]

When the rescue party near the cave after a lengthy trek into the mountains, the stranger's behaviour grows increasingly erratic. Boyd and another soldier, the gung-ho Reich (Neal McDonough), explore the cave and find only human remains (including the tattered remains of a Colonel's uniform). It becomes clear that everyone except Colqhoun has been eaten, leaving the identity of the real culprit in little doubt. Just as Boyd raises the alarm, Colqhoun attacks his comrades, displaying preternatural strength, speed and violence. Boyd is again the last man standing. Desperate to escape, he jumps off a cliff and ends up in a deep pit with a severe leg wound. Next to him lies the body of his dying comrade, Reich. To gain the strength necessary to return to the Fort, he must again drink the blood of the dead. Desperate to alert the others (but also afraid of dying), he reluctantly does so.

Boyd staggers back to Fort Spencer as the only apparent survivor of Colqhoun's vicious onslaught, but his frantic demeanour arouses suspicion, and his tale is not an especially convincing one. (No one save his sister Martha [Sheila Tousey] seems to care that George, who accompanied the rescue party, was also killed: as in many non-fiction accounts of the Donner Party story, Native American deaths are seen as incidental, or irrelevant, when compared to the suffering of whites.)

The only one who believes Boyd is Martha, who tells him that if he wants to stop the wendigo, he must be willing to die himself. The army top brass has also dispatched a replacement for the slain Colonel Hart. To Boyd's horror, this new officer is none other than 'Colonel Ives' – the spitting image of the rabid wildman Colqhoun – neatly dressed in army blues and a great deal more composed than his previous incarnation. No one who has interacted with Colqhoun remains alive save for Boyd and the Fort's resident alcoholic Major Knox (Stephen Spinella), who was so drunk he doesn't recall meeting him. The other soldiers now suspect that Boyd murdered their comrades.

However, when the two men are left alone, 'Ives' freely admits that he and Colqhoun are one and the same and reveals his own backstory. He began his journey West as a sickly tuberculosis patient travelling to a Californian sanatorium, hoping to extend his limited lifespan. After becoming lost without food, he killed and ate the Native American guide who had told him about the wendigo myth, and immediately realised that he had never felt better. After killing and eating five more people in the past three months, Colqhoun now feels reborn, and cannot believe that Boyd, who has also experienced these effects, will not submit to temptation: 'You've tasted it. Felt its power. Yet you're resisting.' When Boyd retorts, 'Because it's wrong', his nemesis smartly responds: 'Ah, mortality – the last bastion of a coward.'

Colqhoun's original motive for travelling to California was a common one during the mid- to late nineteenth century (and thereafter). The wide open spaces and clean air of Southern California were often touted as a restorative tonic. The region was described by the secretary of the Immigration Association of San Bernardino County as 'Nature's Great Sanitarium', and one newspaper editorial claimed that 'There are some thirty or forty thousand people in Southern California who were doomed to death in the eastern climate, and are allowed under these balmy skies to continue their lives to old age.'[61] Colqhoun's previous health problems are reminiscent of the situation faced by one of the lesser-known members of the Donner Party, Irishman Luke Halloran. Halloran was a TB sufferer, who, as Rarick puts it, 'hoped the West would cure him, not kill him', but he succumbed to his illness before the group reached the Sierra Nevada.[62] Colqhoun found in his journey to California exactly the miraculous restoration to health which was associated with the California landscape even in the early days of Westward expansion. Here, however, the California 'cure' is inextricably bound up with cannibalism and monstrosity.

The remainder of *Ravenous* focuses on the attempt by Colqhoun/Ives to persuade Boyd to join him. Fort Spencer's location plays a vital part in this plan. Colqhoun's intention is that once he has 'converted' Boyd and other US army allies, they will feast on the ever-increasing flood of gold-hungry travellers making their way to California. Once General Slauson, the commander of the region, has also been 'turned', the wendigos will have full (and federally sanctioned) control of the major transit route through the mountains. After he finishes outlining his masterplan, Colqhoun stretches his arms wide and gazes with satisfaction at the Californian wilderness in the distance: 'We just need a home. And this country is seeking to be whole. Stretching out its arms and consuming all it can. And we merely follow.'

Despite Boyd's frantic attempts to prevent this horrific scheme from coming to fruition, the closing moments of the film find both men trapped in the lethal embrace of a bear trap. Even as he and Colqhoun breathe their last – each man knowing that if Colqhoun survives only a little longer than Boyd, he will eat his enemy's flesh and survive – we have already seen General Slauson eat from the Fort's communal cooking pot, which is filled with a stew made from human flesh. Regardless of Boyd's final act of courage, California will very likely become the staging post for this latest – and most aggressive – stage of imperial development for the United States. As DiMarco also observes, the immoral self-interest championed by Colqhoun, and the wider systemic problems he represents, looks set to triumph after all.[63] In the final seconds, Martha comes across the duo, realises what has happened and immediately starts to walk towards the mountains. It's a closing image perhaps intended to underline the genocidal consequences which the American take-over would have for California's Native American population.

We are reminded early on in *Ravenous* that the now dominant American culture was forcibly imposed upon the peoples who inhabited that territory beforehand, just as the Spanish imposed their own culture and religion upon the Indigenous population when they first colonised the region centuries before. When Boyd is ordered to report to his commanding officer in the opening minutes, we first see General Slauson supervising orderlies who are moving his desk into an imposing new office: the fine-looking building is presumably a former Mexican stronghold now under American control. During their first meeting, Colonel Hart informs Boyd that Fort Spencer was originally a Span-ish mission: 'We inherited her. Now we're a way station for Western travellers on their way through the Nevadas.' In addition to this brief reference to the Spanish presence in California, when Hart is outlining the 'skeleton crew' who staff the outpost during the winter, he mentions the Fort's Native American servants, George and Martha (as in Washington), last: 'They're both locals, sort of came with the place.' This kind of suggestive 'layering' – in which Spanish/Mexican California is built on/appropriated by white American settlers, in the same way that the Spanish wrested control of the territory from the region's original (Indigenous) inhabitants – is, as we shall see, a consistent theme of the California Gothic, as is the willed amnesia which so often accompanies these actions. Indeed, the unreliable memory of the alcoholic Major Knox means that no one can substantiate Boyd's claim that Ives *is* Colqhoun. Furthermore, the white appropriation of a creature from Algonquin mythology noted by DiMarco, is also suggestive of the ways in which a newer and even more aggressively expansive and rapacious Anglo-American culture will swallow up all that came before, at dire cost to the region's Indigenous inhabitants.

*Ravenous* draws upon two of the most infamous instances of survival can-nibalism in American history. The first is obviously that of the Donner Party. Colqhoun/Ives is essentially a hyperbolic version of Lewis Keseberg (the 'Cain of California', in Starr's words), the last survivor rescued, thereafter accused of killing and eating Tamsen Donner (although as Starr outlines, when McGlashan brought them together many years later, Tamsen's daughter Eliza believed his protestations of innocence).[64] The second instance is the case of a more concretely villainous figure: Colorado mountain-man turned mass murderer Alferd [sic] Packer, who in 1874 admitted eating his companions after they were trapped in a remote cabin for many weeks (he claimed to have done so out of desperation). In *Ravenous*, Manifest Destiny is reimagined as a bloody and darkly ironic foundational horror story in which those at the very forefront of the American colonisation effort – European immigrants in search of a new life, and the soldiers and officers of the US army – are transformed into *actual* cannibals, for whom the mass movement West is an opportunity to feed on the unwary. Greed and self-preservation are presented as the defining characteristics of white America, and the gateway to California looks set to become a slaughterhouse. The film also intersects with many of the elements discussed under the 'California Nightmare' heading in my Introduction.

As in several other narratives discussed in this volume, in *Ravenous* American California is seen as being particularly receptive to dangerous new movements which promise adherents 'rebirth' and an entirely new perspective on life. Colqhoun has characteristics in common with the fictional cult leaders who will be discussed in Chapters 6 and 7. He is a charismatic master manipulator who has been transformed – for the better, as he sees it – by his decision to eat human flesh. He sees Boyd as an ideal potential convert and tries to force him – using both verbal and physical 'persuasion' – to join his cause. Though he ultimately fails in this mission, Colqhoun does manage to 'recruit' Colonel Hart and General Slauson.

Colqhoun also epitomises the fear that the new California will prioritise self-interest and narcissism. For him, survival is worth any degree of moral compromise, and his fellow human beings are either cattle to be consumed or potentially useful allies to be won over to be converted to his horrific cause. For him, the opening of the frontier is foremost an opportunity for personal gratification, and 'progress' is to be exploited to its fullest. The fact that California is a territory in a state of transformational flux – as yet lacking in the traditional military and political structures found on the East Coast – will surely aid the cannibals further as they consolidate their influence over the newest state in the Union.

Finally, there is the Midwestern connection. In Nathanael West's 1939 novel, *The Day of the Locust*, the main protagonist, Tod Hackett, acerbically observes of a certain kind of Los Angeles newcomer that 'they had come to California to die'.[65] The Donner Party, who, like so many of their successors, began their trip in the Midwest – Independence, Missouri, to be exact – are the original 'doomed Midwesterners' so often found in the California Gothic. As Shannon A. Novak and Kelly J. Dixon note of the crude precis of their story which persists to this day:

> This narrative remains simple: Good farming people from the Midwest set out to make new homes on the western frontier. They dally a bit too long, take a wrong turn, and become trapped in the mountains by an early winter storm. To survive, they resort to cannibalism.[66]

Midwesterners do not explicitly feature in *Ravenous*, but the hopeful settlers which Colqhoun knows will soon come streaming towards the Sierra Nevada foothills – and hence, towards Fort Spencer – are an obvious analogue for the naive outsiders who so often pay a terrible price for their dream of achieving the 'good life' in California.

## California Genocide in *The Fog* (1980) and *Winchester* (2018)

I will now discuss two supernatural horror films in which the establishment of American California is associated with even more profound historical wrong-doing. John Carpenter's 1980 film, *The Fog*, like *Messiah of Evil*, depicts coastal California as a locale tainted by callous self-interest and cold-blooded murder. The 2018 film *Winchester*, directed by Michael and Peter Spierig, draws upon the most infamous 'real-life' ghost story associated with the state, that of Sarah Winchester's 'Mystery House'. However, this is a retelling which elides the federally sanctioned genocide of many thousands of Native Americans which accompanied the first three decades of Californian statehood.

In both these films, in different ways, California (and Californians) are haunted by angry ghosts determined to take violent revenge upon those who have materially benefited from their demise. The guilty parties here are not *directly* responsible but are instead family members and descendants whose comfortable present-day circumstances are irrevocably linked to these foundational 'disruptive events'. Sarah Winchester is presented in *Winchester* as an immensely wealthy (if tormented) woman because of the rifles sold by her late husband's company. The townsfolk of Antonio Bay (the setting of *The Fog*) are about to celebrate the centenary of their community, which only exists because their not-so-distant ancestors committed mass murder and theft. In neither of these films is the relative 'newness' of the state any defence against supernatural attack. The bloody circumstances associated with the state's establishment have guaranteed that California has its own ghosts to contend with.

*The Fog* initially seemed to some critics like an odd follow-up to Carpenter's ground-breaking Slasher, *Halloween* (1978), even though, as Robert C. Cumbow observes, the films have more in common than meets the eye: 'Both *Halloween* and *The Fog* tell tales wrought from factual occurrences whose anniversaries are commemorated by a haunting return of fatal figures from the past. In each event, once-human beings are transmogrified into supernatural creatures of abnormal power.'[67] Despite these similarities, studio qualms meant that once initial shooting had concluded, Carpenter and his producer/co-writer Debra Hill were forced to undertake extensive (and gorier) reshoots because of perceived 'problems with the scares'.[68]

Carpenter's inspiration was the sight of a thick fog slowly creeping over Stonehenge when he attended a music festival in England. He was also determined to make a film indebted to the classical ghost story tradition. For this reason, *The Fog* begins with a classic 'spooky tale' framing device: a nocturnal campfire scene during which the supposedly tragic (rather than murderous) origins of Antonio Bay are outlined to local youngsters. It underlines that this is, 'in many ways, a film about narrative – about storytelling and its impact upon our lives'.[69] It is all the more interesting then, that whilst the film's obvious critique of white America in a general (i.e., national) sense has often rightly been noted, the regionally specific nature of this critique has thus far been largely overlooked.

*The Fog*'s basic premise is indeed one that befits an avowedly 'old-fashioned' ghost story. Antonio Bay is a Northern California coastal community which is gearing up to celebrate the 100th anniversary of the event which directly led to the town's establishment. On 21 April 1880, the *Elizabeth Dane*, a clipper ship laden with gold, was engulfed by a sudden fog and dashed on the rocks off nearby Spivey Point. All souls were lost. Despite the warning given by old sea dog Mr Machen (John Houseman) that 'when the fog returns to Antonio Bay, the men at the bottom of the sea will rise up', no one in Antonio Bay is prepared for the terrifying events which are about to unfold. On the night before this fateful anniversary, between the hours of 1:00 and 2:00 a.m., the eerie quiet of the town's empty streets is disrupted by a succession of strange occurrences. Payphones ring in an unearthly chorus. Neon lights flicker and petrol flows from gas pumps. It's a superbly evocative sequence anticipated by the similarly neon-accented nocturnal weirdness found in *Messiah of Evil*.

When local priest Father Malone (Hal Holbrook) discovers a leather-bound journal (written by his grandfather) hidden in the walls of the local church, he realises that the deceased passengers of the *Elizabeth Dane* had good reason to be angry. They were lepers originally confined on an island nearby. Led by a wealthy fellow sufferer named Edward Blake, they asked the fledgling settlement of Antonio Bay if they could set up their own community nearby. However, despite a seemingly amicable initial agreement, the community's leading citizens met in secret on 20 April 1880 (between 1:00 and 2 a.m.) and decided to engineer a shipwreck so that they could be rid of the lepers and steal their gold. Fires left burning at Spivey Point lured the *Elizabeth Dane* towards destruction, and the gold which the greedy settlers recovered from the wreck was used to turn Antonio Bay into a proper township.

It becomes clear that the ghosts want to make sure that 'Six Must Die' to avenge this callous crime. As the 'Night of the Fog' (as it is called in the script) unfolds, a loose coalition of newcomers and townsfolk, including DJ Stevie Wayne (Adrienne Barbeau), her young son Andy (Ty Mitchell), pragmatic local man Nick Castle (Tom Atkins), hitchhiker Elizabeth Solley (Jamie Lee Curtis), town bureaucrat Mrs Kathy Williams (Janet Leigh) and Father Malone, struggle to escape the relentlessly enveloping fog and the vengeful phantoms following in its wake.

*The Fog* has frequently (and persuasively) been interpreted as a critique of the avarice and inherent corruption of the United States. As Steve Smith argues, it hinges upon actively deconstructing Antonio Bay's glib self-celebration and mythologising tendencies.[70] The fact that it is set a hundred years after the establishment of the town charter is, he notes, 'more than simply an index of atmosphere'. Indeed,

> an important strand of Carpenter's film works to undermine the town's mythologized self-image as the very essence of American self-reliance and meritocratic values. If the film turns on something analogous to Freud's 'return of the repressed' [. . .] then what is being repressed is precisely the material conditions that enabled the foundation of the coastal community, and the pretext for its return is precisely the town's complacent self-mythologizing ethos embodied in the centenary celebrations that frame the film's narrative.[71]

According to this reading, although the fog may seem to possess a truly 'inexplicable nature', it can be read 'at the level of allegory' as 'a fictional analogue of the roots in territorial expropriation of the United States itself'.[72]

This interpretation is echoed by John Muir. The film, he argues,

> [is]very much in keeping with Carpenter's negative opinion of America's Capitalist history. In essence, the story is about the underside of the American Dream. The town of Antonio Bay was built on the blood of Blake's men, and on his stolen fortune. For a hundred years, Antonio Bay thrived because its developers had cast themselves as 'winners' and the lepers as 'losers'. Worse than that, their descendants celebrate the conspirators for winning, even holding an extravagant celebration in their honour.[73]

For Kendall R. Phillips, the film is again one in which an attack by supernatural forces is clearly 'predicated upon crimes of the past':

> The town's founding fathers chose instead to kill the lepers and steal their gold and were aided in their evil deed by a mysterious fog that concealed their assault. The parallel here with the long history of American treachery toward indigenous peoples who also had their wealth ransacked and their people killed is clear.[74]

The fact that the centenary celebration for Antonio Bay takes place in 1980, only four years after the United States celebrated its bicentennial with much fanfare and self-congratulation, adds to this suggestion that the film is intended to serve not only as a 'spook ride on film', but as an allegorical critique of the ideological underpinnings of the nation.[75] This detail aligns the film with another major 1980 horror release: Stanley Kubrick's adaptation of Stephen King's 1977 novel, *The Shining*, which is, as critics since Bill Blakemore and Fredric Jameson have noted, saturated with thematic and visual references to the millions of Native Americans displaced and murdered by European colonists and their descendants.[76] However, as Murray Leeder has noted:

> When asked if he intended *The Fog*'s setting as a statement against America, Carpenter came across as slightly defensive: 'Let me also say that every government that has existed most certainly has done the same thing. I'm not simply being critical of the United States' [. . .] Carpenter seems to indicate here that the film not only goes beyond the American context to make a more general claim about how history is controlled by structures of power that work to exclude and repress, but also explores how that repression creates subversive power hovering just below the surface.[77]

Leeder's own reading considers the ways in which the return of a 'repressed history' is 'linked via the ocean, to the disembodied world of communication technology'[78]. He is one of the only critics to consider the possibility that the film also contains elements which point towards a tacit acknowledgement of *regionally specific* history, noting the 'overwhelmingly Caucasian town's Spanish sounding name'.[79] It is a trait which, as he further observes, connects the film to *Poltergeist*'s Cuesta Verde, another white Californian community which is 'built on a heap of lies and the skeletons of betrayed souls and subsequently carries a curse that its inhabitants are unaware of. In both cases, the repressed returns, in skeleton form, to assault the community itself.'[80]

I concur with the critical consensus which persuasively situates *The Fog* as a pointed critique of the contested foundations of the United States. However, the regional details highlighted in the film are much more than just a matter of passing interest. They are a vital facet of the 'old-fashioned' ghost story that Carpenter wants to tell. *The Fog* is, above all else, a *Californian* ghost story, and the film's many visual and thematic references to the region's pre-American past lend the events depicted on-screen a geographically and historically specific historical and cultural resonance.

The most obvious California connection lies within the fog itself. As Marie Mulvey-Roberts observes, Carpenter knew from the outset that presenting it effectively would be key:

Not only was the fog to be a character in the film, but also its leading player. How could Carpenter direct the fog so as to imbue it with charisma and star quality? Was it sufficient for fog in performance to simply be a pulsating and glowing mass? [. . .] the fog can be read not just as a conductor of miasma, but also as a metaphor. Penetrating, invasive, and yet without boundary, this shape-shifter remains the proverbial outsider. Like the Gothic it can conceal that which is actually there, at the same time as accentuating the hidden.[81]

Although Carpenter, as noted earlier, has cited as his inspiration an eerie weather event witnessed in England, Northern California (which is the setting explicitly mentioned in the screenplay and which was also the film's main shooting location) is notorious for its foggy weather, to the extent that the association has become a cliché.[82] Laura Alice Watt notes of weather conditions in the Point Reyes Peninsula (where much of *The Fog* was shot):

A typical day might bring bright sunshine in the morning and turn to dense fog and howling ocean winds by afternoon, making for a damp, cool, and somewhat harsh climate much of the year. But the frequent coastal fog also brings moisture year-round, allowing the grasslands to stay greener much longer than in inland areas.[83]

This propensity towards fog has often had tragic consequences for ships travelling along the regional coastline. It necessitated the construction of *The Fog*'s most resonant visual landmark, the Point Reyes lighthouse, now a major local tourist attraction. Carpenter notes of the lighthouse (which in the film is the location of heroine Stevie's radio station) that the site is considered the 'second foggiest point in California'.[84] It was constructed in 1870 to warn passing ships of the dangers posed by the Point Reyes headlands, which extend 16 kilometres into the sea, and 'pose a threat to ships traveling between San Francisco Bay and locations to the North'.[85] The lighthouse was retired from service only two years before *The Fog* was made.

In his director's commentary, Carpenter claims that the wrecking of the *Elizabeth Dane* was inspired by tales of a real-life California shipwreck. Although he does not specify any one tragedy, there are plenty to choose from. Michael D. White observes in *Shipwrecks of the California Coast* (2014), that the state has seen more than its fair share of shipping disasters, many caused by poor weather conditions:

Over the past four centuries, as California morphed from a remote colonial backwater into an almost irresistible magnet for both people and commerce from all over the world, the number of ships sailing in its waters grew, as did the number of ships in distress, evidenced by disaster after disaster that claimed thousands of lives and millions of dollars in treasure and cargo.[86]

He relates that in one 36-hour period in 1904, four ships were lost thanks to a 'dense fog' that 'fell like a pall' over the entrance to San Francisco Bay.[87] White singles out the Point Reyes Peninsula for particular notice, stating that since 'official record keeping began in the mid-nineteenth century, the fog-shrouded granite rocks of Point Reyes have claimed more than fifty ships'.[88] He notes that these conditions were also obvious during the earliest days of European exploration, citing Sir Frances Drake's description of the Northern California coastline as 'a place beset by "thicke mists", "vile, thicke and stinking fogges" and "contrary winds"'.[89]

One shipwreck which may possibly have inspired Carpenter (it took place in 1881, just one year after the fictional sinking of the *Elizabeth Dane*) is that of the *Erin's Star* cargo bark just off Point Reyes, which White attributes directly to thick fog (the fog whistle did not blow).[90] As Muir notes of the moment in the film when Nick recounts the story of his father's encounter with *another* ghost ship and 'a disappearing Spanish coin minted in 1867', it reminds us that

> the *Elizabeth Dane* is not the only ship in the ocean. Nick's story attempts to extend the horror of the fog by suggesting that ships disappear at sea all the time under mysterious circumstances, that the ocean is a realm of fear and the unknown, and perhaps we should all be afraid of it.[91]

Of course, fear of what might be lurking in the unfathomable depths has long been a staple trope of horror and the Gothic, deployed by authors such as Herman Melville, Edgar Allan Poe, William Hope Hodgson, H. P. Lovecraft and Koji Suzuki. Emily Alder notes of this 'nautical Gothic' tradition, that

> Seafaring itself – or at least its representations in writing – often has strikingly Gothic dimensions. 'The ship,' wrote one late nineteenth-century sailor, invoking the vertigo of nightmares to describe movement through heavy seas, 'appears on occasions to be falling long distances through hideous space.' And Gothic seas need not even be storm-fuelled: 'There is,' wrote another sailor fifty years previously,
> > something in the first gray streaks stretching along the eastern horizon and throwing an indistinct light upon the face of the deep, which combines with the boundlessness and unknown depth of the sea around, and gives one a feeling of loneliness, of dread, and of melancholy foreboding, which nothing else in nature can.

These words belong to Richard Henry Dana, Jr., whose 1840 memoir *Two Years Before the Mast* formed part of the nineteenth-century Atlantic world's vibrant written culture. Dana's language evokes the sea's Gothic potential; as a thing of nature, its unknowable ambiguity, unsoundable deeps, and ominous affect are clearly signalled, and so are its inherent contradictions: the ocean space is boundless yet oppressive, illuminated yet indiscernible, all surface yet all depth.[92]

In presenting us with a supernatural threat explicitly connected to unknowability of the ocean, *The Fog* displays its strong debt to the 'nautical Gothic' tradition. Alder also observes the 'Gothic potential' of the sea found in Dana's bestselling memoir of seafaring life, *Two Years Before the Mast*, a foundational text within Californian literary culture. Dana's volume also helped to draw his fellow Americans towards what was then considered decidedly exotic territory. At the time of his voyage from Boston to the West Coast, California was seen in the United States as a promising but underdeveloped colonial backwater left sorely underutilised by the Spanish and the Mexicans. Gazing at the then 'newly begun' settlement of 'Mission San Francisco', just over a decade before the discovery of gold transformed the region's prospects, Dana predicted that the coastline would be key to its future:

> If California ever became a prosperous country, this bay will be at the centre of its prosperity. The abundance of wood and water, the extreme fertility of its shores, the excellence of its climate, which is as near to being perfect as any in the world, and its facilities for navigation all fit it for a place of great importance

– once, that is, a more enterprising and industrious people than the 'idle, thriftless' native Californians (those of Spanish, Mexican and Native American descent) takes charge, of course.[93]

*The Fog*'s engagement with Californian themes extends beyond these obvious references to the state's rugged coastline and distinctive weather conditions. Several important scenes in the movie were filmed at sites of local historical significance. Granted, this may not have been entirely intentional: Carpenter has said that many of the establishing shots showcasing the lonely splendour of the coastline were shot in response to studio orders to give the film 'more mood, more fear'.[94] Nevertheless, these sites and the other regional locales highlighted in the film have important historical reverberations. During his audio commentary, Carpenter highlights these resonances, indicating that he was aware of these undercurrents.

One such moment occurs when Carpenter notes that the beach where young Andy Wayne makes a find directly connected to the *Elizabeth Dane* (a gold coin that transforms, as a wave washes over it, into part of a wooden ship's nameplate reading 'Dane') is Drake's Bay, the site where, on 17 June 1579, Sir Francis Drake arrived in his ship the *Golden Hind*.[95] Drake and his crew stayed for five weeks in order to repair their battered ship and take on supplies, during which time one of the first major contacts between European explorers and Native inhabitants of California (the Coast Miwok people) took place.[96] Adding a decidedly Gothic resonance to this encounter is the fact that, as Starr notes, the Miwok 'most likely thought that Drake and his men were their ancestors, returned from the dead'.[97] Along with the expeditions which had already been sent from 'New Spain' in the 1530s and 1540s (most famously, those of explorer Juan Rodríguez Cabrillo), Drake's sojourn in California marked the beginning of the centuries-long calamity that would devastate California's Indigenous population. Drake also staked an English claim to California, naming the region 'Nova Albion' (making California the first 'New England') and 'erecting a plate of brass claiming it for the crown'.[98] As Starr notes, although

> Drake's claim on Nova Albion can be seen as mere bravado, it was nevertheless a symbol of great importance as far as California was concerned and has always been treated as such by historians, for it underscored from an English point of view the competition between two great civilizations for California and other regions on the California continent.[99]

In his analysis of *The Fog*, Phillips observes that 'John Carpenter's films are filled with invading forces laying siege', and whilst in some of them these invasions appear to be without clear cause, the film belongs to the subset of Carpenter siege narratives that are instead 'the result of dark forces from the past released in the present'.[100] Phillips continues:

> This is, of course, a classic motif in ghost stories in which some unfettered spirit connected to a tragic past returns to haunt a location. Not only did explorers and settlers push forward to claim the territory once occupied by the wild, primitive and dangerous – forces that linger just past our borders – but the seizing of these wild frontier lands involved countless acts of cruelty and injustice. These injustices do not disappear but are buried in secret places where they await the opportunity to re-emerge.[101]

Though it is relatively brief, the sequence Carpenter shot in Drake's Bay is set the morning after the first deadly manifestation of the ghostly mariners (when they murder the drunken crew of the *Sea Grass*). Andy's discovery of the first tangible relic from the *Elizabeth Dane*, like Father Malone's discovery of his grandfather's journal the night before, provides direct evidence of a connection between the mysterious events occurring in present-day Antonio Bay and the horrific wrong-doing of the town's founding fathers. As such, these artefacts support Phillips's observation that these kinds of historical crimes never entirely disappear, but instead lurk in 'secret places', awaiting rediscovery and re-emergence.

Andy's discovery of the coin/nameplate takes on an even deeper resonance when we consider the local significance of his find. Historically, disappearing coins – one in particular – are associated with Drake's Bay. The explorer's brass plate is said to have featured Queen Elizabeth I's name, the day, the year, Drake's own name and a six pence piece (which had the Queen's image on it), all intended to mark 'the first English claim to the land that would become the United States of America'.[102] As Edward Von Der Porten et al. note: 'Drake's plate and the post on which it was mounted vanished after he sailed off across the Pacific, but its memory survived in the accounts of the voyage.'[103] When it was supposedly 'found' and historically authenticated in July 1936, it soon became 'the state's greatest historical treasure'.[104] As Von der Porten et al. outline, forty years later, however, it became obvious that this supposed 'treasure' was a clever hoax that had unexpectedly taken on a life of its own, perpetrated by scholars belonging to a fraternal order of historians specialising in the study of the American West. Members of the group had manufactured and then 'dis-covered' a fraudulent plaque (which had markings which should have revealed its true provenance immediately) for their own amusement, never imagining that it would be mistaken for the real thing.[105] The mastermind of the hoax was named George Ezra *Dane*, and it was in 1979 (only two years before *The Fog* was filmed) that the first public confirmation of the prank was released.[106] Although this is likely mere coincidence, the fact that the chief hoaxer shared a surname with Carpenter's ghost ship *is* striking: like Andy's discovery in the rock pool, Drake's plate was not what it seemed to be.

Drake's attempt to stake an English claim to California failed, although Anglo-Americans rapidly came to dominate the region following the end of the Mexican-American War and the discovery of gold in 1848. As Leeder notes, whilst the name 'Antonio Bay' hints at a Spanish/Mexican heritage for the town, that heritage is rigorously suppressed within the town itself.[107] Every major character is a white individual of non-Hispanic descent, and there is no explicit mention of a Spanish, Mexican or Native American prehistory for the settlement. Yet, at the same time, there is a very direct connection between events in the film and the state's suppressed/ignored Hispanic and Indigenous past: the prominence granted to the town's church from the beginning of the film.

Although the specific denomination of the church is never explicitly stated, the exterior belongs to the real-life Episcopal Church of the Ascension, located in Sierra Madre, California. Built in 1888, the church was added to the National Register of Historic Places in 1977.[108] Adding a nice touch of nautical Gothic to the building is the fact that the church bell originally belonged to a steamship called *City of Dublin* which was wrecked on the Oregon coastline in 1879.[109]

Antonio Bay's church is of central significance to the narrative of dispossession and revenge dramatised in *The Fog*. The climactic act of sacrificial atonement undertaken by Father Malone, in recognition of his grandfather's participation in the plot to sink the *Elizabeth Dane*, provides the ghostly mariners with their pound of flesh (or rather more than that, given the average weight of a human head . . .). Steve Smith argues that:

> Malone's acceptance of his fate introduces a logic of sacrifice and redemption. Malone's assumption of the sins of his forefathers functions that is, to close the circle, to pay the price demanded of the past, and thereby to free his fellow citizens from their own distant complicity.[110]

Furthermore, he adds, Malone's death also provides a convenient means of bypassing the acceptance of communal guilt, in that 'rather than forcing a recognition of those iniquities, Malone's death prepares the ground for their continued collective avoidance'.[111] Malone's role is also notable in that even before the fog descends, he seems dissatisfied with his position as spiritual leader of the community.[112] He has a drinking problem, and is considered unreliable and erratic by centenary organiser Mrs Williams. When his grandfather's incriminating diary is found, it only seems to confirm the disquiet Malone has already been feeling, verifying his subconscious sense that both church and town have been built on (metaphorically) unhallowed ground. Yet, as is typical in supernatural horror narratives, these warnings are not taken seriously until it is too late: 'Our celebration tonight is a travesty. We're honouring murderers', Malone cries, to little avail.

The ambiguous nature of Father Malone's religious affiliation warrants discussion. Although he possesses many of the clichéd pop culture signifiers of the Roman Catholic clergyman – he harbours doubts about his vocation, has a drinking problem, an Irish name and wears a black cassock – the real-life church in which the film is set is, as previously noted, Episcopalian. More significantly (and confusingly), Malone is said to be the grandson of a priest – Father Patrick Malone, the author of the journal and the founder of the Antonio Bay church – even though Roman Catholic clergyman are forbidden to marry or have children. Malone's religious calling is, nevertheless, presented to us as a family tradition, passed down through the direct paternal line, just like his propensity for guilt. The fact that the film itself seems a little unsure as to what denomination

Malone belongs to means that we have an interesting blurring over of the state's Spanish/Mexican Catholic past. It's a seemingly minor background detail which again gestures towards the real-life origins of present-day California. The Hispanic and explicitly Roman Catholic history of the state prior to American settlement (which was forcibly superimposed over the region's original, Native American history and culture) has often been obscured by the more recent white, Protestant and Anglo-American culture. The central role the church plays in *The Fog* is also a reminder of the foundational role that the Roman Catholic Church played in the Spanish colonisation of California.

The crumbling mission ruins which became subject to considerable nostalgia and conservation efforts in the late nineteenth and early twentieth centuries were, to the ever-expanding citizenry of American California, the evocative remnants of the picturesque but fatally flawed civilisation that had immediately preceded their own, far superior, colonisation effort. Just as the monastic ruins of medieval Britain were fetishized by nineteenth-century writers, architects and artists, so too did American photographers, artists, tourists and even advertisers find the missions irresistible, regarding them as 'romantic subject matter evoking the lost grandeur of the past'.[113] Describing the way in which public attitudes towards the hundreds of Roman Catholic monasteries 'seized by Henry VIII in the 1530s' gradually evolved, Christopher Woodward observes that:

> In the course of three centuries, straightforward greed was followed by ignorance and indifference, and curiosity led to veneration. The changes in attitude to ruins followed the same sequence as in Rome, but there the cycle required more than a thousand years to revolve.[114]

As Kimbro et al. relate in *The California Missions*, if anything, this process was even more accelerated in California, due to both the rapidity with which the mission buildings themselves tended to decay following the advent of Mexican independence in 1821 ('once exposed to the elements, the missions' sun-dried brick walls quickly melted back into native soils') and the speed with which the discovery of gold facilitated rapid 'Americanization'.[115]

In one of the most famous efforts to romanticise the 'Old California' of the late mission era, Helen Hunt Jackson's bestselling novel *Ramona* (1884), it is said of the Moreno house, the bustling but declining Mexican estate in which the narrative is set, that the

> half barbaric, half elegant, wholly generous and free-handed life led there by Mexican men and women of degree in the early part of this century . . . was a picturesque life, with more of sentiment and gayety in it, more also that was truly dramatic, more romance, than will ever be seen again on those sunny shores.[116]

Though Jackson's novel – genuinely progressive for the time – focused on an interracial love story between the mixed-race heroine and a handsome young Native American farmworker, and also critiqued the greed and violence of white settlers – the latter-day romanticising of the missions and of the Mexican and Spanish eras also did much to obscure their inherently imperial, exploitative and oppressive nature.

The network of fortified settlements which underpinned the military, administrative and theological authority of first New Spain and then Mexico in California, began in July 1769 when a land expedition, including the Franciscan priest Junípero Serra, arrived at what is now San Diego Bay and erected a cross 'to mark the founding of mission San Diego de Alcalá. . . . Over the next sixty years, twenty more Franciscan missions would be established along the Alta California coast.'[117] Prominent Californian cities which grew out of Spanish missions include San Francisco, Santa Barbara, Carmel, Santa Cruz, Los Angeles and San Jose. As detailed in *The California Missions*, the mission era only lasted for sixty years. It ended when Mexico gained independence from Spain and revolutionaries demanded that the vast wealth of the church be redistributed.[118] With the passing of the Emancipation and Secularization Decree in 1834, the missions were rapidly dismantled, and 'within a decade some ten million acres had passed in to private ownership, and nearly 15,000 Indians were freed from mission restraints'.[119] As Kimbro et al. have noted, it was only gradually that 'the romantic narrative of the mission past has been supplemented with a wide range of other perspectives':

> Some continue to adhere to the basic tenets of the classical interpretation, maintaining that, in spite of everything, the Franciscan padres and the mission system conferred on the region's native peoples the blessings of civilization – blessings fraught and shadowed perhaps, but blessings nonetheless. Other interpretations offer starkly different views, emphasizing the mission system's catastrophic effect on indigenous populations.[120]

Indeed, this is the view taken by Starr, who notes of the mission system that it was 'a deeply flawed and deficient society':

> The entire relationship of the Spanish settlers – Franciscans and soldiers alike – to the Native Americans was, by contemporary standards, indeed catastrophic. The Franciscans saw themselves as coming to California to save souls, and they must be judged, in part, as the men they truly were – Spanish Catholic missionaries – and by the standards of their time. Yet even a sympathetic observer, acknowledging the benevolent intent of the mission system, must see it by the standards of the twenty-first century, as a violent intrusion into the culture and human rights of indigenous peoples.[121]

The devastating impact upon California's native inhabitants has more recently been highlighted by Benjamin Madley, who views the myriad abuses of the mission system as a precursor to the even more devastating acts of genocide which occurred in the initial decades of the American takeover. The 'California Indian population cataclysm of 1846–1873,' he argues, continued a 'pre-existing trajectory':[122]

> During California's seventy-seven-year-long Russo-Hispanic period (1769–1846) its Indians had already suffered a devastating demographic decline. During the era when Spaniards, Russians, and Mexicans colonized the coastal region between San Diego and Fort Ross, California's Indian population fell from perhaps 310,000 to 150,000. Some 62,600 of these deaths occurred at or near California's coastal region missions, and, in 1946, journalist Carey McWilliams initiated a long debate over the nature of these institutions when he compared the Franciscan missionaries, who had held large numbers of California Indians there, to 'Nazis operating concentration camps.'[123]

Given the foundational significance that the mission system holds in Californian history – and its association with the forced conversion, imprisonment, cultural erasure and violent suppression of the region's Native American population; and the many deaths from disease which resulted from the forced penning together of hundreds of people with little immunity to imported European ailments such as smallpox – the prominent role which Father Malone and the local church play in *The Fog* is all the more suggestive. As Leeder notes, whilst the Church is 'perhaps the institution traditionally most valued in horror films', this is certainly not the case here. Indeed,

> In this premise [it] is not a defense against darkness and evil, but a repository of shameful secrets. It was built with stolen funds, and its walls contain the objects the ghosts want most, a solid gold cross. The cross no longer repels the dead but attracts them; it is not a signifier of the power of Christ but of historical shame.[124]

As well as evoking the frenzy of greed which marked the beginnings of American California – the thirst for gold which transformed a relatively sleepy backwater into a rapidly expanding and actively genocidal American state – *The Fog*'s tale of vengeful ghosts seeking the return of that which is rightfully theirs also subtly evokes the abuses of the pre-American era. If the Spanish era is only very briefly referenced – in the form of the town's name and the Spanish doubloon mentioned by Nick – it is even more telling that the fate of the original inhabitants of coastal California is, on the surface of the film at least, entirely ignored.

However, although the ghosts which terrorise Antonio Bay are white (we never see them in close-up, but we can assume as much from their backstory), the case could be made that their status as lepers has 'othered' them in a manner which means that, as was the case with Native Americans post-1846, their extermination could be justified by the townsfolk. Michelle T. Moran notes that California legislators in the early twentieth century 'called for a leprosy policy that would transport anyone with the disease out of their state and even off the continent'.[125] These proposed measures were

> part of a broad pattern of racial intolerance and racialized notions of disease that circulated along the Pacific coast. Some California medical professionals pronounced leprosy a disease of Chinese immigrants and used the disease as a means to target the population as a physical and moral threat to white residents. [126]

The plotters who profited from the sinking of the *Elizabeth Dane* were not only seeking gold with which to consolidate the fortunes of their fledgling settlement. They also saw Edward Blake and his fellow leprosy patients as a threat to their communal health and security. It is another reminder that although, as previous critics of the film have also noted, *The Fog* certainly belongs to the progressive tradition within American horror cinema, which challenges the heroic light in which the nation still so often views itself, this is also a distinctively *Californian* horror story, and as such, our understanding and appreciation of the film only deepens when considered in relation to the state's unique and often shameful history.

The 2018 supernatural horror film *Winchester* (tagline: 'The House that Ghosts Built') is, allegedly, 'Inspired by Actual Events'. Certainly, the story is one that will be familiar even to those only vaguely aware of the legend behind 'California's most haunted house' (and present-day San Jose's biggest tourist attraction). The story begins in April 1906, as laudanum-addicted San Francisco psychiatrist Dr Eric Price (Jason Clarke) is hired by a lawyer from the Winchester Repeating Arms Company to assess the mental competency of Sarah Winchester (Helen Mirren), the widow of their late president. The Company is concerned because Mrs Winchester, who holds a 51 per cent share of the Company's stock, is spending thousands of dollars every day on a seemingly endless construction project.

Upon moving from New Haven, Connecticut, to Northern California, the widow Winchester purchased a simple eight-room farmhouse and dozens of acres of land, and proceeded to greatly expand the property. The result is, the family lawyer explains, a constantly evolving architectural folly with 'no masterplan'. It is, he continues, 'A house under never-ending construction built on the orders of a grieving widow, whose mind is as chaotic as the house itself.' As is often the case within formulaic supernatural horror films of this sort, the narrative therefore sets up a clash between Price, a cynical sceptic, and Mrs Winchester, a believer in the afterlife who always dresses in mourning garb. Inevitably, although her conviction that ghosts are very real indeed initially seems to him like a sign of mental instability, Price soon realises that Mrs Winchester is saner than he is.

After his unsettling first night in her remarkable house – a confusing melange of rooms, doors, corridors and 'staircases to nowhere', which comes complete with a bell tower that tolls at midnight – Price begins to suspect that there is a method behind its apparent architectural 'madness'. Sarah Winchester is tormented by the deaths, years before, of her beloved husband and child. She believes these losses were the result of a 'curse' attached to the family because their wealth has arisen from profits generated by the Winchester Repeating Rifle, the gun that 'won the West'. As she explains: 'You see, profiting from such a thing as violence and death . . . that is a wickedness that follows you like a shadow.' Her manic construction project has a clear, if unlikely, rationale. The ghosts of the thousands of victims – both innocent and not so innocent – killed by her Company's product have 'unfinished business'. Every night, when the bell tower tolls, they dictate architectural plans to her via automatic writing. The spirits want Mrs Winchester to build exact reconstructions of the rooms in which they died (the film never acknowledges that many, if not most, of those shot dead by a rifle would have surely been killed outdoors), so that they can re-enter our world. When their individual room is finished, most of the ghosts are satisfied and then complete their journey to the afterlife. Those that refuse to leave – who were evil in life and/or still hold a powerful grudge against the Company – are sealed in their rooms by a board studded with thirteen nails.

The most dangerous of the malevolent spirits is Ben Block (Eamon Farren), a Confederate soldier enraged by the deaths of his younger brothers in a battle won by the Union because of their superior Winchester firearms. In retribution, Block stormed the Company's headquarters, murdering fifteen employees before being killed by police officers (who were themselves armed with repeating rifles). Although they encounter complications along the way – mainly due to Mrs Winchester's great-nephew Henry (Finn Scicluna-O'Prey), who is repeatedly possessed by Block – the widow and the psychiatrist eventually vanquish this dangerously unquiet spirit. At the same time, they conveniently come to terms with their own personal losses, because, as Mrs Winchester notes early on, 'grief can be more crippling than arthritis' (another affliction she must cope with).

It is also implied that the upheaval caused by Block's breach of the walls between our world and the afterlife may have caused the 1906 San Francisco earthquake. This immensely destructive real-life event is referenced in the closing titles, although, rather oddly, Price returns to the city without seeming to be aware that much of its infrastructure has been destroyed, with many thousands of lives lost. In the film's final moments, when asked what she is going to do next, Mrs Winchester resolutely replies: 'Rebuild, of course.' The closing credits tell us that she 'continued to build the house 24 hours a day, seven days a week, up to her death in 1922' and that 'The Winchester House remains one of the most haunted mansions in North America.' A picture of the real-life Mrs Winchester briefly appears, to again underline that the film was 'inspired' by supposed historical reality.

Save for the addition of the vengeful Private Block, the character of Dr Price and the demonically possessed Henry (who is here said to be the son of Mrs Winchester's niece Marion [Sarah Snook], a character probably based upon Daisy Merriam, the devoted niece of the real Mrs Winchester), this version of the Winchester legend is otherwise very close to the account of the story that has taken root in the American cultural imagination. As Laura Trevelyan, a descendant of the Winchester clan, has outlined, this 'myth' goes as follows:

> Sarah Winchester was ridden with guilt because her fortune came from Native Americans killed by settlers of the West with their Winchesters. As the story goes, Sarah was haunted by images of death and destruction. After consulting a medium, she was told if she would only keep building, then the spirits of the dead Native Americans would be satisfied. This supposedly explains why Sarah's house in San Jose is vast and unfinished, with staircases that lead nowhere – the tortured woman engaged in a whirlwind of construction, to appease those killed with the rifles which produced her immense wealth. Or did she?[127]

The answer to that final question, as outlined by both Trevelyan and Mary Jo Ignoffo, whose 2010 biography is a definitive study of Sarah Winchester and the legend that attached itself to her, is a resounding 'No'.[128] The basic facts of some of the story outlined in the film are broadly true – Sarah's husband William and infant daughter Annie *did* die decades before she did; she did inherit company stock after she was widowed (though certainly not 51 per cent); and, most importantly, she did move to California, where she 'built, built and kept on building' until she ended up with an 'eight story house' which 'soared into the sky, with cupola's atop turrets, looking like nothing anyone had ever seen before'.[129] However, there is no actual evidence that

Sarah Winchester constructed her house at the behest of spirits, nor that she felt even a glimmer of guilt for the thousands of deaths associated with the Winchester Company firearms. Indeed, the biographical consensus is that she was a retiring but warm-hearted woman whose considerable fortune, life-long interest in architecture and design (she patented several inventions) and, as Trevelyan puts it, refusal to explain to her neighbours 'why she was building this ungainly colossus on their doorstep' meant that 'they tried to come up with explanations of their own'.[130]

Whilst there is no denying that her home was (and remains) a very unusual building, as Ignoffo extensively outlines, rational explanations exist for every supposedly 'uncanny' structural or interior detail found in the house. Many of the supposedly 'spooky' aspects found in the house fittings (such as an alleged fixation with the number thirteen) were opportunistic embellishments added after Winchester's death by John Brown, the canny amusement park operator who took over the property in 1923. Oft-cited oddities such as blocked-off doors and 'stairways to nowhere' belong to parts of the house badly damaged in the 1906 earthquake which were boarded up for safety.[131] Mrs Winchester also tended to seal up parts of the house she was unhappy with, simply moving on to her next home-improvement project. As Christine Junker argues, the obsession with elaborating upon the haunted house narrative associated with the house overshadows the 'progressive potential of Sarah Winchester's architectural project': she is even regarded by some recent commentators as a pioneering female architect and inventor.[132]

Rumours about the house and its reclusive mistress were already appearing in local newspapers before Mrs Winchester's death in 1922, but once it was rented to Brown and transformed into a tourist attraction, the 'legend' really took hold. That process was helped by publicity such as that generated by the 1922 publication in a San Jose newspaper of 'reminiscences' by Edith Daley, a former neighbour, whose introductory remarks make it clear that the house was already a subject of national renown and curiosity. Daley begins with a question:

> The Winchester Mystery House is among America's most famous – and most haunted – houses. It attracts visitors from around the world. Everyone wants to see the curious house built by Sarah Lockwood Winchester. Did she truly believe she would die if she ever stopped building that gargantuan home in San Jose? History – and the house itself – suggest that's true.[133]

Daley's account incorporates many familiar Gothic tropes. For instance, we have a 'towering house' with ominously locked gates and 'queerly placed windows that looked like eyes'[134] (details which also bear a resemblance to Shirley Jackson's description of the monstrously sentient Hill House in her 1959 novel,

*The Haunting of Hill House*).[135] Furthermore, part of what is so unsettling about the Winchester house here is that it is forever expanding: 'With each passing day, the great house grew. It grew top-heavy and lopsided. It grew to become a monstrous crime committed in the name of architecture.'[136]

The 'legend' of Sarah Winchester furthered by Daley and other contributors to the myth – Junker dubs this the 'House that Spirits Built' hypothesis – began to overshadow reality even before she died.[137] Junker suggests that:

> the Winchester mythology is even more interesting given the absolute lack of supporting historical evidence because it demonstrates the cultural desire for a particular type of narrative about houses and their relationship to their inhabitants: in this case, the continued fascination with the Winchester mythology capitalizes on America's complicated relationship with class, the conflation of the white female body with her domestic space, and a cultural desire to acknowledge the wrong-doings of westward expansion without sharing the cultural guilt associated with it.[138]

A similar conclusion is reached by Colin Dickey (2016), who argues that issues related to gender and class, and profound cultural anxiety about the brutal legacy of nineteenth-century American imperialism, explain why this 'lie' came to 'obliterate nearly all truths of the true story'.[139] He asserts that:

> The legend of Sarah Winchester depends on a cultural uneasiness to which we don't always like to admit. An uneasiness about women living alone, withdrawn from society, for one. An uneasiness about wealth and the way the superrich live among us. And, perhaps largest of all, an uneasiness about the gun that won the West and the violence white Americans carried out in the name of civilization.[140]

Dickey's final point was anticipated by Ignoffo, who argues that in the end, the main reason why people cared so much about what Sarah Winchester did with her own house is simple:

> The crux of the Sarah Winchester story is the gun. The awesome and deadly power of the repeater, most often used on the frontier hunting down buffalo or against bandits or American Indians (or when the tables were turned, against the cavalry), simulated outlandish stories about Sarah Winchester and how she used her fortune.[141]

The link between the Winchester rifle, the frontier and the compelling but entirely fabricated ghost story is one that was there from the very beginning.

Given the tragic frequency with which deaths due to gun violence still occur in the United States, as Maria McVarish and Julie Leavitt argue, it is also hardly surprising that a 'popular tourist attraction' which 'neatly consolidates' an ongoing cultural fetishization of 'guns, ghosts and madness' would be irresistible.[142] In their psychoanalytical reading of the narrative, they suggest that

> In lieu of confronting the ghosts of gun violence, the Winchester Mystery House ghost story invents a crazy and superstitious woman who must bear the burden of atonement for violence inflicted by guns, misaligning her with spiritualism, a cultural form of grieving actually considered normal in her time.[143]

However, although the connection between gun violence, gender and the battle between so-called white American 'civilization' and Native American 'savagery' provides a plausible explanation for the continued allure of the story, as was the case with previous critical discussions of *The Fog*, reference to the specifically *Californian* nature of the anxieties which have long-been projected onto the Winchester House is largely absent. Sarah Winchester purchased the site upon which her house was to be erected in 1886. Only a decade before, her new home state concluded a thirty-year extermination campaign against the region's Indigenous population. It was a period marked by murder, devastating disease outbreaks, the American violation of previously agreed legal treaties and, as Benjamin Madley and others have argued, wholescale genocide.

Even when compared to the immense population decline found amongst New England's Native American population in the decades immediately following English colonisation, the collapse of California's Native population in the decades immediately following what demographer Sherburne F. Cook (1976) called, 'The American Invasion', is shocking.[144] As he outlines, whilst both 'Anglo-Saxons' and the Spanish desired to exploit New World resources, and had well-defined administrative policies towards the Native population, their attitudes towards the local population differed substantially in some key respects. The main difference lay in the fact that the English tended to focus upon material wealth, whilst the Spanish also 'availed themselves of human resources' (hence the explicitly theological, 'civilizing' intent of the short-lived mission system).[145] This meant that for the Spanish:

> the aboriginal race was an economic asset and as such was to be conserved. Destruction of individual life occurred only when and if the Indian actively resisted the process of amalgamation or definitely failed to conform to the conqueror's scheme of existence. Wholesale slaughter or annihilation was definitely undesirable.

> The Anglo-American system, on the other hand, had no place for the Indian . . . if there was any conflict whatsoever with the system, the native was to be eliminated ruthlessly, either by outright extermination or the slower method of segregation in ghettolike reservations.[146]

The Anglo-Americans who took control of California in 1846 were also, Cook observes, 'coming fresh from two centuries of bitter border warfare and intolerant aggression', and

> brought with them an implacable hatred of the red race [sic], which made no discrimination between tribes or individuals. All Indians were vermin, to be treated as such. It is therefore not surprising that physical violence was the rule rather than the exception. The native's life was worthless, for no American could even be brought to trial for killing an Indian.[147]

Madley describes the events which began after American settlement got underway as 'The California India population cataclysm of 1846–1873'.[148] During this period, 'perhaps 80 percent of all California Indians died, and many massacres left no survivors or only small children'.[149] Already weakened by the abuses and cultural and physical dislocation of the mission system, California's Native American population was further devastated by a series of disease outbreaks (including a smallpox epidemic) that raged during the 1830s and, according to Cook, killed about 60,000 California Indians.[150] The immensely rapid change in regional demographics which occurred following the discovery of gold also meant that by 1849, 'the non-Indian population had more than tripled in a year'.[151]

As Madley observes, these new emigrants were 'often heavily armed, experienced with paramilitary organizations, and full of fear towards Indians'.[152] There was, he details, wholesale and widespread genocide committed by whites in California after the granting of statehood in 1850, and the 'near annihilation' of the indigenous population was actively facilitated by state and federal policies, as well as the unchecked vigilante violence undertaken by many American emigrants.[153] In short, modern California was constructed upon the graves of thousands of Native Americans, but this crime was of such brutality and historical *nearness* that it has, ironically, all too often been suppressed or ignored by many white Californians until very recently.

In his classic study of witchcraft, astrology and ghost belief in England during the sixteenth and seventeenth centuries, *Religion and the Decline of Magic* (1971), Keith Thomas noted that:

> In medieval England it was fully accepted that dead men might sometimes return to haunt the living. The Catholic Church rationalised the ancient

belief in ghosts by teaching that such apparitions were the souls of those trapped in Purgatory, unable to rest until they had expiated their sins.[154]

Though Protestant attitudes towards the unquiet dead differed from Catholic ones in some important ways, in the seventeenth-century English ghost story, he continues, the ghost always had a reason for coming back – a specific purpose. They were, as in Shakespeare's plays, 'instruments of revenge or protection, they prophesy, or they crave proper burial'.[155]

Although there is no evidence that Sarah Winchester believed that her house was haunted, the legend associated with her unusual architectural endeavours therefore had a specific purpose. Mrs Winchester's ghosts also evoke the horrific but often repressed white atrocities that accompanied the establishment of modern California. Even before her death, she was cast in a role that the expansive and imperialist United States unconsciously deemed to be somehow essential. In Ignoffo's words, 'It was as if she personified a conscience, one that was so guilt-racked over countless violent deaths that she suffered her way into madness in a burgeoning and ghost-infested mansion.'[156] But, of course, the Winchester house was not only, as Daley put it in 1922, 'Among America's most famous – and haunted – houses.' It was also an infamous *Californian* house built at a time when the state was still 'undergoing a vast reorganization in virtually all respects'.[157]

Part of that reorganisation involved a now dominant 'white' California trying to ignore (or worse still justify) the 'genocide hidden in plain sight' which followed the Anglo-American take-over.[158] Although, as Madley notes, 'Californians can no longer elect the perpetrators of genocide to high office', as they frequently did during the late nineteenth century, 'the names of genocide perpetrators and their supporters are inscribed across the state.'[159] He notes that many Californian place names – such as Alpine County's Carson Pass, Alameda's city of Fremont and Lake County's Kelseyville – 'commemorate men directly responsible for leading the killing of large numbers of California Indians, even as they obscure the presence of California Indians'.[160] In the legend of the Winchester Mystery House, as in Antonio Bay, evidence of the murderous misdeeds buried in the regional past is simultaneously everywhere and nowhere.

According to Ignoffo, lurid newspaper speculation about Sarah Winchester's home began in 1895, but it was several years before her allegedly superstitious ways were directly linked to guilt 'surrounding the deaths caused by the repeating rifle'.[161] As she notes, the 'gun guilt' addition to the story coincided with a wider cultural change in attitudes towards gun ownership: 'Up until then, weapons were perceived as a necessity for survival and as symbols of an American identity. As the nation transitioned from an agrarian society to an urban one, widespread gun ownership became a challenge to public safety.'[162] What would also gradually evolve, according to Dickey, were public attitudes 'towards America's westward expansion and Manifest Destiny', so that the Winchester rifle was, in tours of the house, 'now emphasized as the gun that had killed untold Native Americans, all of whom were now haunting the widow who profited from the murder weapon'.[163] One of the fixtures said to support this hypothesis is described by Trevelyan:

> A statue of a Native American, Chief Little Fawn, stands in the grounds of Sarah's home, complete with bow and arrows, as if making his gallant last stand against the rapid fire of the Winchester. Tour guides present this as Sarah's atonement for the slaughter of Indians by the Winchester repeating rifle, her 'tribute' to the dead.[164]

However, this seemingly poignant symbol of a guilty conscience was, she reveals, actually 'a common, cast-iron statue of the day' found in gardens all over the state. Nevertheless, the detail subliminally evokes the near-annihilation of California's Indigenous population, even though that regionally specific guilt has all too often been displaced onto a more appealing (because it is less specific and appears to be less inconveniently *recent*) sense of national wrong-doing.

It should come as no surprise, then, that the film *Winchester* also entirely ignores unpleasant local truths. In making a grieving Confederate soldier the prime instrument of supernatural vengeance, it completely sidelines Native American and other non-white victims of frontier violence. The one scene in which Native American characters appear occurs towards the end of the film, when Price and Mrs Winchester are suddenly able to see for the first time the other ghosts who inhabit the house. Two Native American figures are glimpsed amongst the throng of spirits (along with some enslaved Black people), but unlike the very active (and very vocal) Private Block, the enslaved individuals and the Native Americans remain silent. Their suffering has been totally eclipsed by that of the embittered and entitled white American, who clearly feels that he has been more gravely wronged by the Winchester Repeating Arms Company than they have. There is also no suggestion that Block's desire to destroy the 'vermin' who profited from the death of his kinfolk is anything other than a vicious personal vendetta, or that he in any way embodies the suffering of the many other victims of gun violence. This detail may owe something to the fact that in 2018 (when the film was released) a malevolent and entirely unsympathetic Confederate ghost who (in life) was also a mass shooter, was perhaps deemed a more tonally 'appropriate' villain than a non-white casualty of Manifest Destiny.[165] However, this narrative decision also means that the spectres of those who actually did perish in their hundreds of thousands so that the United States as a whole – and modern-day California in particular – could be established, are briefly evoked only to be dealt with in the most simplistic and condescending terms as silent avatars of patient and passive historical suffering.

Although *Winchester* is (at the time of writing) the most recent, and the most high-profile version of the story to have entered popular culture, Sarah Winchester's unconventional house has been mentioned in many other narratives, including the Stephen King-scripted television miniseries *Rose Red* (2002), which featured a house (and a backstory) that owed much to the legend, but moved the action from Northern California to Seattle. More significantly, the Winchester House is referenced in the most influential American haunted house story of the twentieth century – Shirley Jackson's *The Haunting of Hill House*.

Though only mentioned in passing by aspiring paranormal investigator Dr John Montague, the perpetually confusing floorplan and off-kilter proportions found in Hill House, along with the basic conceit of an eccentric mansion built by a wealthy Victorian to suit his/her unstable mind – was an obvious point of reference for Jackson. In January 1958, when she was beginning to research the novel, Jackson wrote to her parents to ask if they could send on pictures of any suitable 'big old California gingerbread houses', and was duly forwarded a tourist brochure.[166] Jackson said that she remembered 'the winchester [sic] house as a good type house for haunting'.[167] Though she set the novel in rural New England (and was also influenced by other well-known hauntings, including at Borley Rectory in England), her interest in the Winchester House was likely due to more than just its infamous national reputation.

Jackson was a native Californian who came from well-established San Francisco society stock on her mother's side. As Ruth Franklin outlines, Jackson's great-great grandfather, Samuel C. Bugbee, built many of the city's most well-known 'millionaires' palaces' of the 1870s and 1880s, many of which were destroyed by the 1906 earthquake.[168] Though Jackson's family moved to the East Coast when she was sixteen, and she only once subsequently returned to her home state (in the summer of 1939), California remained, as her first biographer, Judy Oppenheimer, notes, 'her Eden, a place . . . she was deeply attached to and would never forget'.[169] Furthermore, as both she and Franklin note, Jackson grew up in the well-to-do San Francisco suburb of Burlingame.[170] This community is only 64 kilometres from San Jose. For Jackson, the Winchester Mystery House was also at one time a relatively local fixture.

However, Jackson would not even have had to travel as far as this to be directly connected to Sarah Winchester. As Ignoffo details, Mrs Winchester owned extensive real-estate holdings in California, amongst them a considerable parcel of land in Burlingame which was wisely purchased just as the community was in the process of becoming one of the most prosperous in the state. Jackson spent much of her childhood living in a house that was only ten minutes' walk from land Mrs Winchester owned. Given that her family moved to Burlingame in 1923 – only a year after Winchester died – it is possible that Jackson was aware of the connection between her own neighbourhood and one of Northern California's wealthiest and most notoriously eccentric residents. In another intriguing coincidence, Ignoffo reveals that Winchester's holdings were, in and around 1908, plagued by the theft of sand and gravel undertaken by unscrupulous local property developers: 'A local resident recalled that it was common knowledge that "half the sidewalks in Burlingame were made from sand stolen from Winchester's beach by a well-known contractor at the time.'[171] The young Shirley Jackson probably played on streets paved with Mrs Winchester's pilfered sand.

In his study of the haunted house in cinema, Barry Curtis notes of such places that 'the laws of nature are suspended – time has been occluded by some traumatic incident that continues to exert a hold on the present through a persistence of energy that can continue to manifest itself'.[172] When it comes to the Winchester Mystery House, the 'traumatic incidents' that have given this largely fictional, but alluring supernatural narrative lasting resonance are not only Sarah Winchester's tragic personal backstory and the national 'gun guilt' and frontier violence said to have tainted her immense wealth. There is also the still largely unacknowledged fate of the many thousands of Native Americans who were exterminated and/or violently displaced by the new American society which so rapidly and forcibly superimposed itself over the prior Mexican, Spanish and Indigenous histories and cultures associated with the region.

As with the sanitised version of local history expounded by the centenary committee in *The Fog*, the inaccurate but nonetheless compelling 'legend' attached to the Winchester Mystery House has therefore endured not only because of its fascinating *national* thematic and historical resonances, but because it presents Californians with a version of their own story that is rather easier to live with than the often appalling realities of early statehood. Here, local (and disconcertingly *recent*) racial atrocities have been safely projected onto the history of the wider United States and discreetly detached from the 'official' story of the Winchester Mystery House. Although Carpenter's seafaring ghosts ultimately destroy the cosy, self-aggrandising consensus that has existed in San Antonio Bay since the sinking of the *Elizabeth Dane* and force the townsfolk to directly confront the historical crime that lies at the very heart of their community, no such reckoning with the horrors of the local past happens in *Winchester*. In *The Fog*, communal guilt is expiated by the sacrifice made by a truly penitent individual (Father Malone) willing to give up his life to atone for the misdeeds of the town's founders. In *Winchester*, the crimes of a nation (and the belligerence of a villainous Civil War veteran) are atoned for by another stoic individual (Mrs Winchester), but there is, crucially, never any sense that her new home state will acknowledge the horrors which accompanied its establishment. Consequently, any gesture towards true catharsis here is unconvincing and shallow.

This evasion is even more striking when we consider that only a few months after *Winchester*'s 2018 cinema release, the state at last formally acknowledged the brutality endured by California's Indigenous peoples in the years just before Sarah Winchester settled there. On 18 June 2019, Governor Gavin Newsom met with tribal leaders to apologise for California's 'history of violence, maltreatment, and neglect' towards Native Americans. He bluntly admitted that 'It's called a genocide. That's what it was. A genocide. [There's] no other way to describe it and that's the way it needs to be described in the history books.'[173] Newsom's office also issued an Executive Order, which declared:

> In the early decades of California's statehood, the relationship between the State of California and California Native Americans was fraught with violence, exploitation, dispossession and the attempted destruction of tribal communities, as summed up by California's first Governor, Peter Burnett, in his 1851 address to the Legislature: '[t]hat a war of extermination will continue to be waged between the two races until the Indian race becomes extinct must be expected'.[174]

The order also decreed that a 'Truth and Healing Council' be established, intended to 'bear witness to, record [and to] examine historical documentation pertaining to the historical relationship between the State of California and California Native Americans in order to clarify the historical record of this relationship in the spirit of truth and healing'. This was another belated indication that the predominately heroic 'story' surrounding the early years of statehood was at last being updated to reflect the real-life foundational horrors which accompanied the establishment of modern California; and which in doing so, also irrevocably influenced the California Gothic.

## Notes

1. Russell, *Book of the Dead*, p. 73.
2. Newman, *Nightmare Movies*, p. 11.
3. Lucas, 'DVD Review: *Messiah of Evil*', online.
4. Ibid.

5. Thrower, *Nightmare USA*, p. 238.
6. Starr, *Americans and the Californian Dream*, p. 415.
7. Ibid. pp. 415–16.
8. As Melissa McFarland Pennell also puts it, 'Perhaps no episode from that colonial past has haunted the New England mind more frequently than did the witchcraft episode that beset Salem Village and surrounding towns in 1692' ('New England Gothic/New England Guilt', p. 41).
9. Ringel, *New England's Gothic Literature*, p. 204.
10. Poole, *Satan in America*, p. 21.
11. McWilliams, *California*, p. 25.
12. Starr, *Americans and the Californian Dream*, p. 126.
13. Ibid. p. 126.
14. Brady, 'Points West, Then and Now', p. 455.
15. Hardesty, 'Historical Perspectives on the Archaeology of the Donner Party', p. 89.
16. Ibid. p. 89.
17. Ibid. p. 90.
18. Ibid. p. 90.
19. Johnson, *'Unfortunate Emigrants'*, p. 11.
20. Ibid. p. 11.
21. McGlashan, *History of the Donner Party*, p. 8.
22. Ibid. p. 8.
23. Ibid. p. 8.
24. Ibid. pp. 7–8.
25. Ibid. p. 9.
26. Ibid. p. 10.
27. Ibid. p. 10.
28. Wallis, *The Best Land Under Heaven*, p. xviii.
29. Ibid. p. xviii.
30. Johnson, 'The Aftermath of Tragedy', p. 76.
31. Starr, *Americans and the Californian Dream*, p. 127.
32. Ibid. p. 127.
33. Stewart, *Ordeal by Hunger*, p. 287.
34. Rarick, *Desperate Passage*, p. 232.
35. Ibid. p. 232.
36. Starr, *Americans and the Californian Dream*, p. 128.
37. Ringel, 'New England Gothic', p. 139.
38. Didion, 'Some Dreamers of the Golden Dream', p. 13.
39. Ibid. p. 29.
40. Lacy, 'Joan Didion', p. 500.

41. Daugherty, *The Last Love Song*, pp. 3–4.
42. *Joan Didion: The Center Will Not Hold* (Dir. Griffin Dunne, 2017).
43. Daugherty, *The Last Love Song*, p. 4.
44. Didion, 'Where I Was From', p. 1085.
45. Ibid. p. 1085.
46. Ibid. p. 1104.
47. Mogen, Sanders and Karpinski, *Frontier Gothic*, p. 159.
48. Ibid. 'Introduction', pp. 14; 18.
49. Ibid. p. 23.
50. Ibid. p. 17.
51. Didion, 'Where I Was From', p. 996.
52. Nowak-McNeice and Zarzycka, 'Californias Everywhere', p. 187.
53. Didion, 'Notes from a Native Daughter', p. 134.
54. See, for instance, the transformation undergone by Jack Torrance in *The Shining*, discussed in Murphy, *The Rural Gothic*, chapter 3.
55. DiMarco, 'Going Wendigo', p. 135.
56. See Murphy, *Rural Gothic*, pp. 108–18.
57. Wallis, *The Best Land Under Heaven*, p. xvii.
58. Starr, *California: A History*, p. 73.
59. Ibid. p. 70.
60. DiMarco, 'Going Wendigo', p. 144.
61. Abel, *Tuberculosis and the Politics of Exclusion*, pp. 5–6.
62. Rarick, *Desperate Passage*, p. 70.
63. DiMarco, 'Going Wendigo', p. 151.
64. Starr, *Americans and the California Dream*, p. 128.
65. West, *The Day of the Locust*, p. 2.
66. Novak and Dixon, 'Introduction', p. 2.
67. Cumbow, *Order in the Universe*, p. 96.
68. All audio commentary excerpts are taken from the version recorded by John Carpenter and Debra Hill for the 2004 Momentum Pictures special edition DVD of *The Fog*.
69. Cumbow, *Order in the Universe*, p. 91.
70. Smith, 'A Siege Mentality?', pp. 35–48.
71. Ibid. p. 37.
72. Ibid. p. 38.
73. Muir, *The Films of John Carpenter*, p. 89.
74. Phillips, *Dark Directions*, pp. 137, 138.
75. Paul Scanlon (1979) quoted in Mulvey-Roberts, 'A Spook Ride on Film', p. 79.
76. See Blakemore, 'The Family of Man', and Jameson, 'The Shining'.

77. Leeder, 'Skeletons Sail an Etheric Ocean', p. 72.
78. Ibid. p. 71
79. Ibid. p. 72.
80. Ibid. p. 77.
81. Mulvey-Roberts, 'A Spook Ride on Film', p. 79.
82. Antonio Bay is described as 'a small Northern California coastal town' in Hill and Carpenter's screenplay.
83. Watt, *The Paradox of Preservation*, p. 42.
84. Carpenter, in *The Fog* audio commentary.
85. 'Visit the Point Reyes Lighthouse', National Parks Service, https://www.nps.gov/pore/planyourvisit/lighthouse.htm (last accessed 23 July 2018).
86. White, *Shipwrecks of the California Coast*, p. 9.
87. Ibid. p. 9.
88. Ibid. p. 10.
89. Ibid. p. 10.
90. Ibid. p. 13.
91. Muir, *The Films of John Carpenter*, p. 88.
92. Alder, 'Through Oceans Darkly', pp. 1–2.
93. Dana, *Two Years Before the Mast*, pp. 77; 217.
94. *The Fog* audio commentary.
95. Starr, *California: A History*, p. 25.
96. Ibid. p. 25.
97. Ibid. p. 25.
98. Ibid. p. 25.
99. Ibid. pp. 25–6.
100. Phillips, *Dark Directions*, p. 137.
101. Ibid. p. 137.
102. Von der Porten et al., "Who Made Drake's Plate of Brass?', p. 116.
103. Ibid. p. 116.
104. Ibid. p. 116.
105. Ibid. p. 116.
106. Ibid. p. 116.
107. Leeder, 'Skeletons Sail', p. 71.
108. Episcopal Church of the Ascension, https://www.ascension-sierramadre.com/welcome.html (last accessed 21 July 2021)
109. 'Episcopal Church of the Ascension', National Parks Service, National Register of Historical Places, https://npgallery.nps.gov/NRHP/AssetDetail/1ddb48f2-55a7-4e26-84aa-8a0b20a14244 (last accessed 21 July 2021).
110. Smith, 'A Siege Mentality?', p. 39.
111. Ibid. p. 39.

112. Also noted by Leeder, in 'Skeleton's Sail an Etheric Ocean', p. 72.
113. Kimbro, Costello and Ball, *The California Missions*, pp. 43–4.
114. Woodward, *In Ruins*, p. 111.
115. Kimbro, Costello and Ball, *The California Missions*, pp. 1; 38.
116. Jackson, *Ramona*, p. 14.
117. Kimbro, Costello and Ball, *The California Missions*, p. 12.
118. Ibid. p. 33.
119. Ibid. p. 33.
120. Ibid. pp. 12; 3.
121. Starr, *California: A History*, p. 41.
122. Madley, *An American Genocide*, p. 3.
123. Ibid. p. 3.
124. Leeder, 'Skeletons Sail an Etheric Ocean', p. 72.
125. Moran, *Colonizing Leprosy*, p. 24.
126. Ibid. p. 25.
127. Trevelyan, *The Winchester*, p. xvi.
128. Ignoffo, *Captive of the Labyrinth*.
129. Trevelyan, *The Winchester*, p. 125.
130. Ibid. p. 126.
131. Ignoffo, *Captive of the Labyrinth*, p. xix (earthquake damage), p. 209 (fabricated obsession with the number thirteen).
132. Junker, 'Unruly Women and Their Crazy Houses', p. 341. Winchester is presented as an unsung pioneer in this respect in 'Mystery House', episode 162 of the design podcast *99% Invisible* (first broadcast in 2015), which draws heavily on Ignoffo's biography.
133. Daley, *Sarah Winchester*, p. 5.
134. Ibid. pp. 11; 15.
135. 'No human eye can isolate the unhappy coincidence of line and place which suggests evil in the face of a house, and yet somehow a manic juxtaposition, a badly turned angle, some chance meeting of roof and sky, turned Hill House into a place of despair, more frightening because the face of Hill House seemed awake, with a watchfulness from the blank windows and a touch of glee in the eyebrow of a cornice' (Jackson, *The Haunting of Hill House*, p. 34).
136. Daley, p. 18.
137. Junker, 'Unruly Women', p. 339.
138. Ibid. pp. 332–2.
139. Dickey, *Ghostland*, p. 53.
140. Ibid. p. 67.
141. Ignoffo, *Captive of the Labyrinth*, p. xiv.
142. McVarish and Leavitt, 'Mourning in the Hollows', p. 156.

143. Ibid. p. 173.
144. Cook, 'The American Invasion, 1848–1870', pp. 3–4. In the conclusion to *An American Genocide*, Madley states: 'The direct and deliberate killing of Indians in California between 1846 and 1873 was more lethal and sustained than anywhere else in the United States and its colonial antecedents' (p. 354).
145. Madley, *An American Genocide*, p. 354.
146. Cook, 'The American Invasion, 1848–1870', pp. 3–4.
147. Ibid. p. 5.
148. Madley, *An American Genocide*, p. 2.
149. Ibid. p. 10.
150. Cook's statistic is cited in Madley, *An American Genocide*, p. 39.
151. Ibid. p. 78.
152. Ibid. p. 84.
153. Ibid. p. 114 ('widespread genocide'); p. 346.
154. Thomas, *Religion and the Decline of Magic*, p. 701.
155. Ibid. p. 712.
156. Ignoffo, *Captive of the Labyrinth*, p. 141.
157. Ignoffo, *Captive of the Labyrinth*, p. 84.
158. Madley, *An American Genocide*, p. 348.
159. Ibid. p. 348.
160. Ibid. p. 348.
161. Ignoffo, *Captive of the Labyrinth*, p. 140.
162. Ibid. p. 140.
163. Dickey, *Ghostland*, p. 66.
164. Trevelyan, *The Winchester*, p. 133. This interpretation of the statue is found in Roger Rule's 2003 novel, *Sarah*, for instance.
165. Block's actions are never ascribed to an explicitly racist motivation: instead, it is said that he wishes to avenge the death of his brothers during the Civil War. This sanitises Block's actions by depicting them as those of a man driven to violence by great personal loss rather than by a poisonously persistent racist ideology.
166. Detailed in Franklin, *Shirley Jackson*, p. 403.
167. Jackson, 'Letter to Geraldine and Leslie Jackson', p. 356.
168. Franklin, *Shirley Jackson*, p. 13.
169. Oppenheimer, *Private Demons*, p. 28.
170. Franklin, *Shirley Jackson*, p. 403.
171. Ignoffo, *Captive of the Labyrinth*, p. 161.
172. Curtis, *Dark Places*, p. 54.
173. Luna, 'Newsom Apologizes', online.
174. Executive Department, State of California, Executive Order N-15-19, 18 June 2019.

# 2

# The Dark Side of 'the Good Life': California and the Birth of Modern Horror

*Chinatown* (1974) is one of the bleakest films about California ever made. Like other 1970s neo-noir films, as Erik Dussere notes, it 'interrogated and undermined the noir detective genre, self-consciously incorporating references to classic hard-boiled films while constructing stories in which detectives are unable to solve the case or become unwitting pawns in a larger plot'.[1] In *Chinatown*, the 'larger plot' in which fast-thinking private investigator J. J. Gittes (Jack Nicholson) finds himself embroiled pertains to the future of Los Angeles.

*Chinatown* screenwriter, Robert Towne, was inspired by a historical epi-sode detailed in Carey McWilliams's *Southern California: An Island on the Land* (1946).[2] The 'Owens Valley Tragedy' began when the city of Los Angeles deliberately created a drought to encourage citizens to vote for the construc-tion of an aqueduct.[3] But as Sam Wasson outlines:

> rather than supply the City of Los Angeles with the water it had paid twenty-five million dollars for, the masterminds brought the aqueduct only as far as the north end of the San Fernando Valley, a hundred thousand acres of which they had clandestinely bought up a year earlier. The newly irrigated land, which they had purchased for a song, netted them an estimated profit of one hundred million dollars. They got rich, but the citizens of Los Angeles were robbed, Owens Valley land workers lost their livelihoods, hundreds of acres were decimated, and 'the rape of Owens Valley', as McWilliams put it, persisted unvanquished. The bad guys won.[4]

*Chinatown*'s chief villain is land developer Noah Cross (John Huston), who lives outside the city in a pretty ranchero-style property. Gittes, who has uncovered Cross's murderous scheme, asks the old man why he is going to all this trouble: 'Why are you doing it? How much better can you eat? What could you buy that you can't already afford?' Cross defiantly responds: 'The future, Mr Gittes! The future!'

Cross is not only an immensely corrupt and powerful figure whose crimes will shape the material infrastructure of Southern California for generations to come. He is also the unrepentant rapist of his tormented daughter, Evelyn (Faye Dunaway), and the father of her child. Money, political clout and the inherent corruption of the young city mean that Cross is not only free to do whatever he likes in a business capacity: he can also engage in consequence-free acts of murder and incest. Cross sees Evelyn and her/his daughter as his own personal property, and clearly feels the same way about Southern California. As he puts it: 'You see Mr Gittes, most people never have to face the fact that at the right time and right place, they're capable of *anything*.'

In the iconic final moments of the film, after Evelyn has been shot dead by police and her child-like daughter has been taken away by Cross, Gittes is advised to embrace the amnesia associated with living the good life in California: 'Forget it, Jake. It's Chinatown.' Yet in classic noir style, there's no getting away from the fact that the rot goes all the way down. Cross will control the future of his helpless daughter/granddaughter just as he has already irrevocably shaped the future of Los Angeles. Even the water in the city's taps is tainted (he owns the department). Furthermore, the even bigger development boom which will be brought about by World War II is just around the corner (the film is set in 1937). The future is indeed coming to Southern California, and soon no one will care (or choose to remember) how it came to be.

The California Gothic often critiques the insistence upon unfettered individual and societal 'progress' which has long been associated with the state. As a result, it has also contributed much to the development of modern American horror fiction and film. As has been well established, the twin horrors of the Holocaust and the atom bomb irrevocably reconfigured the horror and Gothic genres in the years following World War II. From the late 1940s onwards, American horror and Gothic fiction and film more often located dread close to home, and within the darkest recesses of the mind. This new 'horror of the everyday' was also profoundly influenced by Californian settings and themes. Yet, typically, the trend was soon so effectively absorbed into the broader (national) cultural imagination that its *regional* significance has thus far been largely overlooked. This chapter will therefore discuss the ways in which the post-war California Gothic helped to establish some of the most notable themes and preoccupations found within the wider American horror and Gothic traditions during this same period, particularly those pertaining to the unprecedented societal and infrastructural developments which rapidly transformed both the state and the nation at large.

Remi Nadeau's 1963 volume, *California: The New Society*, was published just after the Census Bureau announced that the state had surpassed

New York to become the most populous in the nation. Nadeau resonantly described Californians as 'a people who appear to be moving on the frontier of American culture'.[5] He pointed to the tract home, the backyard swimming pool, the drive-in, the supermarket and the sports car as prime examples of innovations which had originated in California, or were first popularised there.[6] He continued:

> In the past these were continued faint customs brought back from the American frontier. California was out in the provinces; she was absorbed in winning an empire, and she had little of enduring substance to say to the rest of the world. Today California has become the big time.[7]

Nadeau correctly predicted that the state 'may soon be not the outpost but the wellspring of American culture'.[8] His perspective was also a familiar one:

> The fact is that California, perhaps more than any other state, is really a fulfilment of the American dream. Except for some areas of blight, here is the good life – considerable comfort, escape from drudgery and hardship, reasonable leisure time, and the environment to make the most of it. Is this not the American promise – freedom to enjoy life as the fruit of honest labor? Following the American tradition to its ultimate, California is really a sort of secular Kingdom Come.[9]

As Kevin Starr has chronicled, the post-war era was indeed one of 'unprecedented abundance connected to growth' for California – a trend which would continue for the rest of the twentieth century.[10] During this period, 'the national experience and the California experience became, increasingly, a converging phenomenon, building upon the national role played by California in the Second World War'.[11] For Starr, as for Nadeau, understanding the post-war United States is impossible 'without reference to the California experience'.[12] As he puts it:

> From this perspective, the story of World War II and the postwar period edging into the early 1960s asserts once and for all the American dimension of California and the California dimension of America. The dreams of California, in short, were the dreams of the nation, and vice versa. And so were the tensions and ambiguities.[13]

In November 1965, *Los Angeles Times* book critic Robert A. Kirsch devoted a column to Charles Beaumont, who had just published *The Magic Man and*

*Other Science-Fantasy Stories.* Kirsch described Beaumont as the leading light in a new, exciting, and distinctively local literary movement. If there were such a thing as a 'Southern Californian School of writing', he argued, Beaumont was at its very forefront.[14] He saw it as no coincidence that Ray Bradbury, the 'most influential' of this movement, supplied the foreword to Beaumont's collection, nor that Richard Matheson provided the afterword. Beaumont was formed, Kirsch believed, both from 'the mold of his own talents and of the particular setting of ideas, experiences and approaches which may be called the Southern California scene'.[15]

Kirsch made it clear, however, that in using this term, he was not speaking of 'any formal, slavishly imitative circle'.[16] Rather, he continued,

> Schools of writing are critical artefacts contrived to provide some sense of order, some ideas of influence, some notion of continuity. The Bradbury – Beaumont – Matheson – William Nolan – George Johnson group [. . .] is not linked by the traditional and sometimes parochial patterns of regional writing. It is less like the recent Southern Gothic School, than it is the Chicago Renaissance of the 20s and 30s. Thus, when I speak of a Southern California School, I am referring to one source of Beaumont's material. A writer, if he has identity and authenticity as Beaumont does, is produced by constant interaction between discernible environment and the special, individual vision which is his.[17]

Southern California – Beaumont's 'discernible environment' – was, as Kirsch put it, 'new, illusory, open, imaginative, exaggerated, experimental, the land of sports cars and movies, speed and special effects. Above all, it is the terrain of the imagination.'[18] Kirsch directly connected this 'terrain of the imagination' to California's (supposed) lack of history:

> Where the writer does not have the rooted, haunted past, it is the present which provides his sustenance. Perhaps this is why the settled East and the decaying South have not produced the special quality of fantasy which is Southern Californian. Beaumont is interesting for this: but perhaps most importantly because he has transmuted it into the touch of the universal.[19]

In a 1974 column on William F. Nolan, Kirsch further argued that 'the essence of the California School' was 'an unfettered imagination'.[20]

In the 1999 anthology *California Sorcery*, which gathered stories and recollections from authors associated with the Southern California School, Nolan observed that of the twelve authors generally cited as being part of 'The Group' (as this loose assemblage of friends and acquaintances was also known), only one – John Tomerlin – was a native Californian.[21] It was not place of birth, he argued, but 'The fact that we all gravitated to Los Angeles, and produced most of our best work in the Southern California area that justifies the label we now wear.'[22] Their reasons for heading to Southern California (climate aside) echoed Kirsch's assessment:

> Because the area is particularly receptive to creativity. Los Angeles is a totally 'open-minded' city at the cutting edge of modern capital. It is also the entertainment capital of the world; if you wish to write for films or television you must live in Los Angeles. Thus, we were able to write and sell to a variety of West Coast markets while still maintaining our contacts with the New York publishing world. In Los Angeles, there are no creative limits.[23]

Practical considerations – Los Angeles was an obvious destination for any ambitious writer who wished to work in television or the movies – as well as the network of personal connections which sprang up between this group of predominately Midwestern and East Coast creatives, therefore also helped to make Southern California a 'wellspring' for this variety of American cultural expression (to appropriate Nadeau's phrase). As Christopher Conlon notes, it almost seemed as if the most notable of these authors 'had hatched from a single brilliant, fantastically inventive imagination'.[24] 'This', he continues, 'is no accident':

> For these men were, from the early 1950s to the mid–1960s, part of a close-knit brotherhood of writers centered in the Los Angeles area that came to dominate not only printed SF and fantasy, but movies and TV as well – scripting between them many of the period's best-known films (including most of the Roger Corman / Edgar Allan Poe movies), along with classic segments of *Thriller*, *Alfred Hitchcock Presents*, *One Step Beyond* and virtually every episode of *The Twilight Zone*.[25]

Conlon echoes Kirsch's characterisation of Beaumont as 'the headmaster' of the 'Southern California School', describing him as 'the hub of the wheel'.[26] He traces its genesis to the summer of 1946, when Ray Bradbury made friends with Beaumont (then a teenager) after they met in an LA bookshop.[27] By 1952, he continues, Beaumont, who had by then embarked upon his highly successful but tragically abbreviated writing career, had made friends with Nolan, and in turn, Bradbury had just met Richard Matheson.[28] Peripheral members included

*Psycho* author Robert Bloch, and Rod Serling, who invited Beaumont, Matheson and Bradbury to contribute to *The Twilight Zone*.[29] Conlon argues that 'More than any other single program, film, or book of the time, *The Twilight Zone* expresses the heart and soul of the Southern Californian Group.'[30]

The contribution which the Southern California School – or 'The Group'– made to the development of horror fiction in the post-war era is also emphasised by S. T. Joshi. He notes that this 'remarkable group of writers, mostly based in California, effected a revolution in supernatural and non-supernatural horror fiction as dramatic as that engendered by H. P. Lovecraft and his companions a generation earlier'.[31] Joshi observes that they 'all worked seamlessly in the genres of supernatural horror, crime/suspense, science fiction, and fantasy', and that

> these writers, all acquainted with one another and often exchanging ideas dynamically, fostered a modernisation of the supernatural by appeal to science as well as by an appeal to the mundanities of contemporary life in America, with the result that much of their work features a social criticism of the increasing blandness and conformism of their time.[32]

This critique of the 'the mundanities of contemporary life' was often, as we shall see, directly rooted in the massive infrastructural transformations wrought upon the physical and cultural landscape of post-war California.

In this chapter I will begin by discussing the part which California themes and texts played in the establishment of the 'Suburban Gothic' and 'Highway Horror' sub-genres. Then, I will conclude by considering the prominence of the 'rogue white male' trope and the ways in which the cultural construction of the serial killer has been shaped by the frequency with which such crimes occurred in California during the 1970s and 1980s. I have previously discussed some of the texts briefly cited here in relation to these same transformations (most notably, the growth of suburbia and the establishment of the Interstate Highway System). I will not re-hash or refute my previous analysis: I will instead expand upon it by this time focusing upon the California-specific nature of these texts.

## Creeping Terrors: 'Californication' and the Origins of the Suburban Gothic

Matheson's short story 'The Creeping Terror' (first published in 1959 as 'A Touch of Grapefruit') satirises the then-popular notion that California had become an ever-expanding cultural entity which exerted an immense (and not altogether welcome) influence upon the rest of the United States.[33] The 'terror' begins in 1972, when California Institute of Technology physicist Alfred Grimsby realises that 'Los Angeles is alive.' What's more, 'It moves.' Soon, Arizona, Utah, New Mexico and Colorado are inundated with rains so severe that 'several minor religious groups' construct arks. An elderly Nebraska farmer finds an orange tree in his cornfield. The farmer's wife dons sunglasses and shorts, and declares, 'I think I'll drive into Hollywood.' The situation escalates as 'unfathomable citrus tree growth' threatens corn and wheat harvests. The off-kilter behaviour being exhibited by previously staid Midwesterners has the same root cause as the 'alien growth' of the new citrus groves. 'Los Angeles, like some gigantic fungus, was overgrowing the land.'[34]

As Matheson's B-movie-style title indicates, this is yet another post-war invasion narrative featuring a relentless alien menace. Crucially, however, 'the terror' comes from the West Coast of the United States, and not from outer space. The 'Los Angeles Movement' doesn't just *physically* transform the Midwest: it invisibly but permanently alters the people who reside in the 'infected area'. It resembles a comedic version of the alien takeover in Jack Finney's 1955 novel, *The Body Snatchers*. Whilst Finney's invasion most famously manifests itself in the form of the emotionless 'pod people', their conquest also destroys the natural landscape. Once the invaders have fully taken over, they will drain the life out of everything. Even the moon and Mars, were 'alive' before the pods arrived. 'And now . . . it's the earth's turn', Finney's hero, GP Miles Bennell, is told by one of the invaders.[35]

As Mark Jancovich has argued, the alien takeover which transforms Finney's quiet Northern Californian community can be seen as a metaphor for the manner in which the intimacy and warmth of the 'traditional' small-town existence was being eroded by the atomisation and anonymity of contemporary American life.[36] In Matheson's story, the 'Californication' of the United States is a kind of inescapable psychological and environmental terraforming.[37] Although the term 'Californication' was (likely) first used in a book review in *Time Magazine* in 1966,[38] the way in which it was deployed by another *Time* correspondent, Sandra Burton, in 1972, most closely evokes Matheson's satirical take on the state. Burton wrote about the growing fear amongst other Western states that their resources would soon be overwhelmed by the massive population shift west which had already transformed the Golden State: 'Legislators, scientists and citizens are now openly concerned about the threat of "Californication" – the haphazard, mindless development that has already gobbled up most of Southern California.'[39] As Daniel Klug notes, 'Since Burton's introduction of the term, *Californication* has been used as a derogatory term for stereotypes connected to the Californian lifestyle.'[40] The unprecedented growth noted by Nadeau and Starr here becomes an alien virus which relentlessly spreads ever eastwards, in an ironic reversal of Manifest Destiny (a trope found in other California Gothic narratives, as we shall see).

Matheson's tale wryly references many of the clichéd signifiers of the California lifestyle and culture one would expect to encounter at the beginning of the 1960s. 'The LA Movement' results in delusions such as 'Beach Seeking' – a phenomenon in which 'masses of people, wearing bathing suits and carrying towels and blankets, wandered helplessly across the plains and prairies searching for the Pacific Ocean'.[41] Another symptom is a newfound obsession with automobility and a 'maniacal splurge in the building of drive-in restaurants and theatres'.[42] New cults also arise amidst the chaos, divorce sky-rockets and the writers and actors who profit from the boom in film production turn to liberal politics.

By the beginning of 1973, New York has fallen. The last remaining bastions of the old United States are all in New England, because the 'fungus' finds it difficult to adapt to the New England soil. Nevertheless, 'Within three years the entire nation was a part of Los Angeles.' But the invasion doesn't stop there. The story ends on an 'ill-fated' day in 1984, when a tribal chieftain on a remote Pacific Island realises that his own daughter has succumbed to the 'infection'. Soon, the entire world will be absorbed by wider Los Angeles. Southern California has gone global.

Matheson's story humorously highlighted the extent to which the unprecedented changes in living patterns taking place across the United States were pioneered in the wider Los Angeles region. Southern California was at the forefront of post-war suburbanisation. As Kenneth Jackson put it in 1985:

> More than anyplace else, California became the symbol of the postwar suburban culture. It pioneered the booms in sports cars, foreign cars, vans, and motor homes, and by 1984 its 26 million citizens owned almost 19 million motor vehicles and had access to the world's most extensive freeway system.[43]

Starr observes that suburbanisation was a speedy process:

> As of 1950, the vast majority of the 10,586,223 people of California were living in densely settled cities and towns, as they had been doing since the nineteenth century. The planned residential sub-division – developer driven, mass-produced, and uniform in design, readily financed and affordable, marketed to millions of incoming Californians – would not destroy the urban matrix and structure of California life. It would, however, profoundly transform pre-existing communities.[44]

Indeed, he continues, 'values and lifestyles were changing dramatically and quite soon overwhelmed prior Californian identities'.[45] These changes, he notes, began during the war, when eight million new residents moved to the West Coast, many to take up defence jobs. The transition had huge social implications:

> Crime rates soared, especially batteries and sexual assaults, sure signs of a society under stress: a society, in point of fact, that anticipated postwar California in its population surge, prosperity, mobility and instability. The war years, in short, constituted Act One of a drama of accelerated growth and transformation that would continue for the rest of the century.[46]

Published in 1948 and set during the summer of 1936, Shirley Jackson's first published novel, *The Road Through the Wall*, anticipated these changes and, as I outlined in my 2009 book on the Suburban Gothic, established some of the key themes and preoccupations of the sub-genre. The Suburban Gothic 'dramatizes anxieties arising from the mass suburbanisation of the United States and usually features suburban settings, preoccupations, and protagonists'.[47] One if its key thematic conceits is the suspicion that 'even the most ordinary-looking neighbourhood, or house, or family, has something to hide, and that no matter how calm and settled a place looks, it is only ever a moment away from dramatic (and generally sinister) incident'.[48] In the Suburban Gothic, the most insidious dangers come from internal rather than external threats. A setting associated with the sanctity of the middle-class (and almost invariably *white*) nuclear family is here depicted as a locale rooted in dysfunction, mindless conformity and violence of both the human and the supernatural variety.[49]

California was an obvious locale in which to set narratives that dramatised the dark side of suburban living because the region was at the forefront of this revolution. Two foundational examples are Jackson's *The Road Through the Wall* and Matheson's novel, *I Am Legend* (1954). *The Road Through the Wall* depicts a snobbish and self-involved community on the cusp of irrevocable change. The high brick wall which has for years protected the citizens of Pepper Street from the outside world is about to be removed. Pepper Street is located in Cabrillo, a fictional community modelled upon the upscale Northern Californian suburb Burlingame where, as I have noted in Chapter 1, Jackson spent her childhood. Pepper Street is, typically for a Suburban Gothic setting, a liminal space, situated between a row of low-rent apartment houses and a wealthy neighbourhood which is 'so exclusive that the streets had no names, the houses no numbers. The people who owned the wall lived there; so, although no one knew it very surely, did the people who owned some of the houses on Pepper Street.'[50]

In her opening chapter, Jackson establishes the physical and social topography of the neighbourhood, underlining the rigid social hierarchy which defines relationships and status for both adults and children.[51] Jackson was particularly interested in depicting the ways in which the prejudices (both racial and economic) of the adult world are refracted through the behaviour of Pepper Street's youngsters. One of the novel's pivotal figures is Tod Donald, a desperately isolated thirteen-year-old boy: 'Nobody ever noticed Tod Donald very much.'[52] When the youngest child on Pepper Street – Caroline Desmond, the blonde and lavishly dressed little daughter of the family described as 'the aristocracy of the neighbourhood' – goes missing, Mrs Mack, an elderly resident, immediately assumes that outsiders are to blame: '"It's people from outside took her," Mrs. Mack said, nodding her great old head. "People from the other side of the wall."' Another neighbour declares, '"We think she's just gotten lost," [. . .] "This is a nice neighbourhood, not like places where little girls get taken away."'[53]

Variations upon this plaintive refrain – the 'terrible things couldn't possibly happen in a nice neighbourhood like this' fallacy, still so beloved of true crime narratives – repeatedly recur in the Suburban Gothic. As the hours pass, the residents of Jackson's community gather on 'what was traditionally their forgotten village green', husbands staying close to wives, parents keeping a tight hold on their usually lively offspring. Jackson unflinchingly details the self-righteous cruelty which infuses the collective when conditions are *just* right (or rather, wrong). This preoccupation is one of Jackson's most characteristic themes, as the violent behaviour of the villagers in 'The Lottery' (1948) and in *We Have Always Lived in the Castle* (1962) further attest.

When another boy reveals that Tod was acting strangely earlier that afternoon – and the adults finally realise that he is also missing (typically, his parents failed to notice) – the community's suspicion swiftly falls upon the youngster. Then little Caroline's battered body is found by a nearby creek: 'She was horribly dirty; no one had ever seen Caroline as dirty as she was then, with mud all over her yellow dress and yellow socks.'[54] It looks like her head has been bashed in by a rock. When Tod creeps back home later that same night, his guilt is taken for granted, even by his own family. 'Tell me how you killed that little girl', a policeman demands to know.[55] Tod's response is taken as a confession. When the officer leaves him alone for a few minutes, he hangs himself in the dining room, standing on 'his own chair . . . the one he sat on every night at dinner'.[56] This unsettling juxtaposition of the mundane and the macabre is typical of the post-war Gothic and horror tradition. The family dinner table is even more directly connected to murder in Jackson's final published novel, *We Have Always Lived in the Castle*, in which arsenic is added to the communal sugar bowl by another isolated teenager, albeit one whose guilt is in little doubt.

Whether he is guilty or not (the novel is slyly ambiguous on that score), Tod has accepted his role as the street's chosen outcast and justice has been seen to be observed. As Fritz Oehlschlaeger notes, there are some

> remarkable similarities to Jackson's famous story ['The Lottery']. It is about the people of a single street of a small, isolated community, in this case located in California. Its theme is scapegoating, directed by the ordinary middle-class people of Pepper Street at a whole series of victims.[57]

Here, however, the action moves from the rural setting of 'The Lottery' to a suburban community explicitly located just outside San Francisco.

As well as serving as a foundational instance of the Suburban Gothic, *The Road Through the Wall*, Joan Wylie Hall has argued, contributes to a 'prominent theme of much California literature: the loss of innocence in the Eden of the final American Frontier'.[58] She observes of the novel's setting that it 'contains elements of a golden age, but the Eden of the novel is on its way to being lost from the opening page'.[59] Hall also notes that there are some interesting similarities between Jackson's novel and Nathanael West's *The Day of the Locust* (which will be discussed in the next chapter), including the fact that both feature important characters named 'Tod', and that in German, the name means 'death haunted': 'in contrast to Tod Donald, Tod Hackett survives the violent ending of *The Day of the Locust*, but he is injured by a mob that charges against a man who viciously attacks a child star' – meaning that mob 'justice' for violence (or assumed violence perpetrated against a child) features in both novels.[60]

Although it is set several years before the new wave of suburban development which so rapidly transformed the state (and the nation), *The Road Through the Wall*, which was published just as these new transformations were beginning to take hold, established some of the most resonant themes of the Suburban Gothic sub-genre and pointed towards the important role that California-set texts would play in its development. Jackson's core premise – the unease surrounding the imminent removal of the wall which has long separated the poorest parts of the community from the wealthiest – anticipates the strain of middle-class white anxiety about letting the 'wrong element' into the neighbourhood that is expressed much more explicitly in Richard Matheson's *I Am Legend*.

In *I Am Legend*, Matheson, in typical 'Southern California School' fashion, cannily updates a well-worn genre trope – the embattled individual who seemingly finds himself the sole survivor of a global catastrophe – and situates it entirely in and around Compton, in Southern Los Angeles County. The novel envisages a world ravaged by a plague which has killed billions and transformed those who did not die soon after infection into seemingly mindless ghouls. Protagonist Robert Neville characterises them as vampires, but to a modern-day reader, they more closely resemble zombies (it has been observed that George A. Romero's 1968 *Night of the Living Dead* owed much to Matheson). Neville, a suburban husband and father, is immune, but is forced to watch as his wife, child and everyone else die or are (apparently) turned into monsters.

The novel begins in January 1976, as Neville tends to the tedious but essential chores which will hopefully keep him alive for another dreary day. 'Normal' life has been completely upended, and perpetual paranoia is the status quo. As I have previously observed, one of the most striking things about the book is that Neville, whose Aryan credentials are emphasised (he is 'born of English-German stock') often refers to the 'vampires' in terms which compare them to a resentful (and ungrateful) racial or ethnic 'Other'.[61] A key passage comes early in the novel, when Neville, drunk and depressed, facetiously ponders the pathetic but deadly creatures which besiege his home nightly: 'Pore vampires, he thought, pore little cusses, pussy-footin' round my house, so thirsty, so all forlorn. [. . .] Friends, I come here before you to discuss the vampire; a minority element if there ever was one, and there was one.'[62]

As if Neville's clumsy mockery of Black vernacular isn't enough ('Pore little cusses'), he also satirically evokes 'progressive' liberal defences of a misunderstood and disenfranchised minority which must resort to a 'predatory nocturnal existence' in order to survive. When he wakes up, Neville reflects that, 'they'd beaten him, the black bastards had beaten him'.[63] As I noted of this passage in *The Suburban Gothic*:

> Neville's willingness to characterise his struggle for survival in terms so reminiscent of existing racial tensions suggests that he was unlikely to have been a card-carrying liberal, and that now a *really* bad element has moved into the neighbourhood, he can violently express feelings that would perhaps otherwise have been repressed.[64]

When further situated within the racial contexts of post-war Los Angeles, Neville's sentiments (even if expressed as a drunken rant) are even more indicative of the novel's notable contribution to the California Gothic tradition. The location of Neville's embattled suburban home is real: Cimarron Street is a twenty-minute drive from Compton Boulevard. As Robert Yeates, who has also written about the racial contexts of the novel's setting, observes:

> Neville's encounters with the vampires in the city invariably begin with a drive along Compton Boulevard, which runs through the middle of the city of Compton. Whether or not Neville's house is within Compton itself or merely nearby, the repeated reminders of this particular city in Los Angeles County is evocative of racialized spaces.[65]

Starr characterises the move to California made by millions of Americans during the post-war era as another manifestation of a recurrent tendency:

> The Gold-Rush, the 1880s, the early 1900s, the Depression, World War II: California had developed through a series of booms in which large influxes of people in search of a better life – whether imagined as gold, land, employment or merely a second start – had migrated en masse to the Pacific Coast. Through each of these booms, with the possible exception of the Gold Rush, the desire for a new and improved domestic life – visualized as a home of one's own, a garden, family life in a sunny climate – remained consistent.[66]

Mass-suburbanisation did much to help satisfy this demand. Countless new communities sprang up in Southern California, especially within the 'Inland Empire': 'Riverside, San Bernardino, Eastern LA County'.[67] However, for quite some time, the 'dream' of a new home and a fresh start in the suburbs was largely confined to a certain racial and economic demographic only – middle-class white citizens such as Robert Neville:

> Middle-class Americans preferred to live among their own kind of people: people, that is, who looked like they looked, earned what they earned, had been raised the same way they had been raised, and generally shared the same philosophy of life. Home ownership – especially on the mass scale practiced in the new California developments – ensured such a willful segregation. Families voluntarily came to these places to be with their own kind.[68]

The homogeneity of such neighbourhoods was upheld by the financial discrimination that Black (and other minority) aspiring homeowners faced. In Southern California, as elsewhere, 'the poor, the majority of them disadvantaged minorities, were being excluded from the same government assistance that was bringing millions of middle-class Americans, veterans especially, into home ownership'.[69] Nadeau also discussed the racial segregation found in Los Angeles:

> The main reasons for this anomaly are the dominant place of land value in the Southern Californian economy and the general belief that Negro occupancy depresses land value. The veneration of real estate prices is so widespread that it simply overrides the public conscience. The phenomenon is most noticeable among Caucasians with a social-climbing mentality, who have bought what they believe to be a fashionable address, and who fear that their newly won prestige will be shattered by a Negro neighbor.[70]

With these contemporary contexts in mind, it is not difficult to see Neville's anger towards the 'bad element' nightly invading his previously secure neighbourhood as a reflection of the racial tensions which were, during this same decade, directly impacting upon the demographic make-up of Southern California's new suburbs. As Yeates notes:

> The use of Los Angeles in this way can thus be viewed as further evidence that the vampires are representative of African Americans, and that Neville is used by Matheson to demonstrate a racial antagonism at least partially repressed in the city at the time of the novel's publication.[71]

In *Set the Night on Fire: L.A. in the 1960s* (2020), Mike Davis and Jon Wiener argue that there were two different versions of Los Angeles during this time. For Black youngsters in the early to mid-1960s, when 'teenagers in the rest of the country had become intoxicated with images of the endless summer that supposedly defined adolescence in Southern California', everyday life in Los Angeles was far removed indeed from the 'youth paradise' seen in television and film and celebrated in pop music.[72] Moreover, 'edited out of utopia was the existence of a rapidly growing population of more than 1 million people of African, Asian and Mexican ancestry'.[73] 'If these were truly golden years of opportunity for white teenagers, their counterparts in South Central and East L.A. faced bleak, ultimately unendurable futures', they continue.[74] A detail which underpinned the discrimination faced by minorities was 'racially exclusive suburbanisation', which helped create a 'monochromatic society from which Blacks were excluded and Chicanos had only a marginal place'.[75] The result of this

> government sanctioned discrimination during the 1950s had been the creation of a super-ghetto: 75 percent of Los Angeles County's Black population was concentrated in the metropolitan core between Olympic Boulevard on the North and Artesia Boulevard on the South . . . Blacks could not live or be seen at night in any of the dozen or so industrial sub-urbs to its east. A clan of white gangs, the 'spookhunters', patrolled racial boundaries, attacking Blacks with seeming impunity.[76]

The LAPD also brutally and rigorously patrolled the boundaries between 'white' and 'Black' Los Angeles, ruthlessly enforcing 'the unwritten curfew that excluded Black people from white residential districts after dark'.[77]

In *I Am Legend*, the nocturnal 'curfew' pertaining to Cimarron Street impacts solely upon Robert Neville, the last human being left in Los Angeles.

As Matheson establishes in the novel's opening lines, he must always remain aware of the time lest he find himself too far from home when darkness falls: 'On those cloudy days, Robert Neville was never sure when sunset came, and sometimes they were in the streets before he could get back.'[78] But in the sunlight, the tables are turned. In the daytime, Neville equips himself with wooden stakes and 'patrols' the streets of wider Los Angeles, entering homes and businesses at will to exterminate the 'filthy bastards' who now constitute the majority population.[79]

The novel's climactic revelation revolves around the discovery that not all the 'vampires' Neville staked were mindless. Some of them retained (or, thanks to a new pill regimen, regained) their humanity, but Neville killed them because he failed to anticipate a basic biological fact: 'bacteria can mutate'.[80] Neville ultimately takes his own life rather than be publicly executed by the cadre of hybrid human/vampires which is now in charge, knowing that to the 'new race' that has inherited a world 'that was theirs and no longer his', he is a fanatical monster.[81] This suggestive positioning of Neville as both persecuted minority and ruthless enforcer of the (bygone) status quo again takes on enhanced significance when we consider the location of Cimarron Street. As Davis and Wiener note, after the war, the city of Compton was 'subdivided at a furious rate and became the fastest growing suburb in California (until Torrance stole its title)'. Under the leadership of Colonel Clifton Smith, 'the publisher of the Compton Herald Daily and the city's unchallenged political boss', 'the city and its homeowner groups fought every effort by middle-class and skilled working-class Blacks to move into the new Subdivisions'.[82] Nevertheless, demographic changes were well underway: 'By 1959, Compton High School was one-quarter Black . . . By the early sixties, segregation persisted, but now as an internal boundary: the western half of Compton was increasingly Black majority or integrated, while the eastern half remained exclusively white.'[83] I Am Legend's 'last man' is, in a manner of speaking, the last white man in the neighbourhood, the unwitting casualty of rapid demographic changes which not even his best efforts to 'clear' the neighbourhood through violence can thwart.

Andrew Wiese notes that throughout the United States:

> white racism continued to play a leading role in shaping African America suburbanization. Many whites projected their deepest fears about crime, disorder, health, status, and sexuality on to African Americans [. . .] Combined with violent fantasies about the social consequences of racial integration – especially images of rape and miscegenation – economic fear led millions of whites to view black neighbors as something like Visigoths at the gates of Rome.[84]

African American 'infiltration' or 'invasion' of 'white' neighbourhoods was an ongoing concern at the neighbourhood level.[85]

In his dying moments, Neville accepts the logical necessity of his own demise. A new generation of ruthless, sentient and highly organised plague survivors are set on purging the city of the last remaining ghouls, and of Neville himself. Seconds before he dies,

> Robert Neville looked out over the new people of the earth. He knew that he did not belong to them; he knew that, like the vampires, he was anathema and black terror to be destroyed. And, abruptly, the concept came, amusing to him, even in his pain. [. . .] Full circle, he thought while the final lethargy crept into his limbs. Full circle. A new terror born in death, a new superstition entering the unassailable fortress of forever. I am legend.[86]

It's a conclusion which brings to mind the fate of another white, male middle-class Californian: the protagonist of George R. Stewart's elegiac post-apocalyptic novel, *Earth Abides* (1949), which itself had much in common with an earlier tale of California pandemic: Jack London's 1912 'The Scarlet Plague'.[87] The hero of Stewart's novel is a graduate student named Isherwood Williams ('Ish'), who is on a field trip when he is bitten by a snake. When he recovers, Ish realises that during his absence from 'civilisation', 'Super-measles' has swept across the globe. For some time, it seems as if he is the only survivor. However, he eventually finds some fellow survivors, including a mixed-race woman named Emma, who he marries and starts a family with. Ish becomes the leader of a new community located in the suburbs of San Francisco which will likely flourish once their youngsters have fully adapted themselves to the 'new world' left behind in the wake of the pandemic. As he grows old and gradually accepts that the world as he once knew it can never be re-established, Ish takes pride in declaring himself, 'The Last American'.[88]

Ish's fate takes on a particularly revealing regional resonance when we recall that Stewart was drawing upon a real-life Californian 'Last Man' story: that of the Yahi Indian known as 'Ishi'.[89] As Leon E. Stover noted in 1974, Stewart told Ishi's story in reverse: 'the last civilised American' lives to see 'his grandchildren revert to a tribal state of culture'.[90] Furthermore, 'Ishi is the Yahi name for man, Ish the Hebrew.'[91] Ishi's story was most famously detailed in Theodora Kroeber's *Ishi in Two Worlds: A Biography of the Last Wild Indian in North America* (1961). Kroeber and her husband Alfred, one of the founding figures of American anthropology, became aware of Ishi in 1911. He had been hiding alone in the Oroville hills for many years, was emaciated and spoke a language which local Native American tribes could not immediately identify. It was eventually discovered that Ishi was the last surviving member of the Yahi offshoot of the Yana tribe, a nation which had inhabited Northern California for thousands of years before being wiped out by disease and white violence in the years following statehood. In Kroeber's words, Ishi was 'the last wild Indian in North America, a man of Stone Age culture'.[92]

One of the telling things about both Stewart's recasting – or appropriation – of the tragic fate of California's 'last wild Indian' is that his 'Last Man', like Matheson's, finally accepts that the world he was born in is gone forever. As Elizabeth Wells puts it, 'despite Ish's failed effort to revivify a civilizing spirit in his clan, the novel is still optimistic in its distillation of utopian dreams about the continuation of the species'.[93] Like Robert Neville, Ish will also live on as a semi-mythological figure (albeit of the heroic sort) for a few generations at least. This contrasts with the fate of California's real life 'Last Man'. Ishi spent the rest of his life under the supervision of Alfred Kroeber and his colleague Thomas Waterman. He both lived and worked in the Museum of Anthropology in San Francisco – serving as both a janitor and as a kind of living history exhibit – and died there, of tuberculosis, in 1916. Theodora Kroeber notes that for decades after a recording of Ishi's voice was made, it lay 'gathering dust in its waxen grooves along with the ghosts of other Indian voices whose languages are departed with their one-time speakers to the Land of the Dead'.[94] There's a real sense here that, in a familiar formulation, Ishi was perceived of as a ghostly figure even whilst he was still alive: recast as the last of an irrevocably doomed race, sadly, but inevitably, replaced by a hardier strain of (white) humanity.[95]

The projection of his story onto a white Californian in Stewart's *Earth Abides* presents us with a sanitised version of regional history in which the protagonist sagely accepts the certainty of his own demise. There's no need for the brutal extermination tactics which characterised the American settlement of California (or the myriad abuses of the Spanish and Mexican eras). However, this is not quite the case in Matheson: his post-pandemic world is one born of violence, both Neville's and that of his successors. As his love interest/betrayer, Ruth, who is a 'ranking officer' in the new hierarchy, explains, 'New societies are always primitive [. . .] You should know that. In a way we're like a revolutionary group – repossessing society by violence. It's inevitable. Violence is no stranger to you.'[96] Matheson's nightmarish tale is further complicated by the novel's engagement with contemporary anxieties surrounding the disputed right of African Americans (and other racial and ethnic minorities) to access the post-war suburban 'dream' so freely granted to their white counterparts.

These racial tensions are much more explicitly dramatised in the 2021 television series *Them*.[97] Set in 1953 – the year before *I Am Legend* was published – *Them* is about a Black family, the Emorys – Henry (Ashley Thomas), Lucky (Deborah

Ayorinde) and their daughters Ruby (Shahadi Wright Joseph) and Gracie (Melody Hurd) – who leave North Carolina in search of fresh opportunities in California. They also hope to escape memories of a horrific act of racial and sexual violence which took place there. The opening moments of the first episode reference the fact that six million Black Americans left the South during the twentieth century (in the process that became known as the Second Great Migration).

As Isabel Wilkerson has outlined, this mass movement was 'a turning point in history. It would transform urban America and recast the social and political order of every city it touched.'[98] In *Them*, Henry's engineering job in an aerospace plant reflects the prominence of the industry during the period. His hopes for the future resemble those of Robert Joseph Pershing Foster, a Louisiana husband and father (and surgeon) referenced in Wilkerson's oral history. His account also begins in 1953:

> In California, he could stand up straight and not apologise for it [. . .] He was going to be a citizen of the United States, like the passport said. He told Alice [his wife] his decision. They could start out fresh in California, the four of them.[99]

The Emory family are excited about the move, the escape from the South and the move up the ladder which Henry's new job portends; but for Lucky in particular, excitement turns to dread when they learn that Henry has secretly purchased a home in the white neighbourhood of East Compton, despite a real-estate covenant explicitly outlawing such a transaction.

*Them* is largely (though not entirely) related from the perspective of the 'invaders' whose arrival is treated with horror by the rest of the community. 'Who says Compton's theirs?' Henry declares, as hostile white residents watch the family's every move with contempt. The Emorys are in serious peril not only from their new neighbours, but also from the pre-existing psychological traumas which are triggered by this incredibly antagonistic new environment. There is also a supernatural threat to contend with: in a *Poltergeist*-style twist, it later transpires that the land upon which the new suburb has been built was poisoned decades before by a curse.

In *Them*, the middle-class white folk who think of themselves as God-fearing, respectable Americans are the *real* monsters in this California suburb. This basic idea is a central conceit of the Suburban Gothic. Several classic episodes of the original run of *The Twilight Zone* dramatised this notion, but in those narratives (and in later iterations of the 'Monsters-Next-Door' trope, such as *Disturbia* [2007], *The 'Burbs* [1989], *The Lovely Bones* [2009] and *Summer of '84* [2018]), those in peril from such antagonists are also usually white middle-class folks themselves (and their children). *Them*'s vividly stylised focus upon the experience of a Black family terrorised by their white neighbours within post-war suburbia is a decidedly original take on a well-worn theme. Worries about 'property values' provide an initial excuse for their loathsome behaviour, but it is soon made clear that some of the residents are motivated by an even more fanatical sense of white exceptionalism and race hatred. This is particularly true of dissatisfied housewife Betty Wendell (Alison Pill), who uses her influence to foment violence against the Emory family. Within hours of their arrival, the Emorys realise that the discrimination and abuse they hoped to leave behind in North Carolina also flourishes in Southern California. The difference between the polished and well-spoken suburbanites who terrorise the young family in their new home and the bile-spewing redneck racists who subjected Lucky and her baby son to unthinkable violence back in the South is ultimately negligible.

Betty comes from a family which has been in California for several generations – she is proud of the fact that her father operated the Beverly Hills Oil Well. She is also a white supremacist who truly believes that 'Our fathers and grandfathers built the world – this world.' Employing colonial rhetoric, she also tellingly describes herself and her husband Clarke (Liam McIntyre) as 'original settlers' in the suburb (which is only a few years old), and expresses disgust towards the idea of 'Them' (the Emory family) 'on our street'. It's a sentiment which isn't far removed from Robert Neville's visceral loathing of the 'black bastards' he sees as his mortal foes. Neville also consistently refers to the vampires as 'Them', as in the first chapter when he asks, 'did he have to start thinking about *them* again?', in reference to the undead women who besiege his home nightly (italics in original).[100]

Throughout its ten-episode run, *Them* uses tropes and imagery drawn from the horror genre to engage with the often shameful racial realities of post-war California. It is eventually revealed that the land upon which the suburb now sits has been tainted since the late nineteenth century. Two formerly enslaved people (a man and a woman) fleeing the chaos of the Civil War were subjected to supernaturally inspired acts of despicable violence which both anticipate (and intensify) the vile treatment meted out to the Emory family. The show's graphic depiction of the emotional and physical violence inflicted upon its Black protagonists and their ill-fated predecessors was criticised by some commentators, who felt that these scenes were so excessive that they veered towards a commodification of 'Black pain' and trauma.[101] Angelica Jade Bastién argued: 'If anything, it lets modern white people off the hook, providing extremes with which they can distance themselves from their own racism.'[102] It has also been suggested that the show is most effective when depicting the more subtle but no less devastating barriers and microaggressions which torment the family at every turn. As Daniel D'Addario notes of these elements, 'The point is made, elegantly, that the Emorys have left behind the explicit bigotry of the American South for a place where the horrors are more insidious.'[103]

*Them* ends with a bleak final image which makes it clear that even if the supernatural and psychological demons faced by the Emory clan can finally be defeated, the reality of life for members of a Black family attempting to simply live their lives in early 1950s white suburbia remains no less perilous than it was before. As Henry, Lucky and their girls step outside in the aftermath of a shattering supernatural confrontation, they find themselves facing a mob of hostile neighbours who are backed up by gun-toting white police officers. The dream of a fresh start and the desire to attain the good life in California have both been shattered within days of their arrival, and the attractive suburban community that was supposed to be a paradise is instead a neatly manicured hell. In *Them*, we therefore find a timely re-enactment of many of the same themes found seventy years before in the works of Jackson and Matheson, but this time, from a narrative and historical perspective which has thus far been largely overlooked.

## 'The Empty California Sun': Joan Didion's Suburban Gothic

As underlined by *Them*, the Suburban Gothic often returns to the idea that even if a house has very little 'history', the people who live in it have more than enough to compensate, as does the land upon which it sits. This assumption takes on heightened significance within a Californian context because it is often suggested that California has somehow evaded the unpalatable historical baggage associated with 'older' regions of the United States. As Joan Didion put it in 'Where I Was From' (2003):

> One difference between the West and the South, I came to realize in 1970, was this: in the South they remained convinced that they had bloodied their land with history. In California, we did not believe that history could bloody the land, or even touch it.[104]

Didion's 1966 *Saturday Evening Post* article, 'How Can I Tell Them There's Nothing Left?' (reprinted in *Slouching Towards Bethlehem* in 1968 as 'Some Dreamers of the Golden Dream'), is an ominous portrait of an inherently materialistic 'new' California in which this sense of historical dislocation is epitomised by (and perhaps contributes to) a brutal act of spousal murder. In the original *Evening Post* magazine piece, these themes are further underlined by the photographs which accompany the story. The introductory spread, spanning two pages, is headlined by a quote from convicted murderer Lucille Miller, referring to her supposed horror at having to explain to her children that their father has been burnt to death: 'How Can I Tell Them There's Nothing Left?'.

There's nothing left of Lucille's husband, Gordon, but there's also nothing of any emotional worth left in the derelict home once occupied by the Miller family. A black-and-white image of this same house, 'empty now', faces a photograph of the burned-out car in which Gordon perished. The next picture, on the following page, shows Lucille and Gordon on their wedding day, looking young and hopeful. It is set next to a picture captioned 'Desolate Banyan Street is where it happened. At midnight there is no light at all. No cars passed and no help came.'[105] Positioned on the same page is a mug shot of Lucille, who was pregnant at the time of the murder (and for much of the trial that followed). 'How Can I Tell Them There's Nothing Left?' is a classic Suburban Gothic tale lent additional resonance by Didion's deployment of the familiar 'Fallen Eden in contemporary California' theme. Lucille is a classic 'Desperate Housewife', grown tired of her routine, comfortable existence. Gordon is another stock suburban archetype: the anxious and claustrophobic breadwinner.

The couple are not native Californians: Gordon is from Oregon and Lucille is from Manitoba. However, although Lucille is technically not a Midwesterner, she might as well be: 'Of course she came from somewhere else, came off the prairie in search of something she had seen in a movie or heard on the radio, for this is a Southern Californian story.'[106] As Kathleen M. Vandenberg and Christopher K. Coffman put it, 'she had come to the state seeking something that the popular media promised'.[107] The purported artificiality of the couple's existence is contrasted with the primal landscape which surrounds them. The couple resided in the San Bernardino Valley, not far from Los Angeles (an area associated by Starr with post-war suburban growth in the Inland Empire). According to Didion, it is 'in certain ways an alien place'.[108] It is

> a harsher California, haunted by the Mojave just beyond the mountains, devastated by the hot dry Santa Ana wind that comes down through the passes at 100 miles an hour and whines through the eucalyptus windbreaks and works on the nerves. October is the bad month for the wind [. . .] It is the season of suicide and divorce and prickly dread, wherever the wind blows.[109]

As Jan Whitt notes: 'Through the use of disruptive, disquieting images, Didion describes California as a land of terror and a site of humanity's end rather than a place of enchantment, sun worship and hedonism.'[110]

Not only is this then a deeply 'ominous' country, it is also a location which has long attracted naively optimistic seekers of happiness, 'a kind of people who imagined they might live among the talismanic fruit and prosper in the dry air, people who brought with them Midwestern ways of building and cooking and praying and tried to graft those ways upon the land'. Didion famously continues:

> This is the California where it is possible to live and die without ever eating an artichoke, without ever meeting a Catholic or a Jew. This is the California where it is easy to Dial-a-Devotion but hard to buy a book. This is the country in which a belief in the literal interpretation of Genesis has slipped imperceptibly into a belief in the literal interpretation of *Double Indemnity* [. . .] 'We were just crazy kids,' they say without regret, and look to the future. The future always looks good in the golden land, because no one remembers the past. [. . .] Here is the last stop for all those who come from somewhere else, for all those who drifted away from the past and the old ways. Here is where they are trying to find a new lifestyle, trying to find it in the only places they know to look: the movies and the newspapers. The case of Lucille Marie Maxwell Miller is a tabloid monument to that new lifestyle.[111]

In her sharp-eyed critique of Didion's persona and prose style (she is said to put the author in mind of 'a neurasthenic Cher'), Barbara Grizzuti Harrison identifies a distinct note of 'Old California' snobbery and superiority in this passage. She argues that

> Lucille Maxwell Miller is convicted by Didion . . . of wearing polyester and Capris. . . . Lucille Maxwell Miller's real sin – a truly, as it turns out, mortal one – was to live in a subdivision house in San Bernardino Valley and to hope to find 'the good life' there, instead of in Brentwood Park, or Malibu.[112]

Certainly, there is more than a whiff here of patrician disapproval, an implication that the lives being led by Gordon and Lucille and their fellow residents of 'the new California' is fundamentally inauthentic and trite.[113] Characteristically, this 'flotsam of the New California' is also connected to intimations of an apocalyptic reckoning percolating dangerously close to the surface.

The California Eden sought by the Millers and their kind is, it would seem, doomed from the outset, in part by the unwelcoming desert onto which they have unconvincingly 'grafted' their lives, and in part by Lucille's sense of herself (in Didion's reading of the case) as the heroine in a lurid movie, performing actions which have a logic of their own on-screen, but play out very differently in the harsh light of everyday reality. The Millers, we are told, appeared to outsiders to be a happy and materially successful young couple. Upon first moving to California, they lived in

> a modest house on the kind of street where there are always tricycles and revolving credit and dreams about bigger houses, better streets. That was 1957. By the Summer of 1964 they had achieved the bigger house on the better street and the familiar accoutrements of a family on its way up: the $30,000 a year, the three children for the Christmas card, the picture window, the family room.[114]

Now, however, 'They were paying the familiar price for it. And they had reached the familiar season of divorce.'[115]

The Millers' 'season of trouble' is marked by increasingly ominous incidents. The sudden death of the woman whose husband Lucille was having an affair with; migraines and depression for Gordon; a dog accidentally run down; and then, around midnight on that very same day, Gordon's own death in the inferno of a blazing Volkswagen. Quickly, there are suspicions, then a hypothesis – murder clumsily staged to look like an accident – and finally, an arrest. Local detectives examine motel registers and the small print of insurance policies to determine

> what might move a woman who believed in all the promises of the middle class, a woman who had been the chairwoman of the Ontario Heart Fund and who always knew a reasonable little dressmaker and who had come out of the bleak wild of prairie fundamentalism to find what she imagined would be the good life – what should drive such a woman to sit on a street called Bella Vista and look out her new picture window into the empty California sun and calculate how to burn her husband alive.[116]

With the discovery that Lucille and family friend Arthwell Hayton have been having an affair, a reason for the crime appears to have been uncovered. However, as Whitt notes:

> The motive, an affair with the husband of one of her friends, explains the crime, and yet does not explain it. Detectives look for simple causes and effects; Didion, as always, looks for clues to human nature and madness in the 'golden land'. In fact, California becomes a character in Didion's story, a location that seems to have its own terrible energy.[117]

Despite her protestations of innocence, Lucille is painted by both the prosecution and the defence as 'an erring woman, a woman who perhaps wanted too much', and is convicted of murder in the first degree.[118] She ends up in the California Institution for Women, 'not too many miles from where she once lived and shopped and organized the Heart Fund ball'.[119] We are told of the prison that 'A lot of California murderesses live here, a lot of girls who somehow misunderstood the promise.'[120] It's a statement which takes on added resonance when we consider that only a few years after Lucille's incarceration, a group of young women associated with one of California's most notorious crime sprees would be sent to the same prison: Patricia Krenwinkel, Leslie Van Houten and Susan 'Sadie' Atkins, all of whom participated in the Manson Family murders of August 1969, and who, to an even greater extent than Lucille, sorely 'misunderstood the promise'. However, unlike Lucille, a generation older and originally from Canada, Krenwinkel, Van Houten and Atkins were all born in Southern California in the late 1940s. As such, they were true (if extreme) poster children of the new generation for whom the old 'rules' (as Didion put it in 'Slouching Towards Bethlehem') no longer applied.

In his 1962 lecture on 'California and the Human Horizon', Lewis Mumford considered both the 'happy prospects' and the 'fear and dismay' associated with the technological, scientific and communications advances of the era.[121] As Starr puts it in his own analysis of these remarks, they were 'keyed to the impending emergence of California as the largest state in the nation'.[122] Along with the 'population explosion', 'the freeway explosion' and 'the recreation explosion', the 'suburban explosion' is highlighted as one of the myriad 'forms of destruction' which Mumford indicted for creating 'more and more featureless landscapes, populated by more and more featureless people. Never before has a country possessed such a surplus of wealth, energy, food, and natural resources as the United States, and in particular, the state of California.'[123] He compared California with Pompeii, saying that he was haunted by comparisons between this dead city and the 'seemingly live cities we are living in'.[124] Railing against office buildings and the freeway commute, Mumford imagined the weary (male) white-collar worker reaching home at the end of a long day:

> Physiologically the worse for wear, our American finally reaches his dwelling, where he finds a house and a wife in the midst of what is usually called ideal suburban surroundings: a green ghetto, half natural, half plastic, also cut off from human contact, where his wife has for her chief daily companions in her solitude the radio set, the soap opera, the refrigerator, the automatic mixer, the blender, the vacuum cleaner, the automatic washing machine, the dishwasher, and, if she is lucky, the second car. They and their children [. . .]

immobilize themselves before a television screen, where all that has been left out of the actual world, all their unlived life, flickers before their eyes, in images that give a faked sense of the realities they have turned their backs to, and the impulses they have been forced to repress.[125]

'The machine-conditioned American', Mumford added, 'has no life of his own.'[126] He cites Santa Clara and the San Bernardino Valley as prime examples of reckless overdevelopment.[127] Mumford's argument anticipated Didion's depiction of the new suburban lifestyle in Southern California. The horrific crime for which Lucille Maxwell Miller was convicted here represents a violent expression of the dangerously repressed impulses Mumford associated with the 'myriad forms of destruction' brought about by the massive infrastructural changes that transformed California – and the wider United States – in the post-war era.

Towards the end of Didion's article, we are told that the Millers' new house lies empty and is now:

the house on the street with the sign that says PRIVATE ROAD – BELLA VISTA – DEAD END. The Millers never did get it landscaped, and the weeds grow up around the fieldstone siding. The television aeriel has toppled on the roof, and a trash can is stuffed with the debris of family life: a cheap suitcase, a child's game called 'Lie Detector', and the sign that reads ESTATE SALE.[128]

Unintentionally adding to the resonance of this flatly evocative description is the fact that the bottom third of this same page in the *Saturday Evening Post* is occupied by an advertisement for an air conditioning system which promises to 'Cool a houseful of air in 15 minutes.' For the twenty-first-century reader, this promise of an artificially calibrated internal temperature adds another suggestive strand to the unsettling wider resonances of Didion's reportage. The devastating wildfires and energy shortages which are now a regular feature of life in present-day California owe much to precisely this insistence upon material comfort and unfettered consumption.

Didion's ominous take on the Southern California lifestyle has impacted upon later true crime ruminations. In *Dead Girls: Essays on Surviving an American Obsession* (2018), Alice Bolin discusses Didion's influence upon her own perceptions of Los Angeles, which is particularly evident when Bolin describes the restricted geographical orbit of the television news digest *Dateline*:

Many episodes of *Dateline* take place in Los Angeles' outlying areas, suburbs and small towns in Orange County or San Bernardino County or the

Antelope Valley, places where residents might think they are sheltered, just beyond the reach of urban chaos. These are mostly towns developed in the mid-twentieth century, part of that tract-house-studded Sunbelt that saw a huge growth in population with the Cold War aerospace boom. People migrated for the chance to reinvent themselves as members of the all-American middle class in shiny Southern California, a chance to lead lives like the families they saw on television. And for some, that dream was realized: for many of the interviewees on *Dateline*, it seems like they can't believe that their lives have become TV-worthy, like the murder of their family members is the only interesting thing that has ever happened to them.[129]

Bolin's final comment here was anticipated by serial killer Dix Steele in Dorothy Hughes's LA-set novel, *In a Lonely Place* (1947). He thinks of one of the young women he has recently strangled, that 'The only exciting thing that had ever happened to her was to be raped and murdered.'[130]

Also published in 2018 was Michelle McNamara's true crime bestseller, *I'll Be Gone in the Dark*, in which unassuming suburban communities throughout the state (but particularly the wider Sacramento area) are the stalking ground for a ruthless, and at the time that the book was first published, still unidentified burglar, rapist and serial murderer, dubbed by the author the 'Golden State Killer'. In her prologue, McNamara explains that this case 'consumed me the most' because these crimes were denied the prominence afforded those of other Californian serial murderers, such as the Zodiac Killer and Richard Ramirez, the so-called 'Night Stalker'.[131] Neither, she notes, were as active:

Yet the Golden State killer has little recognition. He didn't have a catchy name until I coined one . . . By the time DNA testing revealed that crimes previously thought to be unrelated were the work of one man, more than a decade had passed since his last known murder, and his capture wasn't a priority. He flew under the radar, at large and unidentified.[132]

Several months after the book's release – which followed in the wake of McNamara's own tragic (and unrelated) death – a new round of DNA testing utilising a new technique known as 'genetic genealogy', at last identified a prime suspect: 72-year-old Joseph DeAngelo.[133] In a familiar Suburban Gothic twist, DeAngelo was precisely the kind of insidious internal threat which popular fiction and film have long associated with the milieu. Not only had he worked as a police officer in wider Sacramento during the time he was committing some of his most horrific crimes: DeAngelo had also lived a seemingly conventional suburban existence for many years, and at the time of his arrest lived in Citrus Heights, where four of his attacks took place.[134] 'He was just an average person, an average Joe', an acquaintance told *The New York Times*, apparently without irony.[135]

Later literary, true crime and pop culture depictions of the Californian suburbs as sites associated with murder, madness and repression, built upon the foundations established by Matheson, Jackson and Didion, and further established the state as the most common locale within the Suburban Gothic sub-genre. I have already discussed examples such as *Poltergeist* (1982), *Safe* (1995) and the *Buffy the Vampire Slayer* (1997–2003) in my book on the topic, and so will not dwell upon them again here. Instead, I will briefly consider a more obscure but still grimly fascinating portrait of Californian suburban ennui turned bloodbath: Eric C. Higgs's 1985 horror novel, *The Happy Man: A Tale of Horror*, reprinted in 2017 by Valancourt Books.

In his introduction to the reprint, Higgs explains why he thinks the book has stood the test of time. Mostly, he argues, it is because, 'the secret lives of the normal-seeming, everyday middle class contain an unspeakable darkness that always fascinates, if one cares to dig deeply enough'.[136] His own digging, he continues, started after he moved to Southern California. His sentiments align with those expressed elsewhere in this chapter:

> I was in thrall to the abundant sunshine, wide-open landscapes and ever-widening circle of friends who were cheerfully shouldering their way into dazzling futures. Indeed, 'twas the smiling, sunglass-wearing California that had been as advertised in books and TV and the movies, and not at all dis-appointing. And yet . . . there is always a fly in the ointment, a burr under the saddle blanket. People stubbornly remained people, oblivious to the wonderful stage set that had been prepared for them, and when the young engineer or lawyer or executive would lean close at a backyard pool party where tiki torches cast their wavering glow and the liquor or marijuana had finally taken hold, sometimes they'd say the most dreadful and darkly surprising of things.[137]

*The Happy Man* is about a former naval officer who now works as a mid-level executive. Charles Ripley (the name may be a nod to Patricia Highsmith's psychopathic antihero) and his wife live in a newly established suburb of San Diego called Mesa Vista Estates, which is located right next to 'the tractless wastes of Mexico'.[138] Ripley's complacent but vaguely discontented routine is disrupted by the arrival of a new neighbour, a charismatic software executive named Ruskin Marsh. Marsh and Ripley soon become fast friends, and Ripley finds that the newcomer's influence gradually awakens in him a variety of interests he has hith-erto suppressed. A shared fondness for alcohol, fine dining and extramarital sex progresses to the indulgence of much darker appetites (a turn which is signposted by frequent references to the Marquis de Sade). Marsh and his wife Sybil are, it turns out, members of a very exclusive club. 'The Society of Friends' is, Ruskin say initially, a 'group of people with common interests' dedicated to the pursuit of 'self-knowledge'.[139] The specifics of this pursuit evoke Noah Cross's claim in *Chinatown* that given the right circumstances, people are capable of anything. Indeed, Ruskin even says that the group is about 'Knowing what sort of person you really are. Knowing the sort of things you're capable of.'[140]

The club HQ is based in San Francisco, which geographically aligns it with the Bohemian seekers after forbidden knowledge in Fritz Leiber's *Our Lady of Darkness* (1977) (to be discussed in Chapter 6). The final rite which secures acceptance into its ranks is cannibalism. Sybil and Ruskin have been murdering Mexican migrants captured in the adjoining desert for months, but by the climax of the novel, they intend to feast on Ruskin's girlfriend Angela. Ripley states of this episode that he 'wasn't very hungry', but he nevertheless partakes, knowing that if he refuses, his neck will be next on the chopping board.[141] Although the novel ends with a turn of the tables as Ripley extermi-nates the Marsh family and prepares to carry out a mass shooting at the club headquarters, it is clear he surrendered his soul long before consuming human flesh. Indeed, although he justifies his actions as self-defence, Ripley's rapid transformation into a machine-gun wielding mass murderer suggests that he already had much in common with his smugly homicidal neighbours, even if he is still unwilling to admit to the fact.

The novel also implies that the 'Society of Friends' has taken root in the suburbs of San Diego because of the inherent emptiness of this materially rich but spiritually vapid milieu. In the opening chapter, set after the main events of the novel, the Marsh house is described by Ripley, who has, we later discover, just killed his neighbours, as follows:

> [It] sat there, a plain lump of white stucco giving off no more evil than a Barbie dollhouse, its only glow the Southern California sunshine refracting off its energy efficient windows. Nothing there, not any more than any other house in this development.[142]

## Norman Bates: A Harvest of Bad Seeds

In May 1973, *Time* published an article entitled 'Harvest of Bad Seeds', which discussed a series of rapes and murders that had recently taken place in and around the city of Santa Cruz.[143] A 'succession of co-eds' had disappeared, and the bodies of some of these young women were being found 'weeks or months later, decapitated'. 'In all', the article continued, 'seemingly random murders took the lives of 19 people around Santa Cruz, including a priest who was stabbed to death in his confessional booth.' The 'first break' came in February, when local police arrested a man named Herbert Mullin, who was suspected of having killed ten of the victims. Police had also just caught up with John Phillip Bunyard, who was believed to have been the 'Nob Hill rapist' (he was also later revealed to be a double murderer).

Even more extreme were the crimes of another killer operating in this same area at the same time: 'a 6-ft. 9-in., 278-lb. giant named Edmund Emil Kemper III'.[144] Kemper, we are told, beat his mother to death, mutilated her body, killed a friend of the family and then called the Santa Cruz sheriff's office to confess. He was also 'accused of the rape-murder-mutilations of seven girls who disappeared over the past year'.[145] Kemper and Bunyard had 'histories of severe mental disorder' (Kemper killed his grandparents when he was fifteen but was released from a state mental hospital several years later).[146] Bunyard had also served time in the state's juvenile facilities. Their crimes were said to pose a 'sharp rebuke to the state's correctional facilities', and in particular towards the budget cuts imposed by (then) Governor Ronald Reagan and subsequently by President Nixon.

However, the article's title – which evoked William March's 1954 novel, *The Bad Seed*, in which a psychopathic little girl 'born bad' repeatedly gets away with murder – also implied that finally, permissive California was reaping the consequences of its failure to properly treat and control a new generation of troubled young men whose violent actions were leaving a trail of dead bodies all over the state.

To conclude this chapter on the foundational role which California has played in shaping the modern horror tradition, I will briefly discuss the way in which the state's fictional (and real-life) foregrounding of the figure of the rogue white male (and that of the serial killer), has contributed to the evolution of the modern American horror genre. I first noticed this connection whilst working on *The Highway Horror Film* (2014). Many of these films were either set in California or featured journeys for which the destination was California: it appeared more than any other US state. Just as the Southern states are overrepresented within the backwoods horror/Rural Gothic tradition (for reasons in part to do with the perception of the South as a region that has been 'left behind' by the rest of the United States), California has become the state most associated with highway journeys which end in death, degradation and violence.

This trait is in part obviously related to the wider sense (also referenced in my Introduction above) that California is where seemingly aimless American journeys must come to their inevitable conclusion. As Brian Ireland notes of the road movie genre more generally, 'California is the final destination for many travellers in this genre'; a tendency which he also links to 'the theme of transformation of identity that crops up often in American culture and history'.[147] Additionally, there is some overlap here with the strain of anxiety found within the Suburban Gothic, which is informed by a broadly similar sense of disquiet at the sheer rapidity and immensity of the era's social and environmental changes.

As Edward Dimendberg notes in *Film Noir and the Spaces of Modernity* (2004):

> Cultural historians increasingly have recognized the contradictory character of the 1940s and 1950s, one in which extraordinary American prosperity and supremacy on the international stage coexisted with domestic cultural responses ranging from euphoric celebration to anxiety and fear. From Abstract Expressionism to beat culture to film noir, postwar culture in the United States possessed an often somber underside that contrasts pointedly with the allegedly optimistic public face of the period. Rather than an autonomous or sui generis worldview, a freefloating existential angst, some of the anxiety during this period can be understood as a cultural reaction to rapid and unprecedented changes in the built environment, whose ageing centers were now displaced by an array of modern constructions.[148]

Together with the 'the suburban house, the glass office tower, the public housing project, the superblock, and the shopping center', Dimendberg identifies the freeways as one of 'the period's most representative spatial constructions'.[149] As I outlined in my book on the 'Highway Horror' film tradition, it is a subgenre that arises from anxieties

> explicitly related to the societal impact of mass automobility and the creation of the Interstate Highway System (IHS). In the Highway Horror film, journeys made via the highway inevitably lead to uncanny, murderous and horribly transformative experiences. The American landscape, though supposedly 'tamed' by the highways, is, by dint of its very accessibility rendered terrifyingly hostile, and encounters with other travellers (and with individuals whose roadside businesses depend upon highway traffic) almost always have sinister outcomes.[150]

One of the four main strands of the Highway Horror sub-genre revolves around the serial killer, and it is here that the locational and thematic prominence of California becomes particularly important. Notable examples include John McNaughton's unflinching 1986 classic, *Henry: Portrait of a Serial Killer*, and Dominic Senna's more conventional 1993 film, *Kalifornia*. Both films present us with violent working-class white men whose penchant for inflicting pain upon others prompts them to take to the highways and head West. Although his body count doesn't quite allow him to qualify as a serial killer, the iconic fictional figure whose random acts of horrific violence (most famously) perpetrated upon female victims had the greatest mainstream cultural impact is Norman Bates, and Hitchcock's *Psycho* (1960) can be considered a foundational Highway Horror narrative (along with Steven Spielberg's 1971 Richard Matheson adaptation, *Duel*).

It isn't the only factor contributing to his violence, but Norman's murder of Marion Crane is certainly influenced by the fact that he is a casualty of the 'unprecedented changes in the built environment' identified by Dimendberg, as also being a consistent theme in noir narratives during this same era. The family-run Bates Motel is essentially no longer a going concern because, as Norman (Anthony Perkins) ruefully tells Marion (Janet Leigh), 'they moved away the highway'. Indeed, Marion realises soon after arriving at the motel that if she had only driven a few more miles, she would have reached her intended destination, the town of Fairview in central California. Robert Bloch's 1959 novel on which the film was based was inspired by the notorious real-life case of Wisconsin necrophiliac and murderer Ed Gein. It's unlikely that Bloch intended that the state in which the Bates Motel is located would be considered significant, but nevertheless, given the rapid infrastructural transformations which were sweeping across California at the time, the choice was a timely one. The figure of the psychotic or psychopathic white male who carries out horrific acts of violence against women would become much associated with California during the decade that followed. Indeed, with his mother fixation and necrophiliac tendencies, Bates anticipated real-life successors such as Edmund Kemper (indeed, in the novel, like Kemper, he also decapitates some of his victims).

*Psycho* was not the first Hitchcock film in which a Californian setting featured:

Starting with *Shadow of a Doubt* (released in 1943), some of Hitchcock's most admired films were set principally in the Bay Area. His intimate familiarity with the region allowed him to blend his stories with the area's unique geography. The 'all-American' Santa Rosa is a cozy setting for the dark *Shadow of a Doubt*. Big Basin Park, the Avenue of Tall Trees, San Juan Bautista, Cypress Point, and of course, the streets of San Francisco are central characters in *Vertigo* (1958). *The Birds* (1963) is set in the quaint towns of Bodega Bay and Bodega, with a movie reference to a real-life bird attack near Santa Cruz.[151]

*Shadow of a Doubt* is particularly relevant here, focusing as it does upon the eventful homecoming of Charlie Oakley (Joseph Cotten), a local boy made good who is secretly a sadistic serial killer who preys upon wealthy older women. Here, for the first (but not the last) time in Hitchcock's oeuvre, small-town California is presented to us as the birthplace of a monster. Uncle Charlie is, initially at least, doted upon by his niece (and namesake) Charlie (Teresa Wright) and his loving and overprotective sister Emma (Patricia Collinge), who adores him, but fretfully notes that as a boy his personality was much changed by a serious head injury. Notably, although the film ends with Uncle Charlie's death – he falls out of a moving train whilst trying to kill his niece (who has figured out his true nature) – his wider reputation remains unsullied. Young Charlie and the police are aware of his heinous crimes, but so far as the rest of the Newton family and the town of Santa Rosa know, Charles Oakley was a charming, well-travelled favourite son who died in a tragic accident. Young Charlie's perception of the world, and the people in it, has been forever changed by the realisation that true evil lay close to home all along.

The 'Harvest of Bad Seeds' associated with early 1970s Northern California was, within the public consciousness, largely related to 'stranger killings' carried out against middle-class young white women, even though there were several notorious Californian serial killers who targeted men and boys only (or both men and women), and there have also been several Black serial killers associated with the state. In *Killer on the Road* (2012), Ginger Strand discusses the relationship between the post-war upsurge in serial murder to the advent of the Interstate Highway System:

> Highway violence followed hard on the heels of interstate construction. The nation's murder rate shot up in the sixties and seventies. America became more violent and more mobile at the same time. Were they linked? Did highways lead to highway violence? Yes and no. More highways meant more travel, more movement, more anonymity – all conducive to criminality.[152]

Peter Vronsky (2020) also notes that 'Unlike densely populated Eastern pedestrian cities [. . .] serial murder in California, and, for that matter, most of the United States, was an automotive kind of thing.'[153]

In the 1950s, Strand observes, the compulsive mobility associated with the state was 'frequently invoked to explain why California's delinquency rates were so high: more of the state's residents were recent transplants'.[154] She devotes a chapter to Ed Kemper (himself a murderous juvenile delinquent) and to the murders which took place around Santa Cruz in the early 1970s. It was 'an idyllic coastal resort boasting beaches, redwood forests, and dramatic mountains' which was home to a newly established branch of the University of California system (Kemper's mother Clarnell even worked there as an administrator).[155] Established in 1965, the campus attracted young people from all over for whom hitch-hiking 'was not only central to their low-budget, free-wheeling "lifestyle", it was the perfect expression of counterculture ideals'.[156] Kemper's crimes, involving as they did the calculated targeting of precisely this demographic, meant that the horrified public reaction to his offences anticipated that afforded the even more widely publicised atrocities later committed by the likes of Ted Bundy and John Wayne Gacy. According to Philip Jenkins, the latter two killers

> are so well remembered because they provided faces to what was quite suddenly – between 1976 and 1978 – perceived as a national threat. [. . .] it gave a visible and comprehensible focus to intense fears about violence, specifically directed against women and children.[157]

As Vronsky notes of the Santa Cruz serial murder cluster, it was 'much more puzzling because it was so out of scale to the region's population. The murders were also "witchy" in that California-coast way, kind of like the Manson murders were in the Summer of 1969.'[158] It didn't help that in the 1970s and 1980s there were a succession of new high-profile serial murderer cases in the state. Amongst the most prominent were the still-unsolved Zodiac slayings, believed to have started in 1968, all of which took place in Northern California. These seemingly random shootings and stabbings – and the cryptic letters which the killer wrote to San Francisco newspapers – ensured that the case had a major pop culture impact, which culminated in David Fincher's subtly ambiguous thriller *Zodiac* (2007), in which the obsessional behaviour of the men hunting the killer is ultimately a cause of major disquiet in itself, as though the Zodiac's toxic influence has permeated the very fabric of the places and the people which have become associated with him. In his introduction to the 1985 edition of the book which inspired the film, Robert Graysmith summed up the case in decidedly Gothic terms:

> Witchcraft, death threats, cryptograms, a hooded killer style sought, dedicated investigators, and a mysterious man in a white Chevy who is seen by all and known by no one are all parts of the Zodiac mystery, the most frightening story I know.[159]

Other serial killers operating in California during the 1960s, 1970s and 1980s included Richard Ramirez, Joseph DeAngelo, 'Freeway Killers' William

Bonin, Patrick Kearney and Randy Kraft (their crimes had nothing to do with each other, but they targeted a similar demographic – young men – and stalked the same stretches of new highway), Lonnie Franklin (aka 'Grim Sleeper') and 'Hillside Stranglers' Angelo Buono, Jr, and Kenneth Bianchi. All of these men, with the exception of Franklin, were white.[160]

It is interesting to note, then, that apart from California-set films and true crime narratives which explicitly chronicle or draw upon elements of the crimes referenced above, and the 'Highway Horror' sub-genre movies cited earlier, the only major horror narrative from the 1970s and 1980s which directly incorporates the idea that this kind of violence is somehow an inherent feature of life in present-day California is one in which it is explicitly projected onto a supernatural threat. In Joel Schumacher's *The Lost Boys* (1987), as in Matheson's *I Am Legend*, vampires are real.[161] Here, however, they are still a minority rather than a majority, and the main locus of anxiety involves the notion that the coastal city is 'ground zero' for a very Californian variety of *wrongness* which turns vulnerable young white men into remorseless predators.

*The Lost Boys* is set in a fictional Northern Californian community called 'Santa Carla'. However, the film was shot in Santa Cruz, depicts well-known local landmarks and directly evokes the city's notorious reputation. As Schumacher and others involved with the film have detailed, it was in part this notoriety which led him to believe that Santa Cruz was the ideal location. As he related in an interview:

> When I got there I thought, 'This is exactly where you would go if you were a teenage vampire [. . .] Because you've got the boardwalk, the beach, a lot of transient young people, a lot of drug people, and runaway kids all over the place. Santa Cruz had more murders per capita than anywhere else in the United States. There was a murder outside of our hotel while we were preparing the movie.' The Santa Cruz authorities welcomed the crew, but didn't want to scare any more tourists away, so the town's on-screen name was changed to Santa Carla.[162]

As a local news site notes of the immensely damaging impact which the crimes of Kemper, Mullin and John Linley Frazier had upon the city's reputation, Santa Cruz was indeed dubbed 'The Murder Capital of the World'. Katie Dowd details that this quote was attributed to Santa Cruz District Attorney Peter Chang, who, when attending the scene of the horrific slaying of four young teenagers in the Redwoods State Park in February 1973 (the crime was committed by Mullin) allegedly commented: '"This must be Murdersville, U.S.A." . . . The next day, several wire stories reported Chang had called

Santa Cruz the "murder capital of the world." Chang denied it, but the nickname stuck. It didn't, after all, feel that far off.'[163] The 'murder capital' quote is referenced early in *The Lost Boys*, thereby ensuring that an American audience would (in 1987) have no doubt as to 'Santa Carla's' real-world template, even if they didn't recognise the iconic boardwalk.

The film's main protagonist is teenager Sam Emerson (Corey Haim), who, along with his mother Lucy (Dianne Wiest) and sullen older brother Michael (Jason Patric), has just moved from Phoenix, Arizona to his mother's Californian hometown (a similar travel itinerary is followed by Marion Crane in *Psycho*). Sam brings up the quote shortly after they arrive at his grandfather's ramshackle home: 'Hey Grandpa – is it true that Santa Carla is the murder capital of the world?' Grandpa (Barnard Hughes) admits that there are 'Some bad elements here'. He continues: 'Let me put it this way. If all the corpses buried around here was to stand up all at once, you'd have one hell of a population problem.' It's played for laughs, but Grandpa's response is also a warning. Santa Carla is a stalking ground for predators who target teenagers and children. This is also signposted by the missing person posters plastered on walls and windows in the background of many Santa Carla scenes. They evoke the images of missing children which began to appear on American milk cartons after a spate of high-profile child abductions.[164]

That vampires are involved in these disappearances is left in no doubt. They even have a feral half-vampire child named 'Laddie' (Chance Michael Corbitt), amongst their number (although like Michael and his girlfriend Star [Jami Gertz], he is restored to full humanity at the end of the film). With these real-world associations in mind, the film's most chilling scene is also one of its most subtle. Outwardly respectable electronic store owner Max (Edward Herrmann) is introduced as he stands near the bustling entrance of his boardwalk business one night. A little boy separated from his parents appears in the doorway. Max immediately moves towards the child – in a gesture the first-time viewer may construe as benign – but before he can intervene, Sam's kind-hearted mum Lucy takes charge, and safely reunites the child with his parents. We later find out that Max is secretly the 'King Vampire' of Santa Carla and has been using his unthreatening appearance to prey upon youngsters. Like two of the most notorious serial killers of the same era – Bundy and Gacy – he conceals his monstrous appetites beneath a veneer of white, middle-class entrepreneurial respectability.

Laddie's ultimately reassuring fate defuses the horror which surrounds that of Santa Carla's other missing minors. The outcome for the gang's other victims is much more nebulous, and much more unsettling. This is where Max's role as a 'bad' father figure comes to the fore. In addition to murdering children, he has corrupted the vulnerable teenagers who entered his orbit and were subsequently turned into vampires. He wants to 'turn' Lucy and her sons so that they can all be 'Just one big happy family' – a more 'mainstream' family grouping than his 'single-parent' relationship with the unruly and not always obedient gang of Lost Boys. Neglectful and dysfunctional parenting is a primary theme here. Sam and Michael are brought to Santa Carla because of their parents' divorce, and Sam's friends the Frog brothers (Corey Feldman and Jamison Newlander) operate the family comic-book store whilst their stoner parents lie insensible behind the counter. Again, this is played for laughs, but it emphasises the connection between the violence which blights Santa Carla and the permissiveness of local parents. Their neglect has created the vacuum which allows 'bad' patriarch Max to swoop in.

It's a theme reflected in the film's main plotline, which revolves around Sam's desire to save his brother Michael from vampirism. This development evokes the real-world anxieties referenced in the *Time* 'Harvest of Bad Seeds' article, which focused on the apparently inexplicable acts of horrific violence perpetrated by young men in the Santa Cruz area. Michael becomes associated with the vampires because he is drawn to their apparently consequence-free, thrill-seeking 'lifestyle'. As Sorcha Ní Fhlainn puts it, 'At first, vampirism in this film represents an avoidance of responsibility such as indulging in rebellious fun, getting high, or committing petty crimes, all at a significant remove from parental guidance and rules.'[165] For a moment, this does indeed seem like an attractive alternative to life in a single-parent household which is depending upon the hospitality of his eccentric grandfather. The Lost Boys are depicted as the products of a permissive and chaotic familial and cultural milieu which is still processing the myriad transformations of the post-war era and the hangover left by the late 1960s counterculture. The film even gives the last word to Grandpa, who shows up at the very last minute to save his family by killing Max: 'One thing about living in Santa Carla I never could stomach,' he declares, 'All the damn vampires'.

At this point, it seems as if hippie eccentricity and self-indulgence has been redeemed through its last-minute defeat of the supernatural menace masquerading as a respectable business owner. As Ní Fhlainn suggests:

> Schumacher's film positions hippies and romantics not merely as victims ripe for the taking but rather as innocents capable of protecting the genuine institution of the family (however fractured its state) for the right reasons over capitalistic and political imperatives.[166]

However, there remains the fact that the negligence of the town's adults has still played a substantial role in turning Santa Carla into a fictional version of

'Murdersville, U.S.A.' Furthermore, the *California-ness* of the community has also played an important role in this process. There is clearly an inherent *wrongness* about the city which has made it a perfect home for the vampires. Santa Carla epitomises the culture of transience, gratification and social breakdown which was one of the obvious consequences of the immense social and infrastructural changes which began a generation before. The film also gestures towards an association between the vampires and a more long-standing locus of regional anxiety: the San Andreas fault line. Their lair is hidden in the ruins of a luxury resort which fell into the fault line during the 1906 earthquake.[167] Not for the last time, California is seen as being fundamentally unstable in more ways than one.

In *The Lost Boys*, as in *Messiah of Evil* and *The Fog*, we therefore have another small-town horror narrative in which California-specific cultural and historical anxieties are projected onto a disruptive supernatural or uncanny Other (we will see a more recent recurrence of this theme in Jordan Peele's 2019 film, *Us*, discussed in my concluding chapter). Just as the townsfolk of Antonio Bay refuse to acknowledge the act of mass murder which led to the establishment of their community until forced to do so in *The Fog*, the adults in Santa Carla have either neglected to notice that children and young people are in peril or failed to act until many lives have been lost. Seen in this light, Grandpa's last-minute heroism is also tainted with selfishness. He saves his own daughter and grandchildren but didn't do anything about Santa Carla's 'bad element' until his own loved ones were in imminent peril. Michael has been spared a fate worse than death, but what about the teenagers who weren't so lucky – the potential 'Bad Seeds' no one bothered trying to save?

Kevin Starr ends his volume on the immediate post-war era California (*Golden Dreams: California in an Age of Abundance, 1950–1963*) by discussing the cultural and legal legacy of a figure who arguably anticipated the 'arrival' of the Californian serial killer in the popular consciousness a decade later: burglar, rapist and murderer Caryl Chessman. It was not the first time Starr considered the case. In his previous volume, *Embattled Dreams: California in War and Peace, 1940–1950*, he argued that 'the Chessman case played a major role in defining the 1960s, which in turn played a major role in defining the emergent culture of the United States in the last third of the twentieth century'.[168] *Golden Dreams* ends with a rundown of the furore that surrounded Chessman's May 1960 execution – protests which Starr sees (along with other events and undercurrents around this time) as an ominous portent: 'From this perspective the year 1960, with its dramatic disturbances, possesses in retrospect prophetic suggestions of things to come.'[169] There the book ends. But although Starr concluded Chessman's story in *Golden Dreams*, he never wrote directly about the period between the mid-1960s and the early 1990s in his exhaustively detailed overview of Californian history. The series skipped a generation. It was a striking omission, also noted in a *Los Angeles Times* obituary published after Starr's death in 2017:

> Starr's sprawling series stopped at 1963, skipping the period that included the Watts riots, the Summer of Love, the Manson murders and the passage of Proposition 13, which restricted property taxes. He picked up again with a book that focused on the 1990s. Starr, said his wife, 'couldn't wrap his mind around the '60s and '70s.' 'He was a '50s guy,' she said.[170]

However, although Starr may have been overwhelmed – and perhaps even unsettled – by the prospect of directly engaging with the titanic and at times deeply traumatic social and cultural upheavals which characterised the state during the later 1960s and the 1970s, his work on the decades leading up to this period had already underlined the immensity and importance of the environmental, structural and cultural transformations undergone by California and its people during the immediate post-war era. *Chinatown*'s Noah Cross was correct to believe that controlling the water supply and the land around Los Angeles would grant him immeasurable influence upon 'the future'. Time is the only commodity an immensely wealthy man cannot buy, but there is nonetheless a very tangible immortality to be found in irrevocably shaping the built infrastructure and moral compass of a region in ways that are still felt generations later.

## Notes

1. Dussere, *America is Elsewhere*, p. 116.
2. See Wasson, *The Big Goodbye*, pp. 67–70.
3. Ibid. p. 73.
4. Ibid. pp. 73–4.
5. Nadeau, *California*, p. 291. Kevin Starr's mention of this volume in *Golden Dreams* first brought my attention to Nadeau's work.
6. Nadeau, *California*, p. 8.
7. Ibid. p. 9.
8. Ibid. p. 9.
9. Ibid. p. 3.
10. Starr, *Golden Dreams*.
11. Ibid. p. xi.
12. Ibid. p. xi.
13. Ibid. p. xi.

14. Kirsch, 'Headmaster of the Writing School', p. 8.
15. Ibid. p. 8.
16. Ibid. p. 8.
17. Ibid. p. 8.
18. Ibid. p. 8.
19. Ibid. p. 8.
20. Kirsch, 'William F. Nolan', p. 10.
21. Nolan, 'Remembering "The Group"', p. 27.
22. Ibid. p. 27.
23. Ibid. p. 27.
24. Conlon, 'Introduction: California Sorcerers', p. 1.
25. Ibid. p. 1.
26. Ibid. p. 3.
27. Ibid. p. 3.
28. Ibid. p. 4.
29. Ibid. p. 12.
30. Ibid. p. 14.
31. Joshi, *Unutterable Horror*, p. 561.
32. Ibid. p. 561.
33. Thanks are due here to Mark Jancovich, who helpfully suggested that I include 'The Creeping Terror' in this chapter.
34. Matheson, 'The Creeping Terror', n.p.
35. Finney, *The Body Snatchers*, p. 175.
36. Jancovich, *Rational Fears*, p. 64. Jancovich also refers to 'The Creeping Terror', as 'a social satire of Californian culture' (p. 132).
37. In *City of Quartz*, Mike Davis also argues that in *The Martian Chronicles* (1950), Bradbury had taken 'in a sense . . . the angst of the dislocated Midwesterner in Los Angeles and projected it as an extra-terrestrial destiny' (p. 42).
38. 'Nosepicking Contests: Book Review', *Time Magazine* 87:18 (6 May 1966). See also, 'Californication (word)', Wikipedia, https://en.wikipedia.org/wiki/Californication_(word) (last accessed 14 July 2021).
39. Burton, 'The Great Wild Californicated West', p. 15.
40. Klug, 'These Kind of Dreams', p. 175.
41. Matheson, 'The Creeping Terror', n. p.
42. Ibid. n. p.
43. Jackson, *Crabgrass Frontier*, p. 265.
44. Starr, *Golden Dreams*, p. 5.
45. Ibid. p. 5.
46. Ibid. p. 6.
47. Murphy, *The Suburban Gothic*, p. 2.

48. Ibid. p. 2.
49. Ibid. p. 2.
50. Jackson, *The Road Through the Wall*, p. 6.
51. Murphy, *The Suburban Gothic*, p. 21.
52. Jackson, *The Road Through the Wall*, p. 33.
53. Ibid. p. 177.
54. Ibid. p. 185.
55. Ibid. p. 188.
56. Ibid. p. 189.
57. Oehlschlaeger, 'The Stoning of Mistress Hutchinson', p. 262.
58. Hall, 'Fallen Eden', p. 25.
59. Ibid. p. 24.
60. Ibid. pp. 26–7. Hall also notes that Jackson's husband, the academic Stanley Edgar Hyman, wrote a monograph on Nathanael West (p. 27).
61. Murphy, *The Suburban Gothic*, pp. 32–3.
62. Matheson, *I Am Legend*, p. 26.
63. Ibid. p. 30.
64. Murphy, *The Suburban Gothic*, p. 33.
65. Yeates, 'Gender and Ethnicity', p. 422.
66. Starr, *Golden Dreams*, p. 12.
67. Ibid. p. 13.
68. Ibid. p. 17.
69. Ibid. p. 8.
70. Nadeau, *California*, p. 45.
71. Yeates, 'Gender and Ethnicity', p. 422.
72. Davis and Wiener, *Set the Night on Fire*, p. 1.
73. Ibid. p. 1.
74. Ibid. p. 1.
75. Ibid. p. 9.
76. Ibid. p. 13.
77. Ibid. p. 46.
78. Matheson, *I Am Legend*, p. 7.
79. Ibid. p. 11.
80. Ibid. p. 147.
81. Ibid. p. 153.
82. Davis and Wiener, *Set the Night on Fire*, p. 273.
83. Ibid. p. 273.
84. Wiese, *Places of Their Own*, pp. 98–9.
85. Ibid. p. 99.
86. Matheson, *I Am Legend*, p. 160.

87. Because I analyse 'The Scarlet Plague' and *Earth Abides* in my 2013 book (Murphy, *The Rural Gothic*), I mention them only briefly here.
88. Stewart, *Earth Abides*, p. 297.
89. I am indebted to Prof. Robert Maslan for bringing this connection to my attention after I gave a paper on American plague narratives during the 2017 CRSF conference at the University of Liverpool.
90. Stover, 'Social Science Fiction', p. 22.
91. Ibid. p. 22.
92. Kroeber, *Ishi in Two Worlds*, p. 9.
93. Wells, '*Earth Abides*', p. 480.
94. Kroeber, *Ishi in Two Worlds*, p. 130.
95. See Bergland, *The National Uncanny*.
96. See Matheson, *I Am Legend*, pp. 158; 155.
97. *Them* debuted on Amazon Prime in Spring 2021.
98. Wilkerson, *The Warmth of Other Suns*, p. 9.
99. Ibid. p. 160.
100. Matheson, *I Am Legend*, p. 16.
101. Bastién, '*Them* is Pure Degradation Porn', online; Frazer-Carroll, '*Them* and Us', online.
102. Bastién, '*Them* is Pure Degradation Porn', online.
103. D'Addario, '*Them* is an Unconvincing Examination of American Horror', online.
104. Didion, 'Where I Was From', p. 996.
105. Didion, 'How Can I Tell Them?', pp. 38–9.
106. Ibid. p. 39.
107. Vandenberg and Coffman, 'The Center is Not Holding', p. 21.
108. Ibid. p. 38.
109. Ibid. p. 38.
110. Whitt, *Women in American Journalism*, p. 75.
111. Didion, 'How Can I Tell Them?', pp. 38–9.
112. Harrison, *Off Center*, p. 115.
113. Didion, 'How Can I Tell Them?', p. 38.
114. Ibid. pp. 39–40.
115. Ibid. p. 40.
116. Ibid. p. 43.
117. Whitt, *Women in American Journalism*, p. 79.
118. Didion, 'How Can I Tell Them?', p. 45.
119. Ibid. p. 47.
120. Ibid. p. 47.
121. Mumford, 'California and the Human Horizon', pp. 3–4.

122. Starr, *Golden Dreams*, p. 417.
123. Mumford, 'California and the Human Horizon', pp. 4–5.
124. Ibid. p. 5.
125. Ibid. p. 11.
126. Ibid. p. 11.
127. Ibid. p. 20.
128. Didion, 'How Can I Tell Them?', p. 47.
129. Bolin, *Dead Girls*, p. 125.
130. Hughes, *In a Lonely Place*, p. 428.
131. McNamara, *I'll Be Gone in the Dark*, p. 4.
132. Ibid. p. 4.
133. Wamsley, 'In Hunt for Golden State Killer', online.
134. Haag, 'What We Know About Joseph DeAngelo', online.
135. Ibid.
136. Higgs, *The Happy Man*, p. 6.
137. Ibid. p. 6.
138. Ibid. p. 20.
139. Ibid. p. 103.
140. Ibid. p. 113.
141. Ibid. p. 137.
142. Ibid. p. 14.
143. 'Harvest of Bad Seeds', pp. 22–3.
144. Ibid. n.p.
145. Ibid. n.p.
146. Ibid. n.p.
147. Ireland, 'American Highways', p. 476.
148. Dimendberg, *Film Noir*, p. 8.
149. Ibid. p. 9.
150. Murphy, *The Highway Horror Film*, p. 2.
151. Kraft and Leventhal, *Footsteps in the Fog*, p. 17.
152. Strand, *Killer on the Road*, p. 2.
153. Vronsky, *American Serial Killers*, p. 222.
154. Strand, *Killer on the Road*, p. 36.
155. Ibid. p. 60.
156. Ibid. p. 61.
157. Jenkins, *A Decade of Nightmares*, p. 144.
158. Vronsky, *American Serial Killers*, pp. 223–4.
159. Graysmith, *Zodiac*, n.p.
160. Franklin's crimes, and the official indifference and racism which enabled them, are detailed in Pelisek, *The Grim Sleeper*. Many of the women he murdered were vulnerable sex workers.

161. See Simon Bacon's 'Anywhere-Nowhere, California', for more on the association between vampires and the state.
162. Godfrey, '*The Lost Boys*', online.
163. Dowd, 'Murder Capital of the World', online.
164. LaFrance, 'When Bad News was Printed on Milk Cartons', online.
165. Ní Fhlainn, *Postmodern Vampires*, p. 81.
166. Ibid., p. 82.
167. See also the 'Hellmouth' in *Buffy the Vampire Slayer*.
168. Starr, *Embattled Dreams*, p. 224.
169. Starr, *Golden Dreams*, p. 480.
170. Zahniser and Hamilton, 'Kevin Starr', online.

# PART II

# HOLLYWOOD GOTHIC

# 3

## 'Sunshine isn't Enough': Hollywood Gothic Origins

The 'Hollywood Gothic' presents us with a Los Angeles cityscape populated by men and women whose Tinseltown neuroses render them fatally unable to differentiate between reality and fantasy. Amongst their number, we find doomed ingénues, desperate hangers-on and fallen stars unable to accept that their time in the spotlight has come to an end. Here, Hollywood's unhappy denizens are tormented by visions of what once was, and what will never be. As the name suggests, Hollywood Gothic focuses upon the 'dark side' of a specific commercial and creative industry. Here, the business which has long played a pivotal role in Southern California's cultural and economic development is invariably associated with madness, violence and death. Key locales include opulent mansions whose grandeur conceals death and decay; the private screening rooms and mahogany-panelled backstage offices in which the *real* decisions are made (usually by predatory white men); and the shabby houses, motels and apartment buildings inhabited by those who exist on the industry's margins. Hollywood is here depicted as a location that at first worships and then ruthlessly discards its stars; as a place where youth is adored but cruelly exploited; and where success always comes at an unthinkably high cost.

I will begin my discussion of the Hollywood Gothic by briefly outlining the factors behind the location's rapid establishment as the centre of the global movie-making industry. I'll then consider the reasons why it so rapidly came to encompass both a physical space (the original community which was then absorbed into the wider city of Los Angeles) and a powerful set of ideas which both overlap with and expand upon the California Gothic characteristics outlined in my Introduction. Finally, I will consider the novel which did much to lay the groundwork for the 'Hollywood Gothic': Nathanael West's *The Day of the Locust* (1939). The two chapters which follow this one will concentrate upon films which epitomise the two main types of 'Hollywood Gothic' narrative which followed in the wake of West's acerbically bleak portrait of the industry during the late 1930s. The first type focuses upon the embittered and unstable fallen star, whilst the second details the desperation of aspiring talents who will sacrifice absolutely anything to succeed.

## Hollywood Beginnings

In *Hollywood: The Movie Colony, the Movie Makers* (1941), Leo C. Rosten 'put Hollywood under the microscope of social science', arguing that it was 'an index of our society and our culture'.[1] He emphasised Hollywood's similarity to other industries, arguing that if the motion picture industry was compared to 'other businesses at a comparable time, in their sudden heyday', such as banking, the railroad industry or real estate, 'startling and conclusive parallels' could be found. He also stressed that 'Hollywood was not created out of a void: its characteristics were not invented; its people did not descend from Shangri-La.'[2] Nevertheless, he suggested, 'the aberrations of our culture are more vivid, more conspicuous, and more dramatic in Hollywood than in New Bedford or Palo Alto'.[3]

Rosten was also keen to underline a point important for us to keep in mind during this chapter: 'There are two Hollywoods: the Hollywood where people live and work, and the Hollywood which lives in the minds of the public like a fabulous legend.'[4] 'The legendary Hollywood', he continued,

> is a sort of Venice without the canals, full of glittering conveyances, dazzling maidens, and men like gods. Everyone has flashing white teeth, shapely limbs, three bank accounts, and a suntan. Marble swimming pools abound, there are miles of Byzantine palaces, and champagne flows everywhere.[5]

The Hollywood Gothic, as we shall see, often takes root in precisely this gap between the 'two' sides of Hollywood identified by Rosten. It frequently presents us with close-ups of people and places associated with the glamorous, aristocratic 'legend', but burrows beneath this veneer to expose the corruption and insanity that lies beneath. Additionally, both the place and the 'dream' are in many instances depicted from the jaundiced perspective of marginal characters (often vulnerable young women) whose ambitions are either delusional, doomed or, if attained, destructive for both the individual and those around them.

For Rosten, the core establishing principle which granted the movies a foothold in the hearts and imaginations of Americans everywhere was the recognition that 'No other industry presents so simple an invitation to the ego.'[6] Using an 'imaginary Fanny Jones in any town in the United States' as an example, he succinctly summarised the appealing 'Cinderella Story' of 'magical success' upon which he saw Hollywood's irresistible appeal (and capacity to make actors into new 'folk heroes') resting:

> Her talents may be dismal, her features vegetable, her intelligence uninspired. Yet how plausible is it for her to muse, 'It might happen to me?' And why not? [. . .] Is Fanny Jones astigmatic? She knows that Norma Shearer has a slight squint [. . .] Is Fanny Jones short? They'll photograph her on a box. Is her voice bad? 'They' will change it. Is she fat? They'll put her on a diet. Is she thin? They'll fatten her up [. . .] All that Fanny Jones really needs for a stab at glory is that elusive, undefinable quality for which, she has read, movie producers are always searching in palpatory desperation – 'personality'. And luck.[7]

One of the things that stands out about Rosten's analysis of the 'movie colony' is his awareness of the sheer newness of the industry, and the speed with which Hollywood had established itself as both a real-world business and a symbolic space. Like other commentators, he noted that there are clear precedents for this boom in earlier periods of Californian history (mainly the Gold Rush), but also in the early twentieth-century 'triple bonanza' of movies, oil and real estate, which, from the beginnings of the railroad era in 1876 onwards, transformed a previously obscure settlement into the fastest growing city in the United States.[8]

Los Angeles was also, as James D. Hart notes, unique in that

> as it sprawled outwards, it absorbed small suburbs and separate communities, to become the world's first city that grew up in the automobile age – without a real center and dependent on the private motor car to transport its citizens over its hundreds of square miles.[9]

Hence Reyner Banham's admission that 'like earlier generations of English intellectuals who taught themselves Italian in order to read Dante in the original, I learned to drive in order to read Los Angeles in the original'.[10] Despite Rosten's convincing comparisons to the development of other boom industries, he also acknowledged that Hollywood was in several important ways unique, primarily because of the way in which it combined dream life and real life. Hollywood was always more than just another factory town. It was also a complex set of ideas which rapidly accrued key symbolic and cultural importance. As Lary May puts it:

> Other countries also centralized studios; but in America, the production site was surrounded by a community where the stars really lived the happy endings, in full view of the nation. Here, moviedom became much more

than something seen on the screen or touched in the theatre. At a time when the birth of a modern family and consumption ideas might have remained just a cinematic fantasy, Hollywood showed how it could be achieved in real life. Out in California, stars participated in an exciting existence, free from the former confinements of work and Victorianism.[11]

Hollywood began as a parcel of land purchased in 1887 by a businessman named Horace Wilcox. Wilcox and his wife Daeida intended their new 'city-to-be' (which was, at the time, primarily orange groves and farmland), to be a 'model social community – Christian, righteous, and very dry – no saloons, no liquor stores, with free lands offered to Protestant churches locating within the city limits'.[12] By the time of Wilcox's death in 1892, as Kevin Starr outlines, the settlement had become a respectably populated and predominately white Anglo-Saxon Protestant (WASP) community. By 1900, it had amassed around 500 residents, and was best known as a small but upscale tourist resort.[13] In 1903, Hollywood was incorporated as a city, and by 1904, the new (and soon to be iconic) thoroughfare of Sunset Boulevard linked it to Los Angeles.[14] Starr notes that in these early years, there was nothing particularly unique about the place: Hollywood initially developed along similar lines to 'countless other small Southern Californian towns'.[15]

However, around 1907/8, early indications that the area might be attracting more than just the usual assortment of new businesses and prosperous Yankee settlers arose as the first groups of 'film folk' arrived. Their decision to stay placed Hollywood on 'another course, one that rendered it within the decade America's premier city of dreams'.[16] This is also when Hollywood began to steal the spotlight from the city of Los Angeles. Although Hollywood was only an independent city (and a small one at that) between 1903 and 1910 (when it was incorporated into wider Los Angeles),[17] as Mark Shiel observes, the 'overshadowing of "Los Angeles" by "Hollywood" prevailed until the late 1940s when the studio system began to disintegrate and references to "Los Angeles" became much more frequent in cinema, especially in film noir'.[18] As we shall see, the idea of 'Hollywood' – either as a kind of lost world, or as a burning aspiration, still tends to 'overshadow' the city in Hollywood Gothic narratives.

For Starr, two early geniuses of the film industry – D. W. Griffith and Cecil B. DeMille – helped to create the new capital of the American (and soon, the world) film industry. He cites Griffith's decision to move his then-embryonic Biograph acting troupe from New York to Hollywood in 1910 as a defining moment which facilitated the emergence of 'Hollywood – as a concept, as an industry, as a mythic place.'[19] Griffith, he notes, was also responsible for the first ever 'All California film', *The Thread of Destiny* (1910), which happened to use the region's pre-American history as its subject. It was 'a story of old California' which incorporated then-pioneering outdoor scenes shot in Mission San Gabriel, the first mission established in LA, and also, in 1785, the site of one of the most significant Native American revolts against Spanish rule.[20] The first motion picture made in California therefore contributed to the nostalgic Anglo-American 'cult' of Spanish California established by Helen Hunt Jackson's novel *Ramona* (1884).[21] It's a development which underlines Shiel's observation that during the heyday of the studio system, despite the 'exceptionally heterogeneous' class, gender and racial contexts of the city,

> the majority of films of Los Angeles reinforced its domination by white Anglo-Saxon Protestants. Concentrating their narratives and settings in the increasingly middle-class West Los Angeles, most films aided the dominant culture's suppression and appropriation of the earlier histories of Native American, Spanish and Mexican Southern California.[22]

For Starr, who, throughout his monumental history of the state persuasively argued that the 'California Dream' is itself a central motivating factor in the development of the region, Hollywood was able to 'answer a need for dreams that was basic to America: dreams about mobility, an improved life, romantic love, a better home, a more creative occupation, travel, leisure, excitement of all sorts'.[23] It meant that this 'normal activity' would also have 'major social and cultural consequences for Southern California':[24]

> From the start a land of dreams, a tabula rasa upon and through which fantasy and longings expressed themselves, Southern California found its function and identity further fixed by the presence of Hollywood, which by 1920 or so had become its leading social metaphor. By the mid-1920s myth and reality, dream gesture and landscape had so interpenetrated each other in an actual place – Hollywood and its attendant community of Beverly Hills, plus portions of Santa Monica and Los Angeles – that each aspect of architecture and lifestyle, social psychology and infrastructure, bespoke an integrated condition based upon the Hollywood myth.[25]

In his own discussion of why the movies found such an appropriate home in Southern California, Lary May also highlights this fortuitous alliance between place and industry. Noting that 'a generation of film scholars' had generally focused on two prime reasons as to how this arrangement came about (namely, the temperate climate and SoCal's proximity to Mexico, which facilitated speedy escape from the lawsuit-happy Edison Trust in the early days), he argues that more than just these practical considerations were at play. The 'West Coast production site' would soon 'become more than merely a place to make films. Fan magazines, newspapers and movies themselves would spotlight the comings and goings of movie stars – a life-style that was dramatically different from that of the nineteenth or even early twentieth century.'[26] In his analysis,

> It was not so much the need for sun, or an escape from the now defunct trust that pushed the Big Eight West. More important was the need to find a complimentary locale for the innovations taking place in the film industry after 1914. In terms of costs alone, it paid to move to Los Angeles. This city on the far edge of the continent offered the advantages of a great Boom Town well into the twentieth century. Unlike the older urban areas of the East, it was still in the early stages of growth. Starting around 1900, local elites began to transform the sleepy agricultural town from its Spanish origins into a modern American metropolis.[27]

The sheer 'newness' of LA was also highlighted by Banham in his pioneering architectural history, *Los Angeles: The Architecture of Four Ecologies* (1971). He memorably described LA as

> A city seventy miles square but rarely seventy years deep apart from a small downtown not yet two centuries old, and a few other pockets of ancientry, Los Angeles is instant architecture in an instant landscape. Most of its buildings are the first and only structures on their particular parcels of land; they are couched in a dozen different styles, most of them imported, exploited, and ruined within living memory.[28]

For Banham, the 'splendours and the miseries of Los Angeles, the graces and grotesques' were both 'unrepeatable and unprecedented', rendering the place a more than worthy subject for precisely the kind of historical monograph he was essaying himself.[29] 'Once the history of the city is brought under review', he argued, 'it is immediately apparent that no city has ever been produced by such an extraordinary mixture of geography, climate, politics, demography, mechanics and culture.'[30] Hollywood was, in his view, the 'tertiary industry that sets Los Angeles from every other city that now possesses the same territory', and whilst its economic ramifications were substantial, it is 'the cultural consequences that are now the most important'.[31] He continued:

> Hollywood brought to Los Angeles an unprecedented and unrepeatable population of genius, neurosis, skill, charlatanry, beauty, vice, talent, and

plain old eccentricity, and it brought that population in little over two decades, not the long centuries that most metropolitan cities have required to accumulate a cultured and leisured class. So Hollywood was also the end of innocence and provincialism – the movies found Los Angeles a diffuse fruit-growing super-village of some eight hundred thousand souls, and handed it over to the infant television industry in 1950 a world metropolis of over four million.[32]

Given that the movie industry was one which relied upon creative talents in particular – actors, directors, writers, artists, set designers, make-up artists – as well as technical and business acumen (largely the preserve of the all-powerful producers and studio heads), it is hardly surprising that the birth of Hollywood was quickly succeeded by the birth of the 'Hollywood novel', which rapidly became a distinctive sub-genre of the regional novel in and of itself. Writing in 1987, Nancy Brooker-Bowers observed that 'Over the past seventy years, the Hollywood novel, which features characters in the film industry working either in Hollywood or on location with a Hollywood production company, has developed as an important fiction genre.'[33] In her analysis, it is 'imperative' that novels of this kind are treated separately from other works of Los Angeles-set fiction, 'because their setting – the specific town of Hollywood – has been overwhelmingly influenced by the film industry and the illusions it produces'.[34] This important distinction is one which I shall mostly be adhering to in my own discussion of Hollywood Gothic, which I also view as a distinct (if even smaller) sub-genre, largely film- rather than novel-based, revolving around the darkest possible depiction of the movie industry and those who work in (or aspire to work in) that field.

## Sunshine isn't Enough: *The Day of the Locust* (1939)

*The Day of the Locust* is the prime literary precursor to the emergence of the Hollywood Gothic in its more fecund cinematic incarnation. In what will become a familiar trope, it soon becomes apparent that the primal longings aroused by the movies are in themselves inherently monstrous, destroying both innocent and cynic alike. In Nathanael West's novel, the seductive but dangerous promise of success long associated with California in a wider sense has been lent even greater resonance – and menace – by the fateful convergence of geographical location and creative industry. The California dream had evolved, as did the California nightmare.

Published in 1939, *Locust* was written just before the era between 1939 and 1941 which Rosten suggested might be 'the end of Hollywood's lush and profligate period'.[35] Fittingly, the novel is characterised from the very beginning by the sense that we have entered a chaotic and deeply cynical world. The character around whom the other lost souls in the novel percolate is set designer Tod Hackett (his very name suggests morbid aggression), who has been in Hollywood for less than three months. Like many of the other characters, he is an aspiring nobody, toiling on the margins whilst he dreams of creative glory – which in Tod's case means finally finishing his long-in-gestation apocalyptic painting, 'The Burning of Los Angeles'.

The opening chapter, narrated from Tod's perspective, is filled with details about clothing, props and landscape which suggest that Hollywood is a kind of nightmarish bricolage in which all regard for the boundaries of conventional taste, historical periodisation and logical order have been gleefully jettisoned. As he glances out of his office window on the studio lot, Tod sees an army of extras arrayed in Napoleonic battle-dress pass by, moving 'like a mob': 'The dolmans of the hussars, the heavy shakos of the guards, Hanoverian light horse, with their flat leather caps and flowing red plumes, were all jumbled together in bobbing disorder.'[36] It is a sight which prepares us for the orgy of mob violence with which the novel concludes.

Whilst walking home that same day, Tod observes the evening crowd of Los Angelinos garishly dressed in any fashion they fancy, having variously donned Tyrolean hats, blue flannel jackets and 'sports clothes which were not really sports clothes'.[37] He also notes that

> scattered among these masquerades were people of a different type. Their clothing was somber and badly cut, bought from mail-order houses. While the others moved rapidly, darting into stores and cocktail bars, they loitered on the corner, or stood with their backs to the shop windows and stared at everyone who passed. When their stare was returned, their eyes filled with hatred. At this time Tod knew very little about them except that they had come to California to die.[38]

Variations upon this morbid incantation – 'they had come to California to die' – recur three times in the text, subverting the utopian vision of California as a place of rebirth, rejuvenation and endless personal and economic possibility. Tellingly, Tod always applies this incantation to a specific variety of California newcomer: the ill-fated Midwesterner.

As Mike Davis notes, here, 'Hollywood has become the "dream dump", a hallucinatory landscape tottering on apocalypse.'[39] As was the case with many of the other major authors associated with Hollywood novels of the 1920s and 1930s, West's jaundiced view of the milieu was much indebted to his own experience of the industry and the city of Los Angeles. Tod Hackett is 'portrayed in a situation similar to West's own, brought to the coast by a talent scout for the studios and forced to live the dilemma of reconciling his creative work with his commercial labours'.[40] West's biographer, Jay Martin, writing in 1971, observed that:

> The Hollywood Gold Rush of the 1920s, like that of 1849, had brought with it a mob of pleasure and fortune seekers, active exploiters of Hollywood of the Long Beach oil boom, weary exploiters of the sun, aged citizens of the Midwest, and the sick from all parts of America – as well as those who would prey upon them: confidence men and women of every variety, embezzlers, yoga and faith healers, gamblers, prostitutes [. . .] The grotesque character of this underworld appealed to West's pessimistic view of human life, and when he arrived back in the East he impressed (and often shocked) his friends with tales of the oddities of the golden scene: for him, Hollywood had been a museum of curiosities. He spoke, with obvious interest, of the peripheral characters of Hollywood, of hunchbacks, dwarfs and variously deformed people, told several stories about lesbian actresses and curious sexual practices.[41]

*The Day of the Locust* is an episodic, impressionistic novel in which, as in many of the other 'Hollywood' novels which came before and afterwards, 'the Hollywood "Culture Industry" was synonymous with vulgarity, sham and deception'.[42] Because he is the closest the novel comes to having a central character, it is clear that we are meant to take Tod's perspective on Hollywood seriously. As Thomas Strychacz notes, 'the scenes in which West considers the actual workings of the film industry – the source of the stories that structure the character's consciousness in the novel – are among the most impressive'.[43]

Furthermore, Tod's positioning as an artist who has, his old friends back in art school fear, foolishly 'sold out' and will 'never paint again' is a familiar one.[44] As Davis outlines, this basic premise is itself reflective of a central strand of LA 'mythology', which revolves around the notion of 'the destruction of intellectual sensibility in the sun-baked plains of Los Angeles', a perception which, he asserts, is 'at least partially true'.[45] The city, he continues, has 'for ever more peculiar reasons . . . become the world capital of an immense Culture Industry, which since the 1920s has imported myriads of the most talented writers, film makers, artists and visionaries'.[46] Referring to the hold that both the movie and the aerospace industries have over the intellectual migrants who came to Southern California in search of money and success, Davis lists the metaphors commonly used to describe this dynamic:

> Snared in the nets of Hollywood, or entrapped by the Strangelovian logic of the missile industry, 'seduced' talents are 'wasted', 'prostituted', 'trivialized', or 'destroyed'. To move to Lotusland is to sever connections with national reality, to lose historical and experiential footing, to surrender critical distance,

and to submerge oneself in spectacle and fraud. Fused into a single montage image are Fitzgerald reduced to a drunken hack, West rushing to his own apocalypse (thinking it a dinner party), Faulkner rewriting second-rate scripts, Brecht raging against the mutilation of his work, the Hollywood Ten on their way to prison, Didion on the verge of a nervous breakdown, and so on. Los Angeles (and its alter-ego, Hollywood) becomes the literalized Mahagonny, city of seduction and defeat, the antipode to critical intelligence.[47]

Yet, for all that, as he further observes, 'this very rhetoric' would itself lead to a significant creative and artistic movement in its own right, one which demonstrated 'powerful critical energies at work' and lent itself to particularly 'acute critiques of the culture of late capitalism, and, particularly, of the tendential degredation of the middle strata (a persistent theme from Nathanael West to Robert Towne)'.[48] For Davis, the most 'outstanding' examples of such a critique can be found in LA's distinctive brand of literary and cinematic noir, in which, as he sees it, the city plays 'the double role of utopia *and* dystopia for advanced capitalism. The same place, as Brecht noted, symbolized both heaven and hell.'[49]

Whilst discussing the major Hollywood novels of the 1930s and 1940s – which here, as is generally the case in other commentaries on the trend, are said to include *Locust*, F. Scott Fitzgerald's fragment, *The Last Tycoon* (1941), and Budd Schulberg's *What Makes Sammy Run* (1941) – Springer similarly argues that 'Fictional treatments of Hollywood have generally functioned, with varying degrees of purpose and insight, as commentaries on mass culture, and the tenor of this commentary has largely been critical.'[50] However, he also outlines some important differences between these novels, noting that whilst both Fitzgerald and Schulberg

> center their examination of Hollywood on the personality of a representative central figure [. . .] *The Day of the Locust*, on the other hand, is a markedly decentered narrative, with Tod Hackett providing only a tenuous, connecting presence around which the other characters revolve. Indeed, West's major concern is not on an emblematic central figure at all, but rather Hollywood itself: a unique social and material landscape dominated by a single occupation – movie making – whose excesses and illusions give rise to monstrous expectations and desires, and produce a pervasive sense of reality.[51]

The 'peripheral characters' whom West's authorial surrogate finds himself mixed up with include the opportunistic, promiscuous aspiring starlet Faye Greener and her father Harry, a one-time Vaudevillian reduced to selling home-made silver polish. Tod's perpetually frustrated sexual desire for Faye is the reason why he ends up living in the same shabby apartment building as the father and daughter duo. However, Faye insists upon keeping their relationship 'impersonal', because, she says, he has neither money nor looks. Faye's acting credits thus far extend to a role as a dancing girl – in which, we are told, 'She had only one line to speak, "Oh Mr Smith!" and spoke it badly.'[52] Whilst gazing at the signed photograph she has given him, Tod reflects upon Faye's image in a manner which emphasises the undercurrent of barely repressed sexual violence (on his part) that permeates his fixation upon her:

> She was supposed to look drunk and she did, but not with alcohol. She lay stretched out on the divan with her arms and legs spread, as though welcoming a lover, and her lips were parted in a heavy, sullen smile. She was supposed to look inviting, but the invitation wasn't to pleasure. [. . .] but to struggle, hard and sharp, closer to murder than to love. If you threw yourself on her, it would be like throwing yourself from the parapet of a skyscraper. You would do it with a scream. You wouldn't expect to rise again. Your teeth would be driven back into your skull like nails in a pine board and your back would be broken. You wouldn't even have time to sweat or close your eyes.[53]

Later, Tod berates himself for not having 'the courage to throw himself on her. Nothing less violent than rape would do', and returns again to his brutal rape fantasies towards the end of the novel.[54] The fact that Faye is still a teenager matters little. She is depicted throughout the novel as a character type that would frequently surface in disparaging newspaper reports about Hollywood during the 1920s and 1930s: the cynical, materialistic, none-too-bright starlet who is quick to exchange sexual favours for material and professional advancement.

Although Faye rejects Tod's advances, she soon acquires a new suitor whose Midwestern reserve and loneliness make him the perfect mark. Homer Simpson, a sad-sack Iowan who has been sent to California to rest after suffering a bout of pneumonia, seems to Tod to be 'an exact model for the kind of person who comes to California to die, perfect in every detail down to fever eyes and unruly hands'.[55]

Homer's impetus for moving to the state is one that was still common at the time, although this curative 'myth' was in the process of being superseded by the dreams of Hollywood success outlined by Rosten. Lyra Kilston sums up this long-standing association between Southern California and healthy living as being 'the myth of California as a cure in itself'.[56] She continues:

> By 1860, the notion that health was dependent on place was widely accepted. Eastern American cities, with their humidity, long wet winters,

and dense populations, augured inescapable disease. Doctors prescribed journeys to the West or South West for climatotherapy, citing the 'radically curative and reinvigorating influences' of fresh dry air, ample sunshine, and new scenery. Meanwhile, California's climate cure was exalted in newspaper advertisements, handbooks, and travel guides.[57]

However, despite the promise of renewed vitality and a fresh start, Homer, for whom 'the forty years of his life had been without variety or excitement', soon finds himself carrying out his day-to-day routine with the same 'impersonal detachment' as before.[58] He is repeatedly described in terms which emphasise his seemingly 'mechanical' nature. At one point, he is said to be like a 'badly made automaton', whilst Tod notices upon their first meeting his 'unruly' hands, which are always said to be acting of their own volition. Homer's estrangement from his physical self extends to his repressed sexuality. He is haunted by memories of an episode back in Iowa, during which an intoxicated female hotel guest made sexual advances towards him. He was, characteristically, unable to consummate their encounter.

It is made clear from this that Homer is easy to take advantage of, and will be easily exploited by the more cynical, opportunistic denizens of Los Angeles. Soon after his arrival, he is bullied into renting a cottage in the canyons because most of the other people in his neighbourhood want 'Spanish' houses, but this one is, according to the rental agent, 'Irish' and decidedly 'queer'.[59] Like the buildings and clothing glimpsed by Tod on his way home from the studio, Homer's cottage is a garish mix of styles and themes. Despite its sunny location, it has a thatched roof (which isn't made of straw at all), a door with hinges stamped by a machine to appear 'hand-forged' and a 'Spanish' living room decorated with any manner of unlikely trappings. The bedrooms are decked out in another style entirely, described as having an 'East Coast' theme by the scheming real-estate agent.

Homer's initially uneventful sojourn in LA is interrupted by the intrusion of Harry and Faye. Harry, who has been selling his 'miracle polish' from door to door, collapses in Homer's living room and demands that Faye be summoned. Homer is immediately struck by her beauty, vitality and youth. 'She was as shiny as a new spoon', he notes, and 'although she was seventeen, she was dressed like a child of twelve.'[60] For her part, Faye soon realises that Homer's obvious interest can be turned to her advantage. She tells him, in no uncertain terms, that her goal is 'to be a star someday', or else, 'I'll commit suicide.'[61]

However, her acting ambitions are put on hold when it becomes clear that her father Harry is gravely ill. Observing the sick man as he lies in bed, Tod, typically clear-eyed and cynical, ascribes to him an inherent shallowness of emotional affect:

Harry, like many actors, had very little back or top to his head. It was almost all face, like a mask, with deep furrows behind the eyes, across the forehead and on either side of the nose and mouth, ploughed there by years of broad grinning and heavy frowning. Because of them, he could never express anything either subtly or exactly.[62]

Upon Harry's death, Faye works in a brothel to pay for his funeral expenses (thereby completing a transition from implied to actual sex work which has come to seem almost inevitable). Although Tod describes her as having 'never looked more beautiful', he also says that during the funeral service 'all he could think about was how she had earned the money for her outfit on her back'.[63] Tod also notices an odd scattering of unknown men and women populating the back rows of the church:

He knew their kind. While not torch-bearers themselves, they would run behind the fire and do a great deal of the shouting. They had come to see Harry buried, hoping for a dramatic incident of some sort, hoping at least for one of the mourners to be led weeping hysterically from the chapel. It seemed to Tod that they stared back at him with an expression of vicious, acrid boredom that trembled on the verge of violence.[64]

After the funeral, Tod briefly loses touch with Faye, only to see her one day on the studio backlot, working as an extra. West's description of the various productions Tod passes whilst on the way to find Faye again emphasises the inherent artificiality and temporal and spatial disjointedness of the studio. A group of men and women are sitting on 'a lawn of fiber', 'eating cardboard food in front of a cellophane waterfall'; a little later, an actor dressed as the Greek god Eros lies face down in a pile of old newspapers and bottles. Tod also passes replicas of the wooden horse of Troy, a Dutch windmill and dinosaur bones. As he reaches the top of a hill, he looks down upon a field which represents the final, inevitable studio scrapheap:

He thought of Janvier's 'Sargasso Sea'. Just as that imaginary body of water was a history of civilization in the form of a marine junkyard, the studio was one in the form of a dream dump. A Sargasso of the imagination! And the dump grew continually, for there wasn't a dream afloat that wouldn't sooner or later turn up on it, having first been made photographic by plaster, canvas, lath and paint.[65]

When Tod finally catches up with Faye again, she informs him that she has stopped working in the brothel. She is now living with Homer, who has agreed to bankroll her renewed bid for stardom: 'as soon as she clicked in pictures, she would pay him back with six percent interest'.[66] Faye's delusional fantasy of imminent stardom is fuelled by her belief that success has thus far eluded her because she doesn't have the right clothes. She is an obvious believer in the myth of 'magical success', identified by Rosten as a core contributor to the allure of Hollywood. Faye is convinced that she has that 'elusive, indefinable quality' which will be unleashed upon the world once she is 'discovered'.

Homer is also caught up in this fantasy. The hollowness of his lonely, routine-bound life is for once lessened by his proximity to a lovely young thing who sees him only as a quasi-paternal financial backer. All too soon, however, the 'arrangement' begins to sour, and Faye's boredom makes her cruel. 'At first', West tells us, 'she did it unconsciously, later maliciously.'[67] Even Tod soon begins to feel pity for Homer, whose servility and passiveness mean that he is easy prey for his fickle, materialistic and promiscuous 'protégé'. Recognising that he needs to find a way of ending his own infatuation with her, Tod avoids Faye for several months, instead concentrating on gathering visual references he can use in his art, with a concentration upon 'the different Hollywood churches'. Yet again, West's descriptions here of Hollywood's citizenry evoke mob violence, apocalyptic unease and a sense that the individual has been subsumed into a fickle and potentially aggressive collective: 'He would paint their fury with respect, appreciating its awful, anarchic power and aware that they had it in them to destroy civilization.'[68] He is, however, eventually pulled back into Faye's orbit again when she insists that he join herself and Homer for drinks at an establishment (tellingly) called the 'Cinderella Bar'. During their time there, Faye's thoughtless, domineering treatment of Homer is briefly interrupted when the trio are transfixed by the mesmerising act of a female impersonator who, 'as he crooned was really a woman'.[69] The moment his act ends, however, the young man becomes 'an actor again', tripping over his evening gown and striding off 'swinging his shoulders'. It's an episode which furthers the striking preoccupation with 'acting' and with imitation featured in the novel, in which one façade often hides another, and characters such as Faye and Harry are no longer quite able to distinguish between what is real and what isn't. This dangerous blurring of the boundaries between fantasy and reality is a recurrent theme in the Hollywood Gothic.

There follows an increasingly out-of-control night at Homer's cottage, which begins with a trip to a cockfight and ends when Faye humiliates her host by soliciting sexual favours from Earle Shoop, her cowboy paramour, and his Mexican friend Miguel. Also in attendance at this gathering is Tod's friend Claude Estee, the one character who has attained real success in Hollywood. Early on, we learn that Claude's earnings have enabled him to live in a 'big house' that is an exact replica of a Mississippi plantation. Claude's self-consciously ridiculous facsimile of antebellum living is, in its own way, every bit as garish as Homer's 'queer' little cottage. When Tod attends a party there, Claude greets him by 'doing the impersonation that went with the Southern colonial architecture', which involves pretending to be a Civil War Colonel with 'a large belly', even though 'he was a dried up little man with the rubbed features and stooped shoulders of a postal clerk'.[70] We have here an early appearance of a trope which recurs frequently within the Hollywood Gothic: homes which serve as private stage sets/ worlds for wealthy owners who, because of their Hollywood success, have been granted licence to live out whatever delusional fantasy they wish to indulge in.

Indeed, the Hollywood mansion is a prime visual signifier within the Hollywood Gothic, evoking the classical Gothic castle but at the same time differentiating itself by dint of its newness and its fundamentally inescapable Californian-ness (we also see echoes here of Sarah Winchester's infamous home). These residences are lent an extra sense of unreality by their explicit connection to the world of dreams. As Tod's earlier LA observations have underlined, this is a place where, if you have enough money and will, anything goes. As a result, the city's canyons are lined with 'Mexican ranch houses, Samoan huts, Mediterranean villas, Egyptian and Japanese temples, Swiss chalets, Tudor cottages, and every possible combination of these styles', a hideous melange that Tod characteristically comes to believe that 'only dynamite' can help.[71]

Tod's early visit to Claude's estate also introduces another important visual signifier of the Hollywood Gothic (and the California Gothic more generally): the swimming pool which holds more than just water. Having been invited by crude-talking fellow guest Mrs Schwartzen to survey Claude's garden, Tod finds himself 'pulled along' in her wake:

The air of the garden was heavy with the odor of mimosa and honeysuckle. Through a slit in the blue serge sky poked a great moon that looked like an enormous bone button. A little flagstone path, made narrower by its border of oleander, led to the edge of the sunken pool. On the bottom, near the deep end, he could see a heavy, black mass of some kind.
'What is it?' he asked.

She kicked a switch that was hidden at the base of a shrub and a row of submerged floodlights illuminated the green water. The thing was a dead horse, or, rather, a life-size, realistic representation of one. Its legs stuck up stiff and straight and it had an enormous, distended belly. Its hammerhead lay twisted to one side and from its mouth, which was set in an agonized grin, hung a heavy, black tongue.

'Isn't it marvelous!' exclaimed Mrs Schwartzen, clapping her hands and jumping up and down excitedly like a little girl.[72]

The creature lying at the bottom of Claude's pool is yet another surreal facsimile: a monument to grotesque whimsy that works neither on an 'artistic' level nor as an amusing in-joke. This sight is soon followed by a group outing to the same exclusive brothel in which Faye will later ply her charms. This is a world in which everything can be bought, and in which basic human relationships are all too often reduced to the level of soulless transaction.

It's interesting then that Claude's next appearance in the narrative also involves another dead animal, albeit a real one: the rival bird brutally bested by Miguel's prize-fighting cock 'Juju'. After he and the rest of the men who viewed the cockfight are invited inside for a drink by Faye, Claude, like Tod and Homer before him, is struck by the beautiful young woman. Upon hearing that he works in the movies, Faye outlines how she intends to make a success of her acting career:

> It was all nonsense. She mixed bits of badly understood advice from the trade papers with other bits of the fan magazines and compared these with the legends that surround the activities of screen stars and executives. Without any noticeable transition, possibilities became probabilities and wound up as inevitabilities.[73]

As is the case with Homer's next-door neighbour Mrs Loomis, who has been grooming her little boy, Adore, for stardom, innocence has been superseded by ambition, and self-delusion is the order of the day: 'What's Shirley Temple got that he ain't?', the deluded stage mother declares at one stage. Although every word that Faye utters is 'nonsense', the men watching her pay no heed:

> They were all too busy watching her smile, laugh, shiver, whisper, grow indignant, cross and uncross her legs, stick out her tongue, widen and narrow her eyes, toss her head so that her platinum hair splashed against the red plush of the chair back. The strange thing about her gestures and expressions was that they didn't really illustrate what she was saying. They were almost pure.[74]

As the other men drink in Faye's 'performance', Homer retreats outside, and admits to Tod that he no longer knows how to cope with her behaviour. His distressed reaction includes a bizarre tic, a horribly precise 'manual ballet' in which, yet again, his hands appear to almost act of their own accord.

Tod decides to leave the party after an unsightly brawl breaks out, but returns the next day to see if Homer is all right. In his absence, the evening had further deteriorated, culminating in a violent outburst when Earle discovered

Faye in bed with Miguel. Homer is distraught by the discovery that Faye has left him, and appears to be having a nervous breakdown. The suggestible and sheltered Iowan was ill-equipped to cope with life on the margins of the movie business from the start, and there appears to be no option for him but to return to where he came from. Tod is sympathetic but brutally pragmatic, believing it likely that Faye has returned to her job at the brothel.

Faye's likely fate is a development which again echoes anxieties related to Hollywood and the movie industry which were very much in the air during the 1920s and 1930s. Rosten points out that between 1919 and 1921 alone, the boom brought around 50,000 women to LA, and there was much handwringing surrounding the so-called 'girl problem'. To get around strict vagrancy laws, hundreds of men and women who were at risk of being deemed 'disreputable' and rounded up by the police declared themselves to be 'movie extras'. 'Some', he notes, 'had been employed as extras – for a day or a week; most had not set foot within a studio gate. But they were recorded as "extras" in the police books, and the nation thrilled to tales of movie "stars" caught in raids on brothels or marijuana parties.'[75] It all added further weight to the perception that the movie industry was a threat to the virtue of vulnerable young women.[76] A series of well-publicised and high-profile movie-star divorces, love affairs, drug overdoses, suicides and murders helped exacerbate the sense of scandal. As Rosten suggests:

> The Mid-Westerners who came to Los Angeles to retire, and the tourists who visited it to relax, were awed by the carnival life of the city. They must have been disturbed by the garish houses and the glittering automobiles, by the abandon of the night clubs and the exhibitionism on the beaches – above all, by the loose and lavish use of money. A community populated entirely by entertainers is a ready-made target for hostility. The theatrical profession has always aroused suspicion in the breasts of the moral; acting is the Devil's game, and actors are the children of evil. Hollywood became a synonym for Sodom; the tourists saw sins, but not skills.[77]

In West's final chapter, the novel's preoccupation with violence, mob terror and the terrible-yet-mesmerising implosion of the Californian dream reaches its fateful climax, and the movie-mad streets of LA are engulfed by a riot with decidedly apocalyptic undertones. As Tod, who is again heading back to the cottage in search of Homer, walks downtown, he notices crowds beginning to gather beneath the 'delicate minarets' of 'Khan's Pleasure Palace' (another culturally incongruous building), where the world premiere of a new picture is taking place. The stars will not arrive for several hours, but the crowd has already grown unruly.

Though he initially decides to 'kill some time' by taking in the scene, Tod grows fearful as the undercurrent of anger and aggression surging through the mob grows. Once the stars of the picture arrive, he realises, things are really going to turn nasty:

> At the sight of their heroes and heroines, the crowds would turn demoniac. Some little gesture, either too pleasing or too offensive, would start it moving and then nothing but machine guns would stop it. Individually the purpose of its members might simply be to grab a souvenir, but collectively, it would grab and rend.[78]

The situation is inflamed by the running commentary provided by a radio reporter broadcasting via microphone: 'His rapid, hysterical voice was like that of a revivalist preacher whipping his congregation towards the ecstasy of fits.'[79]

Tod threads his way through the crowd across the street by feigning fellowship with the mob, 'always trying to look as though he were enjoying himself'.[80] From a vantage point atop a wall, he watches as those who join in with the ever-expanding crowd instantly change:

> Until they reached the line, they looked diffident, almost furtive, but the moment they had become part of it, they turned arrogant and pugnacious. It was a mistake to think them harmless curiosity seekers. They were savage and bitter, especially the middle-aged and the old, and had been made so by boredom and disappointment.[81]

It is at this point that Tod ruminates for the final time upon the inner lives of those who have come to California to escape their tedious, humdrum lives, only to discover, once there, that 'sunshine isn't enough':

> Their boredom becomes more and more terrible. They realize that they've been tricked and burn with resentment. Every day of their lives they read the newspapers and went to the movies. Both fed them on lynchings, murder, sex crimes, explosions, wrecks, love nests, fires, miracles, revolutions, war. This daily diet made sophisticates of them. The sun is a joke. Oranges can't titillate their jaded palates. Nothing can ever be violent enough to make taut their slack minds and bodies. They have been cheated and betrayed. They have slaved and saved for nothing.[82]

Tod's physical and emotional detachment is breached when he spots Homer in the throng, clearly in a state of considerable distress. As he tries to manoeuvre him towards a taxi, Tod's bid to leave is again frustrated by another random encounter, this time with Adore Loomis, the aspiring child star. The boy throws a stone at Homer when his efforts to play a cruel practical joke go seemingly unnoticed. Much to Tod's shock, Homer attacks the child. The crowd, enraged, surges forwards, and both men are swept up by the mob as the cry that 'a pervert attacked a child' goes up. Homer disappears into the horde, whilst Tod himself is caught between two masses of people going in opposite directions and is ground between them, 'like a grain between millstones'.[83]

His leg painfully broken, Tod is trapped in a succession of surges and brief moments of relief, during which he sees the horrific sight of a sobbing girl being sexually assaulted by a vampiric-seeming old man. The crowd has given people licence to fulfil whatever lurid desire strikes them in the moment. What's more, upon reaching another 'dead spot', Tod realises that the people caught up in this part of the mob are enjoying themselves. A woman chats to someone whilst paying no attention to the male stranger hugging her around the waist:

> 'The first thing I knew,' Tod heard her say, 'there was a rush and I was in the middle.' 'Yeah. Somebody hollered, "Here comes Gary Cooper," and then wham!'
> 'That ain't it,' said a little man wearing a cloth cap and pullover sweater. 'This is a riot you're in.'[84]

Pulled along still further, Tod clings to railings and tries to escape from the agony of his predicament by thinking about his painting, 'The Burning of Los Angeles', which he has been working on continually since falling out with Faye:

> Across the top, parallel with the frame, he had drawn the burning city, a great bonfire of architectural styles, ranging from Egyptian to Cape Cod colonial. Through the center, winding from left to right, was a long hill street and down it, spilling into the middle foreground, came the mob carrying baseball bats and torches. For the faces of its members, he was using the innumerable sketches he had made of people who come to California to die; the cultists of all sorts, economic as well as religious, the wave, airplane, funeral and preview watchers – all those poor devils who can only be stirred by the promise of miracles and then only to violence . . . No longer bored, they sang and danced joyously in the red light of the flames.[85]

Tod is eventually hauled to safety by a policeman. However, *The Day of the Locust*, characteristically, ends not with any sense of resolution or relief, but on a note of hysteria. Tod finds himself laughing uncontrollably and imitating the noise of the police siren as he is driven away. In West's climactic orgy of communal violence, then, one of the most emblematic rituals associated with movie fan worship – the film premiere – becomes nothing less than a full-on riot, in which both the apparently befuddled innocent (Homer) and the cynical bystander (Tod) have no choice but to surrender to the primal urges of both the crowd and themselves. Tellingly, as throughout the rest of the novel, no actual stars are in attendance here. Nevertheless, the narrative is from the start saturated with an awareness of Hollywood's seductive, insane, over-arching 'dream-life' and a sense that an existence there, even on the margins of the industry, is fundamentally and inescapably chaotic. Indeed, the climax of West's nightmarish vision anticipated two slightly later tales of the terrifying collective power of the mob. The first is Shirley Jackson's parable of ritual human sacrifice, 'The Lottery' (1948), and the second is Ray Bradbury's 'The Crowd' (1943).[86] In this instance, however, the horror of the denouement is intrinsically linked to the very nature of the film industry and to the delusions and mania it inspires. In *The Day of the Locust*, Hollywood is a place in which sex, death and spectacle are intrinsically linked, adoration is swiftly transformed into an ecstatic groundswell of violence, and dreams of stardom lead only to degradation. In this setting even cynics such as Tod Hackett, who think they understand the milieu, can find themselves dangerously, and perhaps even fatally, overwhelmed.

## Notes

1. Rosten, *Hollywood*, p. vi.
2. Ibid. p. 5.
3. Ibid. p. v.
4. Ibid. p. vi.
5. Ibid. p. 12.
6. Ibid. p. 13.
7. Ibid. p. 14.
8. Ibid. p. 18. See also, Hart, *A Companion to California*, p. 242.
9. Hart, *A Companion to California*, p. 243.
10. Banham, *Los Angeles*, p. 3.
11. May, *Screening Out the Past*, p. 167.
12. Starr, *Inventing the Dream*, p. 284.
13. Ibid. p. 284.
14. Ibid. p. 284.
15. Ibid. p. 285.

16. Ibid. p. 285.
17. Hart, *A Companion to California*, p. 190.
18. Shiel, *Hollywood Cinema*, p. 195.
19. Starr, *Inventing the Dream*, p. 291.
20. Ibid. p. 291. The 1785 San Gabriel siege is discussed in Brook, *Land of Smoke and Mirrors*, p. 35.
21. Jackson's 'idealization of a pastoral Californio lifestyle destroyed by rapacious American civilization', is outlined in Brook, *Land of Smoke and Mirrors*, p. 27.
22. Shiel, *Hollywood Cinema*, p. 8.
23. Starr, *Inventing the Dream*, p. 290
24. Ibid. p. 334.
25. Ibid. p. 334.
26. May, *Screening Out the Past*, p. 168.
27. Ibid. pp. 179–80.
28. Banham, *Los Angeles*, p. 3.
29. Ibid. p. 6.
30. Ibid. p. 6.
31. Ibid. p. 6.
32. Ibid. p. 6.
33. Brooker-Bowers, 'Fiction and the Film Industry', p. 259.
34. Ibid. p. 259.
35. Rosten, *Hollywood*, p. 30.
36. West, *The Day of the Locust*, p. 1.
37. Ibid. p. 2.
38. Ibid. p. 2.
39. Davis, *City of Quartz*, p. 38.
40. Ibid. pp. 38–9.
41. Martin, *Nathanael West*, p. 213.
42. Springer, 'This is a Riot You're In', p. 440.
43. Strychacz, 'Making Sense of Hollywood', p. 151.
44. West, *The Day of the Locust*, p. 3.
45. Davis, *City of Quartz*, p. 17.
46. Ibid. p. 17.
47. Ibid. p. 18.
48. Ibid. p. 18.
49. Ibid. p. 18.
50. Springer, 'This is a Riot You're In', p. 440.
51. Ibid. p. 440.
52. West, *The Day of the Locust*, p. 12.
53. Ibid. p. 13.

54. Ibid. p. 63.
55. Ibid. p. 27.
56. Kilston, *Sun Seekers*, p. 9.
57. Ibid. p. 15.
58. West, *The Day of the Locust*, p. 40.
59. Ibid. p. 30.
60. Ibid. p. 47.
61. Ibid. p. 52.
62. Ibid. p. 79.
63. Ibid. p. 88.
64. Ibid. p. 90.
65. Ibid. p. 95.
66. Ibid. p. 99.
67. Ibid. p. 109.
68. Ibid. p. 107.
69. Ibid. p. 113.
70. Ibid. p. 14.
71. Ibid. p. 3.
72. Ibid. p. 16.
73. Ibid. p. 129.
74. Ibid. p. 129.
75. Rosten, *Hollywood*, p. 20.
76. Ibid. p. 20.
77. Ibid. p. 21.
78. West, *The Day of the Locust*, p. 153.
79. Ibid. p. 153.
80. Ibid. p. 154.
81. Ibid. p. 154.
82. Ibid. p. 155.
83. Ibid. p. 159.
84. Ibid. p. 161.
85. Ibid. p. 163.
86. As noted in Chapter 2, Joan Wylie Hall ('Fallen Eden') has noted similarities between the work of Jackson and West.

# 4

# Fallen Stars in *Sunset Boulevard* (1950) and *What Ever Happened to Baby Jane* (1962)

One of the most affecting scenes in *Sunset Boulevard* (1950) begins when Norma Desmond's car pulls up at the gates of Paramount Studios. Norma (Gloria Swanson) is there to visit an old friend, director Cecil B. DeMille. The vehicle is driven by her retainer Max (Erich von Stroheim). By Norma's side sits her lover Joe Gillis (William Holden), a cynical screenwriter. Like Joe, we suspect that Norma's visit will not end well. *Salome*, the script she believes will serve as the perfect vehicle for her triumphant 'return', is terrible, despite Joe's half-hearted edits. What's more, although still beautiful, Norma is fifty: too old to play a young seductress. We watch with the expectation that this encounter will fatally undermine her unrealistic expectations of reignited stardom.

Things get off to a rocky start when a young security guard fails to recognise Norma. However, his older colleague intervenes and respectfully waves them through. Norma grandly sweeps into DeMille's soundstage. Once on set, she is warmly greeted by her old friend. DeMille even ushers her into his director's chair, telling her to watch as he supervises a rehearsal (in fact, he's checking to see who has been calling her on his behalf). As Norma settles into her temporary throne, she disdainfully pushes away a boom mike (a reminder that she blames the coming of sound for ending her career). Then, a lighting technician in the rafters trains his spotlight upon her. For a moment, Norma bathes in its incandescent glow, every inch the screen goddess. A ripple of excitement runs through the soundstage and she is soon surrounded by adoring onlookers. For an instant, her dreams of a glorious Hollywood homecoming almost seem a reality.

The spell is quickly broken. DeMille discreetly orders that the spotlight instead be pointed, 'Where it's needed.' Although he treats Norma with dignity, he obviously has no intention of working with her ever again. DeMille's career is still going strong, but his former protégée will never work in Hollywood again. When Norma is escorted outside, it is clear, as it has been throughout the film, that she is unwilling – or unable – to assimilate into her personal reality any information which conflicts with her own delusional fantasies. Final, mortifying confirmation of the visit's failure comes when Max tells Joe that the phone calls Norma has been receiving from Paramount were entirely unrelated to her screenplay (one of DeMille's underlings wanted to hire her antique car). The Queen of the Silent Screen has been sent back into humiliating exile.

'No one retires voluntarily in Hollywood', observed Leo Rosten in 1941.[1] Hollywood has left Norma behind, but the same cannot be said in reverse. Having once been lauded for her youth, beauty and magnetism, she cannot accept that her cultural and commercial cachet has been fatally eroded. The consequences of this refusal to face reality make *Sunset Boulevard* a 'definitive Hollywood Horror movie', as Richard Corliss has described it.[2] He notes that:

> Practically everything about this final Brackett-Wilder collaboration is ghoulish. The film is narrated by a corpse that is waiting to be fished out of a swimming pool. Most of it takes place in an old dark house that opens its doors only to the walking dead. The first time our doomed hero enters the house, he is mistaken for an undertaker. Soon after, another corpse is buried – that of a pet monkey, in a white coffin. Outside the house is the swimming pool, at first filled only with rats, and 'the ghost of a tennis court'. The only musical sound in the house is that of the wind, wheezing through the broken pipes of a huge old organ.[3]

Both *Sunset Boulevard* and *What Ever Happened to Baby Jane* (1962) reflect Hollywood's often difficult post-war era. As Reni Celeste noted in 2005:

> Film has only in the past fifty years aged sufficiently for the medium to reflect on its own relation to death. Films such as *Sunset Boulevard* (1950) and *Whatever Happened to Baby Jane?* (1962) were not possible before the 1950s. Even though disaster was a critical component of modern stardom from the beginning, and suicide, murder and accidental death intrinsic parts of celebrity, it was not until the 1950s that the aging process of the first generation of stars exposed a glamour worn thin.[4]

In broadly similar ways, they depict the horror and the bitterness that accompanies losing the 'It' factor that once made one a star. What's more, both films also help illustrate an intriguing overlap between the Hollywood Gothic and the classical Gothic tradition.

As David Punter observes of Manfred, the aristocratic villain from Horace Walpole's *The Castle of Otranto* (1764):

What is interesting is the conjunction in Manfred, and after him in so many other Gothic villains, of the feudal baron and the figure of antisocial power. If, as seems likely, the widespread appearance of these figures signifies a social anxiety, then that anxiety clearly had a historical dimension: threat to convention was seen as coming partly from the past, out of the memory of previous social and psychological orders. In other words, it came from the atrophying aristocracy; and if one thing can be said of all the different kinds of fiction which were popular in the later eighteenth century, it is that they consistently played upon the remarkably clear urge of the middle classes to read about aristocrats. *Otranto*'s strength and resonance derive largely from the fact that in it Walpole evolved a primitive symbolic structure in which to represent uncertainties about the past: its attitude to feudalism is a remarkable blend of admiration, fear and curiosity.[5]

The 'Fallen Star' variety of the Hollywood Gothic presents us with a California-specific variation upon this classical Gothic trope. Like Manfred and the dastardly aristocrats who followed in his wake, the spectre of the forgotten or disgraced former star taps into a welter of powerful anxieties. These include uneasiness about the rapidity with which the ingénue becomes the 'has-been', anxieties about female aging and the perceived malleability of the female body, and apprehension about the psychological ramifications of privileged lifestyles founded upon an individual's ability to convincingly play 'make-believe'. The Hollywood Gothic also taps into the broader perception of California as both a land of opportunity and a place where those same dreams, once achieved, immediately become corrupted and corrupting.

Seen through Punter's eighteenth-century Gothic lens, Norma Desmond is a 'threat to convention' because she refuses to accept that her time at the top of her industry's social and economic order has ended. Like Baby Jane Hudson, she is an extreme representative of Hollywood's 'atrophying aristocracy'. Just as the middle classes in the eighteenth and nineteenth centuries loved to read about aristocrats, so too has the public long devoured stories of Hollywood excess and extravagance. The combination of 'admiration, fear and curiosity' Punter identifies within Walpole's attitude towards feudalism aptly describes how Billy Wilder's film depicts Norma. Although she is dangerously insecure and incorrigibly narcissistic, Norma is also someone whom we (and even her victim, Joe) can feel sympathy for. There's a crazed magnificence about her which explains why she became such a big star in the first place.

Drawing upon Rosten, Kevin Starr has also discussed the similarities between Golden Age movie stardom and European nobility: 'Hollywood was a caste apart, fed clothed and housed specially: allowed broad latitude in sexual conduct, marriage and divorce; required only to remain young, glamorous and on view. Hollywood stars thus became an aristocracy, American style.'[6] For Rosten, this 'aristocracy of wealth' was inhabited by a '*nouveau riche*' who were 'young, untrained in the art of the good life, untempered by old codes of behavior'.[7] He argues that this 'aristocratic' role encouraged 'a certain amount of philandering' because whilst 'the nobility of a society are expected to symbolize its virtues, they are also tacitly charged with the duty of violating the stricter taboos from time to time'.[8]

Writing about the establishment of the 'Star System' in *Hollywood Babylon* (1975), Kenneth Anger characterised the 'somewhat disreputable movie performers' who 'found themselves propelled to adulation, fame and fortune' in the late teens and early 1920s as 'the new royalty, the Golden People. Some managed to cope and took it in their stride: some did not.'[9] *Hollywood Babylon* breathlessly detailed a wealth of sensationalist, sexually explicit and humiliating episodes. Many of Anger's most extreme examples involved past-their-best stars whose appetite for sex, drugs or alcohol and inability to cope with life out of the spotlight is said to have led to their deaths.[10]

As Anne Helen Petersen notes, Anger's volume began as a money-making exercise intended to raise capital for his next experimental movie, and 'the salaciousness, the blatant regurgitation of long-dispelled Hollywood rumors, was what resulted in the book's initial ban in the United States and perhaps contributed to its subsequent popularity'.[11] Plumber-turned-comedian Roscoe Arbuckle's rapid fall from grace is given top billing, as the incident which linked Hollywood with 'scandal in the minds of millions'.[12] Whilst researching the book, Anger reportedly

> Pored through newspaper clippings, police files, court reports and mortuary records, he also spoke to butlers, maids, make-up artists, designers, publicists, stand-ins, has-beens, would-have-beens and never-beens: the grapevine. Hollywood did not close ranks to protect the culpable. Old rivalries and jealousies were dragged out of dark corners.[13]

In a chapter entitled 'The New Gods', Anger discusses the lavish spending and opulent tastes attributed to the stars of the 'Roaring Twenties'. Gloria Swanson, pictured in a magnificent flapper-style headdress, is quoted:

> In those days the public wanted us to live like Kings and Queens. So we did – and why not? We were in love with life. We were making more money that we ever dreamed existed and there was no reason to believe it would ever stop.[14]

Manifestations of the 'atmosphere of staggering luxury' include cars, boats and lavishly idiosyncratic homes:

> Spanish-Moorish dream castles like Valentino's hilltop Falcon Lair, with its black marble, black leather bedroom; Marion Davies' hundred-room ocean house at Santa Monica with its all-gold salon, two bars, private movie theater, old masters, and huge marble-bridge-spanned swimming pool: Pola Negri's Roman plunge in her living room and Barbara La Marr's enormous sunken bath with its gold fixtures in her all-onyx bathroom; Harold Lloyd's Greenacres, a forty-room fortress with fountains to rival Tivoli.[15]

As outlined by Petersen, *Hollywood Babylon* was first published in a more outré (and potentially libellous) French edition in 1959, and then 'toned down' and updated for US publication in 1975.[16] It begins with a quote from Aleister Crowley ('Every Man and every Woman is a Star') and a detailed description of D. W. Griffith's 'pasteboard Babylon'. This 'make-believe mirage of Mesopotamia dropped down on the sleepy huddle of mission-style bungalows amid the orange groves that made up 1915 Hollywood', is characterised as a 'portent of things to come'.[17] His final chapter, 'Hollywoodämmerung', opens with a close-up of Marilyn Monroe's corpse and the flat declaration: 'By the sixties, Old Hollywood had died.'[18] A succession of equally degrading and ignominious late 1960s deaths is then outlined, amongst them the demise of the once 'dazzling' Jayne Mansfield who 'career on the skids, crashes to oblivion in June 1967'; the premature passing of some former child actors; silent film star Ramon Novarro's grisly murder; and the accidental overdose of Judy Garland. As Alice L. Hutchison notes, in *Hollywood Babylon*, 'Hollywood's crisis served to intensify the myth and nostalgia for it at the height of its glamour.'[19]

Inevitably (especially given Anger's acquaintance with Manson acolyte Bobby Beausoleil), the horrific murder of Sharon Tate and her houseguests is cited, albeit briefly:

> The '69 Tate massacre was not Old Hollywood. What befell the red house on Cielo Drive resembled the devastation caused by a jet plane crash: the Bad Ship Lollypop piloted by Uncle Sugar. Charlie Manson – programmed puppet, *deus ex-garbage can.*[20]

The book's acidic commentary on Judy Garland's death places pictures of the star in her fresh-faced 1940s prime opposite a full-page image of the star in emaciated middle age. Anger's account of Garland's heart-breaking decline casts the industry as a succubus which feeds upon the young. He also evokes the fate of the doomed 'immortal' goddess in H. Rider Haggard's 1887 classic, *She*: 'She was *hundreds* of years old, the oldest star ever, if you count emotional years, the toll they take, dramas galore for a dozen lifetimes. She was "She", who had stepped into the Flame once too often.'[21]

Anger concludes with images intended to further chronicle Hollywood's present-day decline: the recently restored Hollywood sign (he notes that the 'LAND' has rotted away, so that 'new generations' will no longer be aware of what the sign originally said); the 'empty stages' at Columbia; and another salacious full-spread image: Jayne Mansfield's Chihuahua lying dead in the debris of the car crash which also killed its owner.

Anger's portrait of Hollywood as an industry – and a place – that was on the skids was anticipated by Wilder's film. It may also in part explain Anger's frequent references to Swanson: the movie anticipated many of his own themes. *Sunset Boulevard* is, first and foremost, a film about Hollywood's complex relationship with its own past. It was produced at a time when the industry was in a state of economic and creative crisis. In his chapter on the darkening of Hollywood's 'self-reflexive' tradition, Vincent Brook compares *Sunset Boulevard* with a more optimistic portrait of the industry also released in the early 1950s: *Singin' in the Rain* (1952). Both films, he says,

> reflect, though in opposite ways, the postwar crisis in the movie industry. During Hollywood's 'Golden Age' (1930–46), movies not only rode out the Depression and World War II but experienced their greatest box-office boom. After the war the situation was reversed. [. . .] Hollywood underwent near financial collapse. Owing to a variety of factors – suburbanization, the Baby Boom, the forced divestiture of studio-owned theaters, and, most devastatingly, the advent of television – domestic movie attendance dropped by 50% from the late 1940s to the mid-1950s [. . .] *Sunset Boulevard*'s response to the industry's decline was to view it through a glass darkly, in the process producing one of the first film noirs about Hollywood. *Singin' in the Rain* chose to hype Hollywood with Hollywood. By parodying an earlier industrial crisis – the late-1920s transition to sound, from which the Golden Age emerged – it posited a 1950s overcoming of adversity and a triumphant return to form.[22]

Whilst *Singin' in the Rain* therefore presents us with a very 1950s take on industry woes at the end of the silent era, *Sunset Boulevard* is set in the present and focuses upon a faded star unable to acknowledge her own obsolescence.

Although the character has become a shorthand descriptor for a certain kind of ageing female has-been, Norma Desmond, like the star who played her, was only middle-aged at the time. When Joe castigates her towards the end of the film, he even points this out: 'Norma, you're a woman of fifty. Now grow up! There's nothing tragic about being fifty, not unless you're try-ing to be twenty-five.' Certainly, the actress is past the first flush of youth, but she cannot be considered *old*, nor could the woman who played her: Swanson looked younger than her age. As a result, 'To convey the physical trauma Desmond faces, which is not immediately visually perceptible, she must *tell* Joe of the line on her neck, the damage to her hands, and the problems with the space around her eyes, since none is visible to viewers.'[23] The detail emphasises that Norma's gender has surely contributed to her reluctant exile. Indeed, Max (who was once her husband and director) recalls discovering her when she was only sixteen, meaning that Norma has already been in Hollywood for over thirty years. But although she is only fifty, in an industry founded upon youth and novelty there is no place left for this icon of an earlier age. Despite her deluded efforts, Norma is irretrievably associated with Hollywood's past rather than the endlessly percolating present.

Norma is also not the only casualty of 'progress'. DeMille is still work-ing (as was the case in real life), but the film situates him as a rare survivor of a bygone age. Like her fellow 'Waxworks' – the other forgotten stars of the 1920s with whom she plays bridge (played by real-life legends Buster Keaton, Anna Q. Nilsson and H. B. Warner), Norma was apparently possessed of a type of celebrity tied to a specific time. Max's ignominious latter-day date sug-gests it isn't only actors who can be left behind: directors also fall from grace if they have linked their fortunes to someone whose star billing cannot be maintained indefinitely. Norma's part-insane, part-heroic refusal to accept her fate ultimately transforms her into a classic Gothic villain.

Within the modern American Gothic and horror tradition, characters such as Norma who inhabit their own private worlds often pose a threat to the safety of those who wander into their orbit. One classic example is Norman Bates, as he was originally depicted in Robert Bloch's 1959 novel *Psycho*, a middle-aged loser whose repression of his own sexual impulses is so power-ful that he generates a violently misogynistic alter-ego. Then there is Shirley Jackson's most dangerously wayward protagonist: family annihilator Merricat Blackwood in *We Have Always Lived in the Castle* (1962). Merricat has already murdered (almost) her entire family before the novel even begins. By the denouement, she has finally achieved her dream of living in absolute isolation with her beloved older sister. It is a disturbing fantasy of the desire for absolute stasis fulfilled.

The dangers of arrested development also loom large in the backwoods horror sub-genre, which is characterised by violent encounters between char-acters tied to one specific locale (as is Norma) and those who, like Joe Gillis, are 'just passing through'. Norma's mansion may not be a run-down Texan farmhouse, but it *is* a residence inhabited by someone who, like director Tobe Hooper's characters in *The Texas Chainsaw Massacre* (1974), is infatuated with an industry that no longer wants her – the film business in her case; and the meat industry in theirs. Like her Texan counterparts, Norma is also a nostalgic packrat with a distinctive sense of personal style, although her tastes run more to marble and black velvet than the couches made from human bones favoured by the Texans. A description of the entrance hall to her mansion is provided in the March 1949 version of the screenplay: 'It is grandiose and grim. The whole place is one of those abortions of silent-picture days, with bowling alleys in the cellar and a built-in pipe organ, and beams imported from Italy, with California termites working on them.'[24] Particularly interesting is the mention of showy European luxury (beams from Italy) and their destruction by California's inhospitable insect population – to repurpose Joan Didion, it is as if the 'graft' did not quite take.[25]

Finally, both Norma and her country cousins fatally entrap naive outsiders experiencing car trouble (or rather, as in *The Texas Chainsaw Massacre*, van trouble). Joe only ends up on Norma's doorstep because he is trying to avoid having his car taken away by repo men: 'If I lose my car it's like having my legs cut off', he tells his agent. The sight of Norma's 'great big empty garage' draws him to her property, and then into her life. As Neil Sinyard and Adrian Turner observe, 'Joe's experience in the film can be interpreted as a series of failed escape plans', and the fate of his car is a key symbolic reference point.[26] Noting that it is repossessed anyway, they argue that this humiliation parallels 'Joe's emasculation as Norma begins to direct the rest of his life'.[27] From that point onwards, whenever Joe leaves the house, he is either on foot or being driven by Max. It is an ignominious situation for any young man in early 1950s LA, which already had a fiercely car-centred culture. When Joe does leave for good, it is in the back of a hearse. For him, the road to Sunset Boulevard was always a dead end. Sinyard and Turner also see Norma's 'magnificent old car, synonymous with the extravagant twenties but now antiquated and bizarre on its blocks' as a 'visual anticipation of Norma herself, just as the "cheap new thing" is analogous to Joe and the role he is about to play in Norma's life'.[28] Stalled and rotting vehicles are also a key visual signifier within the backwoods horror movie. *The Texas Chainsaw Massacre* was the first film to use the climactic discovery of the 'car graveyard' (a collection of crudely concealed vehicles obviously belonging to previous victims) as a plot point, but it certainly wouldn't be the last.

It wouldn't be entirely accurate, however, to say that Norma Desmond exists in a state of *absolute* delusion (at least not until the film's final moments). She knows she must engage with the world beyond her driveway if she is to have any hope of recapturing her glory days (as evidenced by the trip to Paramount and the impulsive decision to hire Joe). However, these interactions are both carried out on her terms. Throughout the film – as is underlined by the remarkable closing sequence – Norma expects the world to shape itself around her. And why wouldn't she? She has been granted almost everything she could wish for, in material terms at least. Norma has more money than she can spend thanks to investments rooted in LA's other major boom industries, oil and real estate: 'I own three blocks downtown. I have oil in Bakersfield – pumping, pumping, pumping. What's it for but to buy us anything we want?' she tells Joe.

Norma's greatest possession is her gloomily magnificent mansion. It is described in the script as 'a grandiose, Italianate structure, mottled by the years, gloomy, forsaken, the little formal garden gone completely to seed'.[29] As Sam Staggs chronicles, Wilder and his screenwriting partner, Charles Brackett, had a character – Norma – long before they had any other firm idea. Key to their conception of Norma was the place most associated with the character:

> They envisioned the movie queen sealed away in an immense run-down mansion on Sunset Boulevard; both men had seen such places, they beheld her dusty mementoes, her clutter of furniture sufficient for a remake of *Intolerance*, and they saw the nice young man, maybe from the Midwest, down on his luck, unable to make it in Hollywood.[30]

Additionally, they already also knew how their picture was going to end: 'We had not written the third act yet, but we knew they fished him out of a pool.'[31]

The exterior used for Norma's house was a derelict mansion J. Paul Getty purchased for one of his former wives: it was demolished in 1957.[32] Staggs notes that it become one of the

> most famous shelters in film history, ranking with Tara, Manderley, and the Victorian pile behind the Bates Motel. How appropriate, given Norma's delusions, that her place didn't really exist. Or rather, it existed only in fragments, and they were scattered all over Los Angeles.[33]

As Rosten had observed over a decade before the film was released:

> In Hollywood, as Istanbul or Sioux Falls, the rich hasten to express their wealth, and betray their fitful groping for status, by erecting homes of unnecessary magnitude and splendor. For wealth is a psychological sovereignty, and those within its boundaries live in obligatory palaces.[34]

He notes that Hollywood's 'first batch of movie *arrivistes*' 'built big mansions, fine gardens, and filled their chalets with costly paraphernalia'.[35] DeMille, Mary Pickford, Harold Lloyd, Charlie Chaplin and Carl Laemmle are name-checked, and the architectural influence of William Randolph Hearst's San Simeon is discussed: 'he dazzled their eyes with the magniloquence of his life and the princely abandon of his expenditure'.[36] However, Rosten also notes that as of the early 1940s, architectural trends in the movie colony veered away from this kind of flashy excess:

> The newer movie homes are not exactly modest, but they strive for comfort and graciousness [. . .] It is almost certain that the architectural *faux pas* of the past will not be repeated. The movie people have learned to snicker at Byzantine portals and Moorish patios, they have learned that marble halls and manicured lawns involve exorbitant upkeep, and that taxes, public opinion, and the vicissitudes of movie success conspire to make palaces mock those who built them.[37]

Norma's mansion is therefore another reminder of how out of step she is with contemporary industry mores. The white elephant is inhabited mainly by herself and Max (except for Joe and the chimp, who both die there). The symbolic connection between a house and the psychological state of its inhabitants long-associated with the wider Gothic tradition is obviously perpetuated here: 'Her over-decorated house is an extension of her personality. Norma is wealthy and reclusive, delusional and tragic.'[38] It is also a residence that looked outmoded to contemporary audiences: 'To postwar sensibilities the house looked sinister because of age and heft. In that split-level era when the suburban box was the dream of every family [. . .] old Palazzo like Norma's held value only for the land it occupied.'[39]

In *Sunset Boulevard*, Hollywood also meditates upon the relationship between post-war present and the not-so-distant past by depicting a neglected icon who has become a reluctant casualty of precisely this variety of cultural and historical amnesia, and hunger for what is new. The decision to cast Swanson, a true icon of the silent era, underlines the sheer recency of both American California and of Hollywood as an industry. In his account of Swanson's return to Los Angeles after many happy years in New York, Staggs imagines her resurrecting 'the ghost of young Los Angeles, little more than a country town when Swanson first arrived and now a somewhat sinister world city in the sunshine. And hovering everywhere, the ghost of an earlier self, sure to be encountered at all the wrong moments.'[40] He notes that when Swanson returned in 1949, the state was celebrating the centennial of the Gold Rush.[41]

A background detail which slyly highlights the link between Norma's fate and post-war California's relationship with its own history is the oil painting which conceals her movie projection screen. It is described in the script as a 'big Gold Rush painting' of the 'Carthay Circle School'. As Phoebe S. Kropp notes in her study of Californian culture and memory:

> For some, California history had its genesis in Anglo-Americans' arrival on the scene, which was an open invitation for pioneer stories. Gold Rush stories were the most popular of these origin myths, although these stories centered primarily on Northern California.[42]

Norma's painting, as it is referenced in the script, directly mentions this origin story and its present-day commodification by business interests, with Joe (as in the film's version of the scene) wryly speculating that the painting was presented to her by 'some Nevada Chamber of Commerce'. The detail intersects with a process which was then happening on a local, real-world level. Brook describes one of the ways in which Hollywood attempted to counter its post-war decline by turning to its own history:

> The Hollywood Chamber of Commerce, in an attempt to rebrand the movie capital's image and its tourist appeal, countered with a double whammy of its own: renovation and official abridgement of the Hollywood (née Hollywoodland) sign in 1949, and the inauguration of the Walk of Fame along Hollywood Boulevard and Vine Street in 1958.[43]

The script's sarcastic allusion to 'the Carthay Circle School' is also more than a passing local reference. Carthay Circle was a Spanish revival community established in the early 1920s, which had as its chief feature the Carthay Circle Theatre.[44] Opened in 1926 and demolished in 1969, its celebrated interior 'was a tribute to the early years of California's history, featuring murals illustrating pioneer times by Frank Tenney Johnson and California impressionist Alson Skinner Clark'.[45] Johnson's depiction of the Donner Party adorned the Carthay's curtain: 'Furthermore, the movie shown on opening night was Cecil B. DeMille's *The Volga Boatman*.'[46] The authors of *Theatres in Los Angeles* (2008) note the irony of the fact that 'a theatre that paid such lovely tribute to California's history would become a casualty of the city's lack of respect for its past'.[47] Although Norma's painting in the film is instead a portrait of a Native American chief astride a horse, painted in a style reminiscent of Johnson (who was famed for nostalgic portraits of the 'Old West') it is another reminder that modern-day California was forcibly imposed upon an Indigenous civilisation that was nearly destroyed in the process.

The projector screen concealed behind the painting in the film is another reminder of ephemerality: the 'moving picture' displaced earlier modes of visual representation.[48] Norma, who frequently deploys the gesture-heavy and exaggerated facial expressions associated with silent-movie acting, is herself often framed by Wilder as if she is a figure in a tableau (as in the 'We didn't need dialogue. We had faces!' tirade at the end of this same scene). The conceit suggests a similarity between herself and the romanticised figure in the painting. Both are implicitly seen as belonging to a bygone era of Californian history and have been immortalised by a medium that has itself been superseded.

Although Norma Desmond is the character with whom the film is most infatuated, Joe is the one from whose perspective events unfold. This is highlighted in *Sunset Boulevard*'s famous opening sequence, in which his body floats in Norma's pool as reporters and detectives rush to the scene. Joe's post-mortem voiceover tells us that:

> A murder has been reported from one of those great big houses in the ten thousand block. You'll read about it in the late editions, I'm sure. You'll get it over your radio, see it on television, because an old-time star is involved. One of the biggest [. . .] You see, the body of a young man was found floating in the pool of her mansion, with two shots in his back and one in his stomach. Nobody important, really. Just a movie writer with a couple of B-pictures to his credit. The poor dope. He always wanted a pool. Well, in the end, he got himself a pool – only the price turned out to be a little high.

Joe is another iteration of an important character type already mentioned frequently in this volume: the Midwesterner who pays a high price for their Golden State ambitions. Joe tells us that prior to coming to Hollywood, he worked on a small-town newspaper in Ohio. Despite a few minor credits, this gamble has not paid off. As we flashback to six months earlier, we find him in seedy lodgings. Joe presents his former self as a struggling young writer who 'seemed to have lost his touch'. He's three payments behind on his car, and none of his writing projects seem to be in any danger of taking off. The response he gets when he drops in on a Paramount producer who has helped him out before suggests that he hasn't been producing quality material of late. The producer's forthright script reader, Betty Schaefer (Nancy Olson) calls Joe's new movie treatment 'flat and trite'. His situation has similarities to Tod Hackett's in *The Day of the Locust*. They are both driven young men who came to Hollywood to profit from their artistic endeavours, but find out the hard way that it is much tougher to survive in Los Angeles than they expected.

Joe also has a little in common with Homer Simpson. As West's novel and Wilder's film near their end, both men are on the verge of returning home for good but are violently prevented from doing so – Homer is attacked by the mob and Joe is killed by Norma.

Joe's economic insecurity kick-starts the chain of events which will lead to his murder. His lack of money and industry status has arguably placed him in a situation analogous to that of the sensitive 'damsel in distress' often found in eighteenth- and nineteenth-century Gothic. Norma may be a has-been, but because of her wealth and property she is still much more powerful than Joe, even if initially it seems as if he will be the one doing the exploiting. Joe enters Norma's orbit as a supplicant (he apologises for hiding his car in her garage) rather than as an equal. The scales never quite swing back in the other direction.

Of course, Joe is convinced that he can manipulate the situation to his own advantage. After Norma asks him to look over her sprawling, handwritten script, he believes that he has cleverly turned the tables when he plants the idea in her head of hiring a professional screenwriter. Free rent, a generous wage and a place in which to lie low for a few weeks seems like a pretty good deal, even if his new employer is clearly eccentric.

The reality, as Joe-from-beyond-the grave is all too aware, is very different: what his previous self didn't realise was that he became a character in a Gothic novel the minute he drove onto Norma's property. As earlier critics have suggested, there are obvious similarities here both to Bram Stoker's *Dracula* (1897) – with Joe as a Jonathan Harker figure, menaced by the predatory aristocrat whose home he has freely entered[49] – and Charles Dickens's *Great Expectations* (1861), with Norma, naturally, serving as a silent-film era Miss Havisham, and Joe as a kind of ultra-sardonic Pip.[50] By the end of both these novels, Harker and Pip have been physically and psychologically devastated by their experiences. Things work out even more poorly for Joe Gillis.

As time passes, Joe unwittingly becomes more and more enfolded into Norma's delusional orbit. First, his belongings are moved from his rented room to her guest apartment without his permission. Next, he is moved to a room in the main house next to Norma's personal suite. Norma then buys him a luxurious new wardrobe. Joe is no longer Norma's employee; he is her consort. Max, we later discover, followed this same trajectory in reverse.

Norma's confinement to the house becomes his. Every escape attempt Joe makes is thwarted – by financial inducement, suicide attempt, blackmail and, eventually, murderous violence. Although fresh hope comes into his life because of his new writing partnership with Betty, he cannot bring himself to make a break with Norma. Interestingly, the women are both deeply embedded in the industry (Betty's parents worked at Paramount), had acting dreams (although Betty never made it past the screen-test) and writing ambitions. However, Betty is associated with wholesomeness and innocence (Joe points out that she's only twenty-two), and has a cheery practicality which highlights Norma's narcissism and instability. Decency and madness are, in a nutshell, Joe's romantic choices, and although he ultimately decides to reject them both in favour of going back to Ohio, the madness wins out. As Sinyard and Turner note: 'When Norma shoots him twice in the back and once in the chest and he crashes into the water, it represents his failure to escape from Hollywood, from Norma's mansion, and from Norma's obsessive fantasy world.'[51]

Right at the start of the film, dead Joe wryly mocks the Hollywood ambitions of his past self: the 'poor sap' who always wanted a pool but ended up dead in one. To add insult to injury, it isn't even his own. Dead Joe knows he will only ever be a footnote to Norma's final, most impactful role: that of the insane movie queen who gunned down her hapless gigolo. The location of Joe's death is also worth noting: as Thomas A. P. van Leeuwen notes, 'The pool as a death trap is a popular trope', and Joe Gillis is by no means the only movie character to lose his life in one.[52] Hollywood and swimming pools were, he states, closely associated right from the start. Water is the 'element of dreams', so

> it is logical to assume that in a world where dreams are manufactured, water is of paramount importance. Thus in Hollywood, a place as dry as the nearby desert, the element appears as a dream living in concrete or plastic containers called private swimming pools. Hollywood, mass producer of popular lifestyles, doused its merchandise with generous qualities of water.[53]

By the 1950s, he continues, 'Los Angeles counted more than one million swimming pools, more than the rest of the United States put together.'[54] Certainly, this trend had much to do with the weather and the economic boom, but it also owed much to the example provided by movie stars, who began installing their own private pools during the 1920s and 1930s. Norma's pool, like her house, also serves as a reflection of her psychological state. Initially empty, derelict and frequented only by rats, she refills it for Joe's benefit once they become romantically involved. Joe's fate also underlines the perils of finding yourself dangerously out of your depth in an element fraught with dangers one has sorely underestimated.

When the police prepare to arrest Norma, she has a final moment in the spotlight. Her slender grasp on reality has entirely given way. The arrival of newsreel cameras provides the ever-faithful Max with the means to lovingly 'direct' her final public appearance. After he readies the cameras and lights,

Max gives Norma her cue: 'This is the staircase of the palace . . .' As the description of this spellbinding moment puts it in the script: 'The cameras grind. Everyone watches in awe.' As Norma slowly descends the staircase with uncanny, insane poise, she is swept away by self-aggrandising but apparently genuine emotion. 'You see, this is my life. It always will be. There's nothing else – just us and the cameras and those wonderful people out there in the dark . . . All right, Mr DeMille, I'm ready for my close-up.'

## 'You Weren't Ugly Then: I Made You That Way': The Corruption of Innocence in *What Ever Happened to Baby Jane?*

*Sunset Boulevard* and *What Ever Happened to Baby Jane?* traverse similar thematic territory, which is why Robert Aldrich's 1962 film has often been character-ised as a cruder, crueller imitation of its 1950 predecessor.[55] Their common ingredients include a forgotten female star possessed by unrealistic dreams of a comeback and the fact that the primary location is an outmoded mansion. The main character's attempts to cling to her youthful looks are again a signifier of her inability to accept the reality of her diminished present-day status. Both films also dramatise toxic co-dependence and feature opportunistic male enablers. They both conclude with an impulsive act of murder, and in the final moments of each film, the woman who has committed the crime becomes completely detached from reality, as witnessed by a crowd of onlookers.

Despite these overlaps, there remains much of interest and originality in *Baby Jane*. In part, this is because the film's deranged antagonist displays behaviour which makes Norma Desmond look positively restrained. Baby Jane Hudson (Bette Davis) is an alcoholic, foul-mouthed and deluded grotesque, whilst *Sunset Boulevard*'s fallen star retains her grandeur and charisma a generation after her heyday. *Baby Jane* also revolves around someone who was already a scandalous has-been in her early twenties. More than its predecessor, *Baby Jane* is a film about corrupted innocence. The ways in which show business exploits the young and warps their sense of self is a core facet of the movie's sardonic depiction of life after the cameras have stopped rolling.

Like Henry Farrell's source novel of the same name (1960), the movie opens during the childhood of sisters Jane and Blanche (Joan Crawford): the start date is 1908 in the novel, and 1917 in the film. The prologue sets up the mutually harmful dynamic which will forever define their relationship. 'Baby Jane' is the stage name of Jane Hudson, 'the Diminutive Dancing Duse from Duluth', a show business prodigy whose fame is such that she has her own line of look-alike dolls. The dolls tell us that the childhood of this precocious youngster has already been commodified. However, whilst dolls are inherently malleable, passive objects, the *real* Baby Jane's behaviour suggests that she will not be so easily controlled by others.

The blonde-haired, ringlet-sporting moppet is first glimpsed singing and dancing onstage as her parents watch from the wings. Younger sister Blanche stands resentfully by their side. Responding to popular demand, Jane performs her signature tune, 'I've Written a Letter to Daddy'. She is joined onstage by her father, the enabler behind her rise to show business glory (there's a sense here of unhealthy attachment on both sides). Backstage, the saccharine-seeming young star is anything but sweet. When denied an ice cream, Jane reminds her parents who is really in charge: 'I make the money so I can have whatever I want!' In a family where everyone's livelihood depends upon the celebrity of a little girl, the usual conventions of the parent/child relationship have been overthrown. The star must be given what she wants. Again, the parallels with Norma are evident, but the impact is heightened here because the entitled Diva here hasn't even hit puberty yet.

However, Baby Jane is not the only forgotten celebrity in Aldrich's film. The opening scene is largely relayed to us from Blanche's resentful perspective. Tellingly, Mrs Hudson (Anne Barton) clearly sympathises with her, saying: 'You're the lucky one Blanche, really you are. Someday it's going to be you who's getting all the attention.' She asks that Blanche be kinder to her father and sister when that day comes than they have been to her, but the damage has already been done. Both the Hudson girls have, in their own way, been warped by show business, and Jane's sanity will not survive the transition from vaudeville glory to post-Hollywood obscurity.

The path taken by the sisters – who move from small-town stage to the big screen – recalls the route taken by some of the greatest Hollywood stars of the 1920s and 1930s. Most notably, their trajectory evokes Judy Garland's beginnings as a performer in a family troupe. Like Duluth-born Baby Jane, Garland was also originally from Minnesota. Mention of Duluth also reminds us that what we have here is another Hollywood resident with Midwestern roots.

The next scene in the film, set in 1935, shows us that Mrs Hudson's prediction has come true. Blanche is the one getting all the attention and her sister's screen career is tanking. It opens as Jane's latest performance is being scrutinised by two scathing male executives: 'She stinks, doesn't she?' The fact that the briefly glimpsed movie they are watching is composed of snippets from two of Bette Davis's real-life films, means that, as in *Sunset Boulevard*, the screen history of the actress playing the lead role lends a meta-resonance to the proceedings. However, in *Sunset Boulevard* we see Norma raptly admiring her own performance from the comfort of her living room. It is an exercise in narcissism and nostalgia. The clip that we see is enough to show us that in her 1920s heyday, Swanson/Desmond was possessed of obvious charisma and beauty. Norma may be a deluded eccentric, but she clearly deserved to be a star. The same, importantly, cannot be said of Jane Hudson. As Peter Shelley notes, we see too little of her/Davis's performance to be able to glean any insight into its quality, but the reaction of the men watching it leaves us in no doubt that both she and the film are a disaster.[56] The 'phenomenon' who was once 'known everywhere' (as Farrell's novel puts it) has grown up to be a 'no talent broad' whose career depends upon the generosity of her sister.[57] What's more, Jane's bad behaviour off-screen is a problem (a reminder that the morality clauses associated with the Hays Code were in effect by this time). Blanche is 'the biggest thing in movies', but her insistence that Jane also has to have her own star vehicles is characterised as benevolent but foolish: 'She should have enough sense to know that she can't make a star out of Baby Jane again.'

Later that same night, Blanche is run down by her own car, pinned against the wrought iron gates of her new home. Although we do not see the identity of the driver, the framing implies that resentful family 'bad girl' Jane has caused the accident. The house in which the sisters will spend the next forty years is, we are told, 'a tremendous palace Valentino used to have', described in the script as 'a Spanish-style house'. Like Norma's mansion, the Hudson home is associated with the ostentatious European-style opulence of the silent era. The atmospheric titles return to the image of a shattered Baby Jane doll, making explicit the connection between the toxic commodification of the child star and the shattered body – in Blanche's case – and mind – in Jane's – of the little girls seen in the prologue.

In Shelley's history of 'Hag Horror' (2009), *Baby Jane*, like *Sunset Boulevard*, is cited as a foundational movie. He characterises 'Grande Dame Guignol' as a sub-genre of the wider genres of 'crime, drama, film-noir, horror, mystery, and thriller'. It is said to focus on an older female character (often played by an actress who 'has not worked in some time' or is in her last starring role) and deploys the shock tactics associated with the Grand Guignol. The 'Grande Dames' in such films, he notes, tend to fall into two major categories:

> The role the actress plays in Grande Dame Guignol either presents her as a mentally unstable antagonist or the Woman in Peril protagonist. The grande dame as unstable antagonist may pine for a lost youth and glory, or she may be trapped in idealized memories of childhood, with a trauma that haunts her past. She is akin to Miss Havisham in Charles Dickens's *Great Expectations*, her adult life wasted as she rots away in her unused wedding dress in her room. Like a ghost, the grande dame cannot rest until the

unbalance of the universe is corrected. A refusal to accept reality and the natural process of life exemplifies the fear of aging and death, and implicitly a fear of women.[58]

The most interesting of these films, he continues, 'have characters that possess both these qualities' – who are both antagonist and protagonist.[59] He observes of *Baby Jane* that initially we see

> Bette Davis as the antagonist, tormenting her relatively normal but physi-
> cally disabled protagonist sister Crawford. However, the climax reveals that
> Crawford became disabled when she tried to seek revenge on Davis when
> they were younger. This plot twist makes us re-evaluate Crawford as an
> antagonist and the revelation turns Davis into a passive child, victimized
> and insane.[60]

Shelley makes an important point here. It is ultimately made clear that both Blanche and Jane have behaved badly. When their core personalities were still being formed, Jane's star billing meant that she was allowed to become a spoiled and controlling brat whilst her neglected sister quietly seethed. However, although Blanche isn't entirely blameless, her historical misdeeds pale next to the murderous excesses of Jane. Blanche may have impulsively tried to run down Jane after her drunken sister yet again humiliated her in public, but she clearly has been wracked with guilt ever since, and she was also left unable to walk when her act of rage backfired. Jane is an emotionally and physically abusive sadist. She even beats Blanche's devoted maid Elvira (Maidie Norman) to death with a hammer. The fact that Elvira is Black adds to the sadistic resonance of the scene. She displays great courage in standing up to her cruel white employer, whilst Jane's ruthless brutality suggests that in some subliminal way she always saw 'the help' as disposable.

Jane's inability to move on partially explains why she has become such a toxic, violent adult. As is the case with Benjie Weiss, the child star in *Maps to the Stars* (2014), which will be discussed in the next chapter, Baby Jane is the hapless but dangerous victim of an industry which discarded her when she was no longer needed. The damage done to the young adult who finds herself elevated to unthinkable stardom is bad enough (we might recall that Norma Desmond is said to have been discovered when she was only sixteen), but these pressures are even more pronounced for a younger child. It's another Hollywood Gothic subtext anticipated by *The Day of the Locust*, in which Adore Loomis – the little boy being groomed for Shirley Temple-style star-dom by his pushy Mama – when he is first introduced, imitates the creature from the 1931 film version of Mary Shelley's *Frankenstein*.[61] Like Shelley's creature, Adore has been 'created' by an insanely ambitious parent. Adore also plays a pivotal role in instigating the riot which explodes at the climax of the novel. His cruel prank – the spark that ignites a riot – may be a way of acting out against the adults he is constantly being coached to 'entertain'.

Part of the reason why Jane is so aggressive towards her now physically disabled sister is down to professional jealousy; Blanche has clearly had a much more successful acting career. Jane was a superstar in vaudeville, but neither her fame nor her talent survived the rocky transition to adulthood. Her exile was hastened by the scandal surrounding her presumed responsibility for Blanche's accident. Although there is a brief reference to an old flame of Blanche's in the novel, the film does not say whether either of the sisters have ever been married. It is likely that since the accident, they have each, in their own way, been each other's world, even if Jane has made it an increasingly unpleasant one. Farrell's novel makes it clear that she is not just an abusive drunk, but someone with a serious psychiatric disorder which is only getting worse.[62] In the film, as in the novel, Blanche's willingness to passively tolerate this ill-treatment initially seems baffling (particularly to Elvira). Indeed, the film's basic premise – two sisters, one of them a housebound martyr, the other an unstable psychotic, live a co-dependent existence in a mansion – resembles that of Shirley Jackson's *We Have Always Lived in the Castle* (published in 1962, the year *Baby Jane* was released). However, whereas in Jackson's novel we are only privy to the narrative viewpoint of its unreliable narrator, in *Baby Jane* the perspectives of characters from the outside world also feature.

Indeed, the present-day section of the film – captioned 'Yesterday' – begins as the Hudsons' next-door neighbour Mrs Bates (Anna Lee) and her daughter Liza (B. D. Merrill) watch an old movie starring Blanche. Even though it is punctuated by dog-food commercials, Mrs Bates declares that 'It's still a pretty good picture.' Conversation between mother and daughter turns to speculation about the reclusive celebrity next door. When Liza cattily remarks, 'She must be about 150 by now', Mrs Bates reminds her that Blanche couldn't be much older than herself. It is apparent that contact between the neighbours has been minimal.

We are then introduced to the sisters as they are now. Blanche is in her room watching the same movie, and happily reliving her old role, even if the professional in her cannot help but still second-guess some directorial choices. Suddenly, the door opens and Jane enters, with a scowl on her ludicrously painted face and an omnipresent drink in her hand. Inevitably, she ruins Blanche's moment of contentment by telling her that she is 'an idiot' for watching and switching off the television. Jane is still, we infer, just as spiteful as she was back in her heyday. Thanks to Blanche's disability, she is once again in control, even if her many years as her sister's 'carer' could be seen a form of imprisonment for her too. As is further underlined by the two infamous scenes during which Blanche's food is tampered with (dead parakeet salad, anyone?), her power over Blanche is absolute.

The contrast between the stasis of the lives being led by the Hudson sisters and the busy, conventional lives of their neighbours, heightens our awareness of Jane's growing instability and Blanche's obvious vulnerability. The contrast is also highlighted by the appearance of the Hudson house. As Shelley notes, 'the outmoded set decoration of the house is used as an extension of character'.[63] Wheelchair-user Blanche's room is located on the second floor, but an elevator is never seen or mentioned – an odd detail which adds to our sense of her dependence and isolation.[64] The conceit also leads to the movie's most suspenseful set-piece, during which Blanche crawls with great determination towards the telephone (the scene anticipates kidnap victim Paul Sheldon's similarly pained efforts in Stephen King's 1987 novel, *Misery*).[65]

If Norma Desmond's hopes of a 'return' to the top tier of celebrity seem unrealistic, then Jane Hudson's ambitions are even more deluded. Revealingly, rather than trying to reignite her screen career (possibly because she knows she never had true success there anyway), Jane hopes to bring 'Baby Jane' back by performing in nightclubs and theatres. That a woman in her mid-fifties (Davis was fifty-four at the time, but Jane appears older) believes that anyone would want to see her recreate an act originally performed over forty years before, tells us all we need to know about her tentative grasp on reality. Jane is 'helped' in these ambitions by Edwin Flagg (Victor Buono), whose services as a musical accompanist she secures via a wanted advertisement in a local paper. Edwin is a financially desperate industry hanger-on (his late father was an actor). He still lives with his mother, and we first see him wearing his pyjamas during the day, which suggests that the character is lazy and immature. When Edwin first arrives at the Hudson house, he is taken aback by the bizarre woman who answers the door, but has no idea who she is. As was the case during her earlier trip to the newspaper office, Jane is obliged to identify herself to a stranger: 'I wonder if you can guess who I am?'

Jane's desire to perform again is influenced by the revival of public interest in Blanche and by the discovery that her sister has secretly arranged to sell the house (which belongs to Jane). Her pathetic bid to engineer a comeback can therefore be seen as an effort to regain control by resurrecting the only role in life which has ever brought her recognition and success. It is also implied that Jane's fixation upon her childhood persona is related to an unhealthy relationship with her father. As Shelley notes of their dance onstage at the start of the film, it 'further suggests an inappropriate relationship, since it poses them as a romantic couple, though Jane, as the provider of the family, has, in effect, become an adult figure'.[66] Jane's new costumes, props and the $100 a week she offers Edwin for his services are all paid for with money stolen from Blanche.

Tensions between the two sisters escalate further when Blanche, who is now being deprived of food, searches Jane's room for chocolate and discovers that her own signature is being forged on cheques. She also comes across one of the horror genre's prime visual signifiers of spite: a photograph of herself with the eyes scratched out.

As she prepares for her 'comeback', Jane's abuse of Blanche escalates to outright torture. She beats, starves and imprisons her vulnerable sister. Elvira, as noted earlier, pays for her loyalty with her life. Jane sinks ever deeper into alcoholic self-pity, telling herself, as she pages through an old scrapbook, that 'You could have been better than all of them. But they didn't want that. They just didn't love ya enough.' She coldly dumps Elvira's body in a nearby suburb, but flees when Edwin, who is finally shocked into action after he finds Blanche confined in her bedroom, goes running to the police.

Jane brings Blanche, who is now delirious, to Santa Monica beach, a location she associates with pleasant childhood memories. The film, which has previously mostly taken place in the same few rooms, finally opens up to the natural world, and warm Pacific waves lap against the sand. This is a classic California Gothic dead end. Blanche is obviously in bad shape – she may even be dying – whilst Jane has retreated entirely into her own fantasy world. The impact lies in the sheer incongruity of the scene. Although the sisters arrive at night, as the sun rises the beach fills with a merry assortment of sun worshippers, food vendors and initially unsuspecting police officers. Until a newsflash is heard on the radio, no one even notices the two odd-looking older women sitting on the sand. As in several other narratives discussed in this book, a sunny beachside locale is actively associated with the macabre and the uncanny.

During this scene, Blanche also gives us a reason that explains why she has put up with Jane for all these years. She confesses that she 'crippled myself' when she impulsively tried to run down her drunken sister. Blanche also admits that she only insisted that Jane get movie roles because it made Jane indebted to her – her 'generosity' was really a form of subtle payback for Jane's many childhood tantrums (such as the ice cream episode).

'You weren't ugly then', Blanche declares: 'I made you that way.' Although Blanche's martyr complex is a tad extreme – after all, Jane has just bludgeoned Elvira to death – her admission again makes clear that life in Hollywood has irreparably damaged *both* Hudson sisters. An interesting reading of this same scene by Sally Chivers argues that

> Blanche's confession is not genuine but is instead a ploy to win over Jane to save her own life. The exchange matches previous lies that Blanche has told Jane in an attempt to end Jane's cruelty, and there seems little reason to believe Blanche, now that she is faced with death by starvation or dehydration.[67]

Whatever Blanche's exact motivation, the outcome is the same. Jane's poignant, if unconvincing, suggestion that things could perhaps have been very different between the two of them if only they had been honest with each other – 'You mean all this time we coulda been friends?' – is followed by a characteristically immature attempt to make things right again. In a callback to the opening scene, Jane insists upon buying her semi-conscious sister an ice cream cone. Eventually the nearby police officers recognise Jane's car, realising that a wanted murderer is on the beach. Jane grotesquely pirouettes on the sand as the officers slowly flank her. In the closing moments of *Sunset Boulevard*, Norma Desmond was allowed one final demonstration of her eerie charisma, but the same cannot be said for the Hudson sisters. Jane is finally a demented, homicidal spectacle for an uncomprehending crowd, whilst Blanche lies motionless – perhaps even dead – on the hot sand. Stardom on stage and screen ultimately ruined the lives of both Hudson sisters, setting in motion a decades-long family tragedy which is only now coming to a pathetic close on Santa Monica Beach, as the sun shines cheerily overhead.

## Notes

1. Rosten, *Hollywood*, p. 54.
2. Corliss, *Talking Pictures*, p. 147.
3. Ibid. p. 147.
4. Celeste, 'Screen Idols', p. 32.
5. Punter, *The Literature of Terror*, p. 47.
6. Starr, *Inventing the Dream*, p. 335.
7. Rosten, *Hollywood*, p. 59.
8. Ibid. p. 124.
9. Anger, *Hollywood Babylon*, p. 9.
10. Ibid. p. 6.
11. Petersen, 'What to Do with a Coffin Full of Sugar', p. 82. Petersen's fascinating article discusses Swanson's unsuccessful lawsuit against Anger and his strategically bizarre hate-mail campaign against her.
12. Anger, *Hollywood Babylon*, p. 30.
13. Hutchison, *Kenneth Anger*, p. 198.
14. Ibid. p. 71.
15. Ibid. p. 71.
16. According to Petersen, 'What to Do with a Coffin Full of Sugar', p. 96.
17. Anger, *Hollywood Babylon*, p. 3.
18. Ibid. p. 279.
19. Hutchison, *Kenneth Anger*, p. 200.

20. Anger, *Hollywood Babylon*, p. 286.
21. Ibid. p. 288.
22. Brook, *Land of Smoke and Mirrors*, p. 89.
23. Chivers, 'Baby Jane Grew Up', p. 216.
24. Brackett, Wilder and Marshman, *Sunset Boulevard*, p. 19.
25. Didion, 'Some Dreamers of the Golden Dream', p. 13.
26. Sinyard and Turner, *Journey Down Sunset Boulevard*, p. 275.
27. Ibid. p. 275.
28. Ibid. p. 275.
29. Brackett, Wilder and Marsham, *Sunset Boulevard*.
30. Staggs, *Close-Up on Sunset Boulevard*, p. 25.
31. Quoted in ibid. p. 33.
32. Ibid. p. 83.
33. Ibid. p. 83.
34. Rosten, *Hollywood*, p. 199.
35. Ibid. pp. 200–1.
36. Ibid. p. 204.
37. Ibid. p. 206.
38. Shelley, *Grande Dame Guignol Cinema*, p. 10.
39. Staggs, *Close-Up on Sunset Boulevard*, p. 84.
40. Ibid. p. 55.
41. Ibid. p. 60.
42. Kropp, *California Vieja*, p. 2.
43. Brook, *Land of Smoke and Mirrors*, p. 151.
44. Gebhard and Winter, *An Architectural Guidebook to Los Angeles*, p. 163.
45. Tarbell Cooper, Ronnebeck Hall and Wanamaker, *Theatres in Los Angeles*, p. 55.
46. Ibid. p. 56.
47. Ibid. p. 55.
48. Ames, *Movies About the Movies*, p. 199.
49. Corliss, *Talking Pictures* p. 148. Corliss describes Norma as 'Dracula, or perhaps the Count's older, forgotten sister, condemned to relive a former life, sucking blood from her victim (Holden)'.
50. Sinyard and Turner, *Journey Down Sunset Boulevard*, p. 285: 'There is more than a touch of Miss Havisham about Norma Desmond.'
51. Ibid. p. 282.
52. Van Leeuwen, *The Springboard in the Pond*, p. 156.
53. Ibid. p. 156.
54. Ibid. p. 165.
55. Hereafter I shorten the film title to *Baby Jane*.

56. Shelley, *Grande Dame Guignol Cinema*, p. 24, usefully discusses the real-world contexts of the film clips shown in more detail.
57. Farrell, *What Ever Happened to Baby Jane?*, p. 5.
58. Shelley, *Grande Dame Guignol Cinema*, p. 8.
59. Ibid. p. 9.
60. Ibid. p. 9.
61. West, *The Day of the Locust*, p. 102.
62. Farrell, *What Ever Happened to Baby Jane?*, p. 15.
63. Shelley, *Grande Dame Guignol Cinema*, p. 26.
64. Also noted by Shelley, in ibid. p. 25.
65. In her 2019 article on the film, Mindy Buchanan-King argues that rather than underlining Blanche's physical limitations, this scene shows that she is in fact 'both mobile, and strong in her mobility' ('Joan Crawford', n.p).
66. Shelley, *Grande Dame Guignol Cinema*, p. 24.
67. Chivers, 'Baby Jane Grew Up', p. 224.

# 5

# 'It's a Gateway Part!' Twenty-First-Century Hollywood Gothic

David Cronenberg's film *Maps to the Stars* (2014; scripted by satirist Bruce Wagner), presents us with an intensely bleak portrait of life in twenty-first-century Hollywood. Here, although the times (and the industry) have changed, the locale is again populated by ruthless careerists, delusional psychotics and abusive relationships. The film also presents us with a particularly *haunted* vision of contemporary Hollywood: as Matt Zoller Seitz notes, '*Maps to the Stars* often feels like a ghost story made by people who don't believe in the supernatural.'[1]

The next film discussed in in this chapter, *Starry Eyes* (also 2014, directed by Kevin Kölsch and Dennis Widmyer), presents us with an explicitly super-natural take upon the second type of Hollywood Gothic narrative: that which dramatises the gruelling physical and psychological transformations under-gone by desperate newcomers who have yet to (or will never) 'make it'. These twenty-first-century iterations of the Hollywood Gothic engage with and expand upon the themes most famously dramatised by their post-war predecessors. Additionally, both *Starry Eyes* and the final film discussed in this chapter, the Hollywood Gothic-adjacent movie, *The Neon Demon* (2016, directed by Nicolas Winding Refn), focus upon vulnerable young women undergoing terrifying psychological and physical transformations. These char-acters also fall under the influence of malevolent organisations/forces which promise to help the vulnerable individuals attain their deepest desires. As we shall see, the latter theme indicates the extent to which certain elements of the 'Hollywood Gothic' tradition also intersect with some of the 'Cult California' anxieties discussed in the final part of this volume.

In *Maps to the Stars*, the character who most closely resembles her post-war 'Grande Dame Guignol' predecessors is Havana Segrand (Julianne Moore). Havana is, from the outset, notably insecure. The actress abuses prescription medications, engages in impulsive behaviours and is often depicted in a state of unflattering dishevelment. In one memorable scene, she unselfconsciously engages in a lengthy conversation with her new personal assistant, a young woman named Agatha Weiss (Mia Wasikowska) whilst straining to defecate. Havana's toxic nature is confirmed when she dances with joy upon learning that the son of a rival actress has drowned, because a role she covets is now hers for the asking. Havana is pure celebrity id personified.

However, like her forerunner Norma Desmond, Havana isn't entirely unsympathetic. Her obnoxiousness is rooted in her inability to move past her troubled Hollywood childhood. She is haunted by the personal and filmic past, plagued throughout the film by eerie visitations from the 'ghost' of her late mother, Clarice Taggart (Sarah Gadon). Clarice, a 'dead cult figure', is best known for her role in a 1970s art-house classic called *Stolen Waters* which is about to be remade. Clarice's strange appearances are not likely to be paranormal in nature: they can be interpreted as a manifestation of Havana's mental instability and her inability to come to terms with her mother's emotional and artistic legacy. Clarice's fate – which evokes that of infamous 'Golden Age' casualties such as Frances Farmer – also underscores the way in which industry success can spectacularly backfire for women.[2] Cronenberg famously eschews the supernatural in his films. As he outlined in an interview:

> I said to Bruce: 'I don't believe in an afterlife, therefore I don't believe in ghosts. I do understand being haunted by dead people in your life, but not in the literal sense of actual, physical ghosts.' [. . .] My approach is that ghosts are like memories – you might be haunted by your dead parents, whose voices you can hear in your head, whose presence is almost physical. I know for a fact that is real. But they are not ghosts in a living-after-death kind of way.[3]

Although Havana's luxurious home and obvious (if waning) high status indicate that she has achieved considerable industry success in her own right, Clarice, who died young in a mental institution, achieved a level of critical respect which has apparently escaped her daughter. Havana's celebrity has done nothing to exorcise her personal demons. One critic even describes the character as 'a walking bag of poison'.[4] Havana's resentment towards Clarice is exacerbated by the alleged resurfacing of 'repressed memories' which lead her to believe that Clarice sexually abused her when she was a child. Havana's new 'memories' may be true, or they may be a subconscious means by which she can further disparage her mother's posthumous reputation. It is also later revealed that Havana's therapist Dr Stafford Weiss (John Cusack) has secretly been in a (consensual) incestuous relationship for many decades. He may therefore be projecting his own personal issues onto his needy patient. In the end, it matters little what the exact truth is: what is important is that Havana's relationship with Clarice was a dysfunctional and unhappy one. Havana's celebrity status has only exacerbated matters. Like Baby Jane Hudson, who was fixated upon her father, Havana is petty, insecure, narcissistic and spoilt. Furthermore, because of who she is, she is for the most part able to get away with this behaviour, at least until her brutal comeuppance.

In Chapter 3 above I argued that *Sunset Boulevard* presented us with an updated version of the sinister aristocrat trope so often found in the classical Gothic. Silke Arnold-de Simine has usefully outlined the ways in which *Maps to the Stars* engages with other long-established genre conventions:

> David Cronenberg's *Maps to the Stars* (2014) might be less obviously in the Gothic horror tradition than some of the director's early 'body-horror' films [. . .] but all the elements, put in place by 'Monk' Lewis in 1796, are clearly recognizable and as transgressive as they were then: incest, fratricide/patricide/ matricide/filicide, suicide pacts, abusive mother/father figures, visitations by the dead, repulsive exploitation, mental disintegration and corruption cloaked as redemptive spirituality. In the film, many of these signature Gothic elements have been updated for the spectacularized neoliberal world of 21st-century Los Angeles, a world obsessed with the ever-new, ever-young, and yet spellbound by and enthralled to its own past: Lewis's celebrated monk has become a TV therapist to the stars; redemption is not found in saving your soul but in culti- vating a celebrity status with its empty promise of unconditional devotion; and the stars on Hollywood's Walk of Fame, where Agatha Weiss kneels in adora- tion, are the saints of this new religion.[5]

The film's use of 'signature Gothic elements' related to warped family rela- tionships and psychological instability doesn't only pertain to Havana's storyline. Her plot arc is interwoven with that of two much younger (and even more troubled) children of Hollywood. As a result, the film presents us with a more geographically and thematically expansive view of the Hollywood dystopia theme than *Sunset Boulevard* or *Baby Jane*. Much of *Maps to the Stars* focuses upon a character who has none of the status, wealth or celebrity which Havana has attained, but shares with her a damaged family background. Eighteen-year-old Agatha Weiss is introduced as she gets off the night bus to Los Angeles. She briefly seems like an obvious example of a familiar character type: the naive ingénue who has come to California in search of glamour and opportunity. However, Agatha is no newcomer, and, as her facial scarring and long black gloves suggest, she has secrets of her own.

As her backstory unfurls, we learn that Agatha's upbringing was, if anything, even more warped than Havana's. She is the estranged daughter of Havana's therapist, Stafford, and his wife Christina (Olivia Williams). Several years previously, Agatha discovered that her parents were brother and sister. Already plagued by terrifying delusions of ghostly children, she tried to kill her little brother Benjie (Evan Bird) after performing an impromptu 'wedding ceremony' with him and setting fire to the family mansion (as Arnold-de Simine notes, these elements evoke Edgar Allan Poe's 1839 story, 'The Fall of the House of Usher').[6] The siblings were saved, but Agatha, who was burned in the fire, was diagnosed with schizophrenia, sent to an asylum in Florida and disowned. Upon arriving back in LA, the first thing Agatha does is hire a limo driven by aspiring actor/writer Jerome (Robert Pattinson) to go and visit the empty lot in which the family home once stood. The Hollywood sign looms suggestively over its charred remains, making the connection between the film industry and the dysfunctionality of the Weiss clan explicit.

During Agatha's exile the rest of the Weiss family have prospered. Stafford is, as previously noted, a high-profile celebrity therapist, whilst Benjie is a child star managed by the hard-bitten Christina. Thanks to making contact on Twitter with writer/actress Carrie Fisher (playing herself), Agatha quickly finds work on the periphery of the movie business. She is to become the latest in a long line of 'Chore Whores' (personal assistants) hired by Havana. Agatha is rather like Tod in *The Day of the Locust*, in that scenes revolving round her actions frame the movie, and her relationships with the other characters propel many of the plot developments.

During Agatha's absence, thirteen-year-old Benjie has become an obnoxious, entitled and foul-mouthed teenager. A recent stint in rehab suggests that he has been finding it difficult to cope with stardom and his repressed knowledge of the events which resulted in Agatha's institutionalisation. When he and Agatha are finally reunited – she sneaks into his trailer – it is obvious that the siblings remain close. Agatha claims that she is eager to 'make amends', and explains that she acted as she did because she was 'seeing things' (dead children) and believed that once she and Benjie promised themselves to one another (in a macabre echo of the taboo relationship which exists between their parents) the 'ghosts' would go away. Soon after this meeting, Benjie, who is already under immense pressure to resurrect his struggling career, begins to crack under the strain of celebrity and familial anxiety.

Like Havana and Agatha, he is haunted, tormented by delusions of the resentful 'ghost' of a fan whom he treated with disrespect. Cronenberg has emphasised that Benjie, like Agatha, is both a product and a victim of his context.[7] As his psychological state deteriorates, Benjie chokes a young co-star, believing that he is strangling the 'ghost'. The child lives, but the career-ending incident suggests that despite his callous braggadocio, Benjie feels deeply guilty about his awful behaviour. Cronenberg has stated:

> That's the secret he has. He shares it with his psychiatrist ultimately, but her approach is very benign and clinical. She doesn't get deeply into the real meaning of it, which is that Benjie is quite a sensitive kid and not the crude, tough guy that he likes to pretend to be, which is the role he has created for himself and has to sell to survive. So his fear and this empathy come out in a different way.[8]

By the time Agatha reveals the truth about their parents, Benjie is ready to help her to finish off the job she started four years ago. For the Weiss family, some secrets are simply too toxic to overcome. It doesn't help that Stafford is a conceited charlatan who refuses to treat his own children with honesty or compassion. As Johanna Isaacson notes, 'His therapeutic technique involves a hodgepodge of vaguely orientalist new age bloviated rhetoric, pop psychology, and quasi-sexual massage. Conversations between Havana and Stafford are filled with annoyingly opaque or cliché buzzwords and phrases.'[9] In one of the film's many morbidly comic asides, Stafford spots a copy of one of his own self-help books in Agatha's motel room, and comments, apparently without irony, '*Secrets Kill*. A classic.' As we shall further see in Chapter 7, the alignment between New Age jargon and Los Angeles is also often a dangerous one in 'Cult California' narratives.

Many of the major characters in *Maps to the Stars* are poisonously self-absorbed. Even Jerome, who initially seems like he might potentially be a supportive love interest for Agatha, is only interested in maximising the chances of his own industry success (his opportunistic betrayal of her contributes to Agatha's final psychotic break). The narcissism and insularity of the film industry is here transposed to the realm of poisonous parent/child relationships which ultimately result in the deaths of all three children of Hollywood: Havana, Agatha and Benjie. Havana's parental trauma manifests itself most vividly when she experiences an erotically charged vision of her mother whilst she is engaging in a threesome. It is clear she despises, and yet in some inchoate manner desires, her mother (or perhaps wants to *be* her). Havana's obsession is underlined by her determination to play Clarice's signature role in the remake of *Stolen Waters*. In a Norma Desmond-like detail, despite her fame, she appears to be very lonely. Apart from her agent and the married actor with whom she is having an affair, Havana has few people in her personal life. Like Norma and the Hudson sisters, she lives in an opulent but empty Los Angeles home.

Her only regular companions are her perpetually absent Latinx housekeeper (Havana bitchily castigates the woman for 'having too many kids') and the revolving door of personal assistants. This is where Agatha comes in. Havana is ghoulishly intrigued by Agatha's scars and pats herself on the back for giving her a job. However, although she appears to be a self-effacing and malleable figure, Agatha is a more complicated – and dangerous – individual than her demanding employer anticipates.

In an interesting twist upon the violent acts which take place in *Sunset Boulevard* and *Baby Jane*, this time round the delusional middle-aged diva is the murder victim, not the murderer. The film also reverses the order of the employer/employee murder seen in *Baby Jane*. Havana's fate is sealed when she fires Agatha for unreliability and then screams at her for staining her white couch with menstrual blood. Typically, Havana is too caught up in her own drama to notice that Agatha – who is now glassy-eyed and distant – has slipped into outright psychosis. In a moment of morbid irony, the young woman suddenly bashes Havana's skull in with the Golden Globe awarded to Clarice for *Stolen Waters*. The sense that Clarice is somehow striking out at her daughter from beyond the grave is furthered by the fact that the film previously established clear parallels between Agatha and Clarice: both women have been in a fire (Clarice died in one) and both were institutionalised.

In the film's final scene, Agatha and Benjie complete the 'wedding ceremony' which was interrupted years before, and fatally overdose on the site of their former home. Christina, unable to live with the shame caused by Benjie's attack on his co-star and the possibility that the true nature of her relationship with Stafford is about to come out, sets herself on fire. In a macabre nod to the opening scene of *Sunset Boulevard*, her flaming body is extinguished when Stafford pushes her into the swimming pool. This isn't the only death in a pool referenced in the film: the little boy whose death Havana celebrated also died in one. It's another indication that Cronenberg and Wagner are familiar with the signature tropes of the Hollywood Gothic. In addition, Mark Kermode has persuasively aligned the film with Cronenberg's previous horror movies:

> Beneath the jet-black humour there is real horror – a rampant existential panic that eats away at the lives of the rich and famous, conjuring visions of ghosts from the empty spaces where their souls should be, infecting those who feed upon them and who are desperate to share their disease.[10]

In *Maps to the Stars*, choosing to die on one's own terms is ultimately the only way to escape from the intertwined torments of familial dysfunction and the Hollywood hellscape. When the younger Weiss siblings first reunite, Agatha tells Benjie that she has a job already. He jokingly responds: 'You know, for a disfigured schizophrenic, you got the town pretty wired.' There's an element of truth there. Agatha's actions – murder, arson and suicide – are undeniably extreme, but when we consider the cruelty and cynicism of the town (and the family) in which she grew up, they also make a certain deranged logic. In true classical Gothic style, she is the psychically and physically scarred embodiment of all that has been forcibly repressed on a familial and an industry level. Agatha finally succeeds in bringing about the self-annihilating 'happy ending' which she hopes will banish her Hollywood ghosts for good. In their final suicidal retreat into fantasy, the Weiss siblings, like Norma Desmond and Baby Jane before them, find a kind of macabre sense of completion. As Cronenberg says of the final scene: 'I feel personally that this strange sensual and consensual wedding ceremony is very touching. She's trying to deal with all the madness of her life and her parents' lives, and all the sins of the parents that were visited on her and Benjie.'[11] Agatha's final moments contrast sharply with Havana's fate. Havana's murder is the jet-black punchline to a cruel joke that has been in the making for her entire life.

## 'I Am *Not* a Million Other Girls': *Starry Eyes* and *The Neon Demon*

The aspiring starlet is, like the ambitious young writer (usually male), a staple ingredient in Hollywood-set movies of the non-horror variety, from the two film-related iterations of *A Star is Born* (1937 and 1954), to *Singin' in the Rain* (1952) and, more recently, *La La Land* (2016). James Ellroy's novel *The Black Dahlia* (1987) also uses the ghastly murder of one of LA's most infamously doomed ingénues, Elizabeth Short, as the starting point for a panoramic tale of conspiracy, incest and corruption in high places.

Another acclaimed dramatisation of this trope can be found in David Lynch's *Mulholland Drive* (2001). *Mulholland Drive* is, to begin with at least, a noir-inflected mystery (albeit with a characteristically Lynchian sense of uncanny possibility), but it also deploys familiar horror/Gothic tropes, most notably the doppelgänger. The film's main characters, Betty/Diane Selwyn (Naomi Watts) and Rita/Camilla Rhodes (Laura Harring) have mutable, seemingly interchangeable identities, with Rita at one point donning a blonde wig which makes her look remarkably like Watts's character(s). *Mulholland Drive* also has a famously ambiguous (and much-analysed) ending, which may place it squarely amongst the tradition of narratives in which the main character has really been dead or dying all along, in the style of Ambrose Bierce's famous story 'An Occurrence at Owl Creek Bridge' (1890). Furthermore, there are several scenes – most particularly the jump scare punctuating the superbly ominous Winkie's diner scene – which deploy the tonal and editorial grammar of horror cinema. From the outset, Lynch presents us with a story which subverts conventional narrative expectation, introducing familiar characters and situations – the naive newcomer, the *femme fatale*, the assassin, the botched murder, the mystery that must be solved and the audition that brings the deserving unknown to the gates of stardom – but arranges these elements in such an original and defamiliarising way that they become exhilaratingly unstable, loaded with playful and portentous latent meaning.

*Mulholland Drive* is therefore another film that is both set in Hollywood and about Hollywood. Here, however, the thin line between reality and delusion, which has also been crossed by characters such as Norma, Jane, Havana and Agatha, is transposed to the fundamental meaning of the narrative we have just watched unfold before our eyes. The 'realness' of events is called into question, as is the relationship between sleep and wakefulness and life and death. However, even if we can never be quite sure of the true meaning of what we have seen (or even agree that such a definite point of interpretation can or should be reached), we do have the sense that for Diane Selwyn, the bitterly unhappy actress upon whom much of the second half focuses, dreams of Hollywood fame (and of true love) have curdled. By contrast, her idealised, 1950s-inflected alter-ego/past-self/delusional fantasy, 'Betty', has a dream of an audition which looks set to make her a star (at least until Diane's much grimmer alternate – or perhaps actual? – reality begins to seep in). Betty also gets to rescue her amnesic love interest Rita, and acts out her girl-detective impulses by pursuing an exciting Los Angeles mystery. Diane ends up as a rotting corpse in a seedy Hollywood apartment.

I will now focus upon a more recent (and more explicitly supernatural) exploration of the ways in which the pursuit of Hollywood celebrity corrodes morality and horrifically transforms the female body: *Starry Eyes*. As in *The Neon Demon*, which I will briefly consider at the end of this chapter, *Starry Eyes* is a grim fairy tale set in contemporary Los Angeles. In both films a naive young woman's narcissistic desire for fame leads to grotesque physical and psychological transformation and her own death. These films also suggest that the expectations and appetites associated with their respective (but related) industries – film (*Starry Eyes*) and fashion (*The Neon Demon*) – provide the perfect environment for elitist, self-serving occult practitioners.[12] Additionally, *Starry Eyes* makes literal the metaphorical 'disease' of Hollywood celebrity which Kermode identified in *Maps to the Stars*.

*Starry Eyes* foregrounds from its opening seconds the connection between its main character Sarah Walker's (Alex Essoe) gnawing personal dissatisfaction and her desire to become a movie goddess like the Golden Age icons whose headshots line her walls. As Craig Mann and Liam Hathaway observe, the film treads familiar territory:

*Starry Eyes* is essentially a continuation of cautionary tales such as *Sunset Boulevard* (1950), *The Day of the Locust* (1975), *Barton Fink* (1991), *The Player* (1992), *Mulholland Drive* (2001), and, most recently, David Cronenberg's *Maps to the Stars* (2014). All these films satirize Hollywood's ostensibly attractive allure as a road to destruction, madness, and death, concentrating on protagonists who believe Hollywood will provide the opportunities for fame and fortune they so crave and earn them the respect and admiration of millions.[13]

What makes *Starry Eyes* interesting is precisely this very direct engagement with established narrative conventions. Here, stardom really does transform one into an inhuman monster, and the all-powerful cabal of older white men who control Hollywood are members of a ruthless cult aligned with vaguely Satanic practices.

Sarah is first seen gazing critically at herself in a mirror, intently scrutinising her face and body for flaws. As in the second section of *Mulholland Drive* (when the focus shifts to Diane), the mental toll of life on the margins of Hollywood is emphasised. Sarah is doing all she can to maximise her chances – she takes classes, attends auditions, responds to advertisements – but so far her efforts have gone unrewarded. To pay her way, she works as a waitress in 'Taters', a tacky fast-food restaurant which obliges its female employees to dress in skin-tight clothing. She also has a creepy boss, Carl (Pat Healy). It's an early indication that objectification and exploitation are here seen to define life at every level of the industry for young women.

Sarah is not the only industry wannabe. She is part of a close-knit but competitive group of young actors, writers and directors who have also come to LA in search of Hollywood success. Early on, it is established that she is a fretful and self-critical individual. These internal stresses are exacerbated by life in the city, her demeaning job and her lack of professional success. Sarah is withdrawn in social situations and has a propensity towards self-harm. Her unhappiness is further heightened by the passive-aggressive comments made by her obnoxious frenemy, Erin (Fabianne Therese), a rival actress. Sarah believes that time is running out for her, and that she must aggressively pursue every opportunity.

Then she spots an online casting notice for a horror film. The advertisement runs:

So, you're an actor. You can become other people. But can you be yourself? Can you put your inner being on the screen? Then come try out for Celeste, a young up-and-coming actor in our Tinsel Town terror tale, *The Silver Scream*.

The name of the company, Astraeus Productions, and its symbol – a six-pointed star – indicate that *Starry Eyes* will be gesturing towards the occultism of Aleister Crowley (we might also recall that Kenneth Anger opened the 1975 edition of *Hollywood Babylon* with a quote from Crowley: 'Every Man and every Woman is a Star').[14] This is a Hollywood horror film which, at least at surface level, is about the process of winning a role in a Hollywood horror film. However, *Starry Eyes* complicates its familiar tale of innocence corrupted by effectively depicting Sarah's loneliness and sense of urban alienation. The film is also, particularly in its latter stages, a vividly dramatised body horror narrative (this is where the 'fame as a disease' theme comes in). This facet of the movie is discussed in detail by Mann and Hathaway, who argue that in *Starry Eyes* 'and its ilk, body-horror is reinvigorated for the age of celebrity: it uses the slow and painful destruction of the physical form as a metaphor through which to explore the psychological torment inflicted by a relentless hunger for recognition'.[15] In *Starry Eyes*, the rapid decay and eventual death of Sarah's 'original' human body (and soul) is the price that must be paid if she is to gain admittance to the rarefied realm of the 'star'.

Directors Kölsch and Widmyer make Sarah's decision to accept this horrific bargain understandable – from her perspective at least – by emphasising the dreary nature of her current life in Los Angeles:

> [The city is] introduced as a cold, grey and unwelcoming place; an establishing shot of the Hollywood Hills – complete with the famous Hollywood sign looming ominously from the hillside under cloudy skies – immediately subverts any traditional perception of Los Angeles as 'an endless vista of sun, sand and surf'.[16]

Unlike *Maps to the Stars*, which foregrounds modernist mansions, celebrity homes, studio conference rooms and iconic locations such as Rodeo Drive, much of *Starry Eyes* is set in cramped and dingy shared apartments, on grimy-looking city streets and in Sarah's tacky workplace.

This focus upon the main character's isolation allies *Starry Eyes* with another LA-set horror movie that focuses upon the travails of a solitary young woman working a minimum-wage job to survive: *Entrance* (2012), directed by Patrick Horvath and Dallas Richard Hallam. Initially, *Entrance* doesn't appear to be a horror movie. It provides us with a seemingly low-key portrait of everyday life in a run-down part of Los Angeles. Protagonist Suzy's (Suziey [sic] Block) sense of nebulous unease initially seems like an understandable response to her lonely life in a city which is both densely populated and troublingly anonymous. However, in the final scenes it suddenly becomes clear that Suzy's disquiet was well founded. She attends a house party which descends into murderous brutality when the premises are invaded by a masked killer who has been stalking her the whole time. Her friends are slaughtered one by one. The film ends on an ambiguous note as she is marched to the rooftop by the killer and turns to face him as the sun rises over the uncaring city. However, although Suzy appears to have been singled out at random, in *Starry Eyes* Sarah's desire for success encourages her to make risky decisions. As was the case for Faye in *The Day of the Locust*, Joe in *Sunset Boulevard* and Diane in *Mulholland Drive*, the economic and psychological insecurity of an aspiring talent places them in a highly vulnerable position. Ambition and desperation are always deeply entwined in the Hollywood Gothic. The same can also be said of an earlier Hollywood Gothic-adjacent text I have not had room to discuss here: Horace McCoy's *They Shoot Horses, Don't They?* The 1935 novel focuses upon impoverished and desperate young people on the margins of the movie business – Robert and Gloria, an aspiring director and actress respectively – for whom the brutally exploitative dance marathon, which seems to provide entrants with a rare chance to improve their material and professional prospects, leads only to death.

Because she has been losing hope, Sarah is delighted to receive a callback from Astraeus Productions. Things take on an ominous cast when she sees the girl who entered before her leave in tears. The intimidating casting agents who conduct the audition greet her with a rote incantation which underlines that Sarah is one of many young women with the same dreams: 'When you exit this room, you either will have made a lasting impression, or blended into the sea of thousands of forgotten girls who pass through these halls every day.' The statement is calibrated to tap into the sense of insecurity and exceptionalism felt by Sarah and other ambitious young women – the thousands of modern-day 'Fanny Joneses' longing for their chance to shine. Indeed, the situation appears not to have changed all that much since Leo Rosten noted of aspiring starlets: 'All that Fanny Jones really needs for a stab at glory is that elusive, undefinable quality for which, she has read, movie producers are always searching in palpatory desperation – "personality". And luck.'[17] Sarah is relying upon more than luck and personality – she has worked hard to hone her talent – but her experience at Astraeus shows that her desperate 'stab at glory' still depends upon whether or not industry gatekeepers see in her the 'undefinable quality' which will supposedly make someone a star.

Sarah's earnest reading is met with bored dismissal: 'We saw what we needed.' After she exits the audition, she goes straight to the restroom to privately express her rage and self-recrimination. (As within female-focused body-horror cinema more generally, bathrooms are important here as sites where the 'real' self can be expressed and the rapid deterioration of the physical body becomes vividly apparent). However, as Sarah tears at her own hair, the stall next to her is occupied by the woman who oversaw her audition. This display is just what Astraeus is looking for: 'Maybe we didn't see all that we needed from you after all.' Sarah is called back in to talk about her 'fit', and reluctantly re-enacts her outburst. This time, when she is ushered from the room, the platitude 'we'll be in touch' has the ring of sincerity.

When she is indeed called back, Sarah lets the news go to her head. After her odious boss tells her that she needs to focus on her restaurant job, she quits. When he cautions her that 'There are a million other girls who would beg for a steady job like this', she angrily responds, 'I am *not* a million other girls.'

Audition two is even weirder. Sarah walks into a room lit only by a spot-light. She is asked: 'Would you mind disrobing for us?' – although this is a command rather than a request. As she gingerly stands in the spotlight, Sarah is ordered to 'let your inhibitions go' so that she can 'transform into something else' (the wording, as we shall see, is a form of foreshadowing). Although the prospect terrifies her, once she enters the spotlight, Sarah, like Norma Desmond before her, revels in it, entering a rapturous state (Jesse, the similarly fame-hungry protagonist of *The Neon Demon*, undergoes a similar experience whilst in the spotlight during a climactic fashion show). When the moment passes, she receives the affirmation she has been craving: 'That's what we were looking for, Sarah.'

Whilst the viewer initially perceives Sarah to be a predominately sympathetic figure, as her involvement with Astraeus progresses, it becomes clear that she is also selfish and self-obsessed, and that this is likely part of the reason why she was 'chosen'. An early indication of her capacity for cruelty comes when she attends a pool party with her friends. Erin is jealous of Sarah's callback and passive-aggressively punctures her excitement. When Erin is injured in the pool shortly thereafter, Sarah laughs with delight. That night, she dreams of the spotlight, and the next day brings news that ushers her ever-closer to stardom. The all-powerful 'Producer' has asked to see her in his private office.

As Sarah nervously stands before her friends on the night of the meeting, clad in a red dress, Erin once again tries to undermine her confidence: 'Don't you think you're a little overdressed?' From this point on, *Starry Eyes* leans into its status as a nightmarish fable about the long-time association between Hollywood and the sexual exploitation of vulnerable young women. Although the film's 2014 release predated the public disclosure of one of the industry's most infamous open secrets (the revelation that independent film producer Harvey Weinstein had been sexually abusing women he first encountered within business-related contexts for years), its depiction of Sarah's dehuman-ising, exploitative audition process means that it deserves to be considered a #MeToo-adjacent narrative, and a reminder that predatory male power-brokers have regrettably been a central facet of the industry since it was first established.[18]

The expectation that degrading sexual 'favours' will be exchanged for a shot at stardom comes to the forefront here. After arriving at Astraeus head-quarters, Sarah is ushered into the Producer's leather- and mahogany-lined office. The Producer (Louis Dezseran) is a grey-haired, tanned, expensively dressed older white man who exudes unspoken power and speaks with the same subtly formal diction as his lackeys (indeed, he is 'a stereotypical representation of the Hollywood elite').[19] He flatters her: 'although we interview a lot of young women [. . .] very few of them ever make it to this room'. The Producer also explains a little more about Astraeus, which appears to be a kind of star-manufacturing factory. *The Silver Scream*, he explains, is intended to serve as 'my love letter to this town'. 'Ambition', he declares, 'is the blackest of human desires', and 'This industry is a plague . . . a plague of unoriginality.' As his speech continues, the central plank of the film's premise – the assumption that moral corruption lies at the very heart of Hollywood – is further underlined:

> You cut through the fog of this town and you get desperation. Plastic parishioners worshipping their deity of debauchery. But that's what I find interesting, Sarah – that's what I want to capture in this film – the ugliness of the human spirit.

At this point, Sarah, who as ever is painfully eager to please, responds: 'Yeah, I can see that.' Her hair-tugging is then brought up: it is something she started doing when she was a child, and 'helps me focus on the moment'. Once more linking Sarah's self-harming tendencies with the opportunity to 'progress' in the industry, the Producer claims that his film represents 'a great opportunity for an actress with ambition'. 'That's me!' Sarah exclaims.

Star-struck, she says she will 'do whatever it takes for this role . . . truthfully, I *am* this role.' But the 'role' comes at a price. The charged atmosphere darkens further when the Producer makes it clear that she will be required to prove her desire for stardom by performing a sexual act on him. As he gropes her, he reveals that '*this* is the audition'. He also directly characterises himself as an industry gatekeeper: 'All you need is for me to open them for you. Sarah, I can make you a star.' Deeply shaken, Sarah recoils and leaves. But it isn't long before she begins to reconsider. She admits to her roommate Tracy (Amanda Fuller) that she regrets not doing what the Producer wanted. Although she doesn't quite admit that his demand was a sexual one, the implication is clear:

'There was one final step, and I could have had it too if I was just willing to. . . .' Tracy, shocked by this admission, asks her if she really does wish that she had done what was asked, and Sarah cries, 'It was a *gateway* part!' Her sense of regret is intensified when money troubles mean that she must beg for her old job back and admit that she is indeed, 'a Taters girl'. Tracy reveals what happened at the meeting to the rest of their friendship group. The film's Faustian overtones are made even more obvious when Sarah reveals to another friend, Danny (Noah Segan), that she feels like 'I'm selling my soul already, so it may as well be for something I want.'

Sure enough, Sarah soon willingly returns to the Producer's office, determined this time to do whatever it takes. As she makes her way to the luxury estate on Canyon Drive on foot and by subway (as in *Sunset Boulevard*, not having access to a car in Los Angeles is a signifier of economic and social precarity), the warning that 'There won't be a third opportunity' hangs in the air. What follows when she gets there is essentially a 'selling your soul' sequence, in which she is asked: 'Would you be willing to give up your body to become a vessel for our voice – for my voice? Would you give your old life away for a glorious new life?' The answer, inevitably, is 'Yes'. Sarah is then obliged to 'prove herself' by performing oral sex on the Producer (here, the camera lingers on his gold bracelet and pendant). It is a moment of utterly degrading sexual predation. The Producer croons:

> The gateway is open, Sarah. All you have to do is be willing to step inside forever, and never look back. Kill your old life, Sarah. Bury it in the earth and join us in the skies. Show us the girl I thought you were.

There follow more flashes of light and fragmentary, disorientating hallucinations, and then Sarah wakes up in her own bed. She is stricken with crippling stomach pains, but stumbles to work nonetheless, where her spaced-out demeanour attracts her boss Carl's attention. She slaps him and is fired, thereby cutting off the connection with her 'old' pre-Astraeus life.

From this point on, Sarah becomes increasingly unwell. Tracy urges her to seek medical help, but she pushes aside these well-meaning entreaties, even after humiliating herself at a social gathering. Afterwards, Sarah walks with difficulty through the deserted city streets on the way back to Astraeus headquarters but she is denied entry. The first indications that her 'transformation' may be rendering her dangerous to others comes when she assaults a homeless man en route. Although it initially seems as if her illness may be a psychosomatic reaction to trauma, Sarah is, in a very literal sense, changing. She vomits uncontrollably, stays in her darkened room and begins to physically deteriorate. Her long hair falls out, then her fingernails and teeth, and a black substance seeps from her vagina. She also becomes more alienated from her friendship group, describing them as being 'like a cancer', and throws an envelope of (Astraeus) money at Tracy when her kindly but exasperated roommate tells her to get over the bad audition and find a paying job.

The final stage of Sarah's trip through the 'gateway' comes when she is deathly ill and beset by visions of herself reborn as an eerily beautiful but inhuman figure. When she receives a phone call from an Astraeus representative, she croaks 'I'm dying', only to be matter-of-factly told, 'Yes, you are.' Dreams, she is informed, require sacrifice, 'and so do we. I can give you what you want, Sarah, but you need to embrace who you *really* are. It's time to become one of us. It's time to be *remembered*.' As if she has been given her final instructions, Sarah goes to Erin's house, finding her rival engaged in a cosy moment with potential love interest Danny. Erin initially fails to realise how sick Sarah is: 'Did you actually suck some old movie producer's cock for a role in a movie called *The Silver Scream*?' she asks. Sarah responds mechanically: 'It's a gateway part.' When Erin retorts that it looks more like prostitution, Sarah lashes out with a knife, slashing Erin's face. As if the last remaining tie to her ebbing humanity has been cut loose, she stabs Erin repeatedly and, as the final coup de grâce, pulverises her face. Sarah then kills both Danny and Erin's roommate.

Following this explosion of violence, Sarah is taken to a secluded spot in the Hollywood Hills by a coven of Astraeus associates, all of whom are wealthy older white people. The production company is a long-established Hollywood cult, and their search for a new 'star' has all been leading up to this moment. Sarah is ceremonially buried at the top of the hill, her grave adorned with a fluorescent version of the Astraeus symbol. She is then reborn, working her way out of a kind of birth sac to the cry of 'Hail Astraeus' from above ground.

Sarah – if she can still even be called by that name – claws her way out whilst the sun shines over the city. It is a new dawn and a new life for her. She looks rather like one of the psychotic LSD casualties in Jeff Lieberman's LA-set 'Hippie Horror' classic, *Blue Sunshine* (1977) – completely bald and with long, sharp nails. A gift box left next to the burial site contains a note saying 'Happy Birthday', a gown and a lustrous wig.

The death of Sarah's old self becomes definitive when she makes her way back to her apartment and sequesters herself beneath the covers of her bed once again. When Tracy checks up on her, the 'new' Sarah reveals herself to be bald, completely naked and possessed of dazzling green eyes. She compels her stunned friend to 'Come lie next to me.' Although the command seems like a prelude to seduction, Sarah's 'kiss' sucks out Tracy's life force. In an echo of Fritz Leiber's 1949 story, 'The Girl with the Hungry Eyes', this new 'star' is likely a kind of mass-media vampire/succubus who will feed upon the hapless adoration of her 'fans'. The film ends as the 'new' Sarah narcissistically preens in front of her bedroom mirror, luxuriating in the sight of her heavily made up, glamorously attired reflection. The look is completed by the Astraeus necklace proudly worn around her neck. As Mann and Hathaway put it, 'For Sarah, stardom comes at the price of her mind, body and soul', and this final scene suggests that the 'long dead matinee idols who adorn Sarah's walls' are 'no longer gods, but equals.'[20]

In *Starry Eyes* then, the Hollywood 'fairy tale' identified decades before by Rosten – the dream whereby an ordinary young woman can be delivered from obscurity and elevated to the 'royalty' of movie stardom – becomes indistinguishable from a key trope of the Hollywood Gothic nightmare: the discovery that success irreversibly damages both the individual singled out for 'greatness' and those unlucky enough to fall into his or (much more often) *her* orbit.

The association between an image-based industry and the occult found in *Starry Eyes* can also be found in the recent LA-set film: *The Neon Demon* (2016). Set in the fashion world, this is another nightmarish story about narcissism and the relentless objectification of ambitious and vulnerable young women. Furthermore, as Steen Ledet Christiansen points out, the film 'picks up the same desire for stardom in Hollywood that *Starry Eyes* explores'.[21]

The film's protagonist, Jesse (Elle Fanning), is a sixteen-year-old high school dropout from Georgia, determined to use her only exploitable assets as a means of attaining success and economic security: 'I can't sing, I can't dance, I can't write . . . but I'm pretty. And I can make money off pretty. So . . .' Initially, Jesse seems like an innocent in a world of predators. During the film's opening scene, an aspiring young photographer Dean (Karl Glusman) poses her as a glitter-accentuated, blood-soaked corpse. In its knowing juxtaposition of beauty and death, the tableau immediately suggests that Jesse's California sojourn will not have a happy ending. Mark Featherstone notes of this sequence

> That *The Neon Demon* is concerned with the immortality project based deep inside the fashion industry is evident from the very first moments of the film, where we see Fanning's Jesse draped across a chase lounge [sic] drenched in blood in a pose that recalls some famous Hollywood murder or suicide.[22]

Whilst at the same shoot, Jesse meets make-up artist Ruby (Jena Malone), whose big-sister style solicitude seems to position her as a supportive ally who will help the vulnerable teenager navigate the industry's murky shoals. However, as we later discover, Ruby's interest in Jesse is anything but benevolent. When

Ruby invites the teenager to a glamorous nightclub event, she introduces Jesse to her close friends Gigi (Bella Heathcote) and Sarah (Abbey Lee). They are both established models whose beauty, height and otherworldly poise suggest that they inhabit a different realm from the mere mortals around them. Gigi and Sarah are both intrigued and threatened by the fresh-faced, pastel-clad newcomer. During their first encounter (in the ladies' room), they bitchily size up the competition. Jesse is asked: 'Are you food, or are you sex?' Jesse, who replies that she is still a virgin, seems way out of her depth at this point.

An early indication of the movie's interest in the intersection between the fashion industry and the occult arrives when the stage show Jesse is attending appears to become some sort of preliminary ritual (soundtracked by Cliff Martinez's propulsive number, 'Demon Dance'). Jesse is transfixed by the sight of a female body suspended from the ceiling. The display is accompanied by a hallucinatory light show. The script's references to Crowley are much more explicit than in the film: in the staging directions for this scene, it is said that his famous credo, 'Do What Thou Wilt' is written on the wall of the nightclub.[23]

The first indication that Jesse is a more uncompromising individual than she initially seems comes when she meets with high-profile casting agent Roberta Hoffmann (Christina Hendricks) and immediately disavows love interest Dean when the agent negatively critiques his photographs: 'It was just some guy, he found me online.' The agent says that she sees many small-town girls with big dreams enter her office, most of whom don't make it, but that things will be different for Jesse: 'You – you're going to be great.'

Director Nicolas Winding Refn has described *The Neon Demon* as 'a ceremonial celebration of narcissism' which features 'a lot of blood and high heels'.[24] Like Sarah in *Starry Eyes*, Jesse is singled out for stardom and immediately begins to change (or perhaps it is also the case here that instincts which were already inside her are heightened by her brush with celebrity). Jesse's belief in her own exceptionalism was there even before she is fully exposed to the 'Neon Demon'. For instance, during a later encounter with Ruby's friends, Gigi, who is particularly insecure, declares that 'no one likes how they look'. Jesse immediately and perhaps cruelly responds, 'I do.'

Jesse's penchant for self-adoration is also further accentuated by a transformative experience which takes place during another photo shoot. After being singled out during a casting call by famous photographer Jack Abbot (Desmond Harrington), Jesse, again like Sarah in *Starry Eyes*, is asked to prove her willingness to 'ascend' to the next stage of her career by displaying absolute obedience to the whims of an industry gatekeeper. She is pressured into consenting to a private photo shoot with the much older man. Jesse, looking very childlike, reluctantly complies when Jack demands that she remove her clothing as soon as they are alone. He then slathers her face and neck in gold paint, in an act of both exploitation and adornment. Afterwards, Jesse finds Ruby, who had earlier cautioned her to be wary of Jack, anxiously waiting outside. When she asks how the shoot went, Jesse calmly replies: 'It went good, it was great actually.' The shoot propels her to the next stage of her career. However, Jesse's rapid rise is also noted by her rivals. After the photo shoot, when Ruby meets with Gigi and Sarah in a diner, Sarah bitterly laments that her own 'expiration date' is rapidly approaching: 'Who wants sour milk when you can have fresh milk?' (This further suggestion that Jesse is a product to be consumed is another portent of events to come: as Michael Wheatley notes, 'Winding Refn frequently foreshadows that his story will end in anthropophagy.'[25]) Gigi is less concerned, and points out that new girls like Jesse come and go all the time. Ruby disagrees, declaring that 'She has that "thing"' – in other words, the indefinable but undeniable quality which makes someone a star.

Sure enough, Jesse soon beats out Sarah in a casting call for a leading role in a new fashion show for designer Roberto Sarno (Alessandro Nivola). Sarah responds to Jesse's elevation by angrily smashing a bathroom mirror after the casting call: 'What's it feel like?' Sarah asks, when the teenager enters shortly thereafter, 'To walk into a room, and it's like the middle of winter, and you're the sun?' 'It's everything', Jesse declares. She then nicks her hand on a piece of broken mirror. Sarah suddenly lunges at her in order to suck her blood. Sarah, Gigi and Ruby are more than simply friends: they are a coven of sorts, and Ruby is their leader. Ruby's adherence to Crowley's self-interested tenets is further signposted by a detail which is again mentioned in the script, rather than explicitly referenced in the film: it is noted that the books found in her apartment include *The Holy Books of Thelema* and *Magic and Alchemy*.[26] It is Jesse, however, who initially seems to be undergoing a monstrous transformation. In another echo of the stages Sarah Walker progresses through before being 'reborn' in *Starry Eyes*, Jesse undergoes her final (or perhaps, *almost* final apotheosis) during her catwalk appearance for Roberto, during which she has a pivotal encounter with the 'Neon Demon'. The neon-outlined sequence of tringles which she passes through in this scene represents, according to Winding Refn, 'the face of the Neon Demon', and indicates that 'something is being born' inside of her.[27] The Neon Demon, he continues, is narcissism, and Jesse, like her mythological predecessor, is in love with her own reflection.[28]

Sure enough, it isn't long before Jesse alienates Dean, having bought into designer Roberto's declaration that beauty 'isn't everything – it's the only thing'. Without Dean's emotional support (and his car) she is left even more vulnerable when her scuzzy motel room is breached by predatory intruders (both human and animal). Left with nowhere else to go, Jesse asks Ruby for help. She has no inkling that her new friend's interest in her is primarily carnal, and, as the graphic mortuary scene establishes, likely also necrophilic in nature. Featherstone links the mortuary scene (during which Ruby sexually defiles the corpse of a young woman who resembles Jesse) to the film's wider themes, arguing that

> Winding Refn uses Ruby's mortuary work to foreground the horror of cosmetic surgery in his LA fashion world, which is based on the attempt to eliminate all forms of humanity in the emergence of a kind of fatal utopian form of identity where age no longer exists.[29]

Throughout the film, the use of well-known LA locations adds to the sense of regional specificity. The huge, old-school abode Ruby is housesitting is the well-known Paramour Mansion: her second job as a mortuary make-up technician was shot at the Hollywood Forever Cemetery, where many famous film industry people are buried.[30] Although the mansion initially seems like a sanctuary, after Jesse rebuffs Ruby's aggressive sexual advances it becomes clear that she is once more in danger. She has never been with anyone, Jesse again admits. This may be a further indication that Jesse's capacity for love and desire is primarily directed towards herself, rather than others (Dean, it seems, was ultimately more of a useful resource – he had a car and a camera – than a genuine love interest). Like Narcissus, Jesse is destined to meets her fate in a body of water, albeit one which has been drained: an empty swimming pool.

As she stands on the pool's diving board, clad in a Grecian-style dress, self-adorned with gold facial accents, Jesse presents herself to Ruby like a goddess on a pedestal. Her self-infatuation, courtesy of the Neon Demon's transfiguring power, is now stronger than ever: 'You know what my mother used to call me? Dangerous. "You're a dangerous girl." She was right. I am dangerous. I know what I look like – what's wrong with that anyway? Women would kill to look like this.' Hubris strikes when Gigi and Sarah arrive and, leaping into action as if responding to collective instinct, the predators chase their prey through the mansion's corridors. Cornered, Jesse ends up back at the pool with nowhere to go, as the coven gleefully approaches. Ruby darts forward and pushes her in. In her dying moments, Jesse gazes up at the stars as the life ebbs from her broken young body (shots of the LA nightscape and the moon are a recurring visual motif).

The movie's depiction of the fashion industry as a place where 'fresh meat' is greedily consumed is, like the Faustian-pact trope dramatised in *Starry Eyes*, here rendered a literal rather than a figurative plot development. Jesse's body is devoured by the coven. They also bathe in her blood – an obvious homage to the virgin-murdering proclivities of the youth-obsessed 'Vampire Countess', Elizabeth Bathory. However, some remnant of Jesse's 'essence' appears to live on in the bodies of Gigi and Sarah. This has fatal consequences in Gigi's case: she disembowels herself in a dreamlike state after coughing up Jesse's eyeball during a photo shoot. Sarah has no such misgivings: she calmly picks up the regurgitated eyeball and swallows it, then heads back to take centre stage in the photo shoot. Both her body and career appear to have been rejuvenated by the strategic ingestion of her young rival's body and blood.

As these plot details suggest, *The Neon Demon* is a self-consciously provocative, surreal and hyperbolic movie. Winding Refn has claimed that it is 'a comedy in many ways', and the film clearly revels in its own heightened sense of reality (and artificiality). As the director also states of the film's setting: 'I think LA has two realities: the so-called "real" reality and there's the "artificial" reality. The artificial reality really is the illusion of Los Angeles, and that's something I found really exciting, because it's about mythology.'[31]

As previously noted, *The Neon Demon* is not in a literal sense a film about Hollywood or the film industry, but it clearly deploys and reconfigures the typical settings and situations associated with the 'aspiring starlet' Hollywood Gothic plot: the predatory white male gatekeepers, the luxurious mansion, the pivotal audition, the moment of 'discovery', the fatal swimming pool and the sense that the geographical locale and industry milieu are both corrupt and corrupting. As in *Starry Eyes*, we are presented with a series of important auditions/casting calls which elevate the naive protagonist to an all-consuming and ultimately fatal form of 'stardom' which transforms her into something entirely new. *The Neon Demon* also deploys the 'hopeful young newcomer from out of town' trope seen in *Mulholland Drive* (Betty is said to be from small-town Canada). It also features an image-based industry built upon the toxic fetishization of youth and beauty. In summary then, *The Neon Demon* self-consciously appropriates the characteristics of the Hollywood Gothic in a manner which underlines the extent to which these tropes (and the profound cultural anxieties they contain) have now moved beyond the strict remit of the movie industry. Here, Hollywood's most clichéd, destructive and sadistic obsessions are so pervasive and so powerful that they have spilled into associated industries, and into the wider city of Los Angeles. The reasons why Southern California appears to be a particularly attractive breeding ground for new industries – and new religious movements – which appear to promise new life and new opportunities, will be further considered in the final part of this volume, which focuses upon the prominence afforded to narratives about cults and cult-like organisations within the wider California Gothic.

# Notes

1. Seitz, 'Maps to the Stars', online.
2. The Farmer connection is noted by Seitz in his review (ibid.).
3. Fuller, 'Interview with David Cronenberg', online.
4. Ibid.
5. Arnold-de Simine, 'The Body in the Pool', pp. 73–5.
6. Ibid. p. 73.
7. Cronenberg, in Fuller, 'Interview with David Cronenberg'.
8. Ibid.
9. Isaacson, 'Women Acting Out', online.
10. Kermode, '*Maps to the Stars* Review', online.
11. Cronenberg, in Fuller, 'Interview with David Cronenberg'.
12. Mann and Hathaway, in 'Dreams Require Sacrifice', also see *The Neon Demon* and *Starry Eyes* as belonging to a similar cycle of films critiquing the corrosive effects of Hollywood celebrity (pp. 101; 107).
13. Ibid. pp. 104.
14. Billings and Dhanjal, *Supernatural Signs*, pp. 57–8.
15. Mann and Hathaway, 'Dreams Require Sacrifice', p. 106.
16. Ibid. p. 108.
17. Rosten, *Hollywood*, p. 14.
18. Mann and Hathaway, in 'Dreams Require Sacrifice', also mention this obvious engagement with the film industry's long history of sexual exploitation (p. 110).
19. Ibid. p. 110.
20. Ibid. pp. 106; 107.
21. Christiansen, 'Ominous Metamorphoses', p. 83.
22. Featherstone, 'The Letting Go', p. 282.
23. Laws, Stenham and Winding Refn, *The Neon Demon*, Draft: 11.1.14, p. 10, online.
24. Winding Refn on the DVD audio commentary for *The Neon Demon* (2016).
25. Wheatley, 'For Fame and Fashion', p. 128.
26. Laws, Stenham and Winding Refn, *The Neon Demon*, Draft: 11.1.14, p. 49.
27. Winding Refn, DVD audio commentary (2016).
28. Ibid.
29. Featherstone, 'The Letting Go', p. 283.
30. See https://en.wikipedia.org/wiki/Hollywood_Forever_Cemetery (last accessed 25 September 2021).
31. Winding Refn, quoted in *The Neon Demon* Press Kit, n.p., https://www.wildbunch.biz/movie/the-neon-demon/ (last accessed 25 September 2021).

# PART III

# CULT CALIFORNIA:
# NEW GODS AND NEW SELVES

# 6

# Cult Nightmares in *Our Lady of Darkness* (1977) and *Invasion of the Body Snatchers* (1978)

In his 1978 essay, 'The Suicides of the Temple', Umberto Eco discussed how the Jonestown Massacre was processed by the outside world. For Eco, the 'strangest thing' was that newspapers in the US and Europe reacted as if it were 'an inconceivable event'.[1] To him, Jonestown was, contrastingly, 'a matter of flux and reflux, of eternal returns' which had 'all the characteristics of the millenarian movements throughout Western history from the first centuries of Christianity down to the present'.[2]

Jonestown had also, Eco noted, been anticipated by American popular culture. He cited similarities between Jim Jones and the sex-obsessed cult leader in Harold Robbins's potboiler *Dreams Die First* (1977), and the grail cult in Dashiell Hammett's *The Dain Curse* (1929). Eco also references Ed Sanders's 1971 volume, *The Family*, arguing that in this account of 'Charles Manson's California cult and its degeneration, we find everything already there'. This was, for him, a distinctly *American* story, rooted in a specific geographical and cultural locale. Why, he asked, 'do these things happen, and why in California?'[3]

Eco believed that a combination of elements was to blame, amongst them the progressive attitudes associated with California, the search for deeper meaning characteristic of the United States in the late twentieth century, and the unnerving suspicion in the Golden State that the ground beneath one's feet could give way at any moment.[4] For him, Californian culture represented a potent distillation of attitudes already present within the nation at large. It is characterised as a locale where life is both too easy and too difficult:

a paradise cut off from the world, where all is allowed and all is inspired by an obligatory model of 'happiness' (there isn't even the filth of New York or Detroit; you are condemned to be happy). Any promise of community life, of a 'new deal', or regeneration is therefore good. It can come through jogging, satanic cults, New Christianities. The threat of the 'fault' which will one day tear California from the mainland and cast her adrift exerts a mythical pressure on minds made unstable by all the artificiality. Why not Jones and the good death he promises?[5]

In this chapter, I will focus upon two late 1970s narratives which dramatise Eco's claim that California is indeed dangerously receptive to 'minds made unstable' and cult-like movements which peddle the promise of new gods and new selves. In the California Gothic, as we shall see throughout the next two chapters, the quest for happiness, spiritual fulfilment and freedom from past traumas invariably has horrific consequences.

To begin, I'll outline the reasons why California has for so long been considered 'the cult capital' of the United States and discuss the ways in which this perception has coalesced with the dark side of popular culture.[6] Then, I will discuss Fritz Leiber's urban horror story, *Our Lady of Darkness* (1977), and Philip Kaufman's 1978 film, *Invasion of the Body Snatchers*. The cult-like threats faced in both narratives are irrevocably rooted in the social, architectural and cultural contexts of late 1970s San Francisco.

In his 1953 monograph, *California's Utopian Colonies, 1850–1950*, Robert V. Hine notes that Edenic associations were entwined with European visions of California from the outset:

> Since the fifteenth century, when Garcia Ordonez de Montalvo coined a new word, California, for an imaginary island rich in pearls and gold, the name has called up visions of utopia. [. . .] It is hardly surprising then that even as late as the nineteenth and twentieth century, attempts to reconstruct the Garden of Eden should have flourished along the Western sea.[7]

A 'utopian colony' is, in his definition,

> a group of people who are attempting to establish a new social pattern based upon a vision of the ideal society and who have withdrawn themselves from the community at large to embody that vision in experimental form. The purpose is usually to create a model which other colonies and eventually mankind in general will follow.[8]

Such experiments, he states, were particularly numerous in nineteenth-century America thanks to the lack of government censorship, the 'essential optimism of the era' and the ready availability of 'inexpensive and expansive land'.[9] Although New England was home to many of these groups, California was a particularly attractive locale. Between 1850 and 1950, it 'witnessed the formation of a larger number of utopian colonies than any other state in the union. In this period, at least seventeen groups embarked upon an idealistic community experiment in California.'[10]

Several of the groups Hine discusses broadly conformed to the descriptive criteria which, in the 'common parlance' (as Philip Jenkins puts it), is associated with so-called religious 'cults' (although the preferred academic nomenclature within Religious Studies is the more neutral phrase, 'New Religious Movements', or 'NRMs').[11] To the general public and the mass media, as Jenkins outlines, 'cults are exotic movements that practice spiritual totalitarianism: members owe fanatical obedience to the group and to its charismatic leaders, who enforce their authority through mind-control techniques or brainwashing'.[12]

The 1960s and 1970s were a particularly fecund time for the establishment of cult organisations in the United States in general and in California specifically. However, this boom was not unprecedented. An article in *Time Magazine* in March 1930 declared that 'recent years have witnessed a great burgeoning of California cults', citing, amongst others, splinter groups of Jehovah's Witnesses, the Theosophist colony established at Point Loma, the Rosicrucian Fellowship, the 'Order of the Star in the East', the 'Holy City' (Christian fundamentalists based in the Santa Cruz mountains) and the Besant Society, which believed that 'children born on the Pacific Coast, or in Canada and Australia (or other fresh, unexhausted lands) are creatures of a new, sixth race, capable of seeing ethereal spirits, possessed of clairvoyance'.[13] It was noted that California was a particularly attractive locale for such endeavours:

> Thousands of persons, dissatisfied with the faiths of their fathers, seek new spiritual footholds. Thus, as always in such troubled times, there is a flourishing of cults, of religious novelties and new fashions in faith. Flowery, sun-drenched California, where Nature exhibits herself in mystical opulence, where plenty of people have plenty of money, where there are plenty of invalids contemplating eternity, is particularly propitious for this flourishing.[14]

This assessment anticipated Hine's explanation, in which he establishes that in the late nineteenth century, California underwent a

> population growth and industrial expansion which were roughly analogous to the early nineteenth century in the north Atlantic states. [. . .] Obviously the same factors which stimulated so rapid a growth in population during the American Period in California likewise drew utopian colonies. Mild climate and fertility of soil provided attractive foundations, lavishly advertised by railroads, promoters, and chambers of commerce.[15]

James D. Hart's entry on 'Cults' in *A Companion to California* (1978) similarly noted that

> Cults have flourished in California, particularly in the southern part of the state, perhaps to a large degree because its pleasant climate has already attracted somewhat rootless people searching for an easier life than they had previously known. Lacking established associations, these people also quested for new types of communities.[16]

Jenkins underlines that although 'modern observers tend to assume that the idea of cults is relatively modern, it has deep roots in American history'. He cites the period between 1910 and 1935 (the same era discussed in the *Time Magazine* article) as an 'explosive era for new movements and sects', with the 'most celebrated' said to be 'concentrated in California, which had already staked its irrevocable claim to an image of eccentricity'; although, he adds, 'no region of the country was immune from sensational groups'.[17] Though the 'Satanic Panic' era of the 1980s is often cited, Jenkins continues:

> What is less well known is that similar rumors about bloodthirsty devil cults had also run rampant fifty years previously, and in many ways the first panic served as a foundation for the more recent one. We find in this earlier era the beginnings of the modern mythology about homicidal satanic networks being embedded in American neighborhoods, schools, and churches.[18]

He clarifies that the only precedents for the concept of ritualised cult sacrifice being carried out in the United States in either era were found within the work of horror authors such as H. P. Lovecraft, Robert Bloch and August Derleth.[19]

Nevertheless, sensational news stories about nefarious cult activities in the modern era were influenced by real-world horrors. As Jenkins continues: 'While the Manson case inspired tales of ritual murder gangs, Jonestown contributed to the idea that extreme child abuse was a cult characteristic.'[20] In 1970 – shortly after the slaughter at 10050 Cielo Drive, and several years before the mass murder/suicides in Jonestown – a paperback entitled *Satan's Slaves and the Bizarre 'Underground' Cults of California* was published in the UK. Here, Los Angeles is described as 'a haven for the unstable, the manic depressive, the crank, the exhibitionist, the hedonist'.[21] The book's author, James Taylor, argued that the city 'alone shares the responsibility for attracting the type of individual that is now giving the Golden State a bad name', although San Francisco, which gave 'birth to the hippie movement in its Haight-Ashbury ghetto' is also criticised.[22] He says of the Manson murders:

That the ritualistic mass murder in Benedict Canyon evolved from the Los Angeles scene is really no surprise. For generations, L.A. has been begging for such a 'happening'. One can blame the 'family' for its horrific slaying. One can accuse hippie-ism for its non-conformist attitude to real life. One can conclude that when law and order breaks down to permit drug-taking and free-love communes then one must expect violent insurrection. But can we ever condone the slow disintegration of moral values that has taken us all down the road to brutality and perversion as seen in the Tate slaying? Los Angeles has a lot to answer for – and a lot to offer.[23]

Written in December 1969, before, he admits, anything 'had been proven in court', Taylor's account of the Manson slayings and of the 'family' and other 'Satanic' groups is a lurid, impressionistic cultural artefact, most notable because it so obviously adopts the language of horror-tinged pulp fiction, anticipating the tone of titles such as the influential and widely discredited 1980 Satanic Panic 'memoir', *Michelle Remembers*. The Tate killings, Taylor claims,

> are the final straw to break the apathetic back of the long-suffering American camel. Stories of hippie sex-drug antics in way-out areas of the Golden State have multiplied. And they were frequent enough before Sharon Tate lost her life and unborn baby. The climate of public opinion has long been hardening against hippiedom. The original wonderment and 'smiling youth must have its fling' has vanished. California is steadily becoming more conservative . . . In every region of the State, the daily confrontation of young and old grows more vicious.[24]

Taylor's take on the Manson killings was echoed in Ed Sanders's *The Family: The Story of Charles Manson's Dune Buggy Attack Battalion*, the account, as he puts it, of 'how a group of young Americans became welded together into a war-like clan that killed'.[25] For Sanders, Manson was the negative flipside to the 'noble experiment' of the hippie era. He contrasts Manson's gang with Ken Kesey's 'Merry Pranksters', who 'popularised in 1964–65 the concept of the travelling school bus, painted and decorated artistically, full of decorous wanderers. It was they who experimented in group acid trips, and, more importantly, group mystical experiences under LSD.'[26] They were, Sanders continues, 'essentially good'. Manson, he argues, 'carried this onward, making it evil, slowly changing the colors, the red tempura becoming dog blood, the acid test turning to psychedelic satanism, the filming of happiness turning to the filming of the hapless murder of female Caucasians on the beaches of southern California'.[27] His concluding remarks explicitly link the regional landscape with the malevolent acts recently committed there: 'And only when all these evil affairs are known and exposed can the curse of ritual sacrifice, Helter Skelter and satanism be removed from the coasts and mountains and deserts of California.'[28]

Rebecca Solnit uses imagery associated with cult violence – the infamous 'rattlesnake in the mailbox' which members of the Synanon Foundation (an 'experimental community' started in the 1950s as a drug rehabilitation programme) left for one of its critics in October 1978[29] – as the central organising metaphor for her 2014 essay on the era. As is also the case in this chapter, the year 1978 is cited as a macabre milestone for the state.[30] For Solnit, Kaufman's *Invasion of the Body Snatchers* is the definitive film of that year, because it

> makes an allegory of the fuzzy thinking, fuzzy surfaces, spreading tendrils, and labyrinthine passages that were both the culture and the landscape of San Francisco during the late 1970s. In other words, the city – and by extension, the world – is being eaten by the counterculture, and being taken over by the pods that turn people into affectless ambulatory vegetables.[31]

She sees the transformation undergone by Synanon as one that had parallels throughout the decade: 'The rattlesnake in the mailbox – is that what the 1960s had become? What had begun as one of a host of idealistic and innovative projects during the previous era had gone off the deep end . . . Authoritarian leaders and strange cults proliferated.'[32]

What interests me are the ways this conviction that the 'California Dream' had 'gone off the deep end' was being dramatised within popular culture in the late 1970s. Here, already long-standing European (and later American) perceptions of the region as a place with boundless utopian potential – a perspective which of course ignores the displacement and attempted extermination of California's Indigenous population – are turned on their head. As Krishan Kumar observes, 'like a malevolent and grimacing doppelgänger, anti-utopia has stalked utopia from the very beginning. They have been locked together in a contrapuntal embrace, a circling dance, that has checked the escape of either for very long.'[33]

One of key strands of the California Gothic is the frequency with which the desire for 'enlightenment' and personal growth/happiness becomes associated with violence, death and destruction. Threats to personality, individual personhood and bodily and psychological integrity abound, and physical and mental changes associated with the groups which propagate these beliefs are invariably negative. The state's cultural and physical landscapes are often seen as crucial contributing factors, and the place in which one is, as Eco sardonically put it, 'condemned to be happy', here becomes the spawning ground for a particularly Californian kind of dread.

## 'Their Favourite Guru of the Left-Handed Path':
### *Our Lady of Darkness*

Fritz Leiber was one of the most influential genre authors of the twentieth century. His tales about mercenary heroes 'Fafhrd and the Gray Mouser' (characters he created with his friend Harry Otto Fischer) 'established him as the leading American writer of sword-and-sorcery stories'.[34] He was also an acclaimed science fiction author. It is his pioneering work within the supernatural 'urban gothic' that interests me here. As Brian Stableford observes, Leiber excelled at

> devising hauntings and supernatural creatures specifically adapted to contemporary urban environments. The settings of his stories are city landscapes – tenements, factories, lighted streets – and Leiber proved that such settings could contain supernatural phenomena just as aptly and convincingly as the ancient mansions and stagnant swamps that were still conventional in the weird fiction of the day.[35]

One of his most famous stories, 'Smoke Ghost' (1941), epitomises this approach. The story is about a seemingly ordinary businessman who becomes convinced that a malevolent presence haunts the unnamed city in which he lives and works. He asks his secretary:

> Have you ever thought about what a ghost of our times would look like, Miss Millick? Just picture it. A smoky composite face with the hungry anxiety of the unemployed, the neurotic restlessness of the person without purpose, the jerky tension of the high-pressure metropolitan worker, the sullen resentment of the striker, the callous viciousness of the strike breaker, the aggressive whine of the panhandler, the inhibited terror of the bombed civilian, and a thousand other twisted emotional patterns?[36]

'Smoke Ghost' is one of the most unnerving supernatural horror tales of the twentieth century because the terrifying presence which terrorises the protagonist is the grasping embodiment of modernity itself. It also features themes which would recur over and over in Leiber's horror fiction. All-powerful women with considerable destructive potential are a recurring preoccupation. As Robert Hadji notes, 'the most significant aspect of Leiber's horror fiction, in personal as well as literary terms, has undoubtedly been his continuing fascination with the femme fatale'.[37] This is particularly notable in 'The Girl with the Hungry Eyes' (1949), which was also briefly referenced in the previous chapter. The story is about a photographer who finds himself enthralled and then terrified by a woman who has somehow been shaped by the 'hidden most hungers of millions of men'.[38] As Leiber puts it, she is 'the quintessence of the horror behind the billboard': the personification of contemporary consumer culture at its very worst.

Similarly, in *Conjure Wife* (story 1943; novel 1953), college professor Norman Saylor makes an unwelcome discovery whilst snooping in his wife Tansy's dressing room. He confronts Tansy and learns that she genuinely believes herself to have magical powers. Norman's initial scepticism is soon eroded. Not only is Tansy really a witch, but, unbeknown to their menfolk, the women of the world are all, secretly, capable of summoning magical forces. A series of increasingly alarming mishaps and 'accidents' intrude into his previously orderly and comfortable life.[39] As is common in post-World War II American horror fiction, everyday reality is constantly under threat from sinister elements churning just below the surface of 'ordinary' life.

Leiber's late-career masterpiece, *Our Lady of Darkness*, furthers this sense that 'normality' can at any moment be devastatingly undermined. It was initially published in early 1977 as *The Pale Brown Thing*, a two-part novella in the *Magazine of Fantasy and Science Fiction*, before being expanded for republication under the better-known title later the same year.[40] The novel represents a landmark contribution to the California Gothic canon. As S. T. Joshi puts it, this is 'a novel that simultaneously captured the topography of San Francisco, where Leiber had long resided, and is a grand summation of many of the elements of urban horror that he had introduced in his pioneering short stories of the preceding decades'.[41]

*Our Lady of Darkness* begins with a reference to the 'Levana and Our Ladies of Sorrow' extract from *Suspiria de Profundis* (1845) by Thomas De Quincey, in which he introduces his ancient and all-powerful 'three mothers': *Mater Lachrymarum* (Our Lady of Tears), *Mater Suspiriorum* (Our Lady of Sighs) and *Mater Tenebrarum* (Our Lady of Darkness). One of the great coincidences of modern horror lies in the fact that both Leiber and director Dario Argento (together with co-writer Daria Nicolodi) used De Quincey's concept as inspiration for now-classic narratives released in 1977. In Argento's case, the result was the *giallo* classic *Suspiria*, in which a Berlin ballet school is home to a coven of witches in thrall to the Lady of Sighs. Leiber also locates occult conspiracy in the heart of the modern city. His main character, a recently widowed writer of weird fiction named Franz Westen, is an authorial insert whose life circumstances have much in common with those of Leiber himself.

The city of San Francisco is physically and historically central to *Our Lady of Darkness*. The occult conspiracy Franz finds himself embroiled in is rooted in its landscape, and the key to the secrets he must unravel to survive lies hidden in its *fin-de-siècle* era literary history. *Our Lady of Darkness* is firmly embedded in both the past and the present of California's most bohemian city. This sense of locational specificity is apparent from the outset. The novel begins in Corona Heights, the hilly outcrop located next to the Castro and Corona Heights neighbourhoods. Despite the 'nervous, bright lights of downtown San Francisco', something distinctly 'other' and distinctly piti-less lurks there like a 'great predatory beast'. Corona Heights, we are told, is 'too savage and cantankerous for a park' and so, incongruously, has been developed as a playground instead – thereby juxtaposing the innocence of the city's offspring with the primal landscape in which they play (the 1978 version of *Invasion of the Body Snatchers* also begins in a San Francisco play-ground).[42] The final lines of Leiber's opening inform us that whatever lies within the Heights has 'at last decided on a victim'.[43]

That 'victim' (and our hero) is Franz Westen, introduced as he begins the day in his eccentric old apartment building. Franz is an amiable man in his late forties who was so devastated by the death of his wife, Daisy, that he became an alcoholic. However, Franz has now given up the booze and is happily working on tie-in novels for a trashy television show named 'Weird Underground'. Although he is working below his true potential, the job keeps him busy and allows him to indulge in his love of the occult, and in the work of authors such as Lovecraft, M. R. James and California's own weird-fiction prodigy, Clark Ashton Smith.

Franz's return to the land of the living owes much to the relationships he has built up with the other residents of his late nineteenth-century apartment building on Geary Street. In addition to his friendship with the Peruvian care-takers, Franz is fond of his bachelor neighbours Gunnar and Saul (whose close relationship, he suspects, may perhaps be romantic). Franz has also begun a tentative romance with his younger neighbour Cal (Calpurnia), a musician. Cal is the latest in a long line of Leiber women with extraordinary and potentially terrifying abilities.

Even in these early scenes, Leiber suggests that Franz is overly susceptible to feminine influence. An oil portrait of his late wife hangs above his lonely bed, whilst one side of the mattress is filled with dozens of books 'unconsciously arranged into a female form with long, long legs'.[44] Although Franz initially views this 'Scholar's Mistress' with wry amusement, it will, by the end of the novel, have been transformed into a genuinely threatening presence. In an early indication of Cal's pivotal role in saving Franz from the titular 'Dark Lady', the soothing sound of her music can be heard through the walls of his apartment. Female influence, benign and otherwise, is everywhere in his life.

Franz also projects his fascination with the female form onto a real-life feature of the San Francisco skyline. The Sutro TV tower is described as both 'an obscene embodiment of the blatant world of sales and advertising' and 'a broad-shouldered, slender-waisted, and long-legged' creation which recalls 'a beautiful and stylish woman – or demigoddess'.[45] Completed in 1972, until 2017 the tower was the tallest structure in San Francisco. Like the other (then) recently erected structure which plays a pivotal role in *Our Lady of Darkness*, the Transamerica Pyramid building, it inspired local controversy. City news-paper columnist Herb Caen wrote that he was 'waiting for it to stalk down the hill and attack the Golden Gate Bridge'.[46]

The other city landmark which catches Franz's eye is Corona Heights. It looks, he decides, like 'a raw remnant of up thrust from the earthquake of 1906' – a detail which connects the hill to the primal geographical (and occult) forces which lie just below the surface.[47] It is whilst looking towards the Heights that Franz first sees the terrifying entity which will soon haunt his every waking thought. It initially seems harmless, a 'pale brown rock which detached itself from the others and waved at him'.[48] The entity even evokes the eccentricity of the city's well-established counterculture: 'he smiled broadly at the thought of some hippy type greeting the morning sun with ritual prancing on a mid-city hilltop newly emerged from fog'.[49] It is likely, Franz reflects, someone from Haight-Ashbury: 'a stoned priest of a modern sun god dancing around his little accidental high-set Stonehenge'.[50]

Despite Cal's warning that there have been 'some murders' near the park, Franz puts aside his books and goes there for a hike. One of these volumes is a tome entitled *Megapolisomancy: A New Science of Cities*, by (fictional author) Thibault de Castries. As Franz heads off on his walk, Leiber has already estab-lished the novel's key thematic threads: the presence of dark (and somehow unsettlingly *feminine*) forces hidden in the natural and the built landscape of San Francisco; the cosy yet 'odd' layout of Franz's apartment building; and the suggestion of an association between the city's bohemian underbelly and potentially dangerous occult forces.

Franz explains to Cal that

> this de Castries is very much concerned about the 'vast amounts' of steel and paper that were being accumulated in big cities. And coal oil (kerosene) and natural gas. And electricity too [. . .] But what he was most agitated about was the psychological or spiritual (he calls them 'paramental') effects of all that stuff accumulating in big cities, its sheer liquid and solid mass.[51]

Though de Castries was of European origin, we are told that he settled in San Francisco around 1900 and lived there for the rest of his life. As the novel progresses, it becomes clear that his conviction that the modern cityscape could somehow give rise to 'paramental' forces has some truth in it. The connection between San Francisco's past and present countercultural tendencies is reinforced by Cal's suggestion that de Castries was 'a real proto-hippy'.[52]

As Franz walks across the city, Leiber describes local landmarks in considerable detail. Mentioned again, for instance, is the Transamerica Pyramid building, which Franz believes 'Old Thibault' would have scowled at. His recollections of de Castries's book are stimulated by the sights of the city, and important clues as to the nature of the threat he will soon face are laid out:

> The words came into his head, 'The ancient Egyptians only buried people in their pyramids. We are living in ours.' Now where had he read that? Why, in *Megapolisomancy*, of course. How apt! And did the modern pyramids have in them secret markings foretelling the future and crypts for sorcery?[53]

Upon ascending Corona Heights, Franz gazes out at the city, his perception of the buildings before him again influenced by de Castries's theories – an early sign of the malign influence the man's occult legacy exerts. He spies his own apartment window in the far distance, but is horrified when the 'pale brown shape' previously glimpsed from the reverse vantage point waves at him. Though he tries to convince himself that the figure is probably a burglar 'on hard drugs' (another detail which links occult activity to social disorder), upon returning home, he only finds some oddly unsettling 'crumbles of brownish paper'.

As the novel progresses, Franz becomes yet more drawn to de Castries and his connection to San Francisco's real-life *fin de siècle* Bohemian set – and to the work of Clark Ashton Smith, who was an actual contemporary of Lovecraft and Robert E. Howard. In his canny interweaving of the local literary history with his own unique brand of urban Gothic, Leiber creates a sense of distinct regional specificity. This isn't just a novel set in San Francisco, it is a novel *about* San Francisco.

Once Franz realises that the journal he purchased alongside the de Castries volume belonged to Smith, the interweaving of fact and fiction accelerates. Smith is said to have written that de Castries took credit for the deaths of many of his bohemian contemporaries. Franz is aware of this detail's basis in truth:

> He knew quite a bit about the brilliant literary group centered in San Francisco at the turn of century and of the strangely large number of them who had come to tragic ends – among those, the macabre writer Ambrose Bierce vanishing in revolution-torn Mexico in 1913, [Jack] London dying of uremia and morphine poisoning a little later, and the fantasy poet

[George] Sterling perishing of poisoning in the 1920s. He reminded himself to ask Jaime Donaldus Byers more about the whole business at the first opportunity.[54]

In his discussion of San Francisco's 'Bohemian Shores', Kevin Starr chronicles the unhappy fates which met the poet George Sterling, the journalist and writer Ambrose Bierce and many of their contemporaries, noting of Sterling (who was once a leading light) that by the time of his suicide in 1926, 'The golden age of San Francisco's bohemia had definitely come to a miserable end.'[55] The self-destruction, nihilism and squandered promise which Starr sees as characterising many of the city's leading artistic figures during this period may, he concludes, have had something to do with nature of the state:

> The record of so much desperation makes one wonder whether California was not to blame. As a provincial culture, eager to upgrade itself, it authenticated its artists too easily and they in turn fell into an exaggerated sense of their own importance [. . .] As a region, California offered itself too easily as a self-justifying symbol of spacious identity.[56]

Though he came to prominence during the closing stages of this bohemian era, and knew some its most famous exponents, Smith avoided the tragic denouement that afflicted many of his predecessors and contemporaries. As Joshi outlines, the Auburn native became a literary celebrity when his baroque poetry was championed by Sterling.[57] Hailed by local newspapers as the 'boy poet of the Sierras', Smith's early work garnered commercial success and critical acclaim.[58] Lovecraft liked his poems so much that he wrote him a fan letter, and the two began a friendship which greatly influenced Smith's career. According to Don Herron, Lovecraft 'held Smith in something like awe, considering him the greatest writer of their weird circle'.[59]

Although Smith initially only submitted poems to magazines (with Lovecraft's encouragement), according to Joshi the need for money meant that 'in late 1929 he suddenly began producing stories in substantial numbers. Over the next four years he would write nearly a hundred stories and would vigorously market them to such pulps as *Weird Tales*, *Wonder Stories*, and *Strange Tales*.'[60] As Herron notes, the majority of Smith's prose stories were set in 'other dimensions and spheres' and, in particular, his 'fictional continent of Zothique'.[61] But he did set some in contemporary California, and several of them evoke the unsettling and unwilling proximity to sinister alien realms reminiscent of the best of Lovecraft.

These include 'The Devotee of Evil' (1933), which, as Joshi notes, was inspired by a reputedly haunted house in Smith's hometown of Auburn.[62]

The story, narrated by his recurring protagonist, Philip Hastane, is set in a sinister mansion with a gruesome past, and revolves around the ultimately disastrous occult experiments undertaken by a wealthy Creole eccentric named Jean Averaud, who believes that evil is actually a 'sort of dark vibration, the radiation of a black sun, of a centre of malignant eons'.[63] Averaud bought this house because its dark past suggests that it is one of those special places that are more receptive 'to evil places than others'. He constructs a mysterious 'mechanism' which will allow him to make tangible 'this absolute evil'. Unfortunately for him, he succeeds. The evil he conjures is so all powerful that it leaves him 'petrified into an image of its own essence'.[64] As well as anticipating Leiber by situating cosmic evil in contemporary California, 'Devotee of Evil' features an exotic female character – a 'beautiful mulatess [sic] who never spoke to anyone and was thought to be his [Averaud's] mistress as well as his housekeeper' – who bears a marked resemblance to the mysterious 'Lady of Darkness' associated with Thibault de Castries in Leiber's story.[65]

However, it is Smith's 'The City of the Singing Flame' (1931) which is referenced in Leiber's *Our Lady of Darkness*. As Joshi outlines, the story was inspired by Smith's trips to Crater Ridge, near the Donner Pass.[66] Philip Hastane (who also narrates this story) describes the strange events which occurred when his friend Giles Angarth, an author of 'fantastic fiction' who has been spending the summer in the Sierras, goes missing, along with his illustrator Felix Ebbonly. The answers lie in a journal Angarth sent to Hastane just before his final trip to the mountains, in which Angarth describes coming across two strangely uniform boulders set about five feet apart. The 'greenish-grey stone' they are made from is some queer substance, 'different from everything else in the neighbourhood'.[67] Upon stepping into the gap between the boulders, he is transported to a bizarre new realm. After this initial experience, Angarth becomes obsessed with returning to the other world's teeming 'Titan' city, which is inhabited by a multitude of fascinating beings which, he carefully notes, are 'not monstrous, but have merely developed in obedience to the laws of another evolution than ours'.[68] Upon following the stream of creatures making their way to the city, all of whom are drawn there by an irresistible 'siren melody', Angarth realises that they are travelling to a shrine dominated by the titular 'singing flame'. These 'pilgrims' are then irresistibly compelled to jump into the heart of the fire. Though he is just about able to tear himself away and make his way home, Angarth is unable to stop thinking about what he has witnessed. He invites his friend Felix to come along the next time. The story ends as Angarth describes the circumstances under which Felix hurls himself into the annihilating flame. In his final notes, Angarth says he is going to willingly give himself over to this 'glorious death'. Since 'Real' life has become meaningless, and 'Literature is nothing more than the shadow of a shadow', tomorrow, he concludes, 'I shall return to the city.'[69]

In *Our Lady of Darkness*, 'The City of the Singing Flame' is referred to by Franz in passing as 'that marvellous fantasy'.[70] However, Leiber's references to Smith's life and work are more than mere homage. Although many of Smith's tales are set in exotic secondary worlds, it is 'The City of the Singing Flame' – which opens with detailed descriptions of the rugged Californian landscape – that is explicitly mentioned. Leiber's novel begins with his description of Corona Heights. In both narratives, the primal-seeming California landscape is a site where otherworldly forces gain traction, and naive day trippers stumble across knowledge which changes how they see the world around them. There is also a sense in these stories that creative individuals who make their living by engaging with the fantastical are more susceptible to otherworldly influence than the 'ordinary' person.

In a bid to find out more about the baleful influence which has entered his life, Franz consults his friend Jaime Donaldus Byers, a dedicated libertine well-versed in the lives and proclivities of his *fin de siècle* predecessors. After Franz reveals that he has come to believe that he is being pursued by paramentals, Byers admits that he also owns a copy of *Megapolisomancy* and has researched the man behind the tome. De Castries is cited as the reason why Clark Ashton Smith left San Francisco behind and 'became the hermit of Auburn and Pacific Grove'.[71] It is during this meeting that the decidedly cult-like characteristics of de Castries's bohemian collective begin to emerge.

De Castries, Byers begins, came to turn-of-the-century San Francisco 'like a dark portent from realms of cold and coal smoke in the East that pulsed with Edison's electricity and from which would thrust Sullivan's steel-framed sky-scrapers'.[72] This was an age characterised by immense industrial and technological progress, but also by a wave of spiritual and occult inquiry. De Castries, the dark seer of this new era, brought with him to the West Coast a bag 'stuffed with copies of his ill-printed book' and 'a skull teeming with galvanic, darkly illuminating ideas'. He was also accompanied ('some insist') by a 'large black panther' on a silver leash – though other observers insisted that he was 'accompanied or else pursued by a mysterious, tall, slender woman who always wore a black veil and loose dark dresses that were more like robes, and had a way of appearing and disappearing suddenly'.[73]

After a youth that apparently involved a sojourn in Egypt, de Castries ended up in 'the City by the Golden Gate', having 'acquired a lot of dark, satanic charm from somewhere'. He was looking for 'an elite of scintillating, freewheeling folks with a zest for life at its wildest' and found them. Leiber here again namechecks real-life members of the city's bohemian set: Sterling, Jack London, Bierce, the poet Nora May French (another famous suicide) and even Gertrude Atherton. De Castries is said to have made an immediate impression:

> He was just the sort of human curiosity they (and especially Jack London) loved. Mysterious cosmopolitan background, Munchausen anecdotes, weird and alarming scientific theories, a strong anti-industrial (and we'd say) anti-Establishment bias, the apocalyptic touch, the note of doom, hints of dark powers – he had them all! For quite a while he was their darling, their favourite guru of the left-hand path, almost (and I imagine he thought this himself) their new god. . . . And they were all quite ready to go along (in theory) with his dream of Utopia in which megapolitan buildings were forbidden (had been destroyed or somehow tamed) and parementality put to benign use, with themselves the aristocratic elite and he the master spirit over all.[74]

Adding to de Castries's reputation was his companion, whom he referred to as his 'Queen of Night, Our Lady of Darkness'. Upon hearing these words, it suddenly occurs to Franz that she must be 'one of De Quincey's Ladies of Sorrow, the third and youngest sister'.[75] Reactions to the 'Dark Lady' varied (men were intrigued, women 'uniformly loathed her') and speculation abounded as to the true nature of de Castries's sexual proclivities, especially given San Francisco's reputation as a particularly permissive locale. The 'high point' of his San Francisco adventure, Byers continues, came when he established a 'Hermetic Order' along the same lines of the Order of the Golden Dawn after Aleister Crowley almost broke it up 'by his demands for Satanistic Rituals, black magic, and other real tough stuff'.[76] Crowley is, of course, also referenced in two of the Hollywood Gothic films considered in the previous chapter.

Once the 'Hermetic Order of the Onyx Dusk' was initiated, de Castries revealed his intentions to his eager new acolytes – intentions which resemble those espoused by the leaders of several of the most infamous real-life cults established in California since the mid-nineteenth century:

> As soon as his secret society had been constituted, Thibault revealed to its double handful of highly select members that his Utopia was not a far-off dream, but an immediate prospect, and that it was to be achieved by violent revolution, both material and immaterial (that is, paramental) and that the chief and at first the sole instrument of that revolution was to be the Hermetic Order of the Onyx Dusk.[77]

This campaign to establish utopia via terrorism was to begin with acts of public disorder reminiscent of the actions of the Russian anarchists, albeit with de Castries's 'black magic' thrown into the mix. Bombs were to be set off in San

Francisco's public places and larger buildings, electric lighting was to be sabo-
taged and anonymous letters and phone calls 'would heighten the hysteria'.[78]
The most ambitious of these operations were the group's 'megapolisomantic'
endeavours, which would supposedly cause 'buildings to crumple to rubble,
people to go screaming mad, until every last soul is in panicked flight from San
Francisco'.[79] Crucially, these operations would 'require absolute obedience on
the part of Thibault's assistants', who were dispatched to various locations
around the city to perform odd rituals which would, when performed in the
right order, allegedly help destroy the buildings their leader believed were
poisoning the metropolis. When these initial missions seemed to accomplish
little and his followers drifted away, a vengeful de Castries tried to blackmail his acolytes by revealing scandalous information about them. Despite his
increasing irrelevance, the feeling 'that he was a being with sinister, paramental
powers' was underlined when the 1906 earthquake took place, 'thundering in
brick and concrete waves from the west and killing its hundreds, [when] one
of his lapsed acolytes, probably recalling his intimations of a magic that could
topple skyscrapers, is supposed to have said, "He's done it! The old devil's
done it!"'[80]

The exact nature of the connection between Franz's 'paramental' encounters and de Castries's desire to bring the skyscrapers of San Francisco crashing
to the ground is revealed when Byers relates the occultist's 'last acolyte and
final end'.[81] The tale picks up again in the 1920s, when de Castries was living
in 'downtown cheap hotels' and still brooding about the revenge he wished to
wreak upon those who abandoned him. De Castries also became obsessed with
destroying every copy of his book. At this point, the young poet and writer
Clark Ashton Smith, who is said to have decided to look up acquaintances
of his mentor George Sterling (who here, as in real life, is said to have died a
'nasty' death by suicide), contacts de Castries.

With his old desire to dominate others fired by the presence of this talented
young man, de Castries, for the last time, expounded upon his weird theories
to a receptive listener:

> For several weeks Clark delayed his return to Auburn, fearfully reveling
> in the ominous, wonder-shot, strangely real world that old Tiberius, the
> scarecrow emperor of terror and mysteries, painted for him afresh each
> day – a San Francisco of spectral . . . mental entities more real than life.[82]

However, de Castries was enraged when Smith, who became deeply unsettled
by these conversations, returned back home without warning. In an act obviously reminiscent of the actions of M. R. James's embittered conjurer Karswell

in his 1911 story, 'Casting the Runes', de Castries created a carefully handwritten 'Curse upon Master Clark Ashton Smith and all his heirs', which he then hid in the binding of Smith's journal.[83] This is, of course, the same volume which Franz now owns. But the connections between de Castries and Franz don't end there: after his death, de Castries's cremated remains were scattered late one night by his few remaining acquaintances – amongst them, Dashiell Hammett. The site chosen was the rocky outcrop on Corona Heights where Franz first saw the terrifying 'pale brown thing'. The old man was 'burned wearing a bathrobe he'd worn to tatters . . . a pale old brown one with a cowl'.[84]

Byers reveals that he has been attempting to counteract de Castries's lingering influence for years, and that it was he who graffitied astrological symbols on the Heights as a protective measure. Again, the thematic connection between California's occult past and the troubled late 1970s present is highlighted. Byers regards paramental entities as

> about midway in nature between the atomic bomb and the archetypes of the collective unconscious, which include several highly dangerous characters, as you know. Or between a Charles Manson or Zodiac killer and kappa phenomena as defined by Melita Denning in *Gnostica*.[85]

When he finally leaves Byers's apartment, Franz is in a daze. As he walks back home to 811 Geary Street, he realises that whilst before he had thought of de Castries as 'a mere parochial devil haunting the lonely hump of Corona Heights', now he cannot help but think of a 'ubiquitous demon, ghost, or paramental inhabiting the whole city with its scattered humping hills'.[86] Some of the atoms he shed during his life may even, Franz ponders, be in 'the very air' he is now breathing, as were 'the atoms too of Francis Drake (sailing past San Francisco Bay-to-be in the *Golden Hind*), and of Shakespeare and Socrates and Solomon (and of Dashiell Hammett and Clark Ashton Smith)'.[87]

When Franz attends a concert in which Cal is performing, the final pieces of the puzzle fall into place. He is at first transported by the beauty of the classical music. For the first time since Corona Heights, we are told that Franz 'felt wholly safe, among his friends and in the arms of ordered sound, as if the music were an intimate crystal heaven around and over them, a perfect barrier to paranatural forces'.[88] But when Cal's harpsichord begins to play, he realises why de Castries's occult equations, which did Smith no harm at all, have now been activated. The curse was an equation depending on the precise triangulation of forces related to the city's largest buildings. It failed to work in the 1920s because it depended upon two structures erected long *after* Smith died – the Transamerica Pyramid building and the Sutro TV tower. The final triangulation point is the building containing the room where de Castries spent the final, hate-fuelled years of his life. Upon later flicking through a 1927 city directory, Franz discovers that his own building was once the Rhodes Hotel: 'I live at 607 Rhodes, the place I've hunted for everywhere else. There's really no mystery about it.' He lives 'at the fulcrum of the curse'.[89]

Franz, mentally depleted and emotionally drained, settles in at home to await the return of his friends Cal, Gunnar and Saul, deriving brief solace from a chess match with Fernando, the janitor. Fernando realises that Franz is under occult attack and helps him draw protective pentagrams on the walls. Before he drifts off to sleep, Franz rearranges his 'Scholar's Mistress' on the bed, noting that it is made up of books written by any number of authors associated with the supernatural and the occult. He is seized by a sense of despair, suddenly convinced that

> This city was a mess with its gimcrack high rises and trumpery skyscrapers – Towers of Treason indeed. It had all tumbled down and burned in 1906 (at least everything around this building had) and soon enough would again, and all of the papers be fed to the document-shredding machines, with or without the help of paramentals.[90]

The world now seems a place irrevocably diseased, consumed by a cancer which has been created out of the very materials from which the modern city has been built. As Franz falls asleep to the sound of 'endless sheets of newsprint being crumpled', he finds himself lying next to a presence which at first seems to be his beloved wife Daisy – but it is a version of Daisy which appears to be very sick:

> in the vegetable stage, mercifully tranquilized by her malignancy. Horrible, yet it was still a comfort to lie beside her. Like Cal, she was so young, even in this half-death. Her fingers were so very slim and silken dry, so very strong and many, all starting to grip tightly – they were not fingers but wiry black vines rooted inside her skull, growing in profusion out of her cavernous orbits, gushing luxuriously out of the triangular hole between the nasal and the vomer bones, twining in tendrils from under her upper teeth so white . . .[91]

When he awakes, Franz realises that the nightmare is still unfolding. The paramental entity is in his room, her skeleton the shape of the Sutro TV tower, and 'her thin, wide-shouldered body . . . apparently formed solely of shredded and compacted paper' – paper from the pulp magazines and esoteric volumes with which he has shared his lonely bed.[92] This is the real face of the veiled woman who accompanied de Castries everywhere: Our Lady of Darkness. Just when it seems as if there is no possibility of escape, Franz is saved by the benign and witch-like powers of a woman irrevocably associated with order and goodness. Cal, who sensed that something was terribly wrong, rushes into Franz's room and destroys the entity by instinctively blurting out an impromptu ode to rationality: 'In the names of Bach, Mozart, and Beethoven, the names of Pythagoras, Newton, and Einstein, by Bertrand Russell, William James, and Eustace Hayden, begone! All inharmonious and disorderly shapes and forces, depart at once!'[93] This last-minute deliverance from evil means that even though *Our Lady of Darkness* depicts San Francisco as a locale 'impregnated' (as Franz says of de Castries's burial at Corona Heights) by terrifying 'paramental' forces, it is also something of a love letter to the city, shot through by Leiber's obvious affection for his adopted hometown.

The novel also has some intriguing thematic components in common with the sub-section of American horror films categorised by Matt Becker (2006) as examples of 'Hippie Horror'. Using George A. Romero's *Night of the Living Dead* (1968) as his starting point, Becker argues that late 1960s/early to mid-1970s apocalyptic horror movies such as *Last House on the Left* (1972) and *The Texas Chainsaw Massacre* (1974) ultimately express 'an overriding political ambivalence that was intimately related to a shift in the hippie counterculture's worldview from broad optimism to a foreboding sense of failure and doom'.[94] As he notes, the hippie movement began in mid-1960s San Francisco, 'although its sensibilities quickly spread throughout the country'.[95]

When discussing the process by which the ostensibly non-materialistic, optimistic, pacifist, open-minded and spiritually and sexually liberated movement began to implode under the weight of its own myriad contradictions, Becker cites political scientist Marshall Berman's account of his participation in the 1967 'Exorcism of the Pentagon', 'when a huge throng of hippies amassed to magically "drive out the demons that infused" this symbol of American imperialism "with its evil power"'.[96] Berman, he notes, later recalled that 'Even as we closed in on the Pentagon, we knew that computers were being programmed and orders given inside, and bombs were being dropped half a world away, and people were being killed, and we had no power to stop it.'[97] Becker observes that

> For Berman, the exorcism compelled him to confront not only the powerlessness of the hippies, but also their directionlessness as a movement, and this lack of vision was due, in part, to their mirroring of the very forces they sought to transform . . . In other words, Berman recognised that along with

its culture of peace and love, within the hippie counterculture were strains of malevolence that paralleled those of the 'Establishment'.[98]

In Becker's analysis, as more and more young people embraced the hippie way of life, the 'more diffused, confused, distorted and subdued the revolutionary potential of the hippie's cultural politics became', and the negative transformations became all too apparent on the streets of San Francisco:

> As the population increased, so did the problems. Among the human zoo of the overcrowded Haight were delinquents, psychotics and con artists who jockeyed for space in an environment made increasingly fetid by bad drugs, police harassment, venereal disease – there were dozens of reasons for the degeneration. 'There was a phrase the acid freaks used about a bad trip: they called it a "horror show"', writes Godfrey Hodgson of LSD's occasionally negative effects. 'By 1968 the psychedelic paradise [of the Haight] itself was turning in to a horror show' . . . It was thus not only external traumas that turned the hippie's once-bright hope of a utopian future into a burned-out pessimism. This dystopian reality was also the result of internal malignancies.[99]

Leiber's depiction of late 1970s San Francisco as a city beset by sinister supernatural forces embedded in its infrastructure by a sinister 'proto-hippy', means that his novel vividly evokes the 'dystopian reality' and the 'internal malignancies' that Becker saw arising from the ashes of the late 1960s counterculture. The open-mindedness and experimentalism which in the novel lead to the city's late nineteenth-century bohemian elite falling under the influence of a mesmeric madman, has obvious parallels to the real-life rise to prominence of figures such as Jim Jones, whose San Francisco connections ran deep. The abortive campaign of terror conceived of by de Castries also evokes the many bomb attacks and shootings carried out in the city in the years just before *Our Lady of Darkness* was published. As Brian Burrough has detailed, during the mid-1970s, San Francisco was terrorised by a series of bomb attacks carried out by a radical group operating under the name 'the New World Liberation Front' (NWLF):

> The bombings had become a fixture of daily life in the Bay Area, like the fog. After its debut in August 1974 the NWLF had accelerated the pace of its actions in 1975, detonating thirty-seven explosive devices by the time [Patricia] Hearst was captured, an average of one every week for nine months [. . .] There were so many bombings that an FBI man termed San Francisco the 'Belfast of North America'.[100]

However, unlike the 'Hippie Horror' movies considered by Becker, *Our Lady of Darkness* has little of the nihilism that characterises much bleaker deconstructions of the hippie era, such as *Last House on the Left* and *The Texas Chainsaw Massacre*. Indeed, it concludes on an uplifting note. Salvation here lies in love, the consolations of human connection and in genuine fellowship with one's fellow San Franciscans. Although things will always be, as Cal's wry closing words emphasise, 'a bit chancy', by the conclusion a considerable measure of spiritual and psychic order has been restored to the city. The madness of de Castries has been defeated by goodness and rationality. It is a conclusion which differs greatly from that presented in *Invasion of the Body Snatchers*, which is set in the same city, at the same time, but features a much bleaker denouement.

## 'Pain is Optional': Cult Conspiracies in *Invasion of the Body Snatchers* (1978)

In their 1978 book, *Snapping: America's Epidemic of Sudden Personality Change*, Flo Conway and Jim Siegelman identified a seemingly terrifying new trend.[101] As they explained:

> America has been gripped by an epidemic of sudden personality change. On the surface, it appears like a new age of enlightenment is at hand as people of all ages are discovering new faiths, beliefs and practices that are changing them in ways they never dreamed of.[102]

There was, however, a darker side to this kind of transformation, 'a side that has been largely dismissed, downplayed, or altogether ignored'.[103] The past decade, they continued, had seen a series of 'appalling tragedies' – amongst them the Manson murders, the kidnapping of Patricia Hearst and the bizarre murders carried out by the self-proclaimed 'Son of Sam' – all of them acts intrinsically related to this new 'epidemic'.

'Snapping' is the term Conway and Siegelman use to describe this 'sudden, drastic alteration of personality in all its many forms'.[104] The root cause was said to lie in the myriad of new 'alternative therapies' which had arisen since the late 1960s – amongst them 'Gestalt' therapy, primal therapy and est [sic] (Erhard Seminars Training) – along with the many religious cults founded during the same period. They characterise these movements as a kind of psychological contagion that began on the West Coast and then spread across the rest of the country, penetrating the unsuspecting heartland.[105] According to Conway and Siegelman, 'The children of the seventies', having witnessed the subsidence of the 'great cultural upheaval' of the previous decade, were now seeking out even deeper forms of spiritual fulfilment.[106] What they found instead were 'organiza-tions such as the Unification Church, the Children of God, the International Society for Krishna Consciousness, the Divine Light Mission' and 'the Church of Scientology'.[107] Conway and Siegelman describe how

> In the beginning, the new cults gave little cause for concern . . . they were all simply variations on a familiar American theme: law-abiding citizens exercis-ing their constitutional right to freedom of religion. If those citizens seemed a little strange, at least they didn't get in anyone's way. At worst, the early cult members were mere loose threads in America's colorful social fabric.[108]

But as the 'contagion' spread – the 'industrious and charitable' public image adopted by many of these organisations was supplanted by bizarre and alarming accounts given by the friends and family members of cult devotees:

> These stories told of people who had changed completely, almost over-night. While they claimed to have found true happiness and fulfillment, many seemed to have lost their spontaneity and humor, their free will and their individuality in the process. They had become estranged, present-ing themselves in odd postures ranging from stiff to animated, ecstatic to withdrawn. There was something eerie about them, but it was nothing you could put your finger on.[109]

Let us compare this extract with one of the most oft-cited exchanges from Jack Finney's novel *The Body Snatchers* (1955). It is an ordinary seeming sum-mer afternoon in the Northern Californian town of Mill Valley (it became 'Santa Mira' in the 1956 film adaptation), and local doctor Miles Bennell has been asked to examine Wilma, a usually level-headed local woman who is suddenly convinced that her beloved Uncle Ira has been 'replaced'. She admits that this imposter looks and acts exactly like him, but remains steadfast in her conviction. Now, she says, she has proof:

> 'I've been waiting for today,' she whispered. 'Waiting till he'd get a hair-cut, and he finally did.' Again she leaned toward me, eyes big, her voice a hissing whisper. 'There's a little scar of the back of Ira's neck; he had a boil there once, and your father lanced it. You can't see the scar,' she whis-pered, 'when he needs a haircut. But when his neck is shaved, you can. Well, today – I've been *waiting* for this! – today he got a haircut –'
>     I sat forward, suddenly excited. 'And the scar's *gone*? You mean –'
>     'No!' she said, almost indignantly, eyes flashing. 'It's there – the scar – exactly like Uncle Ira's!'[110]

This sense of paranoid certainty – the conviction that *something eerie, but nothing you could put your finger on* has irrevocably but invisibly transformed a loved one – is the reason why Finney's novel remains one of the most influential pop culture products of the 1950s. As Barry Keith Grant notes of the 1956 film, it

> anticipates the numerous later zombie movies that followed the success of *Night of the Living Dead* (1968), most of which depict the cause as a highly dangerous infection – like 'a malignant disease spreading through the whole country'. It is no surprise, then, that *Invasion of the Body Snatchers* has directly inspired three remakes, each in its own way reinterpreting the basic conceit of the original. They explore questions of technology, gender, selfhood and alienation raised in the original film but cast these in new contexts, demonstrating the story's continued relevance for contemporary viewers.[111]

Philip Kaufman's 1978 film version accomplishes this by moving the original's vision of small-town paranoia to San Francisco, the city at the very heart of the 1960s counterculture. Like its 1956 predecessor, the film depicts exactly the 'sudden dramatic alteration of personality' identified by Conway and Siegelman. It also anticipated the devastating real-world 'contagion' which would soon irrevocably be associated with San Francisco. As Priscilla Wald notes, Kaufman's film 'uncannily foreshadowed the early years of the HIV/AIDS epidemic . . . the pod people forecast and would soon metamorphose into the malevolent, wilful viral-human carriers in the story of disease emergence'.[112] Like *Our Lady of Darkness*, it is another pivotal entry in the 'California Gothic' canon.

Peter Knight notes of the 1956 film, that

> the standard interpretation . . . is that the zombified pod-people represent the dangers of the fearless conformity of totalitarianism in general and communism in particular. More recent readings see the film as a warning about the perils of conformity, not to an alien doctrine, but to the dehumanizing dogma of McCarthyism.[113]

As Annette Insdorf further observes: 'Whether one chooses to see the robotic replicants as representing the conformity of Stalinism or of McCarthyism, the film valorizes the individual of conscience'.[114]

In the late 1970s, Kaufman, in collaboration with screenwriter W. D. Richter, initially planned a remake which would retain the original's small-town setting. However, this version was rejected by the project's financiers. After this setback, it occurred to them to jettison Santa Mira entirely. As Kaufman explained in a 1979 interview:

> We decided that the only way it could really be valid and relevant for today's audiences was to have it played out in a city. You see, twenty years ago, the big cities were places that were secure, really. Small towns were in transition. Now big cities are falling apart, and there is paranoia in the streets. People are distrustful of other people. So we decided to run this theme through the streets of San Francisco.[115]

As a result, in the 1978 version (which Kaufman also viewed as more of a sequel than a remake),[116] small-town GP Miles Bennell becomes City Health inspector Matthew Bennell (Donald Sutherland); Becky becomes Matthew's Civil Service colleague Elizabeth Driscoll (Brooke Adams); and a biologist, and Miles's friend Manny, becomes Dr David Kibner (Leonard Nimoy), a celebrity psychiatrist with a dangerously soothing bedside manner.

In moving the action to San Francisco, Kaufman and Richter do much more than simply allow the basic plotline of the original film to play out on a bigger scale. The 1978 version significantly expands upon the paranoid anxieties of the original film by emphasising the parallels between the pod invasion and the conflicted nature of late 1970s San Francisco. As Kaufman noted:

> We've taken some of the things that were expressed *about* the original film – that modern life is turning people into unfeeling, unthinking pods who resist getting involved with each other on any level – and we've put them directly in the script. Our characters talk openly and directly about the social reality of 'podiness'.[117]

Put simply, although they have much in common, the 1978 film is a specifically *Californian* nightmare which would land very differently had it been set anywhere else, at any other time. Whereas Santa Mira's Northern California location is referenced several times in the 1956 version, the exact location of the town is arguably irrelevant: this could really be any idyllic rural settlement under threat. Political readings aside, the alien threat faced in the source novel is best understood as a metaphor for the often dehumanising technological, social and infrastructural advances which transformed American communities in the post-war era.[118] As Charles Freund notes of the 1956 film:

> Straight out of a Norman Rockwell painting, this community of neighborly Main Street storekeepers and doctors – pushing hand mowers across their spacious lawns and whiling away summer evenings on their

big porches – embodied a cherished American self-image: that we are a homogeneous nation whose traditions and values sprang from the bosom of these small towns . . . The loss of Santa Mira to pod people is more than just an invasion – it's an assault on some basic American fantasies.[119]

If the 1956 film is a *national* nightmare then, the 1978 update is a regional one, saturated with a San Francisco-specific sense of urban disquiet. As David Bates observes:

There is a nice subversion in the use of free-wheeling San Francisco as the setting of Philip Kaufman's masterly remake of Don Siegel's paranoid sci-fi classic, given that the ultimate terror of the story is assimilation to a bland conformity that tolerates no difference: this centre of American counterculture had played out most of its influence by the late 1960s and early 1970s.[120]

Kaufman grounds us in the sights and sounds of the San Francisco cityscape from the outset. During the evocative title sequence, the pod invaders gently blow across the vast expanse of space like deadly tumbleweeds. As they reach our planet's upper atmosphere, the cosmic perspective becomes local. There is a vertigo-inspiring shot – from the pods point of view – of them plummeting through the clouds, until they reach one of the most iconic – and controversial – new landmarks on the city skyline: the Transamerica Pyramid building. We then have a rapid cut to a fog-shrouded Golden Gate Bridge, and then cut to the children's play park in Alamo Square, a real-life city locale which provides one with a panoramic overview of the city below. There is even a sense that the city's famously wet weather may be facilitating the invasion. Damp alien spores are seen dotted on trees, grass, plants and flowers, their jelly-like tendrils eagerly spreading out to 'take over' native plants, before slowly budding into eye-catching but insidious blooms, in an act of instinctive 'ecological imperialism' which will quickly edge out native species.[121] During this same scene, a schoolteacher escorting a group of children encourages her young charges to take these strange new flowers home. Although she has said nothing overtly sinister, from the subtle glance exchanged with the nearby priest (Robert Duvall), incongruously sitting on a nearby swing, we further intuit that something here is not quite right. The teacher and the clergyman are already 'pod people'. The takeover has begun, and the invaders are already embedded in the religious and educational infrastructure of the city.

The film's atmospheric score, sinister sound design and shrewd way of consistently drawing our attention to odd things happening in the background (such as screams which can barely be heard above the traffic and lone citizens frantically running down the middle of the street) furthers this sense that the city has already been irrevocably infected. As Insdorf notes, Kaufman and director of photography Michael Chapman also used subtle camera angles to suggest that someone has already been replaced or will soon become a pod: the fate of everyone but sole survivor Nancy (Veronica Cartwright) is telegraphed by the fact that all the other main characters are glimpsed in a reflective surface at some stage.[122]

There was good reason to set a film about the weirdness – and danger – of contemporary urban life in San Francisco. To say that the late 1970s was a difficult period for the city would be an understatement. As one chronicler of the era suggests:

> Even before Jonestown, San Francisco seemed to be heading for a violent cataclysm. By the late 1970s, the sexual revolution centered in San Francisco had sparked a vehement backlash from defenders of traditional morality, in the city and throughout the country.[123]

Philip Jenkins argues that the late 1970s was a pivotal yet overlooked period in contemporary US history. He cites 1977 as the

> real turning point in domestic policy, the year in which sixties assumptions were widely challenged. In 1977, we see an assault on permissiveness in sexuality and drug use, a counterattack against gains in gay rights, a sharp new opposition to religious experimentalism, and intensifying concern about Communist menaces overseas. At home and abroad, the sixties vision became noticeably grimmer and more threatening. This was far more than just the summer of *Star Wars*, *Smokey and the Bandit*, and *Saturday Night Fever*. The political transformation of the Reagan years is rooted in the social movements of 1977.[124]

He follows this assertion up with an interesting turn of phrase: 'Reaganism did not represent a sudden invasion by a mysterious alien force.'[125] Here, the late 1970s is seen as an overlooked but transformative era, during which the politically and socially conservative forces that would dominate the 1980s were actively reorganising themselves for their own 'takeover'. The sentiment is echoed by Solnit, who notes that

> The 1970s is a decade people would apparently rather not talk about and hardly seem to remember. Perhaps the best thing that can be said about the 1970s is that its experiments – the failed ones that people learned from

and the successful that continued – laid the groundwork for movements to come during the 1980s and after. But in 1978, mostly the mistakes and excesses were on display.[126]

The re-emergence of political and social conservativism as a force to be reckoned with was in part the result of a powerful backlash against many of the most resonant ideas associated with the 1960s counterculture. Nowhere – apart from perhaps the Polanski/Tate residence in August 1969 – was the sense that initial euphoria had mutated into a nightmarish hangover more profound than in San Francisco during the mid- to late 1970s. As Jeffrey Toobin observes in his book about the kidnapping of Patricia Hearst (another infamous California crime story):

> No region symbolized the rapture of the 1960s or the venom of the 1970s more than the San Francisco Bay Area. The Summer of Love, a carnival of music, drugs, and sex in 1967, established the city as the center of the American counterculture . . . Yet, by the 1970s, both San Francisco and Berkeley were wilting under the weight of so many new arrivals. Politics and music yielded, in significant measure, to drugs and violence. And then, in an especially sinister confluence of events, a series of unspeakable crimes beset San Francisco almost simultaneously.[127]

Toobin further notes that along with the Hearst kidnapping (and the victim's notorious 'conversion' to the cause of her captors, the shambolic but ruthless 'Symbionese Liberation Army', or SLA), these crimes included the Zodiac killings as well as the (today) lesser-known 'Zebra' murders, carried out by Black supremacist extremists who shot and killed dozens of (mostly) white pedestrians at random. Because he is focusing upon the Hearst case, which began in 1974, Toobin doesn't mention the bizarre confluence of horrific events which happened in San Francisco in late 1978: the assassination of LGBT rights activist Harvey Milk and Mayor George Moscone in their offices at City Hall on 27 November (by their disgruntled colleague Dan White), and the Jonestown Massacre, which took place only nine days earlier on 18 November. As Solnit says of 1978, 'For San Francisco in particular and for California in general, 1978 was a terrible year in which the fiddler had to be paid for all the tunes to which the counterculture had danced.'[128]

Although the mass suicide/murder of over 900 men, women and children belonging to the 'Peoples [sic] Temple' took place in a jungle compound in French Guyana, the cult had deep-seated connections with San Francisco. Many of the victims were from the city. Until shortly before the cataclysm, the

Reverend Jim Jones was a generally well-regarded member of the city's liberal elite, feted for his outreach work with poor Black neighbourhoods such as the Fillmore District. When discussing the dual assassination of Moscone and Milk, Kevin Starr notes that the impact of the murders was compounded by the fact that the city was 'still reeling' from news of Jonestown. Although the Peoples Temple saga came to a horrific climax many thousands of miles away, he argues that it should still 'be considered part of the California history of this era'. San Francisco, after all, was where the cult 'grew to strength' and where it 'became a force in local politics'.[129] This perspective is also expressed by Tim Reiterman, whose history of the Peoples Temple traces the group's evolution from humble Midwest beginnings to the sickening events in Guyana:

> In Indiana, the Temple was more of a church than a social movement or cult; in California, it was more of a social movement and cult than a utopian community; in Guyana, it would become a utopian community and in some ways the ultimate cult. The most respectable and accurate label in the Temple's early years, even in California, was 'church'. To most people, the California Temple remained a humanitarian, activist Christian church. [. . .] However, in terms of intimacy among members, the Temple most closely resembled a utopian community. Like dozens of communal groups in the nineteenth and twentieth centuries, the Temple came to the West Coast to escape some perceived outside threat and persecution and harbored a self-righteous group mentality that raised natural barriers to outsiders.[130]

As Kaufman observed after the film was released, the horrific climax of Jones's fanatical desire to establish a 'utopian' society in the Guyanese jungle uncannily (and coincidentally) echoed the most resonant themes in his film: 'Jonestown happened just after this film was released, and a lot of people were coming from San Francisco. So there was in the air a kind of strange conformity in the guise of a modern, updated jargon.'[131] Like City Hall assassin Dan White, a socially conservative Catholic who had served the city as a police officer and a firefighter before his election to local government, Jim Jones was a San Francisco insider, albeit one who embedded himself within the city's liberal rather than conservative political infrastructure. Even Mayor Moscone and Harvey Milk were initially supporters of Jones and his seemingly progressive, charity-focused religious movement (David Talbot suggests that Moscone would have lost his mayoral election if Jones had not ordered Temple members to canvass for him).[132] Nor were the politicians the only ones at fault. According to Talbot, 'The city's watchdogs did nothing to alert the public to Jim Jones's growing menace . . . The cult leader won the local media's silence with the same artful combination of seduction and intimidation that he had used on San Francisco's political caste.'[133]

There are no explicit references to Jones or his organisation in the 1978 version of Body Snatchers – it was made before Jonestown happened – but there *is* a clear sense that dark forces have invisibly infiltrated the city's political and social foundations. This thread comes to the fore when we are introduced to Dr David Kibner, the respected local psychiatrist who plays an important role in manipulating the film's main protagonists, Matthew and Elizabeth. As in the original novel, women seem to be more emotionally attuned to the trans-formations that have taken place in their loved ones. After Elizabeth brings home an intriguing new plant from the Alamo Square Park, she soon notices some unsettling changes in the behaviour of her affable but shallow boyfriend, Geoffrey (Art Hindle). She secretly follows him as he travels around the city on a series of mysterious errands, and soon becomes convinced that 'Geoffrey is not Geoffrey.' What's more, she is now certain that he is involved in some kind of mysterious organisation. As she puts it to Matthew, who is her best friend and colleague in the Health Department, 'I keep seeing these people. All recognising each other. Something is passing between them all. Some secret. It's a conspiracy, I know it.'

The coldness and efficiency of the 'new' Geoffrey resembles the behav-iours Conway and Siegelman associated with individuals who have 'snapped'. Describing the transformation which allegedly came over a previously 'ordi-nary' young couple who became members of the Unification Church (aka, the 'Moonies'), they note that 'the Gordons are everyday people – good, decent, healthy. They are also typical cult members. They are college educated and come from upper-middle-class homes.'[134] In the film, Geoffrey, a suit-wearing, sports-loving dentist, is exactly the kind of individual whom the authors would view as a prime candidate for cult 'takeover'. What's more, their description of the mental state which causes someone to 'snap' and break all ties with their previous self resembles the emotional detachment and singlemindedness of the pod person:

> [Snapping] is a phenomenon that occurs when an individual stops thinking and feeling for himself, when he breaks both the bonds of awareness and social relationship that tie his personality to the outside world and literally loses his mind to some form of external or automatic control.[135]

Matthew, a kind but sceptical rationalist, initially downplays Elizabeth's fears. But Elizabeth remains certain that Geoffrey has changed and also becomes convinced that San Francisco is no longer the place that it once was: 'Matthew, I've lived in this city all my life. And somehow today, I felt that everything had changed. People were different. Not just Geoffrey, but *everybody*.' After this exchange, Matthew brings her to a book launch held in honour of his old friend Dr David Kibner, reassuring Elizabeth that the psychiatrist will quickly be able to put her fears into rational perspective. Kibner is indeed calm, charismatic and eerily plausible. He is first seen soothing a terrified woman whose fears are identical to those which are troubling Elizabeth – she believes that her husband is no longer her husband. In a private conversation later the same evening, Kibner tells Matthew and Elizabeth that an outbreak of 'infectious' mass hysteria has begun to afflict residents of the city. He blames it on the transitory nature of contemporary life:

> I've been hearing about it all week – it's getting very popular. People are stepping in and out of relationships too fast because they don't want the responsibility. That's why marriages are going to hell: the whole family unit is shot to hell.

Once it is revealed that Kibner is actually a pod himself, we can consider his seemingly sincere denunciation of contemporary social mores in an entirely new light. Kibner hasn't really provided a rational explanation for an epidemic of understandable emotional turmoil: he's using the professional status of the human he 'replaced' to further the pod cause. As Kaufman puts it:

> [Kibner] was meant to be the most logical, relaxed and reasonable of our characters, but he obviously went to sleep somewhere along the way and woke up on the pod side of things. The message of all religions: Awake. But the reality is that people are lulled into sleep and 'poddom' often by the most 'reasonable' among us. We were thinking of the growing yuppie presence, which evolved into the dot.com boom and which substantially altered San Francisco forever, changing it from the more relaxed Barbary Coast city of bohemians, beatniks, artists, hippies, outcasts, and searchers into a city of strivers.[136]

After Matthew comes face to face with undeniable evidence that Elizabeth's suspicions are true (courtesy of an eerily underdeveloped pod 'body' discovered by his friends Jack (Jeff Goldblum) and Nancy Belicec (Veronica Cartwright), he mistakenly assumes that Kibner's high-profile connections, combined with his own inside knowledge of the city's bureaucratic infrastructure, will help the group to quickly expose the conspiracy. One of Kibner's patients is the Mayor, so Matthew urges his 'friend' to raise the alarm. He also makes futile calls to his own Civil Service contacts. Rather than help in the struggle against the pods, Kibner's position within San Francisco's power elite ensures that the battle is lost before it has even begun. If for some reason the Mayor was not one of the first to be 'taken over', then the 'new' Kibner and his associates will see to it that he does not remain unchanged for long. The fascinating (and coincidental) similarities to the way in which Jim Jones was for years able to operate in plain sight also come to mind during the scene in which Kibner and a group of fellow pods corner Matthew and Elizabeth in an office in the Health Department building. As he prepares to inject them with a sedative which will hasten their 'takeover', Kibner describes what life after being 'replaced' is like. It is exactly the kind of utopian rhetoric that pop culture frequently associates with sinister cults and cult-like organisations: 'You will be born again into an untroubled world, free of anxiety, fear, hate.'

As William Graebner notes of this pivotal scene in his book on the cultural impact of the Patricia Hearst kidnapping:

> These few, brief lines touch on several prominent issues of the decade: the decline of the 1960s counterculture, represented by the word 'love', strongly identified with the Summer of 1967; the emerging religious right; and the sense that Americans, in flight from the social and cultural upheavals of the 1960s, could be tempted to seek comfort – mere survival, mere existence – in an 'untroubled world'.[137]

The SLA, he notes, were seldom described as a cult at the time (although the group did have decidedly 'cult-like' characteristics), but the dramatic 'transformation' undergone by the previously law-abiding young heiress – who when she was finally arrested, famously gave her profession as 'urban guerrilla' – resonated with contemporary fears about 'brainwashing' and 'threats to the modern, unmoored personality'.[138]

As previously indicated, Matthew and Elizabeth are aided in their struggle by free-thinking bohemians Jack and Nancy. Though Goldblum's jittery, paranoid young writer makes the biggest initial impression, Cartwright's character Nancy proves to be much more significant. Nancy is an avid reader of pseudoscience such as Immanuel Velikovsky's *Worlds in Collision* (1950) and she is the first character to seriously consider the possibility of alien invasion, presciently asking: 'Why not space flowers? Why do we always expect them to come in metal ships?' Nancy also declares in an earlier scene that 'Plants have feelings you know – just like people.' She is also the one who figures out that the pods can be evaded if one represses all outward show of emotion. Indeed, imitation soon becomes the only viable survival strategy. In contrast to the arc of the film's other female protagonist Elizabeth (who becomes increasingly passive as the film progresses), Nancy is a resourceful and adaptable individual who is able to survive in San Francisco for some time after the city has been completely colonised by the pods. When the others follow Nancy's example and try to make their way undetected around the decidedly *unheimlich* city, the film's evocation of urban paranoia becomes most pronounced. The city under alien (or 'cult') control evokes in our still-human heroes a sense of profound agoraphobia.

There are distinct historical resonances evoked by the agoraphobic response to the modern city. As Kathryn Milun (2007) outlines, agoraphobia was only publicly recognised as a condition in the late nineteenth century. She describes it as 'a spatial disorder characterized by a phobic inability to walk across wide open urban spaces, or through streets, empty or crowded'.[139] First mentioned in a German psychiatric journal in the 1870s, she continues, it was variously known as 'plaza fright' ( *Platzfurcht*), *peur des espace* (fear of spaces), topophobia or street fear and, perhaps most evocatively, *horreur du vide* (horror of emptiness).[140] Milun links the disorder's rise to public prominence to the era's massive migration from the countryside to the cities, substantial urban growth and the construction of imposing new architectural forms in major cities all over Europe. For nineteenth-century agoraphobics, 'the gigantic squares and boulevards introduced into their cities' became 'hostile environments'.[141] The same is true of the experiences undergone by the main protagonists in Kaufman's film. It begins in one public space – Alamo Square Park – and concludes with a devastating final encounter in another well-known city locale – the street outside City Hall. The film initially alternates between scenes set on the streets and other public places and scenes set in private homes (for instance, immediately after the opening park scene, we cut to Elizabeth entering the distinctive late Victorian home she shares with Geoffrey). Eventually, however, the core quartet of Matthew, Elizabeth, Nancy and Jack are forced to hide in plain sight, on the streets.

The pod takeover has, in a very literal sense, made the city of San Francisco and its inhabitants actively hostile towards the few humans who remain. As the film progresses, all escape routes – by air, sea, or violent resistance – are closed off. Again, it's a state of affairs that evokes the dread which enveloped the real-life city in late 1978. Talbot describes the psychological impact of Jonestown as such: '[it] released a poison gas cloud over San Francisco. There was blood and terror in the air. Even those who loudly denied any guilt were running scared.'[142] He claims that 'In the days after Jonestown and the City Hall assassinations, San Francisco sleepwalked under a dark canopy of clouds that seemed like it would never end. The city was wracked with despair.'[143]

The victory of the pod people also reverses a characteristic highlighted by Yi-Fu Tuan in his landmark human geography text, *Landscapes of Fear* (1979). In his chapter 'Fear in the City', Tuan states that 'An early and essential function of the city was to be a vivid symbol of cosmic order: hence its simple geometric design with walls and streets oriented to the cardinal points, and its imposing monuments.'[144] The key architectural focal point in the 1978 version of *Invasion of the Body Snatchers* is the Transamerica Pyramid building. Completed in 1972, the 48-storey tower, topped by a soon-to-be iconic glass pyramid, was associated by some contemporary onlookers with conspiracy theories related to the lost tribes of Atlantis and the Illuminati. In fact, it was a symbol of corporate might, created by the life insurance company the Transamerica Corporation.[145] As well as making a pivotal appearance in the opening scene, the Transamerica Pyramid building can be spotted throughout the film (just as it repeatedly appears in *Our Lady of Darkness*) – seen from the rooftop of Matthew's apartment building when he privately speaks to Kibner; featured in a poster of the city at night hanging in Matthew's living room; and glimpsed in several other background scenes.

Again, it serves us well to remember that at the time the building was seen by many San Francisco residents as an unwelcome signifier of powerful corporate interests. Within the context of the film, it allies hippie symbology with the world of capitalism. Furthermore, it also subliminally reminds us of the constant presence of the alien invaders: as previously noted, the opening scene suggests that the pods may even have used the unearthly looking building as a navigational reference point.

Tuan argues that the greatest threat to the ideal 'order' of the city has always been chaos – be it due to fire, disease, political unrest or the 'auditory chaos' which represents the soundscape of the messy, ground-level city life: 'An orderly world is threatened by chaos, and every effort is made to contain it.'[146] What we have here, however, is a city in which cult-like order represents the greatest threat of all. As Insdorf perceptively observes, the city grows quieter as the film approaches its bleak conclusion, acting as a 'potent counterpoint' to the pod takeover.[147] Once Elizabeth has been duplicated by the pods, Matthew carries out a desperate act of defiance – he starts a fire which destroys part of the dockside pod cultivation/storage facility. However, the disruption Matthew bravely causes is quickly contained. In imagery which only takes on an even more evocative resonance because San Francisco would soon be considered 'ground zero' for the looming HIV/AIDS epidemic, the pods are using City Hall as the staging post for the imminent takeover of the rest of the United States.[148] There is little to suggest that Matthew's actions will prevent or even delay their inevitable victory.

Ultimately, what is most horrifying about life in Pod City, California, is not everything that has changed, but everything that has not. The pods still show up to work at the jobs once held by the humans they have murdered. They wear their victims' usual clothes and sit at their usual desks and, like Elizabeth's devastatingly emotionless replicant, robotically go through the motions of pre-invasion life. Kibner had earlier claimed that 'Nothing changes – you can still have the same life, the same clothes, the same car.' Matthew immediately responded, 'But what happens to *us*?' It is now clear that nothing, save a physical resemblance and a replicant's 'copy' of the original person's memories and behavioural patterns, remains. Almost all of the human characters are now dead, their dust-bunny style remains neatly swept up by one of the garbage trucks seen busily working away in the background throughout the film.

In the film's final moments, San Francisco becomes a city in which the weirdoes, the bohemians, the idealists and the public servants have all been decisively overtaken by the forces of order, conformity and ceaseless instinctual expansion. The camera, as Insdorf puts it, has previously 'expressed a city in transformation, an urban and nocturnal limbo between a paradoxically heavenly chaos and a peaceful hell'.[149] But now, there can be no doubt that a 'peaceful hell' – the 'untroubled new world' promised by Kibner-the-pod – has triumphed. The film's iconic final seconds underline this profound sense of loss. When Nancy, who has been hiding in plain sight, sees Matthew outside City Hall, she discreetly makes herself known to him. Like the audience, she cannot believe that her resourceful friend has become an emotionless replicant. Surely, like her, Matthew has quietly been 'passing'? But when Nancy greets him, 'Matthew' raises his arm, points an extended finger at her, and emits a horrifying and utterly inhuman shriek. The human counter-revolution is once again over before it ever had a chance.

The fact that the architectural backdrop to this very scene is the building where only a few months after filming concluded one of the city's most devastating crimes would take place, only adds to the scene's eerie significance. Solnit, who also writes about this coincidence, points out that *Invasion of the Body Snatchers* was released less than a month after Dan White's murder spree.[150] When describing the atmosphere at City Hall immediately after the assassination of Milk and Moscone, Talbot writes that 'Now the enormous and beautiful old building felt like a mausoleum.'[151] Kaufman's film ends with a swirling close-up which enters the dark void of Sutherland's gaping mouth. Then the screen goes black. Here, City Hall isn't the only mausoleum: the last survivor of the old (human) San Francisco is about to be exterminated by the alien enforcers of cult-like conformity and an 'untroubled new world'.

## Notes

1. Eco, 'The Suicides of the Temple', p. 311.
2. Ibid. pp. 312–13.
3. Ibid. p. 313.
4. Ibid. p. 315.
5. Ibid. p. 315.
6. See Stark, Bainbridge and Doyle, 'Cults of California', p. 348.
7. Hine, *California's Utopian Colonies*, p. ix.
8. Ibid. p. 5.
9. Ibid. p. 4.
10. Ibid. p. 7.
11. Jenkins, *Mystics and Messiahs*, p. 4.
12. Ibid. p. 4.
13. 'California Cults', *Time Magazine*, p. 62.
14. Ibid. p. 62.
15. Hine, *California's Utopian Colonies*, pp. 9–10.
16. Hart, *A Companion to California*, p. 102.
17. Jenkins, *Mystics and Messiahs*, p. 8.
18. Ibid. p. 12.
19. Ibid. p. 215.
20. Ibid. p. 209.
21. Taylor, *Satan's Slaves*, p. 5.
22. Ibid. p. 6.
23. Ibid. p. 6.
24. Ibid. p. 41.
25. Sanders, *The Family*, p. 11.
26. Ibid. p. 41.
27. Ibid. p. 41.
28. Ibid. p. 412.
29. Janzen, *The Rise and Fall of Synanon*.
30. Solnit, 'Rattlesnake in Mailbox', p. 46. Solnit's excellent essay both intersects with and anticipated some of my own points here.
31. Ibid. p. 33.
32. Ibid. p. 41.
33. Kumar, *Utopia and Anti-Utopia*, p. 99.
34. Stableford, 'Fritz Leiber, 1910–', p. 933.
35. Ibid. pp. 933–4.
36. Leiber, 'Smoke Ghost', pp. 5–6.
37. Hadji, 'Fritz Leiber', p. 262.

38. Leiber, 'The Girl with the Hungry Eyes', p. 27.
39. See chapter 2 of Murphy, *The Suburban Gothic* for more on *Conjure Wife*.
40. Sidney-Fryer, 'Thibaut de Castries, Revenant', pp. ix. The Swan River Press edition of *The Pale Brown Thing* contains an annotated list of the revisions and additions which took place when the original novella was expanded. John Howard quotes (via Leiber scholar, Bruce Byfield) Leiber's own observation that 'the two texts should be regarded as the same story told at different times. If Franz's story is longer in *Our Lady of Darkness*, the reason is that he recalls more the second time he tells it.' See Howard, 'Story-telling, Wonder-questing, Mortal Me', p. 131. I will be referring to the text of *Our Lady of Darkness* throughout this chapter.
41. Joshi, *Unutterable Horror*, p. 690.
42. Leiber, *Our Lady of Darkness*, p. 7.
43. Ibid. p. 8.
44. Ibid. p. 10.
45. Ibid. p. 9.
46. 'Sutro Tower', https://en.wikipedia.org/wiki/Sutro_Tower (last accessed 1 November 2018). The Caen quote cited in this entry was first referenced in 'Sutro Tower' by Louise Rafkin, in 'The Bay Citizen', *The New York Times*, 8 October 2011.
47. Leiber, *Our Lady of Darkness*, p. 13.
48. Ibid. p. 13.
49. Ibid. p. 13.
50. Ibid. p. 14.
51. Ibid. p. 19.
52. Ibid. p. 19.
53. Ibid. p. 28.
54. Ibid. p. 73. Byers was based upon Leiber's friend, the critic and poet Donald Sidney-Fryer, who discusses his own connection to the book in the preface to the Swan River Press edition of *The Pale Brown Thing*.
55. Starr, *Americans and the California Dream*, p. 270.
56. Ibid. p. 286.
57. Joshi, 'Introduction', *The Dark Eidolon and Other Fantasies*, p. x.
58. Ibid. p. xi.
59. Herron, 'Smith, Clark Ashton, 1893–1961', p. 393.
60. Joshi, 'Introduction', *The Dark Eidolon and Other Fantasies*, p. xv.
61. Herron, 'Smith, Clark Ashton, 1893–1961', p. 393.
62. Joshi, 'Explanatory Notes', *The Dark Eidolon and Other Fantasies*, p. 343.
63. Smith, 'The Devotee of Evil', p. 23.
64. Ibid. p. 32.

65. Ibid. p. 22.
66. Joshi, 'Explanatory Notes', *The Dark Eidolon and Other Fantasies*, p. 346.
67. Smith, 'The City of the Singing Flame', p. 54.
68. Ibid. p. 61.
69. Ibid. p. 69.
70. Leiber, *Our Lady of Darkness,* p. 70.
71. Ibid. p. 101.
72. Ibid. p. 102.
73. Ibid. p. 102.
74. Ibid. pp. 106–7.
75. Ibid. p. 108.
76. Ibid. p. 100.
77. Ibid. p. 111.
78. Ibid. p. 111.
79. Ibid. p. 112.
80. Ibid, p. 117.
81. Ibid. p. 121.
82. Ibid. p. 123.
83. Ibid. p. 125.
84. Ibid. p. 132.
85. Ibid. p. 135.
86. Ibid. p. 143.
87. Ibid. p. 143.
88. Ibid. p. 149.
89. Ibid. p. 159.
90. Ibid. p. 174.
91. Ibid. pp. 176–7.
92. Ibid. p. 180.
93. Ibid. p. 182.
94. Becker, 'A Point of Little Hope', p. 44.
95. Ibid. p. 44.
96. Ibid, p. 46.
97. Berman, quoted in ibid. p. 46.
98. Ibid. p. 46.
99. Ibid. p. 47.
100. Burrough, *Days of Rage*, p. 345.
101. Conway and Siegelman, *Snapping*. This volume came to my attention thanks to Joseph P. Laycock's mention of it in 'Where Do They Get These Ideas?', p. 90.
102. Conway and Siegelman, *Snapping*, p. 11.

103. Ibid. p. 12.
104. Ibid. p. 12.
105. Ibid, p. 14.
106. Ibid. p. 28.
107. Ibid. p. 28
108. Ibid. p. 28
109. Ibid, p. 29.
110. Finney, *The Body Snatchers*, p. 11.
111. Grant, *Invasion of the Body Snatchers*, p. 93.
112. Wald, *Contagious*, p. 161.
113. Knight, *Conspiracy Culture*, p. 173.
114. Insdorf, *Philip Kaufman*, p. 107.
115. Freund, 'Pods Over San Francisco', p. 23
116. Grant, *Invasion of the Body Snatchers*, p. 94.
117. Freund, 'Pods Over San Francisco', p. 23.
118. See my own chapter 3 on the 1955 novel in Murphy, *The Suburban Gothic in American Popular Culture*, or Jancovich's discussion of the novel in *Rational Fears*.
119. Freund, 'Pods Over San Francisco', p. 23.
120. Bates, 'Location: Department of Health', p. 76.
121. See Crosby, *Ecological Imperialism*.
122. Insdorf, *Philip Kaufman*, p. 103.
123. Talbot, *Season of the Witch*, p. 311.
124. Jenkins, *A Decade of Nightmares*, p. 6.
125. Ibid. p. 8.
126. Solnit, 'Rattlesnake in Mailbox', p. 34.
127. Toobin, *American Heiress*, p. 13.
128. Solnit, 'Rattlesnake in Mailbox', p. 34.
129. Starr, *California: A History*, p. 331.
130. Reiterman with Jacobs, *Raven*, p. 279.
131. Insdorf, *Philip Kaufman*, p. 130.
132. Talbot, *Season of the Witch*, pp. 278–9.
133. Ibid. p. 289.
134. Conway and Siegelman, *Snapping*, p. 30.
135. Ibid, p. 225.
136. Insdorf, *Philip Kaufman*, p. 106.
137. Graebner, *Patty's Got a Gun,* pp. 141–2.
138. Ibid. p. 140.
139. Milun, *Pathologies of Modern Space*, pp. 2–3.
140. Ibid. pp. 2–3.

141. Ibid. p. 2.
142. Talbot, *Season of the Witch*, p. 309.
143. Ibid. p. 333.
144. Tuan, *Landscapes of Fear*, p. 146.
145. Frantz, *From the Ground Up*, pp. 38–9.
146. Tuan, *Landscapes of Fear*, p. 146.
147. Insdorf, *Philip Kaufman*, p. 104.
148. Wald, *Contagious*, p. 161.
149. Insdorf, *Philip Kaufman*, p. 104.
150. Solnit, 'Rattlesnake in Mailbox', p. 36.
151. Talbot, *Season of the Witch*, p. 331.

# 7

# 'The Usual Utopian Vision': Contemporary Cult California in *The Invitation* (2015), *1BR* (2019) and *The Circle* (2013)

Karyn Kusama's 2015 film, *The Invitation*, evokes the August 1969 murders committed by the Manson Family, particularly the brutal massacre of Sharon Tate and her houseguests. The film also incorporates details associated with the 1978 Jonestown Massacre and with the 1997 'Heaven's Gate' mass suicide (which took place just outside San Diego). As such, it presents us with a notably reflective take on the long-standing association between California and potentially dangerous cults and cult-like organisations which promise to bring about a new world that is superior to the old. As Kusama outlines, the setting is key here:

> It is incredibly specific to Los Angeles. We had moments where we discussed the possibility of shooting elsewhere, and the more we really investigated all of our driving interests in the film, it just became clear that we had to shoot it in Los Angeles, because even though it is a largely interior space, it just feels like there is something about the mythology of Southern California, the sense of self-reinvention that is promised here to so many people who kind of flock to the city, the sense of spiritual quest and spiritual searching and spiritual dwelling and fringe movements that have been born here in Los Angeles.[1]

Kusama's statement recalls an observation made by Carey McWilliams in 1946:

> No single aspect of Southern California has attracted more attention than its fabled addiction to cults and cultists. [. . .] Writing in 1921, John Steven McGroarty said that 'Los Angeles is the most celebrated of all incubators of new creeds, codes of ethics, philosophies – no day passes without the birth of something of this nature never heard of before. It is a breeding place and a rendezvous of freak religions.'[2]

The Manson killings left an indelible impression upon pop culture perceptions of 'cults' associated with the state (even though the vast majority of new religious and 'human potential' movements posed no threat to their followers or to the wider community). 'After Manson', Joseph Laycock observes, 'cult brainwashing was no longer a laughing matter but a source of horror. A collective paranoia played out through numerous horror films of the 1970s in which Satanic cults became a "stock character".'[3] Laycock notes that the pop culture impact of the Manson murders was relatively immediate, and he detects an influence even as early as 1971 in *The Omega Man*, the second film adaptation of Richard Matheson's *I Am Legend*.[4] In *The Omega Man*, Robert Neville, the source novel's suburban Everyman, is reimagined as a military scientist, bullishly portrayed by Charlton Heston, whilst the undead antagonists are a decidedly cult-like band of white-faced ghouls who follow an all-controlling leader. They even call themselves 'The Family', which, as Laycock notes, 'seems an obvious reference to the Manson family, who were convicted in 1971. *The Family* is also the title of Ed Sanders' influential book on the Manson murders, published in 1971.'[5]

There would be many more fiction and non-fiction narratives to come that were inspired by the most infamous American crime story of the late 1960s. As Ian Cooper puts it, 'It should come as no surprise that the Manson Family story has been explored and reworked countless times by writers, musicians and filmmakers.'[6] His 2018 book documents these onscreen manifestations, beginning with the lurid exploitation movies of the early 1970s, before considering the many mainstream horror movies which incorporated aspects of the crimes (in particular the alleged 'ritual murder' component dwelt upon in early accounts of the deadly Tate–LaBianca home invasions).

As the fiftieth anniversary of the murders approached in 2019, the number of narratives inspired by, or dramatising them increased substantially. These included the television crime drama *Aquarius* (2015–16) and elements of season six of *American Horror Story* (2017; subtitled 'Cult' and set in the aftermath of Donald J. Trump's surprise 2016 electoral victory). In 2019, new films included *The Haunting of Sharon Tate* (a supernaturally inflected depiction of the actress's final days) and *Charlies Says*, which focuses on the complex motivations of Manson's female followers. The build-up to the Manson murders is a prime driver of the plot in Quentin Tarantino's *Once Upon a Time in Hollywood* (2019), during which Sharon Tate (Margot Robbie) is depicted as the epitome of youth, beauty and innocence. Her seemingly inevitable doom grants the film's other main plotline – which revolves around male friendship – a degree of poignancy which is then complicated by Tarantino's cathartic reimagining of events on the night of the 8 August 1969.

Emma Cline's novel *The Girls* (2016) also centred on the women who were drawn into Manson's orbit. It is recounted by a troubled older woman who was once a jaded and neglected middle-class runaway. As the novel moves between her hippie past and troubled present, she explains the reasons why she became involved with a group of free-spirited young women in the summer of 1969. Although many of the details (and all the names) associated with the Manson case have been changed, *The Girls*, like *Charlie Says*, attempts to interrogate the reasons why a manipulative charlatan attracted the fanatical devotion of so many lost young women. A devilishly charismatic Manson analogue is also the main antagonist in the convoluted thriller *Bad Times at the El Royale* (2018), set in a rundown hotel/casino located on the California-Nevada border. Finally, Charles Manson and his crimes were frequently evoked as a cultural and criminal turning point in the Netflix TV show *Mindhunter* (2017–19) about the birth of the FBI's Behavioral Science Unit.

*The Invitation* is not yet another dramatisation of the Manson Family murders, but the events do inform its thematic and visual contexts. The film is set in the present and features a cult which is a great deal more formally structured (and widespread) than Manson's impoverished band of misfits. 'The Invitation' (the title refers both to the fictional cult, and to the dinner party invite which brings the main characters together) has thousands of members, and branches in New York, LA and Mexico. Its membership appears to include well-educated professionals ('People like us', one well-heeled devotee declares), and what scant information we learn about the cult's belief system suggests that its core philosophy incorporates elements inspired by real-life groups such as the Peoples Temple, Heaven's Gate and 'human potential' movements such as est and Synanon, all of which began in, or are most associated with, the state of California.

The main protagonist of *The Invitation* is grieving young father Will (Logan Marshall-Green). In the film's opening moments Will and his girlfriend Kira (Emayatzy Corinealdi) drive to a dinner party hosted by his ex-wife, Eden (Tammy Blanchard). Thanks to Will's frequent flashbacks, we learn that their marriage fell apart after the accidental death of their only child. Although Will is rebuilding his life with Kira's help, his melancholy affect suggests that he is still deeply depressed. Eden (whose name evokes the perception of California as an 'Edenic' locale) initially appears to have 'moved on' more successfully. She has found solace in the arms of new husband David (Michiel Huisman). The couple met at a grief support group convened by The Invitation.[7] The dinner party has ostensibly been prompted by Eden's desire to reconnect with Will and the rest of their old friendship group.

The evening's events are depicted from Will's point of view. His fragile emotional equilibrium is threatened by this reluctant return to the place where his son died. We are soon unsure as to whether Will's evident paranoia is a manifestation of mental instability or a sign that something sinister is going on. As Kusama has explained, Will's outsider status is crucial:

He's the disrupter of the group. He's the wet blanket who says, 'Guys, I know you're having a great time, but I'm just not.' That's a very transgressive place to be, and I sympathize tremendously with it. [. . .] And so, I felt like if I could organize the movie around his behavior and the audience's engagement with and alienation from that behavior, a lot of other stuff would fall into place.[8]

This suggestion of narrative unreliability enhances the film's powerful sense of menace. The possibility that Will may be the one who poses a threat to the others is even signposted by an incident that takes place in the opening scene: he uses a tyre iron to kill a wounded coyote.[9]

Eden's large and expensive home has a garden which overlooks the Hollywood Hills and a forbidding front gate. Will explains to Kira that the money came from Eden's family: 'It wasn't ever mine.' The location recalls 10050 Cielo Drive – the Benedict Canyon home in which Roman Polanski and Sharon Tate lived. Eden's home, like theirs, overlooks Los Angeles, and at various points we see the city lights twinkling in the darkness below. This backdrop evokes the opening lines of Manson prosecutor Vincent Bugliosi's true crime bestseller, *Helter Skelter* (1974):

It was so quiet, one of the killers would later say, you could almost hear the sound of ice rattling in cocktail shakers in the homes way down in the canyon. The canyons above Hollywood and Beverly Hills play tricks with sounds. A noise clearly audible a mile away may be indistinguishable at a few hundred feet [. . .] Though the coastal fog was now rolling in from the Pacific Ocean, Los Angeles itself remained hot and muggy, sweltering in its own emissions, but here, high above most of the city, and usually even above the smog, it was at least 10 degrees cooler. Still, it remained warm enough so that many residents of the area slept with their windows open, in hopes of catching a breeze. All things considered, it's surprising that more people didn't hear something. But then it was late, just after midnight, and 10050 Cielo Drive was secluded. Being secluded, it was also vulnerable.[10]

The killings at Cielo Drive are still most infamously associated with the horrific murders of Sharon Tate and her unborn child. However, three of the other four victims were Polanski/Tate houseguests (the other was an acquaintance of the property's caretaker). *The Invitation*'s premise also revolves around a social gathering suddenly disrupted by horrific violence. Tate and her guests were murdered by strangers, whilst in *The Invitation* it is the hosts, Eden and David (and their fellow cult members), who pose the threat.

In addition to Kira and Will, the other guests are: tightly wound academic Claire (Marieh Delfino), joker Ben (Jay Larson), medical professional Miguel (Jordi Vilasuso) and his husband Tommy (Mike Doyle), and livewire Gina (Michelle Krusiec), who spends much of the film waiting for her boyfriend Choi to arrive (an important plot point). Eden seems both delighted and shaken when Will and Kira arrive. Her first gesture towards Will is to wipe a drop of coyote blood from his face. When he and Kira explain what happened, David reassures them: 'That was a good thing. It was a mercy.' It's another clue as to where the evening is *really* going.

As Will tries to reconnect with his old friends, he feels that something is subtly wrong (again, we have that sense of *something eerie, but nothing you could put your finger on* mentioned in the previous chapter). He notices that Eden and David keep their doors and windows locked and that they are fitted with iron bars. David cites a recent home invasion in the neighbourhood by way of explanation. Will's growing disquiet is increased by the presence of two strangers. The first is a dishevelled young woman named Sadie (Lindsay Burdge). David and Eden say they met her whilst staying at The Invitation's compound in Mexico. 'She's helping us out', David declares. The second is an imposing older man named Pruitt (John Carroll Lynch), another fellow cult member.

David urges everyone to raise their glasses 'to new beginnings'. Eden tries to look relaxed, but Will notices that she is anxiously clutching the pearls cinched around her neck. They get a chance to privately reconnect in the kitchen. During this encounter, Will has a flashback to a harrowing incident during which Eden tried to cut her wrists. Although Eden claims to have been 'reborn', this reminder of the profound emotional pain she has suffered in the not-so-distant past undermines her assertion. Like Will, we begin to suspect that her supposed new life is built upon the unhealthy repression of old trauma. 'I've never been better', Eden tells him: 'All that useless pain – it's gone. It's something anyone can have, Will – and I want you to have it too.' When Ben also enters the room, Eden begins to espouse a worldview resembling that expressed by the pod people in *Invasion of the Body Snatchers*: 'I was just telling Will that pain is optional. All those negative emotions, grief, anger, depression – it's all just chemical reactions. It's entirely physical and it's completely changeable.' Ben's crude riposte, 'It sounds fucking crazy', is met with a slap to the face – the first concrete indication that Eden will not tolerate any criticism of The Invitation. The fact that Will and David look alike (both men have brown hair and beards and are dressed in muted earth tones) and are repeatedly seen standing opposite one another, further suggests that Eden has not moved on as much as she likes to claim.

Once everyone settles in the living room, we start to have an idea of what kind of group 'The Invitation' is. David claims that

It's just a bunch of people coming together, they all have lost someone, and they try to help each other. It's really a science, not some weird religious cult or anything. It's smart people, like us, here in LA and New York, thousands of people – you'd be surprised!

He then shows them all a promotional video, narrated by The Invitation's leader, 'Dr Joseph' (Toby Huss), an authoritative man who declares over the opening shots of a beautiful desert compound that 'this is our home in Sonora Mexico, and it is your home too, if you choose it to be. Our home and our family are open to anyone with the desire to help themselves.' The Invitation's aim, he explains, is to rewrite the brain to help it cope with trauma: 'Wherever you are, we transcend', he claims. The final moments of the video show a young woman on her deathbed surrounded by Dr Joseph and other cult members. Joseph assures her that she will soon be reunited with her deceased loved ones: 'Over soon, all of this grief you've chosen. You renounce it. You have made a choice.' As the woman breathes her last, he declares: 'Don't cry – there is no darkness. Just reunion.'

As his guests sit in stunned silence, David happily adds, 'This is what it's all about.' Will angrily says he doesn't understand why David would show something like that at a dinner party. Eden claims that the video was intended to reassure them that 'there's nothing to be afraid of'. Here, death is ominously framed as a 'mercy'. Despite David's claim that The Invitation is 'a science', Dr Joseph's talk of 'transcendence' and 'rewriting trauma' comes straight from the pop culture cult-cliché handbook. His pseudo-scientific pronouncements are calibrated to appeal to vulnerable people who feel they have nothing left to live for. Until he joined, David, was, in his own words, a 'coked-up record producer', unable to cope after the death of his wife. Eden joined to find a way of coping with the death of her son. She unconvincingly adds, 'Look at me now – I'm great, I'm happy.' However, her justification veers into menacing territory when she adds: 'And if anyone tried to take that away from me . . .'

As the film progresses, clues as the true nature of the 'dinner party' continue to accumulate. Will discovers that Eden has phenobarbital in her room. In 1997, thirty-nine members of the San Diego-based Heaven's Gate UFO cult killed themselves with a mixture of this drug and alcohol. It is another reminder of The Invitation's real-life antecedents. However, Will's friends do not take his suspicions seriously: instead, they earnestly inquire about *his* mental state. Will tries to get Miguel and Tommy to admit that there is, at the very least, something odd about Pruitt and Sadie. Tommy acknowledges, 'They *are* a little Mansony', but immediately follows up with: 'This is LA, they're harmless.' The long-standing association between California and eccentric seekers of 'enlightenment' prevents him from considering the possibility that The Invitation might be genuinely dangerous.

The threat lurking behind the group's genial façade becomes even more obvious when Pruitt takes part in a confessional 'game' started by David. 'The point', he says, 'is to be honest. To admit your desires.' Sadie, who goes first, declares 'I wanna tell you all that I love you.' After Gina takes a turn, Pruitt talks about the death of his wife. At first, the others listen sympathetically. Then Pruitt explains that he 'accidentally' beat her to death and was sent to prison. It was, he says, 'by accepting The Invitation and looking only ahead, destroying that horrible part of me that made that moment possible', that he has been 'cured': 'I don't feel guilty anymore. I've chosen to let that go. These emotions are useless, because I'm going to be seeing her again, in a better place than this.'

Pruitt's story is the last straw for Claire, who is the only guest apart from Will who senses that something is wrong. 'It feels like you're selling us something', she tells David, and prepares to leave. Eden and David try to dissuade her, over Will's objections. Pruitt then offers to move his car so that Claire can access her own vehicle. Will is suspicious, but when he tries to check that Claire has left safely, David stands in his line of sight: 'You've been acting so suspicious of our hospitality that frankly it upsets me a little. You seem very distant, just very off somehow.' The iron railings on the window bear a distinctive lantern motif: the cult's logo. The Invitation's malign influence is always working away in the background.

This sense of impending doom is heightened by further visual and thematic allusions to real-life cult nightmares. Much of the film's mid-section takes place in the living room: Sharon Tate and several of her friends were tortured and murdered in her living room. The Invitation, like the Manson Family, has a desert compound (albeit one located in Mexico rather than Los Angeles County, which is where the Spahn Ranch was). Then there's Dr Joseph's description of the group as 'a family', Pruitt's criminal past (Manson and many of his followers had criminal records) and, as with the Tate murders, a powerful cult leader who orchestrates crimes without being physically present when they are carried out. Apart from Will (who is styled to look a little like Manson) and Pruitt, the most obviously 'Mansony' person present is Sadie, whose unkempt appearance, sexual frankness and fanatical devotion to Dr Joseph recall the fanaticism of Manson 'Girls' such as Lynette 'Squeaky' Fromme, Linda Kasabian, Leslie Van Houten, Mary Brunner and Patricia Krenwinkel.

The character's name is likely a reference to Susan 'Sadie' Atkins. According to Bugliosi, Atkins asked her cellmates to call her 'Crazy Sadie', and bragged that she had stabbed Sharon Tate in the stomach and used her victim's blood to scrawl 'Pigs' on the front door of Cielo Drive.[11] Will is rattled by Sadie's sexual advances and her declaration that 'You can hurt me if you want' – a suggestion, perhaps, that like many of Manson's female acolytes, the young woman has been damaged by sexual and emotional abuse before falling under the cult's influence.

As the group then climb the stairs to the dining area (their ascent is shot in dream-like slow motion), Will again tries to convince Tommy that 'Something doesn't feel safe here', only to be told that he is the only one 'freaking people out'. The faint drone of a helicopter can be heard, subtly reinforcing the sense of encroaching calamity. Upstairs, a lavish feast has been laid out. Will is unable to contain himself. He demands that Eden and David explain where Gina's absent boyfriend Choi is. He is shocked and humiliated when Choi (Karl Yune) turns up at that very moment. For a moment, it seems as if the problem here really is all in Will's head. He tearfully admits to Kira that he is 'not ok. My son is dead. Where do I put that?' He has, he continues, 'been waiting to die since the moment it happened'.

As this conversation takes place, we see David lighting a red lantern in the garden. Just when it seems as if Will is about to accept that he has been terribly mistaken, he accidentally opens David's laptop. He comes across another, more alarming video message from Dr Joseph. It is clearly a signal: 'The beautiful moment is upon us. Tonight is the night our fate is made real. The hardest thing is to start. Just take the step.'

Stunned but uncertain as to what this all means, Will is escorted back to the dinner table by Pruitt. Glasses of port are poured, and Eden and David happily toast their guests: 'Raise your glasses. To a better world. To peace!' Will, suddenly convinced that the wine is poisoned, knocks the glasses from everyone's hands. Sadie attacks him, shrieking 'You ruined it!' Will instinctively pushes back, and she hits her head. At this point, everyone looks at Will in absolute horror. He seems dismayed himself. However, unnoticed amidst the uproar, Gina, who had taken a sip of port, lies slumped over the table. The other guests realise that Will was right and panic sets in. There's no cell phone reception, all exits are locked and they are surrounded by homicidal cult members. The truth becomes undeniable when David suddenly guns down Miguel and Choi.

In its final twenty minutes, the film depicts a brutal struggle for survival. David and Eden clearly intended to kill their guests in a manner recalling the mass suicides/murders at Jonestown. When Will foils that plan, a bloodbath reminiscent of the Manson Family murders ensues (Bugliosi wrote in *Helter*

*Skelter* that '10050 Cielo Drive was a human slaughterhouse').[12] Like the Tate/Polanski home invasion, this massacre is carried out at pitilessly close quarters. Victims are stabbed, bludgeoned and shot. Like Tate's houseguest Voytek Frykowski, murdered as he tried to flee, Ben is chased and killed outside (by Pruitt). We have realised by this point that Pruitt murdered Claire as she tried to leave (like Steven Parent, the young man shot to death in the Tate/Polanski driveway, she was the first to die).[13]

After battling a resurgent Sadie, Will and Kira creep through the house in search of an exit. Will overhears David and Eden discuss their original intentions. True to her name, Eden's perceptions were influenced by her belief that she and David were helping everyone ascend to a better world: 'We were supposed to just go to sleep. It was meant to be peaceful.'

She is clearly horrified by the unanticipated bloodbath. David, however, reminds her that 'Dr Joseph said it was gonna be hard, but we'll have to finish it.' Although Sadie is the film's most obvious Manson Girl analogue, Eden's fanatical faith in Dr Joseph and her complicity, up until this point, with the plan to carry out mass murder, also allies her with these women. 'Helter Skelter' (Manson's plan to carry out a series of brutal murders to provoke an apocalyptic race war) was, Sadie Atkins is said to have claimed, about killing random victims so as 'to release them from this earth'. She also declared of her part in the Tate massacre that 'You have to have a real love in your heart to do this for people.'[14] Like Eden and David, Manson's acolytes believed they had been 'chosen' for a special purpose.

As is frequently the case within the horror genre more generally, the death of a loved one leaves those left behind vulnerable to the intrusion and influence of harmful external forces. These forces are often supernatural in nature, but this need not always be the case. Eden's pain is so powerful that it prompts her to commit acts she would previously have considered unthinkable. The Invitation targets people when they are at their lowest point, promising an end to all suffering and reunification with the dead. Eden and Will have both been left devastated by their son's death, and both have made an unsuccessful attempt to 'move on'. However, Eden's coping mechanism involves submitting to a dangerous cult leader whose plan to bring about a 'better world' involves mass murder and suicide.

Will and Kira are cornered by Pruitt, who states, 'There's a plan for us', as he prepares to shoot them. The men fight, but it is Kira who neutralises the threat, bludgeoning Pruitt with a vase. Eden, determined to see the plan through, then wounds Will before shooting herself in the stomach. David is stabbed to death by Tommy.

At this point, it seems as if the danger has passed. As she lies dying, Eden cries for her dead child, admitting, 'I miss him. I miss him so much. I wanted to believe.' To fulfil her final request, Will picks her up and gently lays her down on the lawn, in the same spot where their son died. Eden's last words are characteristically wistful: 'I hope . . . I hope . . .' Her dress (a white, Grecian-style gown now soaked in blood) and place of death may be intended to evoke associations with the final moments of Abigail Folger, who, whilst clad in a long white nightgown, was murdered on the lawn of the Tate/Polanski residence. However, Eden is much more of a villain than a victim. If it wasn't for her involvement with The Invitation, none of her old friends would have been brutally murdered.

For a moment after Eden draws her last breath, the three survivors – Will, Kira and Tommy – stand in stunned silence. Tommy then returns to the house to check on Miguel. Will and Kira hold hands. Then we become aware of police sirens, barking dogs and the drone of helicopters overhead. The camera pulls back to reveal a panoramic shot of the city, and we see countless red lanterns twinkling in the distance. A faraway scream echoes in the night. The massacre at Eden's house was no one-off: Dr Joseph, it becomes clear, was speaking to *all* his followers – thousands of them, in LA, New York and who knows where else – when he ordered them to 'take the step'. Will, instantly grasping the implications, says 'Oh my God', and the screen fades to black.

With this last minute turn of the screw, *The Invitation* consolidates its position as an intelligent and incisive reflection upon the lasting cultural legacy of contemporary California's most notorious cult-related horror stories. As was also the case in *Invasion of the Body Snatchers*, what started in California will likely spread elsewhere. There's also a sense of inevitability to the cult's violence, because it confirms the most paranoid suspicions held by both Will and the viewer. As Laycock notes, decades of pop culture have primed us to believe the very worst about such groups. Unsurprisingly, the 1970s, he continues, were a prime period for the depiction of cult violence in horror cinema.[15] *The Invitation* is something of a throwback to this trend, reconfiguring notorious real-world incidences of extreme cult violence for a twenty-first-century context. *The Invitation*'s sense of grim inevitability also recalls Joan Didion's famous description of life in Los Angeles in the late summer of 1969:

A demented and seductive vortical tension was building in the community. The jitters were setting in. I recall a time when the dogs barked every night and the moon was always full. On August 9, 1969, I was sitting in the shallow end of my sister-in-law's swimming pool in Beverly Hills when she received a telephone call from a friend who had just heard about the murders at Sharon Tate Polanski's house on Cielo Drive. The phone rang many times during the next hour. These early reports were garbled and contradictory. One caller would say hoods, the next would say chains. There were twenty dead, no, twelve, ten, eighteen. Black masses were imagined, and bad trips blamed. I remember all of the day's misinformation very clearly, and I also remember this, and wish I did not: *I remember that no one was surprised.*[16]

Writing about the difficulties of defining California through the state's culture, James Quay asks 'Why California? Of the many places in the world blessed with natural wonders, favorable climates, energetic economies and dynamic populations, why should California hold such a distinctive place in the national and global imagination?' This question, he continues, 'leads us to California's defining cultural feature: its persistence as a location where the deepest human yearnings can be realized'.[17] *The Invitation*, like the other narratives considered in this section, presents us with a nightmarish vision of California as a place where the sincere (if often misguided) desire for a better life and a better self is exploited by seductive and deeply sinister cult and cult-like movements. Like Thibault de Castries in *Our Lady of Darkness* and the alien invaders who quietly exterminate humanity in order to bring about their own version of an 'untroubled world' in *Invasion of the Bodysnatchers*, Dr Joseph and his followers find in California the perfect environment in which to set in motion their own horrific masterplan.

## 'We're Our Best Selves When We Know Our Neighbours Are Watching': *1BR* (2019)

David Marmor's 2019 film, *1BR*, is also set in contemporary Los Angeles. The impressionistic opening sequence features a fleeting glimpse of the Hollywood sign (it is also glimpsed at the beginning of *The Invitation*). This detail reinforces the geographical and thematic link between the events which are about to unfold and the historical/pop culture association between Southern California and nefarious cult activity. The title is a reference to the real-estate abbreviation for 'One Bedroom'. The domicile for rent here is located within a complex named 'Asilo del Mar'. Although the Spanish translation is perhaps a little ominous ('Asylum by the Sea'), for 24-year-old Sarah (Nicole Brydon Bloom), it seems like a perfect place for a fresh start. The name of the complex may also be a clue as to what she is unwittingly getting into: it resembles that of the Del Mar Club, the Santa Monica hotel used as a headquarters by Synanon.[18]

The current tenants are a racially and socially diverse group who seem very welcoming. The only discordant note is the high level of security: the front entrance has a strict 'buzz in and out' door system, and there are cameras throughout the gated complex. Sarah notices elderly resident Edie Stanhope (Susan Davis) stumble for a moment and assists the vulnerable stranger. Sarah doesn't know it yet, but this act of instinctive kindness, along with the fact she is all alone in a new city ('I just moved here, I don't know anyone') make her an ideal new resident.

As in the Hollywood Gothic films *Starry Eyes*, *The Neon Demon* and *Mulholland Drive*, *1BR* is the story of a lonely and isolated young woman whose deepest desire is to 'make it' in Los Angeles. Sarah has no interest in acting, but her ambitions are still related to the entertainment industry: her dream is to be a costume designer. This desire for a backstage role is an indication of her self-effacing temperament: unlike her 'Hollywood Gothic' contemporary Sarah Walker (*Starry Eyes*), *this* Sarah wants to work behind the scenes. However, her ambition also seems vaguely formulated and unrealistic: she has a sewing machine, but we seldom see her at work on it.

Sarah's loneliness is exacerbated by the rocky relationship she has with her widowed father, who is now in another relationship. He worries that she will be unable to manage by herself. As was also the case for Jesse in *The Neon Demon* and Agatha in *Maps to the Stars*, Sarah's economic insecurity is telegraphed by the fact that she lives in a seedy motel. Her unfulfilling temporary job contributes to her dissatisfaction. She spends all day in a grey cubicle performing dull admin. She voices a sentiment previously cited elsewhere in this volume as a means of explaining why someone has moved to California: 'I guess I'm trying to start a new life.'

The fact that Sarah is a newcomer is important. For McWilliams, the city's culture of transience explained the frequency with which new cults sprang up there:

> Migration is the basic explanation for the growth of cults in Southern California [. . .] In the process of moving westward, the customs, practices and religious habits of the people have undergone important changes. Old ties have been loosened, old allegiances weakened. [. . .] Cult movements have moved westwards in America and Los Angeles is the last stop.[19]

Sarah has left everything behind to build a new life in a city that now seems bleak and unwelcoming. The prospect of having to admit defeat and return home is deeply upsetting to her.

For this reason she is delighted when her application to live in Asilo del Mar is approved. The only problem is the no-pet policy. Sarah defiantly sneaks her beloved cat into her new apartment. The welcome she receives is fulsome and apparently sincere. The 'building manager' Jerry (Taylor Nichols), informs her that 'We like to make this place feel like a real neighbourhood.' It's a sentiment reinforced by Brian (Giles Matthey), a young man who is close to Sarah's own age: 'We all kind of take care of each other here', he tells her. 'I like that', Sarah replies. 'LA can be so . . .' – she trails off. 'Lonely?' Brian responds. Again, the connection between a lack of strong personal connections and a vulnerability to cult conspiracy is underlined.

Sarah's delight in her new digs is soon marred by a constant banging noise at night which none of her neighbours seem to hear. She also lacks privacy. She may have her own apartment, but she is constantly bumping into neighbours when she ventures outside. However, Sarah does strike up a friendship with Miss Stanhope and Brian, who seems like a potential love interest. She also makes a new friend at work named Lisa (Celeste Sully). However, these new connections cannot compensate for the noise that keeps her awake every night, or the nasty anonymous note which reveals that someone knows about her cat. It clearly pains Sarah to violate the no-pet code, but the cat is an important source of emotional solace. When she turns down Brian's invitation to a dinner party at his place in favour of hanging out with her friend Lisa, Sarah confides to her colleague that she is thinking of giving up the apartment. She wakes up again the same night to find smoke coming from the kitchen. Her beloved cat has been burned alive in the oven. Sarah is then knocked out with chloroform and tied to a chair. As the assailant injects her with something, she suddenly realises that he is Brian.

*1BR* depicts cult indoctrination in four stages. In the first of these, Sarah is carefully 'chosen' and then manipulated by her new neighbours, who are all members of an authoritarian cult dedicated to furthering their own fanatical ideas about the 'ideal' utopian community. The second stage, which begins when she regains consciousness, takes place over a matter of weeks (or perhaps even months – in a reflection of Sarah's own chronological confusion during this time, the timeline is not made explicitly clear). We realise that the banging on the pipes softened Sarah up by making her tired and even more emotionally fragile. She was originally meant to be taken prisoner at Brian's dinner party. The purpose of this stage is to use intimidation and violence to 'condition' Sarah's behavioural responses to such an extent that she is prepared to become a fully invested member of the group. Sarah awakens in a windowless cell, dressed in a prison-style jumpsuit. She is told that 'no one is coming for you' – the group have closed out her credit cards, sent a resignation letter to her workplace and written a nasty email to her boss, intended to get Lisa in trouble (thereby ending their friendship). Sarah is now more dangerously alone in Los Angeles than ever, except for the fanatical cult members determined to break her down and build her back up again in their own image.

'This programme', Jerry tells her, 'is very simple. You comply, you get rewarded. You don't, you get punished.' At this point, she is reminded of Lester (Clayton Hoff), a neighbour she has always found creepy, who has a missing eye and a mutilated ear. It is now revealed that those injuries were deliberately inflicted upon him because he resisted his 'conditioning'. When Sarah is ordered to place her hands against the walls in a painful 'stress position', she is informed: 'This is for your own good. Someday you'll understand.' The cult views individual suffering as a price worth paying to further the goals of the collective greater good. Locked in her brightly lit cell for twenty-four hours a day, with the same song being played through the loudspeaker on a loop, Sarah quickly loses all sense of time and reality.

Jerry and Brian, who are in charge of Sarah's 'programme', also begin to outline the true nature of the community. Every resident has been through the same behavioural modification process. Even Sarah's seemingly harmless old neighbour was aware of the intention to abduct and forcibly indoctrinate her. Edie visits Sarah to berate her for leaving her family behind for 'selfish reasons', for violating the no-pet rule and for finding escape through alcohol. In words reminiscent of the phrasing also used by David in *The Invitation*, Edie declares of the 'programme': 'It's not crazy – it's science. Jerry knows how to fix bad conditioning.' Sarah is told that total submission will be the only way to escape the horror of her current situation: 'The sooner you give up, the sooner you'll be free.' Her wavering defences are further eroded when her hands are nailed to the wall. When she eventually rips herself free and collapses in a state of delirium, Sarah is deemed to have reached breaking point and is treated with care by female members of the community (who also include a medical doctor).

At this point, stage three of Sarah's indoctrination process begins. She becomes immersed in the teachings of the community and is forced to integrate them into her own worldview. This part of the programme also involves regular sessions in which she is connected to a blood pressure-style monitor which records her physiological reactions to the probing questions she is being asked by Brian and Jerry. To begin with she is ordered to describe all her sexual experiences to date. The apparatus resembles the polygraph-style 'E-meter' deployed within the intensive 'auditing' process undertaken by members of the Church of Scientology. The reasoning behind this intrusive questioning relates to the group's conviction that 'Openness is one of the foundations of this community. We don't keep secrets.' They are convinced that their own enclosed society is superior to the outside world, in which everyone is said to be 'on their little devices, obsessed with themselves. We have to be better than that.' They do, however, have an ominous-sounding plan to change the world, once 'we're ready to handle it'.

In *1BR*, we are told that the community (as the members always refer to it) was founded by a Professor of Behavioural Psychology named Charles D. Ellerby (Curtis Webster), who believed that his research held the key to positively modifying human nature (his initials, 'C.D.E', are on the apartment complex sign, along with the cult's insignia, which consists of overlapping circles). Like 'Dr Joseph' in *The Invitation*, Ellerby is physically absent but represented in pre-recorded video footage, in this case, old television interviews (although he is actually dead, rather than in another geographical location). Again, this detail evokes real-life antecedents: Scientology founder, L. Ron Hubbard, spent his final years in relative seclusion, and was not seen in public for six years before his death.[20] During this period, he 'continued to reign over Scientology with almost paranoid secrecy', relaying his orders to his followers 'in writing or on tape cassettes'.[21] More infamously, Jim Jones recorded many of his sermons on cassette tape, amongst them the rambling, drug-fuelled final monologue during which he ordered his hundreds of followers to poison their children before taking their own lives.

In *1BR*, the community is based around strict adherence to four 'foundations': selflessness, openness, acceptance and security. Ellerby's interviews reveal his certainty that humanity now has the technology (i.e., behaviour modification techniques) which allows us to be moulded into their best selves. The four foundations state that members must always act in the best interests of the community, that 'secrets breed discord' and that members are required to practice 'acceptance' – particularly of punishment administered by other members of the community if one does not follow these teachings. The final foundation is 'security', because, supposedly, 'We're always our best selves when we know our neighbours are watching.' The rationale behind the foundations, as Ellerby puts it, is that 'Soon enough, living the foundation becomes a habit. Then it becomes who we are. And when that happens, we'll make of this world a single, perfect community. Free of loneliness, free of poverty, free of strife.' Yet again, we have the leader of a Californian cult expressing the belief that its dehumanising, authoritarian credo is the key to establishing a 'perfect' new world.

As the months pass, Sarah becomes embedded in the everyday life of the community. She is denied access to the outside world, forced to participate in lengthy interviews with Brian and Jerry and given a job in the community's school, because 'everyone here has a role to play'. Gradually, she becomes more and more compliant. When she asks why she was chosen, the answer is simple: 'Because you needed us.' Sarah finds it particularly difficult to watch when Miss Stanhope, whose health has been deteriorating, is euthanised (by suffocation) as the rest of the community respectfully watches on. This scene resembles one found in another 2019 horror movie about a vulnerable young woman who is gradually indoctrinated by a deceptively welcoming cult community: Ari Aster's Folk Horror film, *Midsommar*. The presence in both films of sequences during which elderly members of the community are murdered/take their own lives because they are seen to have outlived their usefulness emphasises the brutally utilitarian nature of these groups. Sarah is told that Edie 'Can't contribute to the community anymore', and warned not to ruin her final moments by interfering with the ceremony.

A conversation between Brian and Sarah reminds us that he – like everyone else in the complex – was once where Sarah is now. 'At first I thought it was hell', he admits. But then, he claims, 'When you let go, and embrace this community with all your heart, there is nothing we won't do to make you happy.' As a troubled veteran who was suffering from PTSD before he was forced to join, Brian is now fully on board with the community's aims and methods. Assimilation or death appear to be Sarah's only options.

When she finally convinces Jerry that she is ready to become a full-fledged resident, Sarah is branded with the cult's insignia and thrown a 'welcome to the community party'. But her apparent happiness at reaching this final stage of the programme is sullied when Jerry reveals that her future role in the community has been decided upon – she is to be paired off with Lester, whose wife died some time ago. Sarah's acceptance of her place within the community is also shaken when she receives an unscheduled visit from her father, during which he makes a sincere apology for his previous behaviour. To save his life, she has to cruelly reject his apology and order him to leave the complex and never return. Now that her last and deepest ties to the outside world have been cut, Sarah vows to try and make the best of her 'new' life. Lester admits that he spent his first few years as a member of the community either trying to escape or trying to kill himself. Now, he has come to accept that 'This is our life. Nothing can change that. But it can be a good life.'

The fourth stage of Sarah's involvement with the cult begins sometime later. She is now one of the team who monitors residents from the array of closed-circuit TV monitors dotted around the complex (and present in every room). Sarah is obviously by now a trusted and valuable member of the community. Things have even come full circle for her: as the scene opens, she and Brian are watching a stream of unsuspecting applicants enter the complex to view the apartment which has just been advertised for rent – the apartment which is a trap designed to snare vulnerable new recruits. However, Sarah is shocked to see that one of the prospective residents is her old work friend Lisa, who had previously admired the complex. Brian and Jerry swiftly decide that Lisa will make an ideal potential resident. She is an aspiring actress with Hollywood dreams, but these showbiz ambitions have obviously not been realised: as was previously signalled by Sarah's backstage ambitions and Edie's career as a B-movie actress, the desire to find success in Hollywood is here seen to make one particularly susceptible to nefarious cult influence.

Once Lisa moves in the community subjects her to the same well-rehearsed harassment routine they used on Sarah. However, this time Sarah is able to watch the painful 'conversion' process unfold from the other side of the camera: she is working behind the scenes at last. Nevertheless, Lisa is strong-willed and, as Sarah predicted, 'resistant', even when she reaches the still more directly abusive imprisonment phase. Eventually, Sarah is sent into the room to convince her friend that the experience is all for her own good: 'I want to help you. We all do', Sarah tells her: 'I finally have a family that cares about me.' But Lisa, who knows about Sarah's troubled relationship with her father, is quick to reject this platitude: 'You don't have a new family. You just found another Daddy to run your life for you.' This insightful barb breaks through Sarah's months of conditioning.

In the film's final scenes, she finally rebels against the community and tries to help Lisa escape, even killing Jerry, the putative leader of the complex, with his own gun. She uses his key card to make her way through the building's many locked doors, but Lisa is killed along the way. In desperation, Sarah finally tries to convince the rest of the community that 'It doesn't matter who our leader is. The community is all of us', but her efforts are futile. There follows a scene reminiscent of similar mob scenes in both the 1956 and 1978 film versions of *Invasion of the Body Snatchers*, as Sarah is pursued by a horde of relentless cult members who are determined to prevent her escape. Neverthe-less, she finally manages to slip through the last locked door thanks to Lester, who sacrifices his own life so that she can finally reach the outside world.

As Sarah frantically runs down the quiet city streets, it seems for a moment as if she really has managed to evade her captors. But then, in the film's closing seconds, she gradually realises that the other apartment complexes she passes all have a familiar logo on their signage. As CCTV cameras activate and a plethora of alarms start to shriek, it becomes clear that the community operating within Asilo del Mar is definitely not the only one in the neighbourhood. In a con-clusion which has obvious similarities with the final seconds of *The Invitation*, *1BR* ends by making it clear that the cult concerned has a much wider reach than we have thus far suspected. Sarah is free for now, but her fate, even in the minutes to come, is decidedly uncertain. Once more, an organisation based in California which is obsessed with the idea of a bringing about a 'perfect world' by any means necessary seems likely to extend its malign reach beyond the geographical and cultural boundaries of the Golden State.

## 'We Would Have No Choice But to Be Good': *The Circle* (2013)

Dave Eggers's novel *The Circle* belongs to the tradition first established by writers such as Yevgeny Zamyatin, Aldous Huxley, George Orwell, Ray Bradbury and

Margaret Atwood. It also has much in common with the twenty-first-century cult horror narratives just discussed. In addition to drawing upon anxieties inspired by the supposedly utopian late 1960s counterculture, it satirically critiques potentially harmful new technologies and modes of interpersonal interaction. In *Amusing Ourselves to Death: Public Discourse in the Age of Show Business* (1985), Neil Postman famously outlined the key differences between Orwell's and Huxley's competing visions of a totalitarian future:

> Contrary to common belief even among the educated, Huxley and Orwell did not prophesy the same thing. Orwell warns that we will be over-come by an externally imposed oppression. But in Huxley's vision, no Big Brother is required to deprive people of their autonomy, maturity and history. As he saw it, people will come to love their oppression, to adore the technologies that undo their capacities to think. [. . .] In *1984*, Huxley added, people are controlled by inflicting pain. In *Brave New World*, they are controlled by inflicting pleasure. In short, Orwell feared that what we hate will ruin us. Huxley feared that what we love will ruin us. This book is about the possibility that Huxley, not Orwell, was right.[22]

Like Huxley (and like Ray Bradbury in his 1953 novel, *Fahrenheit 451*), Eggers depicts a world in which people happily consent to live in a manipulative and totalitarian one-world state because they have become hopelessly addicted to short-term pleasures and external validation. The fleeting but enthralling sense of belonging provided by insidious new technologies is the Trojan Horse which allows an all-powerful tech company to infiltrate every facet of private, political and public life. In *The Circle*, a more sophisticated version of the abusive behaviour modification techniques depicted in *1BR* is deployed on a global scale and spread via social media platforms and technology. Here, Eggers anticipated the prime concerns of Jaron Lanier's 2018 manifesto, *Ten Arguments for Deleting Your Social Media Accounts Right Now*, in which Lanier pointed out:

> Something entirely new is happening in the world. Just in the past five or ten years, nearly everyone has started to carry a little device called a smart-phone on their person all the time that's suitable for algorithmic behavior modification. A lot of us are also using related devices called smart speakers on our kitchen counters or in our car dashboards. We're being tracked and measured constantly, and receiving engineered feedback all the time. We're being hypnotized little by little by technicians we can't see, for purposes we don't know. We're all lab animals now.[23]

*The Circle* is also a novel about a very *Californian* vision of infinite possibility and human/social perfectibility. Eggers even signposts this aspect of the text by opening with a quote from a canonical work of Californian literature: John Steinbeck's *East of Eden* (1952) – 'There wasn't any limit, no boundary at all, to the future. And it would be so a man wouldn't have room to store his happiness' – an extract which underlines his own novel's sly subversion of the familiar 'California as Eden' theme. The 'technological utopia' represented by his titular tech company represents the newest manifestation of the Californian dream turned nightmare.

We are told that the Circle began when Ty Gospodinov, a 'boy-wonder visionary', devised 'TruYou', a brand-new 'Unified Operating System' which revolutionised the online world and provided the technological and philosophical foundation for the entire company.[24] TruYou is said to have put

> every user's needs and tools, into one pot [. . .] one account, one identity, one password, one payment system, per person. There were no more passwords, no multiple identities [. . .] To use any of the Circle's tools, and they were the best tools, the most dominant and ubiquitous and free, you had to do so as yourself, as your actual self, as your TruYou. Anytime you wanted to see anything, use anything, comment on anything or buy anything, it was one button, one account, everything tied together and trackable and simple.[25]

The Circle has now become a kind of cult which efficiently indoctrinates not only its star-struck employees, but billions of ordinary citizens all over the world. Here, the mass-adoration so often granted to white male 'tech geniuses' such as Bill Gates, Steve Jobs and Elon Musk eventually becomes indistinguishable from the following amassed by actual cult leaders.

*The Circle* is yet another California Gothic story about an idealistic newcomer whose vague but powerful yearning for 'something better' makes them the ideal new recruit for an organisation which will rebuild their personality in accordance with its own core values. The protagonist here, Mae Holland, is introduced as she excitedly begins her first day on the Circle's Northern Californian campus. It is the most exciting and influential tech company in the world. The novel's opening lines capture her idyllic impressions: 'My God, Mae thought. It's heaven.'[26] The Circle has a logo ('a circle surrounding a knitted grid, with a small "c" in the center') which is 'already among the best-known in the world'.[27] Mae is a 24-year-old college graduate who, until just a few weeks ago, was unhappily working as a clerk back in her unremarkable hometown. She can hardly believe that she is now amongst the chosen few working for the company which has been voted the 'the world's most admired company' for four years running.

This opportunity has come about courtesy of Mae's college friend Annie, who has quickly risen through the ranks to become part of the much-admired 'Gang of 40' deemed 'the most crucial minds at the company'.[28] In an early indication of Mae's passiveness, we are told that she only applied to the Circle because Annie suggested it.[29] Like Eden in *The Invitation* or Sarah in *1BR*, she is susceptible to the influence of authority figures who claim to have her best interests at heart.

The avowedly utopian vision of the Circle has been made physically manifest in its beautiful campus, which supplies every amenity, distraction and comfort an employee could possibly want. The grounds are divided into sections named after different historical eras – such as the 'the Old West', 'the Byzantine' and 'the Renaissance'. This brashly ahistorical bricolage is accentuated by the vastly different architectural styles favoured by two of the company's three leaders, fondly known as the 'Three Wise Men'. Although tech genius Ty has disappeared from public view, the older 'wise men', genial frontman Eamon Bailey and finance guru Tom Stenton, have accentuated their personal fiefdoms with *objets d'art* from all over the world. 'That's from some church in Rome', Annie casually tells Mae as she gives her a tour of Bailey's library. The detail recalls the stereotypically Californian indifference towards conventional notions of taste and periodicity that was noted by Tod Hackett when he walked to his apartment building in the opening pages of *The Day of the Locust*.[30] The organisation's indiscriminate cultural appetite is also an indication of its omnivorous nature. The Circle, we are told, has recently 'subsumed Facebook, Google, and finally Alacrity, Zoopa, Jefe, and Quan'.[31]

Although she is a native Californian, Mae is a small-town girl, and has failed to live up to her own high expectations. She is a liberal arts graduate with a massive student loan and reluctantly took up a public service job to repay her debts. In contrast to her burlap-lined cubicle at the utility company, the Circle's idyllic campus casts the rest of the world into negative relief:

> Mae knew that she never wanted to work – never wanted to be – anywhere else. Her hometown, the rest of America, seemed like some chaotic mess in the developing world. Outside the walls of the Circle, all was noise and struggle, failure and filth. But here, all had been perfected. The best people had made the best systems and the best systems had reaped funds, unlimited funds, that made possible this, the best place to work. And it was natural that it was so, Mae thought. Who else but utopians could make utopia?[32]

The Circle seems to Mae like the very embodiment of benevolent technological progress, a company actively working towards the betterment of humanity and the perfectibility of society. The campus – a kind of Edenic California within California itself – is in the (fictional) town of San Vincenzo, which has essentially been colonised by the Circle. This detail recalls the locally transformative impact of real-life Californian tech campuses such as Apple's circle-shaped corporate headquarters in Cupertino, or Facebook's Menlo Park, both of which are also close to the Bay Area. It is said of San Vincenzo that most of it has been 'built or renovated in the last few years – restaurants to serve Circlers, hotels to serve visitors to the Circle, shops hoping to entice Circlers and their visitors, schools to serve children of the Circle'.[33]

Although she quickly settles into her new job on the 'customer experience' team, it takes Mae longer to come to terms with the extent to which the Circle soon dominates every aspect of her life. Participation in the dizzying array of online interest groups (or 'circles') created by company employees is strongly 'encouraged'. It is made clear that a failure to join in will be taken negatively by her supervisors and colleagues. Although this feedback is framed as concern for her social and emotional well-being, the implications are clear. As Dan, Mae's new supervisor, outlines, the Circle sees itself as much more than a traditional place of employment. Deploying the condescending buzzwords typical of Circle employees, he explains that

> We want this to be a workplace, sure, but it should also be seen as a *human*-place. And that means the fostering of community. In fact, it *must* be a community. That's one of our slogans, as you probably know: '*Community First*' [. . .] We're not automatons. This isn't a sweatshop. We're a group of the best minds of our generation. *Generations*. And making sure this is a place where our humanity is respected, where our opinions are dignified, where our voices are heard – this is as important as any revenue, any stock price, any endeavor undertaken here.[34]

Mae is obliged to set up an account on the Circle's social media platform 'Zing' (a satirical amalgamation of Facebook, Twitter and Instagram). The expectation that employees will work to improve their internal 'Participation Rank' (or 'PartiRank') necessitates engaging with posts from other members, even if this takes up many hours in an already busy day.

Soon after Mae begins her new job, Bailey unveils an exciting new technological development. 'SeeChange' is a system of cheap, wirelessly connected and almost invisible cameras which will allow users to stream content anywhere in the world at any time. It is presented to employees at one of the mass gatherings that are a core feature of campus life. SeeChange, Bailey claims, will facilitate democracy by making sure that the repressive suppression of peaceful protest is broadcast to the world, or by ensuring that a vulnerable loved one is benignly watched over. Once these cameras become widely available, 'All that happens will be known.' The Circle's leadership believes that this marks 'the dawn of the Second enlightenment'.[35]

As is the case throughout the novel, advancements which will facilitate the surveillance state are introduced via slogans extolling communal 'betterment'. This is tyranny-in-waiting expressed via self-congratulatory platitudes. Like much of the rest of the world, Mae is dazzled by these innovations, choosing to see them as benign technological interventions which further underline that her new workplace is the most progressive, utopian place in the world. As Margaret Atwood has observed of the novel:

> Some will call *The Circle* a 'dystopia,' but there's no sadistic slave-whipping tyranny on view in this imaginary America: indeed, much energy is expended on world betterment by its earnest denizens. Plagues are not raging, nor is the planet blowing up or even warming noticeably. Instead, we are in the green and pleasant land of a satirical utopia for our times, where recycling and organics abound, people keep saying how much they like each another, and the brave new world of virtual sharing and caring breeds monsters.[36]

Mae loves her new life, but she is concerned about the well-being of her parents (her father has multiple sclerosis) and stressed by the reprimands she receives for not actively engaging with the company's intense online community. After she fails to attend a social event because she is upset by a distressing trip home, Mae is chastised and confesses to her superiors (and to Annie) that the anxiety caused by her father's condition and the high cost of his medical care is weighing upon her. The company swiftly intervenes, at Annie's request, and radically 'improves' the situation. Mae's tearful 'confession' here resembles a seemingly more benign version of the demands made of residents in *1BR*, for whom 'openness' is a foundational principle. As in Asilo del Mar, there can be no secrets in the Circle.

Another indication of the Circle's invasiveness comes when health trackers are given to employees. These trackes are bracelets which monitor heart rate, anxiety levels, BMI, calories burned and electrocardiogram readings. This information is constantly being uploaded back to company servers for analysis and intervention. For Mae, along with her by now extensive interaction with the company's social media platform, the health tracker adds another layer of certainty to her previously aimless life. She is beginning to surrender to the Circle:

> She knew her heart rate and knew it was right. She knew her step count, almost 8,200 per day, and knew that she could get to 10,000 with ease. She knew she was properly hydrated and that her caloric intake that day was within accepted norms for someone of her body-mass index. It occurred to her, in a moment of sudden clarity, that what had always caused her anxiety, or stress, or worry, was not any one force, nothing independent and external – it wasn't danger to herself or the constant calamity of other people and their problems. It was internal: it was subjective: it was *not knowing*.[37]

The only dissenting voice – at first – in Mae's orbit is her ex-boyfriend Mercer, a contrarian craftsman who has remained close to her parents. Mercer reacts angrily when Mae posts a picture of one of his creations to her social media feed without his permission, and sparks a flurry of online interest:

> 'Mae, I've never felt more that there is some cult taking over the world. You know what someone tried to sell me the other day? Actually, I bet it's somehow affiliated with the Circle. Have you heard of Homie? The thing where your phone scans your house for bar codes of every product – ?'
> 'Right. Then it orders new stuff whenever you're getting low. It's brilliant.'
> 'You think this is ok?' Mercer said. 'You know how they framed it for me. *It's the usual utopian vision.* This time they were saying it'll reduce waste [. . .] I mean, like everything else you guys are pushing, it sounds perfect, sounds progressive, but it carries with it more control, more central tracking of everything we do [my italics].'[38]

Although there have already been hints that the Circle takes an uncompromising stance towards corporate rivals and political critics, Mercer is the first to point out that opponents receive a dire comeuppance: 'You think it's just a coincidence that every time some congresswoman or blogger talks about monopoly, they suddenly become ensnared in some terrible sex-porn-witchcraft controversy? [. . .] You're saying this is news to you?'[39] Mae is, however, unwilling – or unable – to accept anything that Mercer says about either the Circle or her own deepening involvement with the company. The impact of Mercer's observations is also lessened by the fact that Mae had previously found him insufferable. After this confrontation, Mae impulsively goes kayaking in San Francisco Bay, 'borrowing' a vessel from the rental place she always uses. She is mortified when the police are called, thanks to the SeeChange camera erected on the property. Although she faces no charges, Mae is summoned by her supervisor the next day and then escorted to Bailey's office for reasons related to the secret 'next phase' of the Circle's messianic devotion to the cause of transparency. Bailey declares that they are going to 'close the Circle at the circle'. He asks her to imagine how people would behave if they acted as if they were being watched every moment of their lives: 'Mae, we would finally be compelled to be our best selves. And I think people would be relieved. [. . .] Finally, finally we can be good. In a world where bad choices were no longer an option, we have no choice but to be good.'[40]

Bailey couches his reproach of Mae in paternalistic terms – the two of them are 'friends', he says, and she should not have hidden anything from him. It's a highly manipulative approach which has the intended effect: 'Mae did feel relief, a surge of it that felt like love [. . .] she wanted to be held by Bailey, to be subsumed by his wisdom and generosity.'[41] Bailey's method of controlling Mae also evokes the other authoritarian 'father figures' previously discussed in this section – Dr Joseph in *The Invitation*, Professor Charles Ellerby in *1BR* and Dr David Kibner in Kaufman's *Invasion of the Bodysnatchers* (all of whom combine the authority bestowed by with their professional credentials with a 'soothing' manner). We might also recall that Jim Jones told his followers to call him 'Dad'.

Mae is asked to publicly discuss her recent behaviour at the company's regular gathering ('Dream Friday') at which new developments and inventions are unveiled. As she sits onstage opposite Bailey, Mae describes the 'awakening' she has experienced over the past week (note the use of religious/spiritual terminology here). She tells the story of her reckless kayaking expedition and, guided by Eamon's carefully pre-rehearsed questions, performatively admits: 'The fact that I thought I was alone, unwatched, enabled me to commit a crime.'[42] Bailey askes Mae to repeat a line she had used in their initial meeting: 'Secrets are lies.' She describes her actions as deeply selfish, because by not recording her kayaking trips, she was also depriving others of this experience. 'Equal access to all possible human experiences is a basic human right', she declares, caught up in the moment. We are told that 'Bailey was looking at her like a proud father.'[43] The presentation eventually leads up to the declaration (again with Mae as the willing mouthpiece) of the following mantra:

SECRETS ARE LIES
SHARING IS CARING
PRIVACY IS THEFT.[44]

The event comes to a rapturous climax when it is revealed that Mae, 'in the interest of sharing all she saw and could offer the world, would be going transparent immediately' – in other words, she has agreed to be the first person to wear a recording device that livestreams (almost) all of her daily interactions and activities in real time.

It is at this point that 'Book II' begins. Mae rapidly becomes a global celebrity and the new face of the company, with many millions of followers who tune in to vicariously participate in her life and that of the company. She is already much enamoured with the Circle: this section outlines the process by which Mae becomes an even more fanatically devoted true believer. However, her exciting new status comes at a high cost. Her parents, reluctant 'co-stars' in Mae's 'reality show' are unsettled by the attention and resent the demands upon their time and energies made by entitled strangers. Mercer is horrified and points this out to Mae, but she refuses to listen. As time passes, the once close relationship she had with her mother and father is fatally compromised by her self-absorption and fanatical commitment to the Circle. Mae soon realises that being 'transparent' means that she must adjust her own behaviour – carefully watch her calorie intake, exercise enough to meet her tracker's precisely calibrated daily expectations and restrict her alcohol intake to avoid setting a bad example for her followers: 'Every day she'd done without things she didn't want to want.'[45] Like Sarah in *1BR*, she is a new recruit (albeit a very willing one) who has risen to a position of considerable responsibility within her new 'community'. As she spends more and more time on the campus, Mae's entire job and her life become indistinguishable.

The Circle has ambitions which go far beyond making a low-ranking employee 'transparent'. Soon, one ambitious local politician after another agrees to stream their own interactions to the public. It rapidly becomes difficult for anyone in public office to refuse, because to do so is taken as an indication that they have things to hide from their voters (the term Eggers uses here is 'Going Clear', which is a term also used by the Church of Scientology, albeit within a different context).[46]

Since her early days at the Circle, Mae has been involved in two on–off romantic relationships. The first is with another campus employee named Francis, who specialises in engineering tracking devices meant to ensure that children (in the first instance) can always be located by their caregivers. As is the case throughout the novel, this seemingly well-intended development soon takes on a sinister resonance. Her second relationship is with a mysterious young man with grey hair who calls himself Kalden, who sporadically turns up at campus events and makes an immediate impression on her. Mae is quickly infatuated with him, but becomes wary when he begins to express concerns about the company's direction. It is Kalden who lays out exactly what 'completion' means:

> Once it's mandatory to have an account, and once all government services are channeled through the Circle, you'll have helped create the world's first tyrannical monopoly. Does it seem like a good idea to you that a private company would control the flow of all information?[47]

Additional – and to Mae, even more surprising – disquiet is voiced by Annie, who is personally devastated when her decision to participate in another company initiative – a combined genealogy and photo-scanning database called 'PastPerfect' – means that deeply troubling family revelations come to the surface.

For a time, it seems as if Mae might begin to rethink her absolute faith in the Circle. She seems horrified when Mercer dies in front of an online audience of millions as the result of a fugitive-tracking demonstration gone wrong, for which she has chosen him to be the primary target. Kalden reveals that he is actually the third 'wise man', technical genius Ty. He tells Mae that she has become the 'benign, friendly face of a totalitarian nightmare', which will soon track every human being from 'cradle to grave, with no possibility of escape'.[48] Bailey is, Ty notes, a true believer, genuinely convinced that 'life will be better, will be perfect, when everyone has unfettered access to everyone and everything they know. [. . .] This is his rapture, Mae! Don't you see how extreme that view is?'[49] Stenton, he continues, is the one who 'professionalized our idealism, monetized our utopia'.[50]

Ty/Kalden begs Mae to read her followers a manifesto he has written entitled 'The Rights of Humans in a Digital Age'. He hopes that because he is the genius who first created the company, his objections will inspire public opposition to the 'completion' process, after which the Circle will be in control of every facet of public, commercial, political and private life. For a moment, it looks as if Mae will help Ty get the message out. However, as the final chapter of the book – titled 'Part III' – begins to unfold, it becomes clear that things have not gone as Ty planned: 'To have gotten so close to apocalypse – it rattled her still.'[51]

In the novel's final pages Mae is sitting by Annie's hospital bedside. Her friend was found catatonic at her desk and remains in a coma. After pretending to cooperate with Ty, Mae went straight to Bailey and Stenton, who swiftly ushered him away, she unquestioningly accepts, to a 'secluded office and no specific duties'.[52] As for Mae, it is obvious that she is even more committed than ever to furthering the goals and philosophy of the Circle. Her closing thoughts about what she believes will be the technological utopia brought about by the company are again described in notably religious terms. She has become a kind of corporate/technological 'Pod Person'. As she thinks about her parents, whom she hasn't seen in many months, she tells herself that:

> They would find each other, soon enough, in a world where everyone could know each other truly and wholly, without secrets, without shame and without the need for permission to see or know, without the selfish hoarding of life – any corner of it, any moment of it. All of that would be, so soon, replaced by a new and glorious openness, a world of perpetual life. Completion was imminent, and it would bring peace, and it would bring unity, and all that messiness of humanity until now, all those uncertainties that accompanied the world before the Circle, would be only a memory.[53]

Although the Circle has come to dominate the world via technological and (ostensibly) non-violent means, Eggers's bleak conclusion has much in common with the endings of *The Invitation* and *1BR*. The utopia-turned-nightmare theme underpinning the 'Cult California' strand of the California Gothic has been updated, thanks to Eggers's satirical take on the state's propensity for pioneering new technologies and new ideas which have the potential to revolutionise everyday life in California and beyond.

Kevin Starr observed in *Coast of Dreams: California on the Edge* (2004) that 'for the past thirty years, California has been rife with experiments in community [. . .] animating these communes was one version or other of the ancient quest – the dream, if you will – of truth, community, and self-esteem'.[54] He cited two prominent 1970s examples of the 'human potential movement': est ('a self-actualization movement based on an almost fascistic concept of power and control') and the drug rehab organisation Synanon, which, as noted in the previous chapter, eventually deployed intimidation and violence against its critics. Starr also states in the same chapter that 'The California coast had always nurtured dreams of technology and science, and, more elusively, the fact and drama of human consciousness, the mind, as a biologically dependent process transcending biology itself.'[55] This crossover between the region's faith in technological forward momentum and the more abstract, but no less idealistic, 'experiments in community' which have been associated with California since the late nineteenth century, is made malevolently manifest in *The Circle*.

Even more definitively than *The Interview* and *1BR*, *The Circle* presents us with a totalitarian and cult-like movement which espouses a dystopian version of stereotypically 'Californian' New Age principles related to 'openness', 'belonging' and 'community', which is well on its way to taking over the rest of the United States and likely the entire globe. It is 'a world moving towards communion and unity', as Bailey puts it.[56] It is a plot development which was anticipated by Jack Finney in *The Body Snatchers*. When Finney's hero, Miles Bennell, realises that for the alien invaders who have quietly and efficiently taken over his small town, Mill Valley is only the start, he asks one of them:

'The world,' I whispered. 'You're going to spread over the *world?*'

He smiled tolerantly. 'What did you think. This county, then the next ones; and presently northern California, Oregon, Washington, the West Coast, finally; it's an accelerating process, ever faster, always more of us, fewer of you. Presently, fairly quickly, the continent. And then – yes, of course, the world.'[57]

## Notes

1. Allen, 'Freedom of Mind', online.
2. McWilliams, *Southern California*, p. 249.
3. Laycock, 'Where Do They Get These Ideas?', p. 88.
4. The first was the movie *The Last Man on Earth* (1964), starring Vincent Price, which is the only adaptation thus far which retains the suburban setting of the novel. See Laycock, 'Conversion by Infection', p. 104.
5. Ibid. p. 104.
6. Cooper, *The Manson Family on Film and Television*, p. 12.
7. Huisman later played a cult leader in the 2020 feminist Folk Horror film, *The Other Lamb*.
8. Radish, 'Karyn Kusama on "The Invitation"', online.
9. The horror film trope of the injured or dead animal on the roadside is always a sign that violence against humans is forthcoming.
10. Bugliosi and Gentry, *Helter Skelter*, p. 3.
11. Ibid. p. 106.
12. Ibid. p. 11.
13. Kusama has confirmed that a shot cut from the final version of the film showed Claire dying at the bottom of a nearby hillside. See Wilhemi, '*The Invitation*: What Happened to Claire Explained', online.
14. Bugliosi and Gentry, *Helter Skelter*, p. 115.
15. Laycock, 'Where Do They Get These Ideas?', p. 86.
16. Didion, *The White Album*, p. 208.
17. Quay, 'Beyond Dreams and Disappointment, p. 4.
18. Janzen, *The Rise and Fall of Synanon*, p. 27.
19. McWilliams, *Southern California*, pp. 270; 271.

20. Lindsay, 'L. Ron Hubbard Dies of Stroke', online.
21. Sappell and Welkos, 'The Mind Behind the Religion', online.
22. Postman, *Amusing Ourselves to Death*, pp. vii–viii.
23. Lanier, *Ten Arguments*, p. 6.
24. Eggers, *The Circle*, p. 19.
25. Ibid. p. 21.
26. Ibid. p. 1.
27. Ibid. p. 2.
28. Ibid. p. 14.
29. Ibid. p. 3.
30. West, *The Day of the Locust*, p. 3.
31. Eggers, *The Circle*, p. 23.
32. Ibid. p. 30.
33. Ibid. p. 161.
34. Ibid. p. 47.
35. Ibid. p. 67.
36. Atwood, 'When Privacy is Theft', online.
37. Eggers, *The Circle*, p. 194.
38. Ibid. p. 59.
39. Ibid. p. 260.
40. Ibid. p. 290.
41. Ibid. p. 291.
42. Ibid. p. 296.
43. Ibid. p. 301.
44. Ibid. p. 303.
45. Ibid. p. 329.
46. See, for instance, Wright, *Going Clear*.
47. Eggers, *The Circle*, p. 401.
48. Ibid. p. 401.
49. Ibid. p. 484.
50. Ibid. p. 484.
51. Ibid. p. 489.
52. Ibid. p. 491.
53. Ibid. p. 491.
54. Starr, *Coast of Dreams*, p. 21.
55. Ibid. p. 27.
56. Eggers, *The Circle*, p. 464.
57. Finney, *The Body Snatchers*, p. 192.

# Conclusion: 'It's Our Time Now': *Us* (2019) and *Desierto* (2015)

The California Gothic narratives discussed here thus far have overwhelmingly dramatised fears and anxieties experienced by white Californians of Anglo-American origin. Yet California is one of the most racially diverse US states. A recent report noted that:

> [n]o race or ethnic group constitutes a majority of California's population: 39% of state residents are Latino, 36% are white, 15% are Asian or Pacific Islander, 6% are African American, fewer than 1% are Native American or Alaska Natives, and 3% are multiracial or other [. . .] Latinos surpassed whites as the state's single largest ethnic group in 2014.[1]

When the initial findings of the 2020 census were released, it was reported that California now 'joined Hawaii, New Mexico and the District of Columbia as a place where non-Hispanic white people are no longer the dominant group'.[2]

As seen in *I Am Legend*, *The Fog* and *Winchester*, in the California Gothic racial unease and guilt about historical crimes and evasions are often projected onto a disruptive (and deracialised) supernatural Other. The almost total 'whiteness' of two of the main varieties of twentieth- and twenty-first-century California Gothic narrative – the Hollywood Gothic and the Cult California narrative – is particularly striking. Here, the perspectives – and fates – of Black, Asian and Latino/x characters are always a secondary focus, if such characters appear at all. Apart from the television show *Them* (2021) – which is in part a pointed corrective to precisely this lack of equitable representation – Gothic unease related to California's rapid post-war growth has usually been dramatised from the perspective of white characters only. *Them* is still unusual in that it directly engages with the question of what the 'California Dream' meant (and continues to mean) for Black Americans and, by implication, for other racial and ethnic groups for whom life in the Golden State has so often been much less 'Edenic' than granted to many white Californians.

I began this book by discussing the reasons why the story of the Donner Party became a foundational 'anti-myth' for the new, white and resolutely 'American' California, and in doing so established several key California Gothic preoccupations. In my concluding chapter, I will focus upon two twenty-first-century horror films which are relayed from the perspective of protagonists whose experiences both engage with and reconfigure these tropes: *Us* (2019), directed by Jordan Peele, and Jonás Cuarón's *Desierto* (2015). Peele's depiction of a resentful 'shadow population' lurking beneath the foundations of middle-class California presents us with an allegorical re-enactment (and critique) of 'Manifest Destiny'. Here, the relentless pursuit of upward mobility, material comfort and opportunity long-associated with California is explicitly linked with complacency, discrimination and an inability to admit that one's own privilege may have come at the expense of others less fortunate.

In the Mexican-made survival horror film *Desierto*, the desperate immigrant's journey towards the 'Promised Land' of California is relayed from a twenty-first-century perspective. The travellers in peril are here Mexican migrant workers desperate to make it across the border. Their already arduous journey soon becomes a nightmarish struggle for survival thanks to the actions of a murderous racist who has taken it upon himself to 'protect' the US-Mexico border. As we shall see, the question, 'Who does twenty-first-century California "belong" to?' lies at the heart of both these films.

## 'From Sea to Shining Sea': *Us*

In *Us*, life in a Northern Californian coastal community is violently disrupted by the intrusion of uncanny and vengeful Others. It is a scenario we have seen before: the same basic premise informs *The Fog* (1980) and *Messiah of Evil* (1973). *Us* also has elements in common with Tobe Hooper's 1982 film *Poltergeist* and Joel Schumacher's 1987 film *The Lost Boys* (discussed in Chapter 2). However, whereas these films focus entirely upon white characters, the family in peril in *Us* is Black. Peele has cited the rarity of this occurrence as a core impetus for the film: 'I realized I had never seen a horror movie of this kind, where there's an African-American family at the center that just *is*.'[3]

The opening scenes of *Us* lay the groundwork for the revelations which will follow. Three successive intertitles appear: 'There are thousands of miles of tunnels beneath the continental United States . . . Abandoned subway systems, unused service routes, and deserted mineshafts . . . Many have no known purpose at all.' Next, there is an extended close-up of a television set tuned to a local news report – 'CAL 11 News Tonight'. The identifying code is clearly meant to be a Californian one, and the number 11 recurs throughout the film.[4]

The identity of the television viewer is at first difficult to discern, but there is a reflection in the screen. A young girl is cutting out paper dolls. Her stuffed toy, a white rabbit, sits by her side. This is young Adelaide/Addie (Madison Curry), and the fact that she is first seen only in reflection is important. A television news report is followed by an advertisement for a real-life fundraising event (to be held in May 1986): the 'Hands Across America' initiative. Addie's paper-doll chain resembles the commercial's logo, a detail which suggests that she is very interested in this endeavour. Subsequent events will bear this out. The commercial asks the viewer to join hands with friends and neighbours so that a human chain can stretch 'From the Golden Gate Bridge all the way to the Twin Towers' and 'From sea to shining sea'. The voiceover plays over a montage showing a multi-racial clasping of hands in various iconic locations. Americans will 'tether themselves together' to fight hunger.

In real life, between 5 and 6 million Americans participated in 'Hands Across America', a figure that was, indeed, technically enough to stretch across the continental landmass.[5] The advertisement's use of the phrase, 'From sea to shining sea', warrants examination. It is most famously associated with the flag-waving hymn, 'America the Beautiful', written by Katharine Lee Bates in 1893. The reference, though fleeting, highlights the ways in which *Us* will seek to reconfigure the mythology of unrestricted and divinely sanctioned Westward expansion. As Diane S. Hope observes, 'America the Beautiful' has a potent patriotic appeal:

> In hindsight, we can see that the North American experience was shaped by conflicted dreams of an abundant, lush, and spectacular land that would reward its destroyers with riches. Such dreams and fantasies worked to push domination of the continent ever westward. It was a mythology, after all, propagated as a godly mission and a manifest right. [. . .]
>
> Perhaps no other reservoir of images has maintained the popular appeal as the lines written in 1893 by Katharine Lee Bates in her patriotic hymn, 'America the Beautiful' [. . .] The song's familiar combinations of beauty, religiosity, and manifest destiny in verbal descriptions of North America have entered the symbolic environment as sentimental visual icons [. . .] Less often visualized are the stanzas that bless incursions into the wilderness and material success [. . .] The song is a standard of popular culture patriotism and wraps the ideology of manifest destiny, democratic ideals, and capital around images of the land as ever beautiful and ever bountiful.[6]

As we shall see, the grown-up version of the little girl watching this advertisement, now known as 'Red' (Lupita Nyong'o) is a visionary leader with an instinctive understanding of the power of symbolism drawn from this same 'reservoir' of patriotic imagery. Red also believes that she was chosen by God. For the abandoned community which Red leads, America the 'ever bountiful' (to paraphrase Hope) was only ever this way for those lucky enough to live above ground.

After the 'Hands Across America' television spot, there follows an advertisement for Santa Cruz beach, highlighting the narrative centrality of this locale. Santa Cruz, as noted in Chapter 2, was strongly associated with the earliest days of the serial killer 'epidemic' in the United States.[7] A fictionalised version of the Santa Cruz boardwalk was also depicted as an enticing but deadly location in *The Lost Boys*. The Santa Cruz here therefore resurrects the real-life notion that there is an inherent *wrongness* about the area, which is why so many notorious crimes occurred there.[8] Additionally, this locational overlap with *The Lost Boys* provides us with a hint about the nature of the story which is about to unfold. *Us* also revolves around a 'lost' child irrevocably transformed by her foray into the 'dark side' of the Santa Cruz/Santa Carla experience. Like Schumacher's juvenile vampires, Peele's feral revolutionaries are associated with an underground lair. In the California Gothic, trouble in every sense of the word is often found just below the surface of everyday life.

The gender of the child enthralled by the television in this opening scene also recalls *Poltergeist*, which similarly opens with an extended close-up of a television set, laying the groundwork for the abduction of little Carol Anne Freeling (Heather O'Rourke) by the 'TV people' whose corpses fester beneath the foundations of the SoCal suburb of Cuesta Verde. In both films, paternal complacency also leaves a child vulnerable to dangerous external influences. Carol Anne creeps through the house to converse with her new 'friends' through the television set her dozing father Steve (Craig T. Nelson) has left switched on. A more explicit instance of paternal neglect leads to Addie's abduction in *Us*. Disquiet about the powerful (and potentially harmful) influence which ideas gleaned from television can have upon susceptible youngsters also links both films. Young Addie's rage-filled future self, Red, will recreate the striking visual metaphor of the 'Hands Across America' advertisement by violent means. Furthermore, Red's revolution may also be a pointed riposte to the arguably simplistic aims of the initiative: as Erick Neher notes, '[t]he rise of the Tethered might thus be seen as a reaction to a smug, failed attempt to help society's less fortunate'.[9]

*Us* and *Poltergeist* also have in common a focus upon a middle-class family placed under siege by justifiably angry entities from just below the (literal and metaphorical) surface of everyday life. The mortal remains of the ghosts in

*Poltergeist* were crassly bulldozed into the foundations of the suburb in which the Freeling family live. In *Us*, the 'Tethered' live in squalor whilst their doubles thrive above ground, blissfully unaware of the 'have-nots' below their feet. In both films, the targeted abduction of a little girl is the method by which the 'shadow population' begins to strike back against their oblivious oppressors.

In the scene which follows the television-focused opening moments of *Us*, an on-screen chyron informs us that it is 1986. Today is Addie's birthday, and she and her bickering parents Rayne (Anna Diop) and Russel (Yahya Abdul-Mateen II) are visiting the Santa Cruz boardwalk. Russel guzzles beer and reacts childishly when Rayne briefly leaves their daughter in his care. Whilst he is distracted, Addie finds herself drawn towards the beach. She notices an attraction called 'Vision Quest: Find Yourself'. The attraction's livery incorporates clichéd Native American motifs and a fake sequoia tree. When Addie enters, she finds herself in front of a series of trick mirrors and becomes disorientated when the lights suddenly go out. As she peers at one of the mirrors, we see her reflection moving – but before we or Addie can grasp what is happening the scene ends, and the film's initially cryptic opening titles – depicting rows of rabbit cages in a utilitarian classroom – unfurl.

The main action then moves to the present day. It begins as the thirty-something woman who appears to be grown-up Addie (I will here refer to her as 'Adelaide') travels with her family to her late mother's home. The Wilson clan consists of Adelaide, her husband Gabe (Winston Duke) and their children – teenager Zora (Shahadi Wright Joseph) and youngest child Jason (Evan Alex). There is clearly some reluctance to return 'home' on Adelaide's part. She is unsettled by the prospect of going to Santa Cruz beach to meet friends but is guilt-tripped into doing so by Gabe. Peele again works revealing details into these scenes. Young Addie's favourite toy, the white rabbit, is briefly referenced. Jason is an aspiring firebug who wears a mask slung around his neck (meaning that he is, in a sense, 'two-faced'). Zora, a gifted athlete, has just given up running, because, she glibly announces, it isn't worth the effort if she won't ever be good enough for the Olympics.

Although no details about the professions of Gabe or Adelaide are given, the family clearly have a comfortable middle-class lifestyle. As Richard Brody observes: '[a]voiding the stereotypes of black Americans in movies, Peele instead knowingly depicts them as a stereotype of a financially successful, socially stable, and cinematically average American family'.[10] Books and paintings displayed in the vacation house suggest that Adelaide grew up in an intellectually nourishing environment. However, Gabe aspires to an even higher standard of living. He proudly reveals that he has purchased a second-hand motorboat and is teased by the rest of the family. 'You're all spoiled', he retorts. The desire to better one's material circumstances is felt by all the characters in this film.

Flashbacks from Adelaide's (apparent) childhood show that although she soon returned to her parents physically unharmed, the psychological trauma caused by her 'disappearance' resulted in the need for counselling. The Wilson family's trip to the beach to meet up with friends Kitty and Josh Tyler (Elisabeth Moss and Tim Heidecker) underlines the mystery surrounding her traumatic experience beneath the boardwalk. The Tylers are white and they are also wealthier than the Wilsons. For Gabe, this economic disparity inspires envy.[11] Kitty, who is fond of day drinking, cheerfully reveals to Adelaide that she has 'had a little work done' and wanted to be an actress before she had children (the notion that a person has missed out on a more desirable life is an important one here). Adelaide admits that she finds casual conversation difficult: 'I have a hard time just talking.' Throughout their time at the beach, she remains uneasy. When Jason is drawn towards the same tunnel young Addie entered in 1986 (now rebranded 'Merlin's Castle'), she is terrified. Although Jason has an unsettling encounter with a man wearing a red jumpsuit, he is unharmed. Nevertheless, Adelaide insists that the family return home.

It is later that same night that the film morphs into what at first seems like a classic home-invasion narrative, albeit one with an uncanny twist (the film's debt to these conventions has already been widely noted).[12] Adelaide reveals to Gabe that the return to Santa Cruz has stirred up troubling memories. She attempts to describe her childhood experience in the hall of mirrors, explaining that 'There was another girl in there. She looked like me. Exactly like me.' Although Gabe tells her what she saw was 'just a reflection', Adelaide is convinced that 'She's still coming for me.' Again, Gabe downplays her unease. At that very moment, however, the lights go dark, and Jason solemnly declares: 'There's a family in our driveway.'

Sure enough, there is a hand-holding group of four standing in the shadows – a 'Boogeyman's family', as Jason puts it. Gabe refuses to take Adelaide's panic seriously and goes outside to confront the trespassers (as he grows more fearful, his manner becomes more self-consciously and comically 'street'). The trespassers ignore his empty threats and Gabe finally tries to call the cops. But it is too late for outside intervention. After a signal from Red, their leader, the trespassers deftly break into the Wilson home – all except Red, who locates the 'hide a key' rock and calmly enters as though she were stepping through her own front door. It is obvious that the intruders are no ordinary criminals. In fact, they are doppelgängers who look almost identical to the entire Wilson family – clad in bright red jumpsuits (accessorised with sandals, bronze scissors and a Michael Jackson-style single glove) and displaying decidedly aggressive body language.

Considering *Us* in terms of its engagement with many of the conventions of the home invasion sub-genre helps illuminate some of the ways in which it also engages with the California Gothic tradition. Following the global economic crash of 2007/8, in addition to a boom in haunted house movies, there was a striking resurgence in the number of home invasion films that were released.[13] These included titles such as *Kidnapped* (2010), *Trespass* (2011), *In Their Skin* (2012), *Mother's Day* (2010), *The Bleeding House* (2011), *Entrance* (2012), *The Purge* (2013), *Hate Crime* (2013), *Home Sweet Home* (2013), *Home Invasion* (2016) and *You're Next* (2011). Michael Fiddler's useful outline of the uncanny resonances of the home invasion movie helps explain the crossover between the haunted home and the 'invaded' home:

> The antagonist of the piece, the Other, crosses the threshold. What follows is a prolonged violent confrontation between the protagonists and the antagonist within the domestic setting. This simple setup has been explored in a range of ways. [. . .] The 'invasion' can either be the sole focus of the film, as in *Panic Room* (2002) or can appear within a wider narrative, as with *A Clockwork Orange* (1971). [. . .] in each of their varied ways, these examples show how the presence of the invader within a domestic setting disrupts boundaries. The normative understandings of 'home' are problematized. The unheimlich atmosphere that is engendered by this unwelcome presence breaks down conventional categorizations of the internal and the external, as well as that of the family unit itself.[14]

The typical pre-2008 American home invasion narrative was about a middle-class white family being terrorised by violent criminals (usually resentful working-class white men – this same dynamic is also found in most backwoods horror films). The white-collar patriarch often 'regains his masculinity' by violently besting the intruders who have threatened his family and home. The frequency with which these films depict middle-class white families being terrorised by working-class criminals reflects a trend which Steve Macek ascribes to racial and locational politics:

> If Hollywood over the past few decades of conservative ascendancy has increasingly framed the city as hostile territory, it has also tended to present the sparkling clean, well-lit world of the suburban middle-class family as 'under siege' from a range of sexual, criminal and moral threats that are typically urban in origin.[15]

Given the inaccurate but widespread assumption that 'suburban middle classes' always equals 'white', it is hardly surprising that American films of this type tend to be racially homogeneous. Home invasion narratives in which the home being invaded belongs to a Black family (or to a family from another non-white racial group) are still rare, although there are some examples, including the exploitation thriller *Fight for Your Life* (1977), *Breaking In* (2018) and *The Intruder* (2019).

The antagonists in a home invasion narrative typically have two basic motives: they will either be economically motivated 'have-nots' or sadists with no mercenary motive who want to terrorise and murder their victims – as in *The Strangers* (2008), *Funny Games* (1997/2007) and *Angst* (1983). In *Us*, it is quickly established that this is a 'haves versus have-nots' style narrative. Gabe tells the intruders, 'We don't have anything here – this is our Summer home.' This is again a common trope: *Funny Games*, the *Straw Dogs* remake (2011), the 2009 remake of *Last House on the Left*, *In Their Skin* and *You're Next*, all feature protagonists whose secondary address is invaded. The fact that the Wilsons have a vacation home (even if it has been inherited) confirms that they possess a degree of economic privilege denied their attackers. The use of this trope recalls Aviva Briefel and Sianne Ngai's important observation that 'horror film presents owning a house in particular as a form of proprietorship that automatically entitles the buyer to the experience of fear, as if fear itself were a commodity included with the total package'.[16] They argue that

> In restricting their presentation of fear or anxiety to figures we immediately recognize as privileged, the past two decades of horror and slasher films suggest that being frightened is paradoxically a sign of empowerment. Victims in these films are consistently white, suburban residents engaged in the middle-class routines of moving to a single-family home, celebrating holidays, or going on vacation. The characters who seem to have the most claim to being afraid are thus themselves owners or future inheritors of property, as if the entitlements of material ownership automatically extend to the psychological or affective realm.[17]

From the perspective of Red, the leader of the doppelgänger family (and Adelaide's double), their breach of the Wilson home is, crucially, all in the cause of reclaiming what is rightfully hers/theirs. The Wilsons may not be white, but they are still an unmistakably middle-class family engaging in the recognisably 'middle-class routine' of a nice vacation by the shore. Gabe's sweatshirt indicates that he attended a prominent HBCU (Howard), and Addie is said to have trained as a dancer when she was a teenager, whilst their children seem to want for nothing. To apply Briefel and Ngai's analysis here, this degree of privilege is precisely what gives the Wilsons 'the claim to being afraid'; as Adelaide knows only too well, they have so much that can be taken away from them.

After Red and her family have restrained their doubles, she explains why they are there. Red has a strained style of speech which suggests that she has not spoken out loud in many years: 'Once upon a time, there was a girl, and the girl had a shadow. The two were connected; tethered together. So whatever happened to the girl happened to the shadow.' Red and her fellow 'Tethered' are, it seems (possibly), clones of some sort who have been living parallel lives below ground that are a twisted parody of those experienced by their above-ground originals. Gabe, missing the point as ever, tries to mollify Red by offering her material goods – money, the family car, his new boat. In Peele's script, it is noted at this point that 'Gabe . . . been in denial of the supernatural element at play.'[18] He asks, 'What are you people?' His query is repeated by Red, who then declares, in a key line, 'We're Americans.' She might equally have declared, 'We're Californians.' Red then orders Adelaide to 'tether' herself to the heavy living-room coffee table with handcuffs.

After Adelaide is 'tethered', the differences and similarities between the Wilson family and its doubles become more noticeable, as each of the Wilson clan is paired off with (or attacked by) their counterpart. Gabe's double, Abraham, is a violent, hulking brute. Zora's double, Umbrae, is a smirking psychopath who runs even faster than she does. Jason's double, Pluto, is also fascinated by fire, which explains why he wears a mask – his face is covered in burn scars. Apart from Red, who does the talking for all of them, none of the other doppelgängers can speak.

Although it isn't definitively confirmed until the film's closing scene, as has been hinted from the outset, 'Red' is the 'original' Addie – the little girl we met in the 1986 opening sequence. The 'original' Addie was accosted by her double in the hall of mirrors and dragged to the grim underground compound inhabited by the 'Tethered'. Addie's resourceful double – her 'shadow' – dressed herself in Addie's clothing and went back upstairs to be 'found'. 'Addie's' odd behaviour and speech difficulties were not caused by trauma: until she resourcefully instigated the switch, she was a mute second-class citizen who lived in squalor below ground. Adelaide the adult – the once 'tethered' child who stole the life of her duplicate – has tried to forget her origins. However, her reluctance to return to the boardwalk and her fear that her life is about to be taken away from her by 'the girl in the mirror' indicates that she is (at least subconsciously) aware that the comfortable life she has been living for many years was never rightfully hers. Meanwhile, although the original Addie – now called 'Red' –absorbed the feral mannerisms of her new community, she also held onto her memories and channelled her sense of rage and dispossession into a belief in her own special destiny. Red has now united the 'Tethered' in a common revolutionary purpose.

Red's status as leader of this rebellion is discussed by Soraya Nadia McDonald (note: she refers to Red as 'Adelaide'):

> Even when forced to live a life in the shadows, Adelaide has never, ever allowed herself to forget the life that came before it. For the original Red, assimilation means becoming Adelaide seamlessly. It's something to strive toward, a practice to be perfected with conscientiousness and repetitions. But for the real Adelaide, assimilation below ground means relinquishing her true identity. It means giving up. It means resignation and defeat. And because she refuses to do any of those things – Adelaide is, after all, a little American black girl with a heritage of fight and resistance encoded within her very bones – she grows up to be a revolutionary. The image of a black woman as a violent, murderous revolutionary is quite rare.[19]

Adelaide's unsuccessful bid to escape from her origins is signalled by her choice of clothing. Whilst Red, like her followers, is clad in a crimson jump-suit, Adelaide dresses in white – the colour of innocence and of forgetting. However, by the end of the film, her clothing is heavily blood-stained, symbolising the violent return of guilty knowledge which has hitherto been repressed. Adelaide's association with 'whiteness' also aligns her life trajectory with the complacency and willed amnesia of white California, which, as we have seen throughout this volume, has often failed to recognise the genocidal crimes (and other racially and economically inclined injustices) which haunt the state's past, present and probable future.

*Us* is ultimately a film about a very Californian preoccupation: the desire to secure the 'good life' no matter the cost to those who have deliberately been prevented from even trying to attain it in the first place. Adelaide appears to 'have it all', but she knows deep down that she only moved up in the world (literally) because she stole the life of her double. Red lived in the sun (as young Addie) for nine years, but this existence was violently snatched away. Nevertheless, her time above ground has, as McDonald puts it, ensured that 'she grows up to be a revolutionary'. The invasion of the Wilson home makes it clear that the rest of the Tethered will now take by force that which had previously been denied them, just as Adelaide did all those years ago.

However, it takes some while for the Wilsons (and the viewer) to realise that this threat to the status quo isn't unique to their own family. After they are left alone with their doubles, they all manage to trick, outrun or temporarily overpower their foes, and the family escape in Gabe's motorboat. However, once the action shifts to the Tyler residence – a luxurious bayside home – the film shifts gear. This is no isolated incident: the Tyler's have their own doppelgängers, and Kitty, Josh and their twin daughters are swiftly overwhelmed by their murderous doubles.

The Wilsons arrive in the immediate aftermath of the attack and instantly discover that the duplicates of the Tyler clan are intent on wiping them out too. There follows another brutal confrontation between a 'human' and a 'Tethered' family. Zora and Jason are adept at fighting for their lives, using aspirational household items – a golf club, a trophy – with which to bludgeon their foes. Adelaide is briefly captured by Kitty's deranged double, Dahlia, who, in a twisted echo of the cheerful vanity of her 'original', gazes, first raptly and then with total self-loathing, at own scarred face in the mirror (a twisted echo of Kitty's facelift). Dahlia clearly wishes to cut Adelaide's face too but she stops herself. It is an indication of the absolute control Red has over her followers. Dahlia has obviously been ordered to leave Adelaide's fate up to her leader.

The Wilsons kill off (most of) the Tyler doppelgängers, and then find themselves the sole (living) occupants of this desirable home. During this moment of respite, we receive firm confirmation via a television news report that these attacks are also taking place in the outside world. The police lines are busy, and there have been violent 'incidents' on the boardwalk (which suggests that Santa Cruz is at the epicentre of the disturbance). 'Someone said they were coming from the sewer', a shaken bystander says to a reporter.

As well as causing havoc and 'stabbing people', the individuals running amok are said to be forming a lengthy human chain, something which would, Gabe rightly observes, 'take a shitload of co-ordination'. Adelaide, galvanised by a sudden realisation, takes charge, announcing, 'We've got to go.' She decides, 'We need to move and keep moving. We'll take the coast. Go to Mexico', but Gabe and the children are reluctant to leave the comforts of the Tyler home. 'Woah, woah, woah', Gabe says, 'We have everything we need here.' However, Adelaide has realised that what she knows, Red knows. It is only a matter of time before Red tracks them down: 'They've been planning this. They have the upper hand.' She tells Gabe, 'You're not in charge anymore.' This statement shows how the Wilson family dynamic has evolved in response to the night's events. Adelaide is now as assertive as her nemesis, whilst Gabe and the children have also shown themselves to be as capable of violence as their counterparts. Furthermore, like Red, Adelaide is now the undisputed leader of her family, relegating Gabe to the same subordinate position occupied by his dim-witted double, Abraham.

At Adelaide's urging, the Wilson's take the luxury car which belonged to their dead friends and hit the road, repelling an attack from one of the surviving Tyler doppelgängers as they exit. They must also deal with Zora's double, Umbrae, who ambushes them on the roadside. In another indication of the latent violence of the Wilson kids, Zora, who has insisted on driving, mows Umbrae down without hesitation. Afterwards, Adelaide gazes upon the girl's twisted body. The interlude implies that she possibly feels some degree of empathy towards the insane child who is an exact double of her own daughter. Only moments before, Zora bragged that she had 'the highest kill count in the family'. Her violence, like that of the rest of the Wilson family thus far, has been in the cause of self-defence, but it is again clear that Adelaide's above-ground family can be just as violent as their 'shadows' if they need to be. Indeed, the escalating aggression of the Wilson family evokes a theme found in two Wes Craven films: *The Hills Have Eyes* (1977) and *Last House on the Left* (1972). In *The Hills Have Eyes*, a family travelling to California in their motorhome makes an ill-advised detour through the Nevada desert and is besieged by a clan of cannibalistic mutants. In *Last House on the Left*, a seemingly 'civilised' upper-middle-class couple wreak bloody revenge upon the family of low-life criminals who raped and murdered their beloved daughter. In both films, civility and squeamishness are rapidly jettisoned when the middle-class family is threatened by its 'uncivilised' Other. In *Us*, the lines between 'civilisation' and 'savagery' are blurred to an even greater extent by the fact that Adelaide, the mother of the 'good' family, is secretly one of the 'Others'.

As the Wilsons drive through Santa Cruz in the early hours of the morning, the quiet streets are filled with detritus which attests to an outbreak of major civil disorder. Too late, they realise that Red has staged another ambush. Pluto sets their car on fire, but thanks to Jason's ability to manipulate his double's imitative behaviour, the youngster is burned to death himself. Jason is snatched by Red, who has been hidden in plain sight all along. Adelaide realises she must face her worst fears and head below ground to save her child. In an echo of Red's familiarity with the hide-a-key back at the vacation house, she quickly finds the hidden wall which leads to the Tethered compound. She descends on an escalator, ending up in an empty space which is described in the script as looking like 'a publicly funded underground tunnel'. The Tethered are below ground no more, but dozens of white rabbits – the same animals seen in the title sequence – have been released from their cages. The rabbits, we now realise, were a primary food source, and young Addie's stuffed toy – a white rabbit – was another indication of the eerie connection which existed between the two little girls even before the switch took place.

Red and Adelaide have their final confrontation in an empty classroom. Red, who is now the only surviving member of her family, is making paper dolls, an obvious call-back to her younger self's engagement with the same activity back in 1986. When she begins to speak (unlike Adelaide, Red loves a good monologue, which is another indication of her 'above ground' origins) – we are finally provided with more details about the backstory of the Tethered. Red forcefully asserts their personhood: 'We're human too, you know.' She continues:

> It was humans that built this place. I believe they figured out how to make a copy of the body, but not the soul. The soul remains one, shared by two. They created the Tethered so they could use them to control the ones above. Like puppets. But they failed, and they abandoned the Tethered. For generations the Tethered continued without direction. They all went mad down here. And then . . . there was us.

Here, Red's messianic sense of mission is once more apparent. She even deploys language reminiscent of that used by some of the cult leaders I have discussed in the previous chapters. Red claims that she and Adelaide were 'born special', and that their lives intersected back in 1986 because 'God wanted us to meet that night.' Flashbacks to that evening show the two girls simultaneously experiencing the same urge to travel towards one another. The original Red (who is now grown-up Adelaide) headed up the escalator, whilst young Addie (the future Red) entered the tunnel. Grown-up Red tells Adelaide that she has never stopped thinking about the fact that the two of them could simply have gone back above ground together. Instead, she was dragged to the compound and forced to remain with the Tethered, who seem to have spent their days and nights mindlessly imitating the actions of their above-ground selves, devoid of any sense of purpose or individual identity. That is, until the night of what Red calls 'the miracle', which appears to have heralded a kind of collective awakening for the community. When Adelaide was fourteen and took part in the ballet recital (which she had earlier described to Kitty as 'her peak'), Red was simultaneously compelled to perform for the Tethered. The experience changed her life trajectory and that of her 'people': 'That's when I saw God and he showed me my path. You felt it too.' The Tethered, changed by what they saw, surrounded Red: 'They saw that I was different. They saw that I could deliver them from this misery. I found my faith and I began to prepare. It took years to plan.' Red explains that she doesn't just want to kill the woman who stole her life: she 'wants to make a statement the whole world can see'.

The women fight and their brutal struggle is intercut with flashes of their respective dance recitals. It becomes clear that in her version of the recital, young Red told the story of abduction. Although Red initially has the upper hand, Adelaide prevails, strangling her nemesis with her own handcuffs. As Red painfully breathes her last, she looks younger and more vulnerable than before. Adelaide's face is contorted into a grimace of delight, and she utters animalistic grunts. It is as through is slipping back into her instinctive Tethered behaviours. A sudden noise reveals that Jason, whom Red had stashed in a nearby locker, has seen the entire episode unfold.

Adelaide tries to convince her son that everything can go back to normal now, but he still looks terrified. The two of them ascend and reunite with Zora and Gabe. As the Wilson family leaves Santa Cruz in a commandeered ambulance, they pass a line of Tethered individuals standing hand-in-hand next to the boardwalk's big wheel. Corpses are strewn everywhere. Reaffirming her place as leader of the family, Adelaide drives. Jason sits in the front seat, as though warily keeping an eye on her. A final flashback confirms that Adelaide was indeed once one of the Tethered, and that she kidnapped the 'original' Addie so that she could take her place.

In the final pages of Matheson's *I Am Legend*, Robert Neville ultimately discovers that his understanding of the post-plague world was dangerously incomplete. Up until then, he considered himself the last surviving representative of 'normalcy' and humanity, but he comes to accept in his final moments that he is actually a dangerous aberration. It's a typical 'Southern California School' twist: that which appeared to be 'the norm' was in fact anything but. *Us* manipulates our narrative sympathies in a similar way, initially depicting Adelaide as a loving wife and mother haunted by a traumatic childhood experience. But from Red's perspective, Adelaide is a monster. Red despises the woman who for decades has enjoyed the privileges she has been denied from the moment she was dragged underground, and has clearly passed this sense of resentment and dispossession on to her followers. However, as viewers, we may also ask ourselves whether we can condemn a little girl, destined to spend her life underground, for trying to better her circumstances, even if her successful bid to 'climb the ladder' ruins the life of her unwitting double?

Adelaide's trajectory post-life swap suggests that if the other Tethered were given the same opportunities for self-improvement, they could also be 'exactly like you' (as Red puts it). The 'new' Adelaide was raised by a caring mother who seems to have implemented the advice of the therapist, who told her she should encourage her troubled child to engage with the arts so that she could 'learn to tell her own story'. Being raised in a loving and cultured home has transformed the mute little girl Adelaide once was into a woman who has, at least to outward appearances, successfully been assimilated into the world above. Grown-up Red believes that she and Adelaide are 'special' and implies that this mysterious shared quality has helped each of them to adapt to their radical new surroundings. The fact that young Adelaide/Red was able to organise the (in her words) 'insane' ranks of the Tethered into an army capable of following her orders, suggests that once her fellow compound dwellers were presented with a vision of life beyond the tunnels, they too were capable of literally and figuratively rising above their pre-ordained station.

The importance of being able to tell one's own story is also emphasised here. Adelaide does so through dance (during the pivotal teenage dance recital, and her balletic but vicious final battle with Red). However, she is still unable – even by the end of the film – to fully articulate her experiences though language. Adelaide has spent twenty-five years hiding who (and what) she is, and it is even possible that until Red came back into her life, she had no conscious memory of her true origins. Her story has been painfully repressed, and as such, cannot be spoken aloud. In contrast, Red has used *her* story – that of a little girl ripped away from everything she loved – as the fuel which lights the flames of revolution. She knows, thanks to her television watching days, that a narrative must capture public attention if it is to make an impact: hence Red's canny use of distinctive costuming and props and her determination to make sure that 'everyone is watching'. Red instinctively understands the power of presentation.

Apart from the few details mentioned in Red's monologue, Peele keeps the backstory of the Tethered vague. From a purely practical perspective, it makes little sense that scientists would at some point create a vast underground community of clones and then leave their unstable subjects entirely unsupervised for decades. Indeed, this aspect of the film has attracted criticism. Richard Lawson concludes his review of the film by suggesting:

> *Us* is, I think, among other things, a vague statement on inequity and class struggle, framed as a sort of unconscious Eloi vs. Morlocks system of oppression that breaks into terrible rebellion. That's certainly a worthy allegory to tackle in this age of economic and social atomization. But Peele is both too literal and not specific enough in that inquest, showing us some hard, tangible things, while remaining coy about what those things really are and what they might mean.[20]

Tasha Robinson rightly notes that there don't appear to be any actual impediments which prevent young Addie from just making her way back home.[21] Red and Adelaide both find their respective ways above and below ground without encountering any security measures. The Tethereds' internalised sense of inferiority and lack of vision seem to be the main forces keeping them below ground. They do not have the guile or the sense of destiny which prompted young Red to seize her chance. They may somehow even have been 'bred' to accept their place. That changes, of course, when their own messiah/Moses figure, Red, takes control of the Tethered narrative.

These apparent lapses in narrative logic also make more sense when we interpret *Us* as a satirical social allegory operating in the tradition of Rod Serling's television series *The Twilight Zone* (1959–64). It's 'the statement the whole world can see' – as Red puts it – that really matters, not the finer points of internal plot logic. Indeed, Peele has said that *Us* was inspired by the 1960 *Twilight Zone* episode 'Mirror Image', which was one of many original series scripts written by Serling.[22] Peele is also, in a very literal sense, Serling's successor: he executive-produced the 2019–20 revival of *The Twilight Zone* and hosted each episode.

The 'Mirror Image' episode is about a young woman named Millicent Barnes (Vera Miles), who is obliged to spend the evening in a bus depot waiting for her journey to begin. A series of uncanny incidents leads her to believe that she is being stalked by a malevolent double from a parallel universe. Millicent's erratic behaviour escalates to such an extent that the staff and other passengers eventually come to believe that she is having a mental breakdown. In the episode's final moments, she is taken away by the police just as the male passenger who has tried to help her spots his own eerily grinning doppelgänger. In adapting this same basic scenario for a twenty-first-century audience, and in making the character who comes face-to-face with her own sinister double a Black woman, Peele imbues Serling's original scenario with additional resonances pertaining to issues of identity, class politics and the high costs of 'fitting in' to the dominant culture. McDonald persuasively argues that assimilation is a key theme here:

> The Wilson family of *Us* are not immigrants, but they are invested in an Eisenhower-era ideal of normalcy that is quickly becoming outdated: a married couple with two kids, a house, and a vacation home. They are black, and so they are Americans in a country that does not always fully regard black people as such – and thus are immigrants in their own nation, in a way. For the Wilsons, assimilation is mostly economic, finding ways to signal that they, too, are the American Dream. [. . .] Everything about them says we're perfectly typical. We belong. Except one of them doesn't. . . . [t]he real Adelaide illustrates the dark destructiveness that lies beneath the surface of assimilation. When as a child (in the '80s) she wanders into a hall of mirrors, labeled as an Indian 'Vision Quest' that will lead her to 'find

herself,' Adelaide encounters a little girl who looks exactly like her. The girl, Red, strangles Adelaide and drags her down to the underworld of the tethered, a world defined by deprivation [. . .] Above ground, Red assumes Adelaide's identity. [. . .] For both Adelaide and Red, assimilation involves erasure and survival.[23]

In the closing moments of *Us*, the Wilson family's vehicle grows smaller and smaller as the camera ascends and they drive into the California countryside, hoping to find sanctuary across the border in Mexico. The anthemic ballad 'Les Fleurs', sung by Minnie Riperton, starts to play. The music rises to an emotive swell as the camera slowly pulls back to reveal, first, a lush green panorama of forests, fields and mountains, and then the sight of smoke and helicopters hanging over the city in the distance. A red line of the Tethered extends across the landscape and towards the city. This is, clearly, not an incident solely confined to Santa Cruz. She may be dead, but Red's plan to make a statement the world can see has clearly borne fruit. Even without their visionary leader, the Tethered are laying claim to a world they see as rightfully theirs. Assimilation is no longer an option: this is a revolution. It's a conclusion underlined by the song choice. 'Les Fleurs' finds Riperton 'imagining herself a flower budding into bloom, a hippy-dippy metaphor for every soul realising its true potential'.[24] The final sentence of Peele's script states that 'The line goes on and on and on, towards the rising Sun' (making it clear that the Tethered are heading East). The text which appeared at the beginning of the movie takes on an even more ominous meaning: 'there are millions of miles of tunnels all over the continental United States'.

Yet again, a dangerous movement which began in California looks set to spread to the rest of the United States. In *Us*, this movement inspires a bloody conflict between those who until now have been denied access to the opportunities and the privileges of the 'world above', and those whose unthinking enjoyment of middle-class life in the sun is now under direct threat. As Peele has explained:

This movie is about this country. We're in a time where we fear the other, whether it's the mysterious invader that we think is going to come and kill us and take our jobs, or the faction we don't live near, who voted a different way than us. We're all about pointing the finger. And I wanted to suggest that maybe the monster we really need to look at has our face. Maybe the evil, it's us.[25]

However, Peele's outline of the film's meaning has regional as well as national relevance. The California setting in which *Us* takes place and its references to previous California Gothic narratives are more than incidental details or wry homage. As the California Gothic has suggested from the outset, there are always 'losers' for whom the 'good life' granted to the more privileged – or the more aggressive – has come at an unacceptably high cost. In *Us*, the complacency and arrogance associated with this status quo is violently overthrown, and the ranks of the forgotten and the dispossessed will soon stretch from sea to shining sea.

## 'Leaving is a Form of Dying': *Desierto* (2015)

In June 2015, Donald J. Trump announced that he would once again seek election to the office of President of the United States. After claiming that his opponents had no idea how to defeat ISIS (Islamic State), Trump turned to an issue closer to home – immigration. 'The US has become a dumping ground for everyone else's problems', he claimed:

> When Mexico sends its people, they're not sending their best. They're not sending you. They're sending people that have lots of problems, and they're bringing those problems with us. They're bringing drugs. They're bringing crime. They're rapists. And some, I assume, are good people.[26]

Trump's controversial take on Mexican migration and his pledge to build an impenetrable border wall helped propel him to a surprise victory just over a year later. This was not the last time that he used dehumanising language when referring to Latino migrants. In a 2018 meeting with Californian officials opposed to the state's 'Sanctuary city' policy, Trump said of undocumented immigrants: 'These aren't people. These are animals.'[27]

Mexico's September 2016 selection for Best Foreign Language Film at the 2017 Oscars was Jonás Cuarón's *Desierto*, in which the humanity of migrants making their way to the United States is pointedly contrasted with the violence of a white American who believes he is entitled to murder undocumented immigrants.[28] In Mexico, the film's trailer was soundtracked with an anti-immigrant speech from Trump.[29] However, as Lee Bebout and Clarissa Goldsmith note, 'Throughout the twentieth and twenty-first centuries, the image of the Latinx migrant has been deployed to conjure, depict, and isolate social problems in the U.S. white imagination.'[30] Trump's rhetoric was extreme, but it was also nothing new.

*Us* features an American family who flee violence in California in the hope of finding safety in Mexico. *Desierto* focuses on the horrific ordeal endured by a Mexican migrant trying to make his way back to his family in California.

Like *Us*, *Desierto* foregrounds the perspective and the personhood of those who have so often been excluded from dominant, white-centred notions of Californian history and identity. It does so in part by adopting the narrative framework of the backwoods horror movie.[31] *Desierto* also has elements in common with the real-life horror story discussed in my first chapter: that of the Donner Party. This notorious historical episode involved ill-fated travellers (many of them recent immigrants) whose already difficult journey was halted just short of California by a combination of colossal misfortune and fatal miscalculation. A desperate and protracted struggle to survive ensued. The same basic plot summary can be given for *Desierto*. However, in this case the migrants are prevented from safely reaching their destination by racial violence. Furthermore, the hostile frontier landscape in which Cuarón's migrants fight for their lives is not the Sierra Nevada mountains, but the Sonoran Desert.[32]

Cuarón has said that as a Mexican who has lived in the United States for many years, he wanted to make a film which drew upon the sharp rise in anti-immigrant sentiment associated with Trump's campaign:

There started to be a really strong rhetoric of hatred towards immigrants. I became interested in doing a project about this subject but wanted to do it in a new way. I didn't want it to be a cliché film. That's what started [me] to talk about these issues through the [genre of] a horror movie or an action movie.[33]

When asked which films of this type were particularly important to him, he cited Steven Spielberg's 1971 television movie, *Duel*, a foundational 'Highway Horror' film (which is set in California and based upon the story of the same name by Richard Matheson):

I saw it when I was a kid and I loved it. I re-watched it eight or ten years ago, and I was really amazed, not only by its simplicity and how it manages to keep you gripped to your seat with such a simple narrative, but how, at the end, it's just a story of a truck chasing a car, but it can become a story about so many other things.[34]

Like *Us* then, *Desierto* owes much to its predecessors. In *Duel*, as in *Desierto*, strangers engage in a brutal life-and-death struggle. However, whilst the motives of the truck driver who repeatedly tries to run Spielberg's protagonist, David Mann (Dennis Weaver), off the road remain unknown, from the moment that the killing starts in *Desierto*, we are left in no doubt as to why the gun-toting antagonist Sam (Jeffrey Dean Morgan) is murdering innocent migrants. As Bebout and Goldsmith note:

> At first glance, *Desierto*'s political imagination and the cultural work it performs appear to be clear. By drawing upon the migration and horror film traditions, the film seeks to depict the horror and violence of migration. In this vein, Sam embodies the manifestation of the violent potential of U.S. border policy and the nation's history of nativist vitriol. The horror film becomes the logical extension of dehumanization and terror characterizing Latinx migration experiences in the United States and depicted in the Latinx migration genre.[35]

Gael García Bernal (who plays the main protagonist, Moises) believes that Sam is 'a manifestation of the horror of hate speech. I think that's what he is. [. . .] The monster is the hate narrative that exists. The heroes are the migrants.'[36] Dawn Keetley has also argued that *Desierto*'s antagonist epitomises a new trend in horror cinema, the trope of the 'white-male-as-monster':

> You might respond that white men have always been horror movie monsters. I would argue, though, that until now, they have always had some kind of characteristic that pushed them toward a less- (or more-) than human condition, toward the unnatural, the monstrous [. . .] *Desierto*'s Sam, on the other hand, is just a plain, all-too-human man – a man who is filled with a hatred that the film does little to nothing to explore or explain. And *Desierto* isn't alone in offering the white man as (very human) monster. In fact, I think that the rise of the white man as horror movie monster is one of the significant trends of our decade.[37]

Keetley suggests that the current prominence of such figures owes much to the current state of US politics:

> It's hard not to see it as connected in some way with the ascendency and election of Donald Trump, although it clearly preceded him. Could one argue that the white-male-as-monster (which is part of a discourse that's much bigger than the horror film) contributed in small part to the white anger that helped get Trump elected? Or is the white male as monster a representation (and rebuke) of those angry Trump voters? Conversely, are these white men as monsters being taken by some as heroic, sympathetic?[38]

*Desierto*'s monstrous white man is indeed certainly connected to contemporary racial and political anxieties, but the antagonist – and the basic premise – also hearken back to the earlier tradition of backwoods horror films which I discussed in *The Rural Gothic in American Popular Culture* (2013). As I detailed there, American backwoods horror movies can generally be divided into two main sub-types. The first sub-type 'Type 1', refers to *Deliverance*-inspired or influenced films in which the antagonists are resentful white working-class men who represent corrupt and degenerate versions of the resilient and self-supporting frontiersman.[39] The second sub-type, 'Type 2' films, tend to feature 'degenerate' and cannibalistic family groups (*The Texas Chainsaw Massacre* is the foundational narrative here). 'Type 1' films usually depict 'duelling conceptions of masculinity – urban and rural' – facing off against each other in a wilderness environment (usually, though not always, a forest).[40]

The victims in both kinds of film are always naive outsiders who are travelling through an unfamiliar and unforgiving North American wilderness. These protagonists, who are usually 'just passing through' on the way to somewhere else are attacked by vicious locals who in part resent them because they possess a degree of geographical mobility, economic security and educational attainment which they themselves lack. Furthermore, as in *Desierto*, the villains in 'Type 1' films often use the weapons and tactics previously used to hunt animals against human prey. In *Desierto*, Sam is clearly very familiar with the border landscape in which he undertakes his murderous 'hunting' trips. He has a home-field advantage, just like his counterparts in *Deliverance* (1972), *Trigger Man* (2007), *Southern Comfort* (1981) and the Australian film, *Wolf Creek* (2005).

There is a crucial difference between *Desierto* and earlier backwoods horror movies, however. In the latter, the (main) victims being hunted by white, working-class aggressors are themselves invariably white and English-speaking, but are rendered 'Other' in the eyes of their attackers by dint of their urban or suburban origins and apparent privilege. Although Sam in *Desierto* is (to all outward appearances) a blue-collar rural American, he is still, by dint of his race and his citizenship, possessed of more agency and opportunity than the weary migrants who must risk their lives to live and work in the United States even before someone starts shooting at them. Sam loathes the migrants because to him they are faceless 'vermin' whose entry into 'his' country sorely offends his sense of personal and national exceptionalism. It is also clear that taking on the role of murderous gatekeeper has given Sam a sense of purpose and power which is probably otherwise absent in his life.

*Desierto* was filmed in Mexico and is told largely (though not entirely) from the perspective of the migrants. The film opens with an extended shot of the Sonoran Desert. The noise of the truck in which the migrant group is being transported is the first thing we hear, and then the vehicle is seen in the distance, the lone human presence in a beautiful but hostile landscape.

The first line – part of a prayer in Spanish mumbled by one of the young women in the truck – underlines the emotional and familial costs of migration: 'Leaving is a form of dying.' She is reciting a version of the 'Migrants Prayer' ('La Oración del Migrante'), a prayer associated with the dangers faced by migrants making their way to the United States. Marc Silver's 2013 documentary, *Who is Dayani Cristal?*, is about the attempt to trace the final journey undertaken by a young man who was found dead in the desert near Tucson, Arizona. Gael García Bernal and the documentary's crew traced the man's route across Central America and 'towards the stretch of desert known as the corridor of death'.[41] Paul Theroux notes that a version of the prayer was found in 'the pocket of a migrant' whose death is mentioned in the documentary.[42] *Desierto* therefore underlines from the outset the plight of those making the dangerous journey North in real life. Here, the 'corridor of death' becomes an actual killing field after the truck breaks down many miles from the border. The thuggish people smugglers make it clear to their passengers that they will have to continue on foot. The smugglers are nervous because it is rumoured that a rival gang was recently gunned down in this same area of the 'Badlands'. 'The United States is that way', one of them says dismissively, pointing towards the border.

Sam (whose name may be a reference to 'Uncle Sam')[43] is introduced in a manner which underlines his debt to the backwoods horror trope of the frontiersman-gone-bad. He is an accomplished outdoorsman with a pick-up truck and a well-trained hunting dog, 'Tracker'. Sam also wears a cowboy hat and has two flags that were adopted by Donald Trump's MAGA movement displayed on his vehicle: a Confederate Battle flag and a sticker with the Gadsden flag. He is stopped by an officer from the US Border Patrol as he heads towards the border fence. Although the officer clearly distrusts him, he is allowed to continue on his journey. Sam's contempt for the Border Patrol implies that he finds their policies too lax for his liking. As throughout much of the film, Sam's narrative perspective is interwoven with that of the migrants. Although he is a pitiless killer, Sam is a heavy drinker who is likely attempting to compensate for his own inadequacies by targeting strangers whose deaths are unlikely to be noticed, much less investigated. As the flags on his truck indicate, his hatred is also rooted in the belief that the United States is meant only for (white) people like him.

Moises, the character played by García Bernal, is a husband and father whose motives for crossing the border highlight the long-standing links between California and Mexico. His wife and young son still live in Oakland and Moises is determined to be reunited with the child, even though his wife is convinced that he will use his deportation as an excuse to disappear from their lives. Before being removed from the United States, Moises had a job and a well-established life in California. He had even applied for a residence visa. However, he was deported after being stopped for a broken headlight. The other migrant whose backstory is detailed is a young woman named Adela (Alondra Hidalgo), who tells Moises that she had no desire to leave home, but her parents believed that their home village was too dangerous and paid a male neighbour to accompany her on the trek North. She later reveals that this neighbour, Ramiro (Óscar Flores Guerrero), has been sexually abusing her throughout the journey.

A few hours after the group starts walking, one of the traffickers spots Sam's truck and urges caution. It is too late for that, however. Sam has set himself up on a nearby ridge, and quickly kills almost all the travellers with his high-powered hunting rifle: 'Welcome to the land of the free!', he crows. Moises, Adela and two of the other travellers survive the initial onslaught because they had been lagging behind. Although they briefly escape Sam's notice, Tracker the dog picks up their scent. At this, his owner wearily responds, 'Jesus Christ. They just keep coming.' Tracker soon kills Ramiro, and then leads Sam to the last remaining member of the people-smuggling gang. Sam shoots the young man in the head.

When Sam sets up camp for the night, Adela and Moises hide amidst a rocky outcrop and discuss how they came to be in this position in the first place. 'If only they knew what things are like here', Adela says, in bitter reference to her parents' belief that she will have a safer life in the United States. Moises declares his intent to return to his son – he even carries the child's toy bear as a talisman. Despite what his wife thinks, he will make his way back to Oakland: 'I don't want to disappear.' Sam, meanwhile, is drinking by the campfire and drunkenly conversing with his canine companion. The heat, 120 degrees Fahrenheit in the daytime, is starting to get to him, but he is perhaps also referring to his situation in a more general sense when he says: 'I gotta get out of this hell.'

Adela and Moises seize the initiative when daylight arrives. At her suggestion, they steal Sam's truck (using the talking bear carried by Moises to lure Tracker in the wrong direction). Their plan initially succeeds, but jubilation turns to terror when Sam shoots Adela and the truck crashes. Upon realising that she is in no condition to run, Moises leaves Adela behind. Staying with her would mean certain death for the two of them. Fleeing through a field of prickly cactuses, he uses the flare gun taken from Sam's truck to kill Tracker. Sam's reaction – hysterical rage – underlines his warped sense of empathy. He was clearly attached to his dog but has killed a dozen innocent people (and probably more before that) without remorse.

Upon nearing the border fence, Moises tries to wave down a Border Patrol car, but they don't see him. A desperate final battle ensues between the two men. Sam's tactical advantage has finally been eroded by the death of his dog. Eventually, as they grapple on top of some high rocks, Sam falls, badly breaking his leg.

At last, Moises has possession of the rifle. Speaking in Spanish (as he and the other Mexican characters have done so throughout), he responds to Sam's cries for help by saying, 'You killed them all – as if we were animals.' He then screams with rage. It's a moment which evokes the final seconds of *Duel*, during which the film's previously mild-mannered suburbanite yells in primal joy after his nemesis has driven over a cliff edge. However, whereas the motives of the antagonist in *Duel* remained unspoken, from the outset of *Desierto*, Sam has made his rationale for murder obvious. In his final scene he is a grovelling, abject figure, begging for mercy from the man he has just spent twenty-four hours trying to kill. Yet his monstrous sense of entitlement is still evident: 'Don't you dare leave me!' Moises decides not to shoot Sam, instead saying, 'Let the desert kill you', before making his way back to Adela. Like his many victims, Sam will die an anonymous death in the desert: just another disappearance in the Badlands.

Moises carries Adela on his back as he desperately tries to make it to the border. Like his biblical namesake, he is determined to reach the Promised Land. His humanity and bravery are in stark contrast to Sam's cruelty and cowardice. As they reach a seemingly endless expanse of salt flats, Moises frantically says to Adela (who may already be dead) that all they need is 'Just one last push. We're almost there.' They duo are dwarfed by the stunning but indifferent landscape. Dusk falls, and finally he sees headlights in the distance. The highway, the route to safety, is 'right there'. However, the film ends whilst Moises is still painfully struggling towards their destination. His final words are 'One last push. Carry on. Come on, Carry on.' A slow pan across the screen emphasises the sheer size of the desert and prompts us to wonder how many other desperate travellers are out there, risking their lives in a bid to make it to the United States. We will never know if Moises makes it back to his family in Oakland.

Despite the central role which Mexicans and Californians of Mexican and Spanish descent have played in the history and development of California pre- and post-American statehood, the Mexican and Spanish periods of Californian history are often only gestured at in the California Gothic, either referenced via Spanish place names, or in the missions which once existed where a 'white' community now sits (as is the case in *Ravenous* and *Buffy the Vampire Slayer*, in which we are told that the site upon which Sunnydale now sits was once occupied by a Spanish mission destroyed by an earthquake in 1812).[44] It is a pattern replicated within American horror more generally: '[w]ith the exception of George Romero, Robert Rodriguez, and Guillermo del Toro, U.S. horror films have rarely been produced by, directed by, or star Latinx'.[45] (Here, it is worth mentioning again that *Desierto* is a Mexican production, with a Mexican director and a largely Mexican cast and crew.)

As David E. Hayes-Bautista outlines in his study of Latino identity in the region, from the very beginnings of 'American' California there was a 'clash of narratives' between those who felt that the 'the new state of California was not going to be for Latinos – the "native Californians," or Californios – but only for the "American" population', and Latinos for whom the term '"America" was largely a geographical expression, for the modern nation-states of Mexico, Venezuela, Argentina' and other states which did not, as of the early nineteenth century, yet exist.[46] He notes that for Latino delegates at the 1849 California Constitutional Convention, who had also 'been active participants in government when Alta California was still part of Mexico', their 'vision of California's future as part of the United States was based on their understanding of Mexico's constitution and government, and their vision of "America" presumed the values of self-government with freedom and equality for all'.[47] However, between the Declaration of Independence in 1776 and California's Constitutional Convention in 1849, 'the definition of "American" had largely changed in the US, from the universalist ideal of individual liberty and freely chosen self-governance to a nativist definition that limited "American" to members of a self-perceived national ethnic group: white, preferably Anglo-Saxon, Protestant, and English speaking'.[48]

Hayes-Bautista further observes that the 'universalist vision of "American California" championed by the Latino delegates and a significant proportion of the Atlantic American ones' initially prevailed, and that the 1849 California Constitution 'abolished slavery, (theoretically) opened suffrage to non-whites, guaranteed legal protection for married women's property rights, and stipulated that all legal documents be published "*en inglés y en español*" (in English and Spanish)'.[49] However, subsequent decades saw the brief pre-eminence of the nativist and virulently anti-immigrant 'Know-Nothing Party'[50] and a rise in such sentiments in the aftermath of the Civil War, as well as anxiety about rising immigration from Southern (Catholic) Europe. These factors, combined with the aftermath of the 1910 Mexican Revolution, during which 'nearly a million Mexicans fled their homeland', further eroded the 'universalist' vision of California.[51]

In her history of the eugenics movement in the United States, Alexandra Minna Stern observes that although 'Eugenics historiography' was, to begin with, centred on the East Coast, the movement soon gained a major foothold in the West, and in California in particular.[52] She notes that

> the 'West' spawned metaphors and myths for the initial generation of American eugenicists who updated the Manifest Destiny doctrines of the 1840s with a twentieth-century medical and scientific vocabulary to expound on the noble Westward march of Anglo-Saxons and Nordics.[53]

Stern devotes a chapter to 'eugenic gatekeeping' on the US-Mexico border, and when discussing the origins of the US Border Patrol she observes that whilst the organisation's mythology 'symbolically erased the presence of living Indians in the borderlands', 'it was also driven by myopic visions of the nation's racial and demographic future. [. . .] patrolmen and their superiors were charged with protecting the "American" family-nation from potential contamination from alien outsiders'.[54] She argues that the 'strategies of surveillance, detection and interception that continue to this day' created a 'regime of eugenic gatekeeping on the U.S.-Mexican border that aimed to ensure the putative purity of the "American" family-nation while generating long-lasting stereotypes of Mexicans as filthy, lousy and prone to irresponsible breeding'.[55]

Sam is not a member of the US Border patrol. As previously noted, the tense encounter he has with one of its officers suggests that he holds the organisation in contempt. But he does see himself as a 'gatekeeper'. He justifies his monstrous actions by telling himself that he is protecting his home from the 'faceless hordes' across the border. However, it has been persuasively suggested that the film's focus upon Sam's killing spree, to the exclusion of other factors which make undocumented migration across the US-Mexico border such a dangerous endeavour, is misleading. Bebout and Goldsmith point out that Moises and the other migrants were in peril even before Sam started shooting:

> In truth . . . they have been in danger since they undertook the journey just as slow violence has spurred and shaped their migration experiences. [. . .] Sam's murderous hunt highlights for the audience migrant vulnerabilities: Sam is the cause of danger for the precarious lives of the crossers. This representational sleight of hand is a dangerous move because the audience may focus on the psychopathic and sympathetic killer gringo and forget about the actual killers: economic policies, immigration policies, underground migrant policies, and the desert, to name a few.[56]

*Desierto* also emphasises the contrast between the ways in which different waves of migration/immigration (and different groups of migrants/immigrants) have been treated at various points in Californian history. As discussed in Chapter 1, whilst the ordeal undergone by the Donner Party was initially treated by some commentators as a lurid and shameful spectacle, as the decades passed, their story was gradually 'rehabilitated' by writers such as Charles McGlashan and George R. Stewart (and by accounts written by some of the survivors themselves). California, then as now, attracted immigrants from all over the world (and migrants from all over the continental landmass of North America, including Mexico).

Yet, as Stern notes, the treatment of migrants from Mexico – which has centuries-long familial, linguistic, political and cultural ties with California – has often been notably hostile, and Mexicans (and Californians of Spanish and Mexican origin) have historically (and even up to this day, as Donald Trump's rhetoric underlined) aroused unease amongst certain sections of the white (Anglo-American) community. She argues that one of the reasons why 'eugenics prospered in California' was because for many of the Europeans who settled in the Pacific West from the late 1800s onwards, the act of 'civilizing what they saw as fertile but under-utilized terrain meant applying modern science, above all, the maxims of heredity and biology, to graft a new polis onto the Spanish and Mexican past'.[57] *Desierto*, like *Us*, foregrounds the question of who, exactly, should be entitled to live and prosper in the state, but in a manner which underlines the importance of these long-standing neighbourly tensions and ties.

It is a question which will likely take on enhanced significance in the future, thanks to a trend confirmed by the initial results of the most recent California Census: California's demographic boom is over, at least for now. As *The New York Times* reported in April 2021:

> California remains the nation's most populous state, an immense, churning window into a majority-minority national future. But new data from the Census Bureau . . . confirms what demographers have suspected for years. The boom is gone. Dampened by declining birthrates and federal policies that drastically slowed immigration, California's population increase of 6.1 percent over the past decade was the smallest in at least a century and less than the 7.4 percent national average, according to the census.

Births, the report continued, had 'declined by more than 15 percent in the past decade'.[58]

Expensive housing, ageing baby boomers and the slowdown in immigration are all cited as key factors. So were environmental concerns: the extreme weather patterns caused by global warming have in recent years had a particularly devastating impact upon California. Wildfires in particular have become much more frequent, destructive and intense.[59] As a 2020 report in the *Los Angeles Times* put it, 'Fire season in California looks different these days. Temperatures are hotter. Fires are bigger and more destructive. Air quality is the worst in decades.'[60] Although the report was referring to the region's seismic instability rather than climate change, an observation made by Marc Reisner in his 2003 volume, *A Dangerous Place: California's Unsettling Fate*, comes to mind:

> The most striking thing about modern California is not that it has trans-formed itself, in two long human lifespans, from a seamless wilderness into the most populous and urban of the fifty American states. [. . .] Nor is it even that so many people are pouring in from everywhere that California is about to become the first state without a white – at least Caucasian – majority. All that is peripheral to the most fateful upshot of this state's cen-tury and a half of frantic growth: most of its inhabitants have settled, and will continue to settle, where they shouldn't have.[61]

What does this mean for the future of the California Gothic? As we have seen, my analysis has focused upon the foundational horrors of the American takeover, the infrastructural transformations of the post-war era, the high costs of the Hollywood Star system and the dangerous allure of organisations which promise a better world and a better you. The racism, violence and exclusion faced by non-white Californians and others for whom the utopian promise of the state has so often been a misleading mirage, has been another important consideration. As Camille Suárez, a history professor who was asked to com-ment upon the state's 'slow growth future' pointed out: 'From the days of the Gold Rush in the mid-19th century, the idea of a "California dream" has been accessible only to certain people and may feel even further away for many.'[62]

The reader will have noticed that there is a considerable degree of repeti-tion within my conception of the 'California Gothic'. These elements include the recurrent appearance of coastal communities with hidden secrets, the fre-quency with which desperate newcomers find out the hard way that California is anything but a paradise, and the horrors which ensue when the pursuit of 'stardom', or of personal/communal betterment, is malevolently exploited. I have come to believe that this is a regionally specific version of the tendency first identified by Philip Fisher within a national context. In *Hard Facts: Setting and Form in the American Novel* (1987), Fisher discussed the ways in which the nineteenth-century American novel (particularly the popular novel) drama-tised the 'central hard facts of American history'. These were, he stated:

> the killing of the Indians, which gave a 'clear land' where a 'New World' might be built; the slavery that was a moral and rational outrage [. . .]; and

finally, the severe evacuation and objectification of the self that followed from the economic and future orientated world of capitalism and the city.[63]

'Popular forms', he continued

> are frequently repetitive, and they are frequently read almost obsessively, as detective novels, westerns, romances and pornography are, becoming what might be called a diet of reality that returns again and again to the same few motifs so that they might not slip away. [. . .] Repetition is in the service of working through or at least in the service of refusing to forget. All three acts, recognition, repetition and working through, are features of cultural incorporation. Only a few facts keep on being remembered as who we are and these facts are incorporated and then, after a time, felt to be obvious and even trite.[64]

It is all, he goes on, part of 'the framework of national self-imagination'.[65]

Within the California Gothic then, the obvious repetition of key themes and tropes can also be seen as a way of 'working through' or 'refusing to forget' the 'hard facts' which accompanied the establishment and development of modern (American) California. It seems likely that the sub-genre will in the future engage with the current 'hard facts' which are even now rapidly reshaping the state's environmental, demographic, political and economic prospects.

'Much has been written about the California dream, a concept which is embraced by those people who have achieved certain advantages. Little has been written about the California nightmare.'[66] Philip Fradkin made this observation in 1995: rather more has been written about the 'California nightmare' since then, and surely will be in the future. It is my hope that this volume plays a part in establishing the California Gothic as a topic amply deserving of academic attention.

## Notes

1. 'Just the Facts: California's Population', *Public Policy Institute of California*, https://www.ppic.org/publication/californias-population (last accessed 13 August 2021).
2. Schneider, 'Census Shows US is Diversifying', online.
3. Hiatt, 'The All American Nightmares of Jordan Peele', online.
4. The significance of the '11:11' synchronicity is discussed by Jeffries in 'Jordan Peele (Dir.), *US*', p. 296; and by Booker and Daraiseh, 'Lost in the Fun House', p. 123.
5. https://en.wikipedia.org/wiki/Hands_Across_America (last accessed 25 February 2021).

6. Hope, 'Environment as Consumer Icon', pp. 166–7.

7. Vronsky, *American Serial Killers*, p. 223.

8. Booker and Daraiseh, 'Lost in the Fun House', briefly mentions the locational overlap with *The Lost Boys* in terms of the film's 'debt to the dark side of 1980s popular culture' (p. 125).

9. Neher, 'Interpreting Horror', p. 114.

10. Brody, 'Review: Jordan Peele's *Us*', online.

11. See Olafsen, 'It's Us', for more on Gabe's attempts to 'keep up' with Josh Tyler (p. 27).

12. See Booker and Daraiseh, 'Lost in the Fun House', p. 121; Eric Kohn, '"Us" Review', online; Yamato, 'This is Us', online; and Brody, 'Review: Jordan Peele's *Us*', online.

13. I expand upon this observation in Murphy, 'It's Not the House that's Haunted', pp. 235–53.

14. Fiddler, 'Playing *Funny Games*', p. 282.

15. Macek, *Urban Nightmares*, p. 234.

16. Briefel and Ngaî, 'How Much Did You Pay for This Place?', p. 71.

17. Ibid. p. 71.

18. Peele, *Us*, p. 50, online.

19. McDonald, 'Free to Be You and Me', p. 45.

20. Lawson, 'Jordan Peele's *Us* Stabs Itself in the Foot', online.

21. Robinson, 'Does the Ending of Jordan Peele's *Us* Play Fair?', online.

22. As outlined in Hiatt, 'The All American Nightmares of Jordan Peele', online.

23. McDonald, 'Free to Be You and Me', p. 45.

24. Chick, 'Minnie Riperton', online.

25. Robinson, 'Jordan Peele's Us', online.

26. Philips, 'They're Rapists', online.

27. Korte and Gomez, 'Trump Ramps Up Rhetoric on Undocumented Immigrants', online.

28. Hecht, 'Oscars: Mexico selects "Desierto"', online.

29. Ibid.

30. Bebout and Goldsmith, 'On the Border Between Migration and Horror', p. 147.

31. Bebout and Goldsmith also discuss the film's debt to the slasher and 'road movie' genres, and usefully outline the ways in which the film is indebted to the conventions of the Latinx migration genre ('On the Border Between Migration and Horror').

32. 'Sonoran Desert', https://en.wikipedia.org/wiki/Sonoran_Desert (last accessed 2 May 2021).

33. Flores, 'Interview with "Desierto" Director Jonás Cuarón', online.

34. Giroux, 'Interview: How Jonas Cuaron's "Desierto" was Inspired by "Duel"', online.
35. Bebout and Goldsmith, 'On the Border Between Migration and Horror', p. 148.
36. Crucchiola, 'Gael García Bernal On His New Film *Desierto*', online.
37. Keetley, 'Cuaron's *Desierto* and the Rise of White Man as Monster', online.
38. Ibid.
39. Murphy, *The Rural Gothic*, p. 147.
40. Ibid.
41. *Who is Dayani Crystal?* (dir. Marc Silver, 2013), https://whoisdayanicristal.com/about (last accessed 10 August 2021).
42. Theroux, *On the Plain of Snakes*, p. xx.
43. Also noted by McDonagh, 'Film Review: Desierto', online.
44. As outlined in Season 4, episode 8, 'Pangs', https://buffy.fandom.com/wiki/Sunnydale_Mission (last accessed 11 August 2021).
45. Bebout and Goldsmith, 'On the Border Between Migration and Horror', p. 150.
46. Hayes-Bautista, *La Nueva California*, pp. 1–2.
47. Ibid. pp. 2–3.
48. Ibid. p. 3.
49. Ibid. p. 5.
50. Ibid. pp. 6–13.
51. Ibid. p. 17.
52. Stern, *Eugenic Nation*, p. 6.
53. Ibid. p. 6.
54. Ibid. p. 77.
55. Ibid. p. 59.
56. Bebout and Goldsmith, 'On the Border Between Migration and Horror', p. 166.
57. Stern, *Eugenic Nation*, p. 85.
58. Hubler, 'Why California's Growth Has Slowed', online.
59. Gabbert, 'Data Shows the Worsening Trend of California Wildfires', online.
60. Krishnakumar and Kannan, 'The Worst Fire Season Ever. Again', online.
61. Reisner, *A Dangerous Place*, p. 3.
62. Suarez was quoted in Ronayne, 'Awaiting Census Count', online.
63. Fisher, *Hard Facts*, p. 7.
64. Ibid. p. 7.
65. Ibid. p. 8.
66. Fradkin, *The Seven States*, p. xviii.

# Bibliography

Abel, Emily K., *Tuberculosis and the Politics of Exclusion: A History of Public Health and Migration to Los Angeles* (New Brunswick, NJ: Rutgers University Press, 2007).

Alder, Emily, 'Through Oceans Darkly: Sea Literature and the Nautical Gothic', *Gothic Studies* 19:2 (November 2017), pp. 1–15.

Allen, Nick, 'Freedom of Mind: Karyn Kusama on *The Invitation*', *RogerEbert.com*, 6 April 2016, https://www.rogerebert.com/interviews/freedom-of-mind-karyn-kusama-on-the-invitation (last accessed 9 July 2021).

Allmendinger, Blake (ed.), *A History of California Literature* (New York: Cambridge University Press, 2015).

Ames, Christopher, *Movies About the Movies: Hollywood Reflected* (Lexington: University Press of Kentucky, 1997).

Anger, Kenneth, *Hollywood Babylon* (London: Arrow Books, 1991 [1975]).

Arnold-de Simine, Silke, 'The Body in the Pool: Reflections on David Cronenberg's *Maps to the Stars*', *Studies in Gender and Sexuality* 17:1 (January 2016), pp. 73–5.

Atwood, Margaret, 'When Privacy is Theft: Dave Eggers's "The Circle"', *The New York Review of Books*, 21 November 2013, https://www.nybooks.com/articles/2013/11/21/eggers-circle-when-privacy-is-theft/ (last accessed 9 July 2021).

Bacon, Simon, 'Anywhere-Nowhere, California: The Real, The Imaginary and the Lonely Vampire in the Golden State', in Katarzyna Nowak-McNeice and Agata Zarzycka (eds), *A Dark California: Essays on Dystopian Depictions in Popular Culture* (Jefferson, NC: McFarland, 2017), pp. 115–26.

Bastién, Angelica Jade, '*Them* is Pure Degradation Porn', *Vulture*, 14 April 2021, https://www.vulture.com/article/review-them-amazon-series.html (last accessed 13 July 2021).

Banham, Reyner, *Los Angeles: The Architecture of Four Ecologies* (Berkeley: University of California Press, 2009 [1971]).

Bates, David, 'Location: Department of Health, 101 Grove Street at Polk', in Scott Jordan Harris (ed.), *World Film Locations: San Francisco* (Bristol: Intellect Books, 2013), p. 76.

Bebout, Lee, and Clarissa Goldsmith, 'On the Border Between Migration and Horror: Rendering Border Violence Strange in Jonás Cuarón's *Desierto*', in Frederick Luis Aldama (ed.), *Latinx Ciné in the Twenty-First Century* (Tucson: University of Arizona Press, 2019), pp. 147–70.

Becker, Matt, 'A Point of Little Hope: Hippie Horror Films and the Politics of Ambivalence', *The Velvet Light Trap* 57 (Spring 2006), pp. 42–59.

Bergland, Renée L., *The National Uncanny: Indian Ghosts and American Subjects* (Hanover, NH: University Press of New England, 2000).

Billings, Arlene, and Beryl Dhanjal, *Supernatural Signs, Symbols and Codes* (New York: Rosen Publishing Group, 2011).

Blakemore, Bill, 'The Family of Man', *The San Francisco Chronicle Syndicate*, 29 July 1987.

Bolin, Alice, *Dead Girls: Essays on Surviving an American Obsession* (New York: Harper Collins, 2018).

Booker, M. Keith, and Isra Daraiseh, 'Lost in the Funhouse: Allegorical Horror and Cognitive Mapping in Jordan Peele's *Us*', *Horror Studies* 12:1 (2021), pp. 119–31.

Brackett, Charles, Billy Wilder and D. M. Marshman, *Sunset Boulevard* [typescript draft], 21 March 1949.

Brady, H. Jennifer, 'Points West, Then and Now: The Fiction of Joan Didion', *Contemporary Literature* 20:4 (Autumn 1979), pp. 452–70.

Brands, H. W., *The Age of Gold: The California Gold Rush and the New American Dream* (New York: Anchor Books, 2003).

Briefel, Aviva, and Sianne Ngaî, '"How Much Did You Pay for This Place?": Fear, Entitlement, and Urban Space in Bernard Rose's *Candyman*', *Camera Obscura: Feminism, Culture, and Media Studies 37* 13:1 (January 1996), pp. 71–91.

Brody, Richard, 'Review: Jordan Peele's *Us*', *The New Yorker*, 23 March 2019, https://www.newyorker.com/culture/the-front-row/review-jordan-peeles-us-is-a-colossal-cinematic-achievement (last accessed 30 September 2021).

Brook, Vincent, *Land of Smoke and Mirrors: A Cultural History of Los Angeles* (New Brunswick, NJ: Rutgers University Press, 2012).

Brooker-Bowers, Nancy, 'Fiction and the Film Industry: A Brief History of the Hollywood Novel and a Bibliography of Criticism', *Literature/Film Quarterly* 15:4 (January 1987), pp. 259–68.

Buchanan-King, Mindy, 'Joan Crawford: Problematizing the (Aging) Female Image and Sexuality in *Whatever Happened to Baby Jane?*', *Quarterly Review of Film and Video* 37:5 (2020), pp. 408–30.

Bugliosi, Vincent, with Curt Gentry, *Helter Skelter: The True Story of the Manson Murders* (London: Arrow Books, 1992 [1974]).

Burrough, Bryan, *Days of Rage: America's Radical Underground, the FBI, and the Forgotten Age of Revolutionary Violence* (New York: Penguin, 2015).

Burton, Sandra, 'The Great Wild Californicated West', *Time Magazine*100:8 (21 August 1972), p. 15.

'California Cults', *Time Magazine* 15:13 (31 March 1930), pp. 62–4.

Celeste, Reni, 'Screen Idols: The Tragedy of Falling Stars', *Journal of Popular Film and Television* 33:1 (2005), pp. 29–38.

Chick, Stevie, 'Minnie Riperton: Ten of the Best', *The Guardian*, 29 June 2016, https://www.theguardian.com/music/musicblog/2016/jun/29/minnie-riperton-10-of-the-best (last accessed 30 April 2021).

Chivers, Sally, 'Baby Jane Grew Up: The Dramatic Intersection of Age with Disability', *Canadian Review of American Studies* 36:2 (2006), pp. 211–28.

Christiansen, Steen Ledet, "Ominous Metamorphosis in *Starry Eyes*', in *The New Cinematic Weird: Atmospheres and Worldings* (Lanham, MD: Lexington Books, 2021), pp. 67–88.

Conlon, Christopher, 'Introduction: California Sorcerers', in William F. Nolan and William K. Schafer (eds), *California Sorcery: A Group Celebration* (Forest Hill, MD: Cemetery Dance, 1999), pp. 1–26.

Conway, Flo, and Jim Siegelman, *Snapping: America's Epidemic of Sudden Personality Change* (Philadelphia and New York: J. P. Lippincott, 1978).

Cook, Sherburne F., 'The American Invasion, 1848–1870', in *The Conflict Between the California Indian and White Civilization* (Berkeley: University of California Press, 1976), pp. 255–364.

Cooper, Ian, *The Manson Family on Film and Television* (Jefferson, NC: McFarland, 2018).

Corliss, Richard, *Talking Pictures: Screenwriters of Hollywood* (London: David and Charles, 1973).

Crosby, Alfred, W., *Ecological Imperialism: The Biological Expansion of Europe, 900–1900* (New York: Cambridge University Press, 2004).

Crow, Charles, 'Homecoming in the California Visionary Romance', *Western American Literature* 24:1 (Spring 1989), pp. 3–19.

Crucchiola, Jordan, 'Gael García Bernal on His New Film *Desierto* and the Responsibility of Privilege', *Vulture*, 14 October 2016, https://www.vulture.com/2016/10/gael-garca-bernal-on-his-new-film-desierto.html (last accessed 3 June 2016).

Cumbow, Robert C., *Order in the Universe: The Films of John Carpenter* (Lanham, MD: Scarecrow Press, 2000).

Curtis, Barry, *Dark Places: The Haunted House in Film* (London: Reaktion Books, 2008).

D'Addario, Daniel, '*Them* is an Unconvincing Examination of American Horror: TV Review', *Variety*, 8 April 2021, https://variety.com/2021/tv/reviews/them-amazon-lena-waithe-1234944373/ (last accessed 13 July 2021).

Daley, Edith, *Sarah Winchester: My Neighbor* (Concord: New Forest Books, 2018).

Dana, Richard Henry, Jr., *Two Years Before the Mast* (London: Reader's Digest Association, 2000 [1840]).

Daugherty, Tracy, *The Last Love Song: A Biography of Joan Didion* (New York: St. Martin's Press, 2015).

Davis, Mike, *City of Quartz: Excavating the Future in Los Angeles* (London: Verso, 2006).

Davis, Mike, and Jon Wiener, *Set the Night on Fire: L.A. in the Sixties* (London: Verso, 2020).

Deverell, William, and David Igler (eds), *A Companion to California History* (Oxford: Wiley Blackwell, 2014).

Dickey, Colin, *Ghostland: An American History in Haunted Places* (New York: Viking, 2016).

Didion, Joan, 'How Can I Tell Them There's Nothing Left?', *Saturday Evening Post*, 7 May 1966, pp. 38–47.

'Notes from a Native Daughter', in *We Tell Ourselves Stories in Order to Live: Collected Nonfiction* (New York: Everyman's Library, 2006), pp. 131–41.

'Some Dreamers of the Golden Dream', in *We Tell Ourselves Stories in Order to Live: Collected Nonfiction*, pp. 13–29.

'Where I Was From', in *We Tell Ourselves Stories in Order to Live: Collected Nonfiction*, pp. 949–1106.

*The White Album* (New York: Simon and Schuster, 1979).

DiMarco, Danette, 'Going Wendigo: The Emergence of the Iconic Monster in Margaret Atwood's *Oryx and Crake* and Antonia Bird's *Ravenous*', *College Literature* 38:4 (Fall 2011), pp. 134–55.

Dimendberg, Edward, *Film Noir and the Spaces of Modernity* (Cambridge, MA: Harvard University Press, 2004).

Dowd, Katie, '"Murder Capital of the World": The Terrifying Years When Multiple Serial Killers Stalked Santa Cruz', *SFGATE*, 2 August 2020, https://www.sfgate.com/crime/article/santa-cruz-kemper-mullin-frazier-murders-12841990.php (last accessed 2 December 2020).

Downey, Dara, 'Emma Frances Dawson's California Gothic', in Monika Elbert and Rita Bode (eds), *American Women's Regionalist Fiction: Mapping the* Gothic (Basingstoke: Palgrave Macmillan, 2021), pp. 287–303.

Dussere, Erik, *America is Elsewhere: The Noir Tradition in the Age of Consumer Culture* (Oxford: Oxford University Press, 2014).

Eco, Umberto, 'The Suicides of the Temple', in Leonard Michaels, David Reid and Raquel Scherr (eds), *West of the West: Imagining California* (Berkeley: University of California Press, 1989), pp. 311–16.

Eggers, Dave, *The Circle* (London: Hamish Hamilton, 2013).

Elbert, Monika, and Rita Bode (eds), *American Women's Regionalist Fiction: Mapping the Gothic* (Basingstoke: Palgrave Macmillan, 2021).

Farrell, Henry, *What Ever Happened to Baby Jane?* (London: New English Library, 1960).

Featherstone, Mark, '"The Letting Go": The Horror of Being Orphaned in Nicolas Winding Refn's Cinema', *Journal for Cultural Research* 21:3 (2017), pp. 268–85.

Fiddler, Michael, 'Playing *Funny Games* in *The Last House on the Left*: The Uncanny and the "Home Invasion" Genre', *Crime Media Culture* 9:3 (2013), pp. 281–299.

Finney, Jack. *The Body Snatchers* (London: Gollancz, 2010 [1955]).

Fisher, Philip, *Hard Facts: Setting and Form in the American Novel* (New York: Oxford University Press, 1987).

Flores, Estefani, 'Interview with "Desierto" Director Jonás Cuarón', *Hola Cultura*, 13 October 2016, https://www.holacultura.com/interview-with-desierto-director-jonas-cuaron/ (last accessed 3 June 2021).

Fradkin, Philip L., *The Seven States of California: A Natural and Human History* (Berkeley: University of California Press, 1997 [1995]).

Franklin, Ruth, *Shirley Jackson: A Rather Haunted Life* (New York: Liveright, 2016).

Frantz, Douglas, *From the Ground Up: The Business of Building in the Age of Money* (Berkeley: University of California Press, 1993).

Frazer-Carroll, Micha, 'Them and Us: Why Amazon's New "Race Horror" Show is Worse than Copycat Programming', *The Independent*, 9 April 2021, https://www.independent.co.uk/arts-entertainment/tv/features/them-amazon-prime-video-jordan-peele-b1829136.html (last accessed 18 September 2021).

Freund, Charles, 'Pods Over San Francisco', *Film Comment* 15:1 (January–February 1979), pp. 22–5.

Fuller, Graham, 'Interview with David Cronenberg', *Film Comment*, 26 February 2018, https://www.filmcomment.com/blog/interview-david-cronenberg-maps-to-the-stars/ (last accessed 1 July 2021).

Gabbert, Bill, 'Data Shows the Worsening Trend of California Wildfires', *Wildfire Today*, 31 March 2020, https://wildfiretoday.com/2020/03/31/data-shows-the-worsening-trend-of-california-wildfires/ (last accessed 17 November 2021).

Gebhard, David, and Robert Winter, *An Architectural Guidebook to Los Angeles* (Salt Lake City, UT: Gibbs Smith, 2003).

Ginsberg, Lesley, 'Mary Austin's California Gothic', in Monika Elbert and Rita Bode (eds), *American Women's Regionalist Fiction: Mapping the Gothic* (Basingstoke: Palgrave Macmillan, 2021), pp. 305–22.

Giroux, Jack, 'Interview: How Jonás Cuarón's "Desierto" was inspired by Stephen Spielberg's "Duel"', *Slashfilm*, 21 October 2016, https://www.slashfilm.com/547115/desierto-jonas-cuaron-interview/ (last accessed 3 June 2021).

Godfrey, Alex, '*The Lost Boys*: Joel Schumacher on Making the Coolest Vampire Movie of All Time', *Empire Online*, 23 June 2020, https://www.empireonline.com/movies/features/lost-boys-joel-schumacher-making-of-interview-feature/ (last accessed 2 December 2020).

Graebner, William, *Patty's Got a Gun: Patricia Hearst in 1970s America* (Chicago: University of Chicago Press, 2008).

Grant, Barry Keith, *Invasion of the Body Snatchers* (Houndmills: BFI/ Palgrave Macmillan: 2010).

Graysmith, Robert, *Zodiac: The Shocking True Story of America's Most Elusive Serial Killer* (London: Titan Books, 2007 [1976])

Haag, Matthew. 'What We Know About Joseph DeAngelo, the Golden State Killer Suspect', *The New York Times*, 26 April 2018, https://www.nytimes.com/2018/04/26/us/joseph-james-deangelo.html (last accessed 15 October 2020).

Hadji, Robert, 'Fritz Leiber', in Jack Sullivan (ed.), *The Penguin Encyclopedia of Horror and the Supernatural* (New York: Viking, 1986), pp. 262–3.

Hall, Joan Wylie, 'Fallen Eden in Shirley Jackson's *The Road Through the Wall*', in Bernice M. Murphy (ed.), *Shirley Jackson: Essays on the Literary Legacy* (Jefferson, NC: McFarland, 2005), pp. 23–33.

Hardesty, Donald L., 'Historical Perspectives on the Archaeology of the Donner Party', in Kelly J. Dixon, Julie M. Schablitsky and Shannon A. Novak (eds), *An Archaeology of Desperation: Exploring the Donner Party's Alder Creek Camp* (Norman: University of Oklahoma Press, 2011), pp. 89–100.

Hardesty, Donald L., et al., *The Archaeology of the Donner Party* (Reno: University of Nevada Press, 1997).

Harrison, Barbara Grizzuti, *Off Center: Essays* (New York: Dial Press, 1980).

Hart, James D., *A Companion to California* (New York: Oxford University Press, 1978).

'Harvest of Bad Seeds', *Time Magazine* 101:19 (7 May 1973), pp. 22–3.

Hayes-Bautista, David E., *La Nueva California: Latinos from Pioneers to Post-Millennials*, 2nd ed. (Oakland: University of California Press, 2017).

Hecht, John, 'Oscars: Mexico Selects "Desierto" for Best Foreign Language Category', *Hollywood Reporter*, 14 September 2016, https://www.hollywoodreporter.com/movies/movie-news/oscars-mexico-selects-desierto-foreign-928823/ (last accessed 30 September 2021).

Herron, Don, 'Smith, Clark Ashton, 1893–1961', in Jack Sullivan (ed.), *The Penguin Encyclopedia of Horror and the Supernatural* (New York: Viking, 1986), p. 393.

Hiatt, Brian, 'The All-American Nightmares of Jordan Peele', *Rolling Stone*, 29 January 2019, https://www.rollingstone.com/movies/movie-features/director-jordan-peele-new-movie-cover-story-782743/ (last accessed 18 June 2021).

Higgs, Eric C., *The Happy Man: A Tale of Horror* (Richmond, VA: Valancourt Books, 2017 [1985]).

Hine, Robert V., *California's Utopian Colonies, 1850–1950* (New Haven, CT: Yale University Press, 1966 [1953]).

Hope, Diane S., 'Environment as Consumer Icon in Advertising Fantasy', in Mark Meister and Phyllis M. Japp (eds), *Enviropop: Studies in Environmental Rhetoric and Popular Culture* (Westport, CT: Greenwood Publishing, 2002), pp. 161–74.

Howard, John, 'Story-telling, Wonder-questing, Mortal Me: The Transformation of *The Pale Brown Thing* into *Our Lady of Darkness*', in Fritz Leiber, *The Pale Brown Thing* (Dublin: Swan River Press, 2016), pp. 131–42.

Hubler, Shawn, 'Why California's Growth Has Slowed (And Why Demographers Aren't Surprised), *The New York Times*, 26 April 2021, https://www.nytimes.com/2021/04/26/us/us-census-california.html (last accessed 17 November 2021).

Hughes, Dorothy B., *In a Lonely Place*, in Sarah Weinman (ed.), *Women Crime Writers: Four Suspense Novels of the 1940s* (New York: Library of America, 2015 [1947]).

Hutchison, Alice L., *Kenneth Anger: A Demonic Visionary* (London: Black Dog Publishing, 2004).

Ignoffo, Mary Jo, *Captive of the Labyrinth: Sarah L. Winchester, Heiress to the Rifle Fortune* (Columbia: University of Missouri Press, 2010).

Insdorf, Annette, *Philip Kaufman* (Urbana: University of Illinois Press, 2012).

Ireland, Brian, 'American Highways: Recurring Images and Themes of the Road Genre', *Journal of American Culture* 26:4 (2003), pp. 474–85.

Isaacson, Johanna, 'Women Acting Out in (Cognitive) *Maps to the Stars*', *Blindfield: A Journal of Cultural Inquiry*, 16 August 2016 https://blindfieldjournal.com/2016/08/16/women-acting-out-in-cognitive-maps-to-the-stars/ (last accessed 1 July 2021).

Jackson, Helen Hunt, *Ramona* (New York: Signet Classics, 1988 [1884]).

Jackson, Kenneth, *Crabgrass Frontier: The Suburbanization of the United States* (New York: Oxford University Press, 1985).

Jackson, Shirley, *The Haunting of Hill House* (New York: Penguin, 1987 [1959]).
'Letter to Geraldine and Leslie Jackson, 14th January 1958', in Laurence Jackson Hyman (ed.), *The Letters of Shirley Jackson* (New York: Random House, 2021), pp. 356–61.
*The Road Through the Wall* (New York: Penguin, 2013 [1948]).

Jameson, Fredric, 'The Shining', *Social Text* 4 (Autumn 1981), 115–25.

Jancovich, Mark, *Rational Fears: American Horror Genre in the 1950s* (Manchester: Manchester University Press, 1996).

Janzen, Rod, *The Rise and Fall of Synanon: A California Utopia* (Baltimore, MD: Johns Hopkins University Press, 2001).

Jeffries, Judson L., 'Jordan Peele (Dir.), *Us* (Motion Picture), Universal Pictures', *Journal of African American Studies* 2 (2020), pp. 288–96.

Jenkins, Philip, *A Decade of Nightmares: The End of the Sixties and the Making of Eighties America* (Oxford: Oxford University Press, 2006).
*Mystics and Messiahs: Cults and New Religions in American History* (Oxford: Oxford University Press, 2000).

Johnson, Kristin, 'The Aftermath of Tragedy: The Donner Camps in the Later Years', in Kelly J. Dixon, Julie M. Schablitsky and Shannon A. Novak (eds), *An Archaeology of Desperation: Exploring the Donner Party's Alder Creek Camp* (Norman: University of Oklahoma Press, 2011), pp. 63–88.

Johnson, Kristin (ed.), *'Unfortunate Emigrants': Narratives of the Donner Party* (Logan: Utah State University Press, 1996).

Joshi, S. T., 'Introduction' and 'Explanatory Notes', in Clark Ashton Smith, *The Dark Eidolon and Other Fantasies* (New York: Penguin, 2014), pp. ix–xxiii; 339.
*Unutterable Horror: A History of Supernatural Fiction*, Vol. 2: *The Twentieth and Twenty-First Centuries* (Hornsea: P. S. Publishing, 2012).

Junker, Christine R., "Unruly Women and Their Crazy Houses: Sarah Winchester's Unconventional Domesticity', *Home Cultures: The Journal of Architecture, Design and Domestic Space* 12:3 (2015), pp. 329–46.

Karpel, Craig, 'California Evil', in *Esquire: The Magazine for Men*, March 1970.

Keetley, Dawn, 'Cuaron's *Desierto* and the Rise of White Man as Monster', *Horror Homeroom*, 28 August 2017, http://www.horrorhomeroom.com/cuarons-desierto-rise-white-man-monster/ (last accessed 11 August 2021).

Kermode, Mark, '*Maps to the Stars* Review: Cronenberg Enters the Dark Heart of Hollywood', *The Guardian*, 28 September 2014, https://www.theguardian.com/film/2014/sep/28/maps-to-the-stars-review-david-cronenberg-dark-heart-hollywood (last accessed 2 July 2021).

Kilston, Lyra, *Sun Seekers: The Cure of California* (Los Angeles: Atelier Editions, 2019).

Kimbro, Edna E., and Julia G. Costello, with Tevvy Ball, *The California Missions: History, Art, and Preservation* (Los Angeles: Getty Publications, 2009).

Kirsch, Robert A., 'Headmaster of the Writing School', *Los Angeles Times*, 1 November 1965, p. 8.

'William F. Nolan at Head of His Class', *Los Angeles Times*, 6 December 1974.

Klug, Daniel, 'These Kind of Dreams: Dystopian Depictions of California in the Music Video "Californication"', in Katarzyna Nowak-McNeice and Agata Zarzycka (eds), *A Dark California: Essays on Dystopian Depictions in Popular Culture* (Jefferson, NC: McFarland, 2017), pp. 174–83.

Knight, Peter, *Conspiracy Culture: From Kennedy to the X-Files* (London: Routledge, 2001).

Kohn, Eric, '"US" Review', *IndieWire*, 9 March 2019, https://www.indiewire.com/2019/03/us-review-jordan-peele-sxsw-1202049907/ (last accessed 30 September 2021).

Korte, Gregory, and Alan Gomez, 'Trump Ramps Up Rhetoric on Undocumented Immigrants: "These aren't People. These are Animals"', *USA Today*, 16 May 2018, https://eu.usatoday.com/story/news/politics/2018/05/16/trump-immigrants-animals-mexico-democrats-sanctuary-cities/617252002/ (last accessed 11 August 2021).

Kowalewski, Michael, 'Contemporary Regionalism', in Charles L. Crow (ed.), *A Companion to the Regional Literatures of America* (Oxford: Blackwell Publishing, 2003), pp. 7–24.

Kraft, Jeff, and Aaron Leventhal, *Footsteps in the Fog: Alfred Hitchcock's San Francisco* (Santa Monica, CA: Santa Monica Press, 2002).

Krishnakumar, Priya, and Swetha Kannan, 'The Worst Fire Season Ever', *Los Angeles Times*, 20 September 2020, https://www.latimes.com/projects/california-fires-damage-climate-change-analysis/ (last accessed 30 September 2021).

Kroeber, Theodora, *Ishi in Two Worlds: A Biography of the Last Wild Indian in North American* (Berkeley: University of California Press, 2011 [1961]).

Kropp, Phoebe S., *California Vieja: Culture and Memory in a Modern American Place* (Berkeley: University of California Press, 2006).

Kumar, Krishan, *Utopia and Anti-Utopia in Modern Times* (Oxford: Blackwell, 1987).

Lacy, Robert, 'Joan Didion: Daughter of Old California', *Sewanee Review* 122:3 (Summer 2014), pp. 500–5.

LaFrance, Adrienne, 'When Bad News was Printed on Milk Cartons', *The Atlantic*, 14 February 2017, https://www.theatlantic.com/technology/

archive/2017/02/when-bad-news-was-printed-on-milk-cartons/516675/ (last accessed 14 July 2021).

Lanier, Jaron, *Ten Arguments for Deleting Your Social Media Accounts Right Now* (New York: Vintage Digital, 2018).

Laws, Mary, Polly Stenham and Nicolas Winding Refn, *The Neon Demon*, Draft: 11.1.14, http://www.whoaisnotme.net/scripts/TND_2014_UD.pdf (last accessed 9 November 2021).

Lawson, Richard, 'Jordan Peele's *Us* Stabs Itself in the Foot', *Vanity Fair*, 20 March 2019, https://www.vanityfair.com/hollywood/2019/03/jordan-peeles-us-stabs-itself-in-the-foot (last accessed 18 June 2021).

Laycock, Joseph P., 'Conversion by Infection: The Sociophobic of Cults in *The Omega Man*', *International Journal for the Study of New Religions* 1:2 (2010), pp. 103–20.

'Where Do They Get These Ideas? Changing Ideas of Cults in the Mirror of Popular Culture', *Journal of the American Academy of Religion* 81:1 (March 2013), pp. 80–106.

Leeder, Murray, 'Skeletons Sail an Etheric Ocean: Approaching the Ghost in John Carpenter's *The Fog*', *Journal of Popular Film and Television* 37:2 (2009), pp. 70–9.

Leiber, Fritz, 'The Girl with the Hungry Eyes' [1949], in Jonathan Strahan and Charles N. Brown (eds), *Fritz Leiber: Selected Stories* (San Francisco: Night Shade Books, 2011), pp. 19–33.

*Our Lady of Darkness* (Glasgow: Fontana, 1978).

*The Pale Brown Thing* (Dublin: Swan River Press, 2016).

'Smoke Ghost' [1941], in Jonathan Strahan and Charles N. Brown (eds), *Fritz Leiber: Selected Stories* (San Francisco: Night Shade Books, 2011), pp. 5–18.

Lindsay, Robert, 'L. Ron Hubbard Dies of Stroke: Founder of the Church of Scientology', *The New York Times*, 29 January 1986, https://www.nytimes.com/1986/01/29/obituaries/l-ron-hubbard-dies-of-stroke-founder-of-church-of-scientology.html (last accessed 23 December 2020).

Lucas, Tim, 'DVD Review: *Messiah of Evil*', *Sight and Sound*, January 2010, http://old.bfi.org.uk/sightandsound/review/5268 (last accessed 23 July 2021).

Luna, Taryn, 'Newsom Apologizes for California's History of Violence against Native Americans', *Los Angeles Times*, 18 June 2019, https://www.latimes.com/politics/la-pol-ca-gavin-newsom-apology-california-native-american-tribes-061818-story.html (last accessed 28 July 2020).

Macek, Steve, *Urban Nightmares: The Media, the Right, and Moral Panic Over the City* (Minneapolis: University of Minnesota Press, 2006).

Madley, Benjamin, *An American Genocide: The United States and the California Indian Catastrophe, 1847–1873* (New Haven, CT: Yale University Press, 2016)

Mann, Craig, and Liam Hathaway, 'Dreams Require Sacrifice: Fame, Fortune and Body Horror in *Starry Eyes*', in Katarzyna Nowak-McNeice and Agata Zarzycka (eds), *A Dark California: Essays on Dystopian Depictions in Popular Culture* (Jefferson, NC: McFarland, 2017), pp. 101–14.

Marling, William, 'The Hard-Boiled California Novel', in Blake Allmendinger (ed.), *A History of California Literature* (New York: Cambridge University Press, 2015), pp. 199–212.

Martin, Jay, *Nathanael West, The Art of His Life* (London: Secker and Warburg, 1970).

Matheson, Richard, 'The Creeping Terror', in *Shock! Thirteen Tales to Thrill and Terrify* (New York: Dell, 1961), pp. 139–53.
  *I Am Legend* (London: Victor Gollancz, 2011 [1954]).

May, Lary, *Screening Out the Past: The Birth of Mass Culture and the Motion Picture Industry* (New York: Oxford University Press, 1980).

McDonagh, Maitland, 'Film Review: Desierto', *Film Journal International*, 12 October 2016, http://fj.webedia.us/reviews/film-review-desierto (last accessed 16 October 2021).

McDonald, Soraya Nadia, '"Free to Be You and Me": The Doubled Characters of *Us*', *Film Comment* (May–June 2019), pp. 44–7.

McGlashan, Charles, *History of the Donner Party: A Tragedy of the Sierras* (New York: Dover, 2013 [1880]).

McNamara, Michelle, *I'll Be Gone in the Dark: One Woman's Obsessive Search for the Golden State Killer* (London: Faber and Faber, 2018).

McVarish, Maria, and Julie Leavitt. 'Mourning in the Hollows of Architecture and Psychoanalysis', in Adrienne Harris, Margery Kalb and Susan Klebanoff (eds), *Ghosts in the Consulting Room: Echoes of Trauma in Psychoanalysis* (London: Taylor and Francis, 2016), pp. 156–80.

McWilliams, Carey, *California: The Great Exception* (Berkeley: University of California Press, 1999 [1949]).
  *Southern California: An Island on the Land* (Salt Lake City: Peregrine Lake Books, 2010 [1946]).

Milun, Kathryn, *Pathologies of Modern Space: Empty Space, Urban Anxiety, and the Recovery of the Public Self* (New York: Routledge, 2007).

Mogen, David, Scott P. Sanders and Joanne B. Karpinski (eds), *Frontier Gothic: Terror and Wonder at the Frontier in American Literature* (Madison, NJ: Farleigh Dickinson University Press, 1993).

Moran, Michelle T., *Colonizing Leprosy: Imperialism and the Politics of Public Health in the United States* (Chapel Hill: University of North Carolina Press, 2012).

Muir, John, *The Films of John Carpenter* (Jefferson, NC: McFarland, 2000).

Mulvey-Roberts, Marie, 'A Spook Ride on Film: Carpenter and the Gothic', in Ian Conrich and David Woods (eds), *The Cinema of John Carpenter: The Technique of Terror* (Wallflower Press: London, 2004), pp. 78–90.

Mumford, Lewis, 'California and the Human Horizon', in *The Urban Prospect* (New York: Harcourt, Brace and World, Inc., 1968), pp. 3–23.

Murphy, Bernice M., *The Highway Horror Film* (Basingstoke: Palgrave Macmillan, 2014).

'"It's Not the House that's Haunted": Demons, Debt and the Family in Peril in Recent Horror Cinema', in Murray Leeder (ed), *Cinematic Ghosts: Haunting and Spectrality from Silent Cinema to the Digital Era* (London: Bloomsbury, 2015), pp. 235–53.

*The Rural Gothic in American Popular Culture* (Basingstoke: Palgrave Macmillan, 2013).

*The Suburban Gothic in American Popular Culture* (Basingstoke: Palgrave Macmillan, 2009).

Nadeau, Remi, *California: The New Society* (New York: David McKay and Company, 1963).

Neher, Erick, 'Interpreting Horror: Jordan Peele's *Us*', *Hudson Review* (Spring 2019).

Newman, Kim, *Nightmare Movies: A Critical Guide to Contemporary Horror Films* (New York: Harmony Books, 1998).

Ní Fhlainn, Sorcha, *Postmodern Vampires: Film, Fiction, and Popular Culture* (Basingstoke: Palgrave Macmillan, 2019).

Nolan, William F., 'Remembering "The Group"', in William F. Nolan and William Schafer (eds), *California Sorcery: A Group Celebration* (Forest Hill, MD: Cemetery Dance, 2001), pp. 27–8.

Novak, Shannon A., and Kelly J. Dixon, 'Introduction', in Kelly J. Dixon, Julie M. Schablitsky and Shannon A. Novak (eds), *An Archaeology of Desperation: Exploring the Donner Party's Alder Creek Camp* (Norman: University of Oklahoma Press, 2011), pp. 1–30.

Nowak-McNeice, Katarzyna, and Agata Zarzycka, 'Californias Everywhere', in Nowak-McNeice and Zarzycka (eds), *A Dark California: Essays on Dystopian Depictions in Popular Culture* (Jefferson, NC: McFarland, 2017), pp. 184–192.

Nowak-McNeice, Katarzyna, and Agata Zarzycka (eds), *A Dark California: Essays on Dystopian Depictions in Popular Culture* (Jefferson, NC: McFarland, 2017).

Oehlschlaeger, Fritz. 'The Stoning of Mistress Hutchinson: Meaning and Context in "The Lottery"', *Essays in Literature* 15:2 (Fall 1988), pp. 259–65.

Olafsen, Harry, '"It's Us": Mimicry in Jordan Peele's *Us*', *Iowa Journal of Cultural Studies* 20:1 (Spring 2020): pp. 20–33.

Oppenheimer, Judy, *Private Demons: The Life of Shirley Jackson* (New York: Fawcett Columbine, 1988).

Peele, Jordan (dir.), *Us* (2019), https://www.scriptslug.com/assets/scripts/us-2019.pdf (last accessed 30 September 2021).

Pelisek, Christine, *The Grim Sleeper: The Lost Women of South Central* (Berkeley, CA: Counterpoint, 2017).

Pennell, Melissa McFarland, 'New England Gothic/New England Guilt: Mary Wilkins Freeman and the Salem Witchcraft Episode', in Monika Elbert and Rita Bode (eds), *American Women's Regionalist Fiction: Mapping the Gothic* (Basingstoke: Palgrave Macmillan, 2021), pp. 39–56.

Petersen, Anne Helen, 'What to Do with a Coffin Full of Sugar: Gloria Swanson, Kenneth Anger, and Self-Authorship in the Star Collection', *Moving Image* 13:2 (Fall 2013), pp. 81–98.

Philips, Amber, 'They're Rapists: President Trump's Campaign Launch Speech Two Years Later, Annotated', *The Washington Post*, 16 June 2017, https://www.washingtonpost.com/news/the-fix/wp/2017/06/16/theyre-rapists-presidents-trump-campaign-launch-speech-two-years-later-annotated/ (last accessed 11 August 2021).

Phillips, Kendall R., *Dark Directions: Romero, Craven, Carpenter, and the Modern Horror Film* (Carbondale: Southern Illinois University Press, 2012).

Poole, W. Scott, *Satan in America: The Devil We Know* (Lanham, MD: Rowman and Littlefield, 2009).

Postman, Neil, *Amusing Ourselves to Death: Public Discourse in the Age of Show Business* (London: Methuen, 1985).

Poston, Dudley L., Jr., and Rogelio Sáenz, 'The US White Majority Will Soon Disappear Forever', *The Conversation*, 30 April 2019, https://theconversation.com/the-us-white-majority-will-soon-disappear-forever-115894 (last accessed 13 August 2021).

Punter, David, *The Literature of Terror*, Vol. 1: *The Gothic Tradition* (London: Routledge, 2014).

Quay, James, 'Beyond Dreams and Disappointment: Defining California Through Culture', in William Deverell and David Igler (eds), *A Companion to California History* (Oxford: Wiley Blackwell, 2013), pp. 3–21.

Radish, Christina, 'Karyn Kusama on "The Invitation", Working as a Female Director, and Ambiguous Endings', *Collider*, 8 April 2016, https://collider.com/the-invitation-karyn-kusama-interview/ (last accessed 7 July 2021).

Rarick, Ethan, *Desperate Passage: The Donner Party's Perilous Journey West* (New York: Oxford University Press, 2008).

Reisner, Marc, *A Dangerous Place: California's Unsettling Fate* (New York: Pantheon Books, 2003).

Reiterman, Tim, with John Jacobs, *Raven: The Untold Story of the Rev. Jim Jones and His People* (New York: Penguin, 2008).

Rice, Richard B., et al., *The Elusive Eden: A New History of California* (Long Grove, IL: Waveland Press, 2019).

Riley, James, *The Bad Trip: Dark Omens, New Worlds and the End of the Sixties* (London: Icon Books, 2019).

Ringel, Faye, 'New England Gothic', in Charles L. Crow (ed.), *A Companion to American Gothic* (Oxford: Wiley Blackwell, 2013), pp. 137–50.

*New England's Gothic Literature: History and Folklore of the Supernatural from the Seventeenth Through the Twentieth Centuries* (Lewiston, NY: Edward Mellen Press, 1995).

Robinson, Tasha, 'Does the Ending of Jordan Peele's *Us* Play Fair with the Audience?', *The Verge*, 25 March 2019, https://www.theverge.com/2019/3/25/18281033/jordan-peele-us-movie-twist-ending-reveal-questions-explained-analysis (last accessed 18 June 2021).

'Jordan Peele's *Us*', *The Verge*, 22 March 2019, https://www.theverge.com/2019/3/9/18257721/us-review-jordan-peele-get-out-lupita-nyongo-winston-duke-elisabeth-moss-tim-heidecker-horror (last accessed 30 September 2021).

Ronayne, Kathleen, 'Awaiting Census Count', *US News and World* Report, 24 April 2021, https://www.usnews.com/news/politics/articles/2021-04-24/awaiting-census-count-california-ponders-slow-growth-future (last accessed 30 September 2021).

Rosten, Leo C., *Hollywood: The Movie Colony, the Movie Makers* (New York: Harcourt, Brace and Company, 1941).

Russell, Jamie, *Book of the Dead: The Complete History of Zombie Cinema* (Godalming, Surrey: FAB Press, 2005).

Sanders, Ed, *The Family: The Story of Charles Manson's Dune Buggy Attack Battalion* (London: Rupert Hart-Davis, 1972).

Sappell, Joel, and Robert W. Welkos, 'The Mind Behind the Religion: Chapter Four: The Final Days: Deep in Hiding, Hubbard Kept Tight Grip on the Church', *Los Angeles Times*, 24 June 1990, https://www.latimes.com/archives/la-xpm-1990-06-24-mn-1016-story.html (last accessed 23 December 2020).

Schneider, Mike, 'Census Shows US is Diversifying, White Population Shrinking', https://apnews.com/article/census-2020-house-elections-4ee80e72846c151aa41a808b06d975ea, 13 August 2021 (last accessed 13 August 2021).

Seitz, Matt Zoller, 'Maps to the Stars', *Roger Ebert.com*, 28 February 2015. https://www.rogerebert.com/reviews/maps-to-the-stars-2015 (last accessed 1 July 2021).

Shelley, Peter, *Grande Dame Guignol Cinema: A History of Hag Horror from 'Baby Jane' to 'Mother'* (Jefferson, NC: McFarland, 2009).

Shiel, Mark, *Hollywood Cinema and the Real Los Angeles* (London: Reaktion Books, 2012).

Sidney-Fryer, Donald, 'Thibaut de Castries, Revenant', in Fritz Leiber, *The Pale Brown Thing* (Dublin: Swan River Press, 2016), pp. ix–xv.

Sinyard, Neil, and Adrian Turner, *Journey Down Sunset Boulevard: The Films of Billy Wilder* (Ryde, Isle of Wight: BCW Publishing, 1979).

Smith, Clark Ashton, 'The City of the Singing Flame', in *The Dark Eidolon and Other Fantasies*, ed. S. T. Joshi (New York: Penguin, 2014), pp. 52–69.

'The Devotee of Evil', in *The Dark Eidolon and Other Fantasies*, ed. S. T. Joshi (New York: Penguin, 2014), pp. 21–33.

Smith, Steve, 'A Siege Mentality? Form and Ideology in Carpenter's Early Siege Films', in Ian Conrich and David Woods (eds), *The Cinema of John Carpenter: The Technique of Terror* (Wallflower Press: London, 2004), pp. 35–48.

Solnit, Rebecca, 'Rattlesnake in Mailbox: Cults, Creeps, California in the 1970s', in *The Encyclopedia of Trouble and Spaciousness* (San Antonio, TX: Trinity University Press, 2014), pp. 32–47.

Springer, John, 'This is a Riot You're In: Hollywood and American Mass Culture in Nathanael West's "The Day of the Locust"', *Literature/Film Quarterly* 24:4 (1996), pp. 439–44.

Stableford, Brian, 'Fritz Leiber, 1910–', in E. F. Bleiler (ed), *Supernatural Fiction Writers*, Vol. 2: *Contemporary Fantasy and Horror* (New York: Charles Scribner's Sons, 1985), pp. 933–9.

Staggs, Sam, *Close-Up on Sunset Boulevard* (New York: St Martin's Griffin, 2003).

Stark, Rodney, William Sims Bainbridge, and Daniel P. Doyle, 'Cults of California: A Reconnaissance in Space and Time', *Sociological Analysis* 40:4 (1979), pp. 347–59.

Starr, Kevin, *Americans and the California Dream, 1850–1915* (New York: Oxford University Press, 1986).

*California: A History* (Modern Library: New York, 2007).

*Coast of Dreams: California on the Edge, 1990–2003* (New York: Vintage, 2006).

*Embattled Dreams: California in War and Peace, 1940–1950* (New York: Oxford University Press, 2002).

*Golden Dreams: California in an Age of Abundance, 1950–1963* (New York: Oxford University Press, 2004).

*Inventing the Dream: California Through the Progressive Era* (Oxford: Oxford University Press, 1985).

Stern, Alexandra Minna, *Eugenic Nation: Faults and Frontiers of Better Breeding in Modern America* (Oakland: University of California Press, 2015).

Stewart, George R., *Earth Abides* (London: Orion, 1999 [1949]).

*Ordeal by Hunger: The Story of the Donner Party* (New York: Houghton Mifflin, 1988 [1936]).

Stover, Leon E., 'Social Science Fiction', *CEA Critic* 37:1 (November 1974), pp. 21–4.

Strand, Ginger. *Killer on the Road: Violence and the American Interstate* (Austin: University of Texas Press, 2012).

Strychacz, Thomas, 'Making Sense of Hollywood: Mass Discourses and the Literary Order in Nathanael West's *The Day of the Locust*', *Western American Literature* 22:2 (Summer 1987), pp. 149–62.

Sykes, Brad, *Terror in the Desert: Dark Cinema of the American Southwest* (Jefferson, NC; McFarland, 2018).

Talbot, David, *Season of the Witch: Enchantment, Terror, and Deliverance in the City of Love* (New York: Free Press, 2012).

Tarbell Cooper, Suzanne, Amy Ronnebeck Hall and Marc Wanamaker, *Theatres in Los Angeles* (Chicago: Arcadia Publishing, 2008).

Taylor, James, *Satan's Slaves and the Bizarre 'Underground' Cults of California* (London: New English Library, 1970).

Theroux, Paul, *On the Plain of Snakes: A Mexican Road Trip* (New York: Penguin Books, 2019).

Thomas, Keith, *Religion and the Decline of Magic* (London: Penguin, 2003).

Thrower, Stephen, *Nightmare USA: The Untold Story of the Exploitation Independents* (Godalming, Surrey: FAB Press, 2007).

Toobin, Jeffrey, *American Heiress: The Wild Saga of the Kidnapping, Crimes and Trial of Patty Hearst* (New York: Random House, 2016).

Trevelyan, Laura, *The Winchester: The Gun that Built an American Dynasty* (New Haven, CT: Yale University Press, 2016).

Tuan, Yi-Fu, *Landscapes of Fear* (Minneapolis: University of Minnesota Press, 2013 [1979]).

Vandenberg, Kathleen M., and Christopher K. Coffman, 'The Center is Not Holding: Joan Didion and the California Dreamer', in Katarzyna Nowak-McNeice and Agata Zarzycka (eds), *A Dark California: Essays on Dystopian Depictions in Popular Culture* (Jefferson, NC: McFarland, 2017), pp. 15–24.

van Leeuwen, Thomas A. P., *The Springboard in the Pond: An Intimate History of the Swimming Pool* (Cambridge, MA: MIT Press, 1998).

Von der Porten, Edward, et al., 'Who Made Drake's Plate of Brass? Hint: It Wasn't Francis Drake', *California History* 81:2 (Spring–Fall 2002), pp. 116–33.

Vronsky, Peter, *American Serial Killers: The Epidemic Years, 1950–2000* (New York: Berkley Books, 2020).

Wald, Priscilla, *Contagious: Cultures, Carriers, and the Outbreak Narrative* (Durham, NC and London: Duke University Press, 2009).

Wallis, Michael, *The Best Land Under Heaven: The Donner Party in the Age of Manifest Destiny* (New York: Liveright, 2017).

Wamsley, Laurel, 'In Hunt for Golden State Killer, Investigators Uploaded his DNA to Genealogy Site', *The Two-Way*, NPR, 27 April 2018, https://www.npr.org/sections/thetwo-way/2018/04/27/606624218/in-hunt-for-golden-state-killer-investigators-uploaded-his-dna-to-genealogy-site (last accessed 15 October 2020).

Wasson, Sam, *The Big Goodbye: Chinatown and the Last Years of Hollywood* (London: Faber and Faber, 2020).

Watt, Laura Alice, *The Paradox of Preservation: Wilderness and Working Landscapes at Point Reyes National Seashore* (Berkeley: University of California Press, 2017).

Wells, Elizabeth, '*Earth Abides*: A Return to Origins', *Extrapolation* 48:3 (2007), pp. 472–81.

West, Nathanael, *The Day of the Locust* (London: Penguin, 2018 [1939]).

Wheatley, Michael, 'For Fame and Fashion: The Cannibalism of Creatives in Chuck Palahniuk's *Haunted* and Nicolas Winding Refn's *The Neon Demon*', *Exchanges: The Interdisciplinary Research Journal* 7:2 (2020), pp. 115–33.

White, Michael D., *Shipwrecks of the California Coast: Wood to Iron, Sail to Steam* (Charleston, SC: History Press, 2014).

Whitt, Jan, *Women in American Journalism: A New History* (Champaign: University of Illinois Press, 2008).

Wiese, Andrew, *Places of Their Own: African American Suburbanization in the Twentieth Century* (Chicago: Chicago University Press, 2004).

Wilhemi, Jack, '*The Invitation*: What Happened to Claire Explained', *Screen Rant,* 7 July 2020, https://screenrant.com/invitation-horror-movie-what-happened-claire-explained/ (last accessed 30 September 2021).

Wilkerson, Isabel, *The Warmth of Other Suns: The Epic Story of America's Great Migration* (London: Penguin, 2010).

Woodward, Christopher, *In Ruins: A Journey through History, Art, and Literature* (London: Vintage, 2002).

Wright, Lawrence, *Going Clear: Scientology, Hollywood and the Prison of Belief* (New York: Random House, 2017).

Wyatt, David, *The Fall into Eden: Landscape and Imagination in California* (Cambridge: Cambridge University Press, 1986).

Yamato, Jen, 'This is Us', *Los Angeles Times*, 14 March 2019, https://www.latimes.com/entertainment/movies/la-ca-mn-jordan-peele-us-lupita-nyongo-winston-duke-20190314-story.html (last accessed 30 September 2021).

Yeates, Robert, 'Gender and Ethnicity in Post-Apocalyptic Suburbia', *Journal of the Fantastic in the Arts* 27:3 (2016), pp. 411–34.

Zahniser, David, and Matt Hamilton, 'Kevin Starr, Author of California Histories and Former State Librarian, Dies at 76', *Los Angeles Times*, 15 January 2017, https://www.latimes.com/local/lanow/la-me-ln-kevin-starr-obit-20170115-story.html (last accessed 2 October 2021).

# Index